THE
HANDY
WISCONSIN
ANSWER
BOOK

About the Authors

Terri Schlichenmeyer is an award-winning, self-syndicated book reviewer. In addition to several columns written each week, she's contributed to several *Uncle John's Bathroom Readers* and other trivia-type books. You can read Terri's book reviews in more than 200 newspapers and magazines throughout the world. Terri has been reading since she was three years old; she reads four or five books a week and never goes anywhere without a book. She lives on a Wisconsin prairie with two (not-spoiled) dogs, a handsome redhead, and 15,000 books.

Mark Meier was born and raised in a western Wisconsin community near La Crosse. Despite his travels, the "Coulee Region" will always be his home. Mark earned a B.S. degree in philosophy, holds a black belt in Tae Kwon Do, and is a licensed private pilot. He published the science fiction series "Ebony Sea" under the pen name Marc Meiner, and he contributed to the fiction anthologies *Shadows and Teeth* and *Lost and Found*. He produces a news/talk show on local radio 1410-WIZM and lives with his wife, Linda, and their dog, Stitches.

THE
HANDY
WISCONSIN
ANSWER
BOOK

Terri Schlichenmeyer and Mark Meier

VISIBLE
INK
PRESS

Detroit

ALSO FROM VISIBLE INK PRESS

THE HANDY WISCONSIN ANSWER BOOK

Visible Ink Press®
43311 Joy Rd., #414
Canton, MI 48187–2075
Visible Ink Press is a registered trademark of Visible Ink Press LLC.

Most Visible Ink Press books are available at special quantity discounts when purchased in bulk by corporations, organizations, or groups. Customized printings, special imprints, messages, and excerpts can be produced to meet your needs. For more information, contact Special Markets Director, Visible Ink Press, www.visibleink.com, or 734–667–3211.

Managing Editor: Kevin S. Hile
Art Director: Mary Claire Krzewinski
Typesetting: Marco Divita
Proofreaders: Larry Baker and Chava Levin
Indexer: Shoshana Hurwitz
Cover images: Shutterstock.

Library of Congress Cataloging–in–Publication Data

Names: Schlichenmeyer, Terri, author. | Meier, Mark, 1964– author.

Title: The handy Wisconsin answer book / by Terri Schlichenmeyer and Mark Meier.

Description: Canton, MI : Visible Ink Press, [2019] | Includes index. | Identifiers: LCCN 2018061426 (print) | LCCN 2019003212 (ebook) | ISBN 9781578596980 (ePub) | ISBN 9781578596614 (pbk. : alk. paper)

Subjects: LCSH: Wisconsin–History. | Wisconsin–Miscellanea. Classification: LCC F581 (ebook) | LCC F581 .S35 2019 (print) | DDC 977.5–dc23

LC record available at https://lccn.loc.gov/2018061426

10 9 8 7 6 5 4 3 2 1

Printed in the United States of America.

Table of Contents

Acknowledgments

Thanks to Susan T. Hessel for your excellent memory on one of La Crosse's biggest mysteries! Thanks to the guys at the Clark County–UW Extension for their over-the-phone help. You guys ROCK!

—Terri

I would like to thank Roger Jänecke and the entire team at Visible Ink Press for the opportunity to coauthor this book, and Terri Schlichenmeyer for bringing me aboard.

No author writes in a vacuum, and my various critique groups have contributed greatly to my portion of this project. There are far too many to name individually, but one person needs to be mentioned: Peter Donndelinger, who has repeatedly saved me from embarrassment. His knowledge of sports far exceeds mine.

—Mark

DEDICATIONS

To Mom. You and Mumpsy started this. It's all your fault.

—Terri

For my parents, Wayne and Karen, who early on instilled in me an appreciation for the written word.

—Mark

Photo Sources

ABC Television: p. 298.
Scott Ableman: p. 214.
Keith Allison: p. 235.
I. M. Bondarenko: p. 76.
Frank Bryan: p. 226.
Stephanie Caine: p. 275.
Carnby (Wikicommons): p. 330.
Chris 7 (Wikicommons): p. 310.
Compujeramey (Wikicommons): p. 253.
Cousin's Subs: p. 155.
Alan De Smet: p. 305.
DLZ28 (Wikicommons): p. 211.
Dutch National Archives, The Hague, Fotocollectie
     Algemeen Nederlands Persbureau: p. 282 (top).
Anthony Earl: p. 126.
Chris Evans: p. 210.
Adam Fagen: p. 213.
Federal Bureau of Investigation: p. 338.
Francis M. Fritz: p. 353.
Heritage Hill State Historical Park: p. 37.
jbspec7 (Wikicommons): p. 269.
Johnmaxmena2 (Wikicommons): p. 221.
KDTW Flyer: p. 184.
Library of Congress Prints and Photographs Divi-
     sion: pp. 65, 129, 318.
LuxAmber (Wikicommons): p. 342.
Mark Meier: pp. 157, 160, 163, 164, 198.
Mark Moen: p. 296.
Metro-Goldwyn-Mayer: p. 356.
Mike Morbeck: p. 255.
Morrison_2001 (Wikicommons): p. 270.
New York Public Library: p. 33.
Nobel Foundation: p. 80.
Steve Paluch: p. 206.

Paramount Records: p. 69.
The Project Gutenberg EBook of Woman's Work in
     the Civil War: p. 50.
Jim Roberts: p. 19.
Royal Broil (Wikicommons): pp. 35, 166, 244, 264,
     333.
Terri Schlichenmeier: pp. 8, 72, 77, 93, 199, 290,
     322, 325.
Kevin Schuchman: p. 291.
Shutterstock: pp. 3, 5, 9, 11, 13, 15, 17, 26, 40, 42,
     56, 61, 85, 88, 91, 95, 98, 104, 111, 116, 120,
     139, 143, 145, 150, 153, 169, 173, 175, 179, 182,
     192, 194, 202, 217, 232, 243, 247, 251, 260, 261,
     277, 301, 302, 307, 313, 315, 320, 327, 354, 357.
State Historical Society of Wisconsin Visual
     Archives: p. 46.
Sulfur (Wikicommons): pp. 48, 82.
Marion S. Trikosko: p. 363.
UCinternational: p. 219.
U.S. Air Force: p. 67.
U.S. Army: p. 44.
U.S. Congress: p. 125.
U.S. Department of Defense: p. 287.
U.S. Department of Health and Human Services: p.
     130.
U.S. Marine Corps: p. 186.
U.S. Senate Historical Office: pp. 123, 131.
VancityAllie (Wikicommons): p. 282 (bottom).
Allan Warren: p. 360.
Wikicommons: pp. 53, 141, 266.
Public domain: pp. 28, 30, 45, 62, 188, 225, 238,
     249, 252, 256, 273, 284, 294, 316, 348, 350, 362.

Timeline

Year(s)	Event
Circa 10,000 years B.C.E.	Melting glaciers sliding south left their marks on the terrain in what eventually became Wisconsin. The Great Lakes are formed.
10,000–8,000 years B.C.E.	Humans first appeared in the area now known as Wisconsin.
1634	Jacques Marquette and Jean Joliet were the first "official" Europeans to arrive in what would eventually become Wisconsin.
17th Century	The Iroquois Wars are fought on and off throughout the century, ending around 1701.
1746–1747	Wisconsin Potawoatomi join the fight in the French and Indian War.
Spring and summer 1832	British soldiers fought with Black Hawk's Sauk soldiers in the Black Hawk Wars.
Early 1800s	The first European immigrants migrated to the area.
1820s	Mining became a major industry.
1835	Wisconsin's first brewery opened in Mineral Point.
October 25, 1836	Original territorial legislature met in new purpose-built capitol.
September 1839	First state capitol building completed.
1840	Wisconsin's dairy industry began when Anne Picket makes cheese for neighbors to preserve milk.

Year(s)	Event
February 11, 1842	Territorial legislator James Vineyard shot and killed fellow legislator Charles Arndt.
May 29, 1848	Wisconsin officially became a state.
June 7, 1848	Wisconsin's first governor, Nelson Dewey, took office.
March 20, 1854	Republican Party is formed at Ripon College.
1861–1865	Wisconsin sent 91,000 residents to fight in the Civil War.
October 7 and 8, 1871	The Great Peshtigo Fire killed some 800 people and destroyed tens of thousands of acres of timber.
June 12, 1899	Wisconsin's deadliest tornado crossed three counties.
1900	Alvin Kraenzlein became Wisconsin's first Olympic Games winner.
April 18, 1901	First MLB team named "Milwaukee Brewers" played their first official game.
1903	First Harley-Davidson motorcycle made available to the public.
February 26, 1904	A gas lamp started a fire that gutted most of the state capitol building.
September 1, 1904	George Poage became the first African American Olympic medalist.
December 26, 1904	Largest snowfall recorded in Wisconsin near Neilsville.
September 17, 1907	Harley-Davidson incorporated.
1917–1918	Wisconsin sent 125,000 of its citizens overseas to fight in World War I.
January 1919	Wisconsin joined thirty-eight other states in banning alcohol.
August 11, 1919	The Green Bay Packers formed, taking their name from the Indian Packing Company.
1933	Prohibition was abolished in the state.
April 6, 1933	Deepest snow recorded in Wisconsin in the Flambeau Reservoir.
July 13, 1936	Hottest day recorded in Wisconsin occurred in Wisconsin Dells.
November 11, 1940	"The Day the Duck Hunters Died."
December 7, 1941	Fifty-six Wisconsinites were killed at Pearl Harbor.
1941–1945	Wisconsin sends more than 300,000 citizens to fight in World War II.

Year(s)	Event
January 3, 1947	Senator Joe McCarthy began serving as a U.S. senator.
1948	Wisconsin celebrated its centennial year with a huge state fair in West Allis.
June 1950–July 1953	Wisconsin sent more than 130,000 of its citizens to fight in the Korean War.
April 6, 1953	County Stadium, home of the Milwaukee Brewers, is completed.
1955–1975	Wisconsin sent 57,000 of its young men and women to fight in the Vietnam War.
April 30, 1961	The Menominee Indians, as a tribe, were abolished by House Concurrent Resolution 108.
June 1, 1965	Curly Lambeau died. Two months later, New City Stadium is renamed Lambeau Field.
December 3, 1967	The Green Bay Packers played what became known as the Ice Bowl.
March 19, 1969	Milwaukee Bucks used their first-round draft pick on Lew Alcindor (Kareem Abdul-Jabbar).
1970	The Seattle Pilots moved to Milwaukee and were renamed the Brewers.
May 1, 1971	Lew Alcindor changed his name to Kareem Abdul-Jabbar.
April 8, 1973	Thirteen inches of snow postponed the season opener for the Brewers by five days.
November 2, 1974	Hank Aaron signed with the Brewers.
June 16, 1975	Kareem Abdul-Jabbar was traded to Los Angeles.
February 15, 1980	Eric Heiden won the first of five individual gold medals in the 1980 Olympic Games.
1982	The Brewers played in the World Series for the first time, losing to the Cardinals in Game 7.
December 1, 1985	The Green Bay Packers played what became known as the Snow Bowl.
1987	A cardboard hat inspired Ralph Bruno to make the first "Cheesehead Hat."
1988	The first issue of *The Onion* was created at the University of Wisconsin.
September 13, 1992	Brett Favre took over for the injured Don Majkowski and received his first snap for the Green Bay Packers.

Year(s)	Event
1993	California surpassed Wisconsin in milk production for the first time.
December 26, 1993	LeRoy Butler performed the first of what would later be called the Lambeau Leap.
1994	Bonnie Blair became the first to win gold in the same event three Olympic Games in a row.
February 4, 1996	Coldest day recorded in Wisconsin occurred in Couderay.
February 1, 2001	County Stadium is demolished. The Brewers began playing in Miller Park.
March, 2004	Brett Favre named "Toughest Guy in America" by *Men's Journal*.
April 13, 2006	Largest hailstone recorded fell in Jefferson County.
June 5, 2012	Governor Scott Walker won his recall election.
June 22, 2013	Ryan Braun was suspended from MLB for sixty-five games for "unspecified violations" of the sport's drug use policy.
2014	The Milwaukee Brewers' "melt down season."
February 27, 2015	Travis Kvapil had his stock car stolen in Atlanta, Georgia. The following day the car was recovered.
October 19, 2018	The Milwaukee Bucks opened their regular season at the new Fiserv Forum facility.

Introduction

Mention you are from Wisconsin to anybody who's never been there and by the look on their face you know instantly what they're thinking: cows, cheese, and "Yeah, you betcha."

But here's the (not-so) secret you know that they don't: yes, Wisconsin has cows—over a *million* of them, producing America's second-highest amount of milk and milk products. Yes, Wisconsin has cheese—hundreds of yummy varieties, from common cheddar to the kinds of fancy cheeses you'd find in boutiques; cheese perfect for grilling, salads, pizza, burgers, crackers, casseroles, and for just plain eating. And yes, Wisconsinites can be heard muttering, "Yeah, you betcha," but we're also a state that talks, thinks, moves, plans, plays, and acts progressively.

Our state motto *is*, after all, "Forward."

Long before that motto was put into place, Wisconsin was a forward land: here, you'll find hills and valleys, caves and flat farmland, woods and rivers; many of these features, thanks to glaciers that oozed through the state millions of years ago, create Wisconsin's beautiful terrain. We enjoy gorgeous summers that green up the land, and we proudly withstand cold and snow like champs. That's what we have today; it's what the earliest residents lived in, and that's what European explorers found some 400 years ago, when they first came to what would ultimately become a U.S. state. We just know that makes for some good hiking, spelunking, camping, swimming, and water-sliding!

And yet—we're not just about fun.

Wisconsin farmers are among the hardest working bunch in the country. While it's true that dairy farmers have quietly been getting out of the business in alarming numbers, it's not just dairying that Wisconsin claims. Other crops, such as soybeans, hay, oats, and corn come from Wisconsin, as well as hemp and other important crops. There are nearly 70,000 farms in the state, utilizing more than a million acres to produce the crops that we and other states rely on.

We're a diverse group, representing Caucasian, African American, Hmong, and Hispanic residents; people from around the world have come to Wisconsin from the state's very beginning. With them, they brought cheese (from England), lefse (from Norway), beer (from Germany), and casserole (from France). They brought bowling, polkas, and curling from their home countries.

Many brought businesses along with them, too.

Through the years, Wisconsin businesses and institutions have been innovative and cutting-edge. A Wisconsin business was the first in the country to have an escalator in its stores; certain employee benefits were also launched in Wisconsin. Our state has contributed widely to the entertainment industry through filming locations, concert venues, and the invention of instruments; and some of Hollywood's best-loved stars, singers, and performers came from here.

Our public schools can count a lot of "firsts," including the first kindergarten in America. Our university system is second to none. Award-winners come from our state. Wisconsin played important parts in anti-slavery efforts and in civil rights. And on that note, as for politics, well, you'll be surprised at what's happened in Wisconsin at the beginning of statehood, in the twentieth century, and now!

And yet life in Wisconsin isn't all seriousness. We know how to have fun—from Summerfest to Oktoberfest, from hiking to biking, and from snow skiing to water sliding. Our major cities are open for visitors, whether it's for a weekend or forever. Wisconsin's tiniest towns are welcoming, and many of them know how to throw excellent parades. If it's fun, we do it. If it's a challenge, we accept it. If it's a sport, we've tried it, from lacrosse to football. And on that note, it's rumored that many Wisconsinites bleed "green and gold"—which means there'd better be nobody who even *begins* to talk smack about our Packers, Brewers, Bucks, or Badgers!

The Handy Wisconsin Answer Book offers hundreds and hundreds of question-and-answer-type entries designed to tell a story, delight a reader, and inform anyone who wants to know about this awesome state. You'll find quirky things in these pages, things that will surprise you, and maybe a few arguments. If you don't know where to begin, just pick a page, or check out our comprehensive index, browse around, peek at pictures, learn something new.

Be aware that you might question our categorization (a politician, for instance, in a chapter not about politics). You might wonder why we included some topics and not others. Hey dere, we freely admit that there's just no way to cover every single little thing that makes Wisconsin great, don'tchaknow, and to keep this book absolutely, completely updated would be impossible. We did our best, and we had fun doing it.

Will you like this book?

Yeah, you betcha.

WISCONSIN BASICS

Why is Wisconsin called "Wisconsin"?

Wisconsin's name comes from a Native American word, but no one knows for certain which tribe contributed. It may be from an Algonquian word for "long river." It might be from the Chippewa-Ojibwa-Anishinabe word "Ouisconsin," which means "gathering of waters." It may come from a poor French translation of the Miami word "Mesconsing," which also refers to the Mississippi River, which flows along much of Wisconsin's west side.

Even the spelling of the state has changed over the years. In the 1600s, French explorers spelled it "Oiusconsin" and "Misconsing," the latter of which was explained by confusion of the pronunciation of the letter "M." Even during the War of 1812, soldiers spelled the state "Ouisconsin," but that changed around the time miners came to do business in the 1820s. By then, government officials had occasionally used the spelling we know. One of the first printed versions of the state's name came from Governor James Duane Doty, who created a map of the state in the early 1800s, and spelled the state's name as "Wiskonsan," but a government document dated February 1, 1830, mentioned "Wisconsin." This back-and-forth, according to conflicting sources, apparently happened through the mid-1800s; by the time Wisconsin achieved statehood, its familiar way of spelling was firmly in place.

Who lived in Wisconsin before the first settlers?

Scientists and archaeologists say that people lived in the Great Lakes area about 10,000 to 12,000 years ago. They were the Paleo-Indian people and information about them is sketchy, since they left no written record of their daily lives. Rock art, arrowheads, and burial mounds are the best information we have of those very early people.

Long before French and English trappers came to Wisconsin in search of furs, several specific Native American tribes lived in the state. While it's impossible to know exactly which tribe or tribes were first, it's believed that the Oneota, the Menominee, the Chippewa, the Potawatomi, and the Ho-Chunk were among the original tribes in Wisconsin. The Menominee, it should be noted, is the only modern state tribe whose story says they have always lived in Wisconsin.

Life for them, and for all native Wisconsin people, changed in 1634, when French fur trader Jean Nicolet and missionary Jacques Marquette arrived on what would be Wisconsin's shores, and were followed by other explorers of the area, and by fur trappers and traders. The abundance of fur available for trapping was the focus of those early white visitors until the early 1800s, when settlers began to arrive.

When did Wisconsin officially become a state?

The answer to when Wisconsin became a state is a long one. The area we now know as Wisconsin was originally in the Northwest Territory and was acquired through negotiations with the British after the Revolutionary War in an agreement known as the Treaty of Paris of 1783. At that time, mostly just Native Americans, explorers, and trappers lived in the Northwest Territory.

In 1800, this large swath of land to the east of the Mississippi became a part of the Indiana Territory, through an act of Congress. The Indiana Territory had its own appointed officials, including a representative; Congress also immediately made land easier to purchase, setting up the opportunity for the area to become settled.

In 1809, the land we know as Wisconsin officially became part of the Illinois Territory but when Illinois became a state in 1818, what would eventually become Wisconsin was enfolded as part of the Michigan Territory. When Michigan became a state in 1836, part of the area west of the Mississippi joined the Iowa Territory.

At that point, President Andrew Jackson appointed a new governor and secretary, and Wisconsin became an official territory—a status that lasted until May 29, 1848, when Wisconsin became a state.

Where is Wisconsin on a map?

Wisconsin is in the upper midwestern part of the United States, just west of Lake Michigan and south of Lake Superior. It shares borders with Michigan, Iowa, Minnesota, Indiana, and Illinois. On the west side is the Mississippi River; on the east side is Lake Michigan. Wisconsin's geographical coordinates are 43.7844° N, 88.7879° W.

How many counties are there in Wisconsin?

There are seventy-two counties within the boundaries. The largest, with almost 1,545 square miles (2,486 square kilometers), is Marathon County; the smallest in area, with just 249 square miles (400 square kilometers), is Pepin County. The county with the largest population is Milwaukee County. The least-populous county is Menominee County.

When was each county created, and what are the respective county seats?

Wisconsin's first counties were Brown and Crawford Counties, both established in 1818 back when Wisconsin was still a Territory. The last county established in the state was

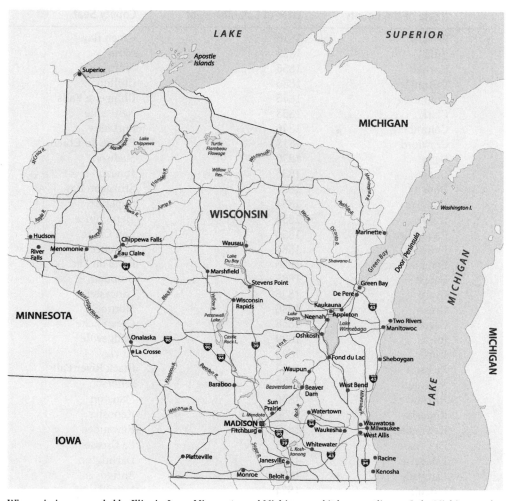

Wisconsin is surrounded by Illinois, Iowa, Minnesota, and Michigan, and it has coastline on Lake Michigan and Lake Superior.

Menominee, which was created in 1959 and now basically outlines the area known as the Menominee Indian Reservation.

Other counties occurred as following (including all county seats):

Wisconsin Counties

Name of the County	Date of Establishment	County Seat
Adams	1848	Friendship
Ashland	1860	Ashland
Barron*	1859	Barron
Bayfield**	1945	Washburn

3

Name of the County	Date of Establishment	County Seat
Brown	1818	Green Bay
Buffalo	1853	Alma
Burnett	1856	Siren
Calumet	1836	Chilton
Chippewa	1845	Chippewa Falls
Clark	1853	Neillsville
Columbia	1846	Portage
Crawford	1818	Prairie du Chien
Dane	1836	Madison
Dodge	1836	Juneau
Door	1851	Sturgeon Bay
Douglas	1854	Superior
Dunn	1854	Menominee
Eau Claire	1856	Eau Claire
Florence	1881	Florence
Fond du Lac	1836	Fond du Lac
Forest	1885	Crandon
Grant	1836	Lancaster
Green	1836	Monroe
Green Lake	1858	Green Lake
Iowa	1829	Dodgeville
Iron	1893	Hurley
Jackson	1853	Black River Falls
Jefferson	1836	Jefferson
Juneau	1856	Mauston
Kenosha	1850	Kenosha
Kewaunee	1852	Kewaunee
La Crosse	1851	La Crosse
Lafayette	1846	Darlington
Langlade	1879	Antigo
Lincoln	1874	Merrill
Manitowoc	1836	Manitowoc
Marathon	1850	Wausau
Marinette	1879	Marinette
Marquette	1826	Montello
Menominee	1959	Keshena
Milwaukee	1834	Milwaukee
Monroe	1854	Sparta
Oconto	1851	Oconto
Oneida	1885	Rhinelander
Outagamie	1851	Appleton
Ozaukee	1853	Port Washington
Pepin	1858	Durand
Pierce	1853	Ellsworth
Polk	1853	Balsam Lake
Portage	1836	Stevens Point

The counties of Wisconsin.

Name of the County	Date of Establishment	County Seat
Price	1879	Phillips
Racine	1836	Racine
Richland	1842	Richland Center
Rock	1836	Janesville
Rusk***	1901	Ladysmith
Sauk	1840	Baraboo
Sawyer	1883	Hayward
Shawano	1853	Shawano

Name of the County	Date of Establishment	County Seat
Sheboygan	1836	Sheboygan
St. Croix	1840	Hudson
Taylor	1875	Medford
Trempealeau	1854	Whitehall
Vernon****	1851	Viroqua
Vilas	1893	Eagle River
Walworth	1836	Elkhorn
Washburn	1883	Shell Lake
Washington	1836	West Bend
Waukesha	1846	Waukesha
Waupaca	1851	Waupaca
Waushara	1851	Wautoma
Winnebago	1840	Oshkosh
Wood	1856	Wisconsin Rapids

*Bayfield County was called La Pointe County until 1866.
**Barron County was originally Dallas County, until 1869.
***Rusk County was known as Gates County until 1905.
***Vernon County entered the state as Bad Axe County and was renamed in 1862.

What is the highest point in Wisconsin?

Timm's Hill in Price County in north central Wisconsin is the highest point in the state, with an elevation of 1,951.5 feet (595 meters).

What is the lowest point in Wisconsin?

It may seem to be cheating, but the lowest point in Wisconsin is underwater in Lake Michigan, at about 580 feet (177 meters) above sea level.

Where is the center of Wisconsin?

Wisconsin's central point is located in Wood County, a few miles southeast of Marshfield.

What's unique about Wisconsin's geography?

By the end of the last ice age, perhaps some 12,000 years ago, the area we know as Wisconsin had undergone a radical change. Before the glaciers, the topography of Wisconsin was basically flat, with the occasional gently rolling hill. As glaciers scraped their way south, they created lakes (15,000 of them!), moraines, bluffs, sandstone rock formations, rich farmland, and more flat land. Glaciers covered almost the entire area except the Driftless Area of Wisconsin—in the southwestern part of the state—which never saw glaciers at all.

Basically, Wisconsin is divided into three geographical areas:

- To the far north is the Lake Superior Lowland, which is bordered by Lake Superior and gently slopes upward from the south. This area is small; no more than 20 miles (32 kilometers) from the edge of the lake.

- Just below that is the Northern Highland, characterized by more than a million acres (404,700 hectares) of forest, including the Chequamegon-Nicolet National Forest, which is the only forest managed by the U.S. Forest Service. This area covers most of the northern part of the state.

- The Central Plain includes rich farmland and rock formations, such as the Wisconsin Dells.

- The Eastern Ridges and Lowlands, which includes a ridge that runs all the way to New York. Agriculturally, this area is known for its rich farmland.

- The Western Upland is a mix of many kinds of geography, including limestone formations and sandstone hills, steep ravines, and flat farmland.

There are mountains in Wisconsin: Rib Mountain, known as a great area for skiing; Thunder Mountain, Lookout Mountain, Timms Hill, and Harrison Hill.

The glaciers left many rivers: The Wisconsin River, Mississippi River, Chippewa River, Pine River, Menominee River, St. Croix River, the Kewaunee River, Wolf River, and the Kinnickinnic River.

At its widest, Wisconsin's borders are 295 miles (475 square kilometers) apart; at its longest point, the state is 320 miles (515 kilometers) in length, for a total land amount of 54,314 square miles (140,673 square kilometers).

Some of the 15,000 lakes left by the glaciers: Lake Michigan, Lake Superior, Devil's Lake, Castle Rock Lake, Lake Winnebago, and Lake Mendota.

Overall, nearly half of Wisconsin is covered in woodland. Of the state's 65,503 square miles (91,952 square kilometers), 45 percent of it is farmland.

What's unique about Wisconsin's geology?

Wisconsin geologists have surveyed and noted more than a hundred official outcroppings of rock formations in the state, as well as dozens of different kinds of rock. Many of the outcroppings can be visited, but many more can't, due to road and highway location and gravel mining. As for general geology, well, you walked on it today and can visit it in any park in the state.

Wisconsin's geological terrain ranges in age from nearly three billion years old (Bayfield and Ashland Counties and along the Black River) to relative young'uns that are a mere 440 million years old. You may be surprised to learn that some of the older rock that lies beneath the surface of Wisconsin came from volcanic sources, once upon a time. Glaciers formed some of the state into the valleys and rivers (particularly in the central and eastern parts), while a notable absence of glaciers is to blame for other parts of Wisconsin's rocks and caves, particularly in the southwestern sections.

Forty-five percent of Wisconsin is devoted to the agriculture industry. Forty-six percent of the state is woodland.

7

Wisconsin isn't necessarily known for its rock formations, made when glaciers came through the area tens of thousands of years ago, but we have 'em! This one stands near Camp Douglas, just off I-90.

How many lakes can be found in Wisconsin?

If you like to swim or go boating, you're in luck! There are some 15,000 lakes in the state of Wisconsin. Alas, nearly half of them are so small that they don't even have names.

Created some 12,000 years ago when glaciers slid through Wisconsin, Lake Winnebago near Oshkosh, at nearly 140,000 acres (56,656 hectares), is the state's largest lake. Thirty miles long and 10 miles wide (48 by 16 kilometers), the water is an average 15 feet (4.6 meters) deep and is a great place for fishing. Camping is also available along Lake Winnebago.

Pentenwell Lake is the state's second-largest lake. Located in Wood, Juneau, and Adams Counties, Pentenwell is a man-made lake created in 1948 by Wisconsin River Power Company in conjunction with a hydroelectric plant. Pentenwell Lake is 42 feet (12.8 meters) deep at its deepest and offers just over 23,000 acres (9,300 hectares) of swimming, boating, and canoeing. Be aware that Pentenwell Lake's waterways can bloom with algae and the Wisconsin DNR recommends that humans and pets avoid that.

How much riverway is there in Wisconsin?

A lot! With nearly 13,000 rivers and streams, Wisconsin boasts 84,000 miles (135,185 kilometers) of riverway within its borders! That includes more than 10,000 miles (16,100 kilometers) of trout streams; more than 500 miles (805 kilometers) of rushing whitewater; and one of the nation's longest free-flowing (non-dammed) streams, the Baraboo River.

Some 4,700 dams dot Wisconsin's waterways, and a little over half are owned by private entities and individuals: the state owns less than twenty percent of the river dams here and governments own about 16 percent of the dams.

At 430 miles (692 kilometers) in length, the Wisconsin River is the state's longest river. It meanders from the northeast part of the state nearly to the southwest corner, and was formed over the course of millions of years, first by glaciers and then by glacial melting. The Wisconsin River has been known by this name since before European settlers arrived: in 1673, explorer Jacques Marquette recorded its name as the "Meskousing" River, which is a variation on the current spelling.

The Rock River is 299 miles (481 kilometers) long and flows from Wisconsin into Illinois. Sauk and Fox Indians were said to have referred to the river as "rocky waters," which means the Rock River has lived up to its name for centuries.

At about 225 miles (362 kilometers), the Wolf River in Wisconsin's north is another notable river here. If whitewater rafting is your thing, here's your river; if you'd rather fish, you'll find walleye and sturgeon in the Wolf River. And if you'd rather hike and take in the scenery, the Wolf River boasts 24 miles (39 kilometers) of nationally designated scenic waterway.

At 182 miles (293 kilometers), the Fox River is Wisconsin's fourth-longest river. Scientists believe that humans have been living along the Fox River for nearly 10,000 years.

You can't talk about Wisconsin without a good discussion of the Mississippi River which, along with the St. Croix River, forms most of Wisconsin's western border; 200 miles (322 kilometers) of Wisconsin, in fact, consists of Mississippi waterway.

Formed some 100 million years ago, the Mississippi River actually starts in Minnesota's Lake Itasca, with a tiny bit of water you can literally walk over. From there, the

Wisconsin's waterways are not only fun to be on, they're relaxing to sit near. This waterfall is along Highway 27 in Merrillan.

9

river flows more than 2,300 miles (3,700 kilometers) to the Gulf of Mexico in Louisiana. Thirty-three rivers and countless streams drain into the Mississippi from its head to its mouth. The Mississippi is one of the Top Five Largest Rivers in the world; even so, it isn't the nation's longest river; the Missouri River is just slightly longer.

Today's Mississippi is essential to the economic health of the entire upper Midwest. Twenty-nine locks and dams help some 175 tons of freight up and down the river each year, until the river is frozen in the northern climates. Sixty percent of the grain grown and sold in the United States is transported down the Mississippi River each year.

What's the weather like up there?

If you like a change in season, you're in luck! Wisconsin definitely has four distinct seasons.

The hottest summertime temperature of 114 degrees was recorded on July 13, 1936, in Wisconsin Dells. Ask any farmer and you'll hear stories of ferocious cold, but the coldest temperature recorded was –55 degrees F in Couderay (Sawyer County) in early February 1996. The record for total snowfall was achieved in Hurley (Iron County) when a total of more than 23 feet (7 meters) of snow fell during the winter of 1996–97.

Wisconsin's average high temperature is about 82 degrees in the summer. Wintertime low temps will hover around 0 degrees. Overall mean temperature is 40 degrees in the northern part of the state and 48 degrees in the southern parts.

In the northern half of Wisconsin and particularly along the northern Lake Michigan areas, the freeze season runs roughly November through the first part of April, although a late-August freeze is not unheard of. That's good ice fishing weather! In the southern half of the state, the freeze season is approximately December through later March, although in some years winter has been known to last until nearly May.

Bring your umbrellas when you're in Wisconsin: average rainfall is just under a meter of rain, and runoff ultimately empties either into Lakes Superior and Michigan or into the Mississippi River, either directly or through many tributaries. Average snowfall in Wisconsin depends on where you are: in the southern areas, a total of 30 inches (76 centimeters) of white stuff is about what you'll get in a winter season, while far northern parts of the state could see 160 inches (406 centimeters) of snow. Snow will last on the ground more than twice as long in the north as in the south (140 days versus about 65 days).

Wisconsin weather isn't all about good news, though: in an average year, residents will see 30 tornadoes in the northern part of the state and 40 tornadoes in the southern half. Frequency of tornadoes peaks in the months of June and July and they're often accompanied by thunderstorms with lightning, hail, and high winds. Thundersnow, by the way, is not uncommon in the winter months.

What is Wisconsin's state motto?

Wisconsin's state motto is "Forward." It was adopted in 1851 and reflects what officials hoped would be the optimism of Wisconsin residents then and into the future.

What is on Wisconsin's state flag?

The motto is on the state flag, along with a sailor and a miner (to indicate the diversity of employment in the state), and a badger along the top of a shield, which displays a U.S. flag in the center surrounded by four segmented parts to show Wisconsin's industries, circa 1863: agriculture, mining, navigating, and manufacturing. Along the bottom of the shield are a cornucopia and a pile of lead, to signify the bounty in the states' food products and minerals.

The state flag of Wisconsin was designed in 1863.

Until the Civil War, Wisconsin didn't have a flag. Union soldiers asked for one, so it was designed in 1863. A few revisions have been made to the flag over the years but except for the addition of the words you'll see across the top of today's flag and "1848" on the bottom, the flag we fly today would be familiar to soldiers on the battlefield more than 150 years ago.

When you say "Wisconsin" ...?

You're only saying one of the states' many names. Because of Wisconsin's reputation for awesome dairy products, it's known as America's Dairyland or The Cheese State. Affectionately, residents are called "Cheeseheads." Wisconsin is also known as The Badger State, originally because of the miners who once made their living underground. Historically speaking, Wisconsin was called The Copper State due to its early fame for mining, but that moniker hasn't been used for many decades.

What is the state bird?

Though Wisconsinites like to joke that the state bird is the mosquito, the real state bird is the American robin (*Turdus migratorious*). Known for its orange-red breast and its distinctive song, the robin is a migratory bird and generally escapes Wisconsin winters, although it's not uncommon to see them year 'round.

It's not spring without robins in Wisconsin, and we all eagerly await their return. Male robins are brighter than the females—she's a bit "muted" in color—and both have a wide range of vocalizations. Robins will usually nest two or three times in a season; there are generally four eggs in a nest on the first go-around, with fewer eggs in subsequent nestings. Technically speaking, a robin is a member of the thrush family, but that didn't matter at all to English settlers, who saw the red breast of the American robin and were reminded of their red-breasted robins from back home—even though the two birds are not related.

In the late 1920s, the Conservation Chairman of the Wisconsin Federated Women's Club polled schoolchildren around the state to gather opinions and nominations for a

11

state bird. Overwhelmingly, the children loved the robin. Still, Wisconsin had no official state bird until June 4, 1949, when the robin became it.

What is the state flower?

The state flower is the wood violet (*Viola papilionacea*), as voted by schoolchildren on Arbor Day in 1909. Commonly found in wooded areas, meadows, and perhaps even back yards, the wood violet blooms in the spring and early summer. Its delicate purple flowers are a favorite for small bouquets and nosegays but they don't live long after being plucked. The best part: wood violets are not just pretty to look at: the leaves of the wood violet are edible!

The wood violet, so beautiful in our state, is obviously a big favorite: Illinois, Rhode Island, and New Jersey also call it their state flower.

What is the state food?

There are several answers to this: Wisconsin's state fruit is the cranberry. Cranberries are grown in water-filled bogs and are harvested through the water. You'll find cranberry bogs dotting the state, but they are primarily found near the Tomah and Wisconsin Rapids areas. Most people think of Thanksgiving when they think of cranberries, perhaps because the fruit is harvested in the late fall, but they're tasty any time. Also look for craisins—yum!

The state grain is corn. In 2016, Wisconsin farmers grew 573 million bushels of corn, at about 56 pounds (25.4 kilograms) per bushel, making for a nearly $2 billion overall crop. In 2016, according to the Wisconsin Corn website, Wisconsin was ranked eighth in corn production in the United States, with Dane, Rock, Grant, Dodge, and Lafayette Counties leading the way. More than four million acres (1,619,000 hectares) of corn were planted in Wisconsin in 2016, half of which was used to feed livestock. And that acreage amount is not including corn on the cob, which you'll find at nearly every roadside farm market throughout the summer months.

The state pastry is the Kringle, a baseball-mitt-sized pastry with fruit and/or nut filling and drizzled with icing. Wisconsin's Danish immigrants brought the Kringle to the state with them in the early 1800s and, in fact, some recipes in use today are nearly identical to those 200-year-old recipes. Racine is known as "The Kringle Capital of the World," in case you're wondering.

The state beverage is, of course, milk, which was—very surprisingly—not the state beverage until 1987! That's despite the fact that Wisconsin *is* America's Dairyland and has been one of the leaders in the nation in milk production for generations. You'll find milk in cold glasses fresh from the fridge, but also in butter, cheese, ice cream, many baked goods, milk powder, and lots of other products.

Does Wisconsin have a state dairy product?

Of course! In 2017, a group of fourth-graders from Mineral Point Elementary School asked lawmakers to make cheese the Official State Dairy Product.

It was a good choice: thanks to its 1.3 million dairy cows, Wisconsin manufactures some 11 billion pounds (5 billion kilograms) of cheese per year. That's slightly more than 25 percent of the cheese consumed in the United States annually. Ninety percent of Wisconsin's milk goes toward making Wisconsin cheese.

The only limit to cheese flavors is the imagination: you can get cheese with vegetables, sausage, bacon, or pepperoni in it. You can get the classics: mozzarella (the number one cheese made in Wisconsin), Colby, and cheddar. You can get stinky cheese, hard cheese, or soft cheese. You can get it in squeaky curds, strings, whips, bricks, or wheels.

By the way, Wisconsin leads the nation in the number of dairy goats, too, with more than 44,000 milking nannies in the state.

What is the Wisconsin state tree?

Known for their brilliant red leaves in the fall, the *acer saccharum,* or the sugar maple was voted as the Wisconsin state tree in 1893 by the state's schoolchildren but it wasn't quite made official then. In 1948, another poll of children was taken and they, too, said that the sugar maple should become Wisconsin's state tree, even though the white pine had its fans (perhaps because of Wisconsin's logging industry). The state legislature, in 1949, agreed with the children and Chapter 218, Laws of 1949, made it official.

The sugar maple, sometimes called the hard or rock maple, is one of Wisconsin's premiere hardwood trees. In the late winter or early fall, depending on your location within the state, you'll notice the tree's beautiful colorful leaves of yellow, orange, or red. The following early spring, sap can be harvested from the maple tree with the use of a

Founded in 1968, family-owned Ehlenbach's Cheese Chalet in DeForest sells a selection of some 250 varieties of Wisconsin cheese—cheese heaven for anyone visiting there!

tap and a bucket. The sap is then boiled down to make maple syrup; it takes 34 gallons (129 liters) of raw sap to make one gallon of maple syrup.

Sugar maple trees can live to be 300 to 400 years old.

What is Wisconsin's state fish?

Named the Wisconsin state fish in 1955, the muskellunge, or musky (*Esox masquinongy Mitchell*), is a member of the pike family. It's believed that its name comes from "masquinongy," meaning deformed pike, which is an apt description: built like a torpedo with a long, long body and a flat snout filled with teeth, the musky is an exceedingly strong swimmer that lives mostly in Wisconsin's northern lakes and rivers. Catch one of these fighting bad boys on a hook, and you've got a battle ahead of you!

What are the Wisconsin state rock and the Wisconsin state mineral?

The Kenosha Gem and Mineral Society proposed red granite as the state rock in 1971. They made the suggestion to promote Wisconsin's geology and, because Wisconsin has a strong mining background, for its significance in state history. Red granite is native to Wisconsin.

The Wisconsin state mineral is galena, or lead sulfide, chosen for its abundance and for its historical significance in the state, due to Wisconsin's legacy in mining. Aside from farming, one of Wisconsin's earliest industries—particularly in the southwest portion of the state—was lead mining. In the very early 1800s, in fact, the populations of Grant, Iowa, and Lafayette Counties combined were more than that of Milwaukee at the time! Mining was so important to Wisconsin's origins that you'll still see vestiges of it on the state seal, the state flag, and on Wisconsin's coat of arms.

What is Wisconsin's official state soil?

Antigo silt loam (*typic glossoboralf*) was designated as Wisconsin's state soil in 1983. Created by glaciers, it's the most common kind of soil in Wisconsin and it's very important to cropland and woodland alike.

What is the official Wisconsin state animal?

Again, this is a multi-answer question:

Since 1957, the badger (*Taxidea taxus*) has been the official state animal, perhaps in part because of Wisconsin's early mining history: badgers live subterraneously; miners make their livings underground. The comparison drawn was obvious.

Badgers are stout, low-to-the-ground mammals that were practically made to dig, with powerful forelimbs and long sturdy claws. For the most part, they're solitary and shy, spending all but a fraction of their day in their den. When they do venture forth, they hunt small mammals, birds, and grubs for dinner. If you spot a badger, steer clear of him! Badgers prefer to avoid people but, if cornered, they're fierce fighters and they aren't to be messed with.

Since 1985, Wisconsin's state dog has been the American Water Spaniel, thanks to eighth graders at Washington Junior High School in New London. According to the Wisconsin Blue Book, just five dog breeds are native to the United States, and the American Water Spaniel is the only one native to Wisconsin. New London's Dr. Fred J. Pfeifer is credited with developing the breed, and standardizing it; he finally registered the American Water Spaniel with the AKC in 1920 with recognition two decades later.

The American Water Spaniel is absolutely a hunting dog and makes an excellent family pet. Regulation coat is tightly curled with a protective undercoat; standard colors are liver and chocolate, sometimes with a white spot on the chest.

Among a zoo of state animals, the badger is the official state wildlife mammal of Wisconsin, as well as the mascot of the University of Wisconsin—Madison.

The state domestic animal is the dairy cow (*Bos Taurus*), which should surprise no one. The surprise is that the dairy cow didn't get her due until 1971, when she was given the honor (and yes, it's "she," since dairy cows are inherently milk-giving female bovines). The average dairy cow turns her dinner into between 6 and 7 gallons (23 to 26 liters) of milk per day.

The state wildlife animal is the Whitetail deer (*Odocoileus virginianus*), and has been since 1957, even though the animals have been around since, presumably, before people.

The Whitetail deer—so named because of the white underside of its tail that flashes when the deer senses danger—can run up to 40 miles (64 kilometers) an hour at its fastest. It can easily jump 9-foot fences and Whitetails have been clocked at 13 miles (21 kilometers) per hour swimming in the water. Fawns are born generally in the early spring; most of the time, a doe will have one fawn, but multiples are not uncommon.

The state symbol of peace is the mourning dove (*Zenaidura macroura*), which is a small grey bird with black spots, about the size of a pigeon, that makes a soft cooing sound that differentiates itself from pigeons (mourning doves are members of the dove family). When groups of mourning doves take flight, you may hear a loud "whistle." They prefer woodland or prairies' edge to live and mate—the latter of which they do multiple times throughout a long nesting season lasting roughly April to September. Although they were once relatively scarce, the mourning dove population has returned to population levels that give researchers confidence.

The mourning dove became a Wisconsin's state symbol of peace in 1971; ironically, it became a game bird in late 2003.

The state insect is the honeybee (*Apis milliferra*), as it's been since 1977, thanks to the third-grade class of Holy Family School of Marinette and the Wisconsin Honey Producers Association.

Honeybees are not loners: up to 80,000 individual insects live in a single hive, along with a queen, whose sole responsibility in life is to lie around and lay eggs. In her 8 years on earth, a queen can leave a half-million larvae behind, the majority of which are sterile female worker bees whose job it is to work on behalf of the hive, maintaining the comb, caring for eggs, keeping the temperature regulated, and defending the hive. Fossilized records of the very first bees indicate that they've been around for some 40 million years and have remained unchanged for three-quarters of that.

Consider this: the honeybee wasn't the only insect up for honors as the state insect. Other also-rans were dragonflies, ladybugs, and the mosquito!

Wisconsin even has a state fossil?

It might come as a surprise that an area so far from the sea would have an extinct marine arthropod as its state fossil, but that's what Wisconsin has: the trilobite (*Calymene Celebra*), the state fossil since 1985.

Many millions of years ago in the Paleozoic Age when salt water covered the area, trilobites—which grew up to 14 inches (36 centimeters) in length and were related to the crabs, lobsters, and arthropods you might recognize today—were common in what would one day become Wisconsin. Like most arthropods, the trilobites outgrew their shells and had to abandoned their too-small ones in order to grow new ones; thus, one animal might have been responsible for several fossils, over time.

Today, if you look hard, you might still see a trilobite fossil in one of the states' rock formations.

What is the Wisconsin state dance?

When immigrants came to Wisconsin in the mid-1800s, they brought with them a fad that had been burning through Europe—particularly in Germany and Poland. In the polka, dancing couples move their feet, fast, to 2/4 time and a lot of oompa-oompa'ing, since no polka music is complete without accompanying accordion or concertina.

Because German and Polish heritage runs strong in Wisconsin, the Polka was designated as the state dance in 1993. There were a lot of people who supported that idea: it was originally put forth by a group of schoolchildren from Madison; polka boosters, a regional folk museum, and other supporters seconded the motion.

Learning to polka is easy, by the way, and can be done even by small children; in its most basic form, it's really little more than a hop-hop on one foot, then hop-hop on the other although more elaborate polkas take some learning.

Yes, Wisconsinites take their polkas seriously. If you don't believe us, visit the Wisconsin Polka Hall of Fame in Hartford.

Polka dancing originated in Europe, arriving with German and Polish immigrants settling in Wisconsin. Since then, the polka has become the official state dance.

Also note that Wisconsin has an official state waltz, written by composer Ethwell "Eddy" Hanson of the New London / Waupaca area. Though Hanson penned the waltz in 1951, it didn't enter into the record books as official state waltz until 2001.

What are the words to the official Wisconsin state song?

When it was first written, "On Wisconsin" was meant for use at the University of Wisconsin, as a fight song. The words were:

> On, Wisconsin! On, Wisconsin! Plunge right through that line!
> Run the ball right down the field, a touchdown sure this time.
> On, Wisconsin! On, Wisconsin! Fight on for her fame,
> Fight! Fellows! Fight! Fight, fight, we'll win this game.
> On, Wisconsin! On, Wisconsin! Stand up, Badgers sing!
> "Forward" is our driving spirit, loyal voices ring.
> On, Wisconsin! On, Wisconsin! Raise her glowing flame!
> Stand, fellows, let us now salute her name!

The tune, originally intended for the University of Minnesota, was written by William T. Purdy and was presented at a football game in 1909.

In 1913, J.S. Hubbard and Judge Charles T. Rosa rewrote the song to be more like a state song than a cheer. The words they proposed were:

17

On, Wisconsin! On, Wisconsin!
Grand old badger state!
We, thy loyal sons and daughters,
Hail thee, good and great.
On, Wisconsin! On, Wisconsin!
Champion of the right,
"Forward," our motto
God will give thee might!

While it may be argued that the first version is sung more often, the second version was officially adopted as the Wisconsin state song in 1959.

What is Wisconsin's State Ballad?

Absolutely different from Wisconsin's official state song, Wisconsin's state ballad came to be in 2001 when Erma Barrett of Juneau County wrote lyrics and her granddaughter, Shari Sarazin of Mauston, composed the music for "Oh, Wisconsin, Land of My Dreams."

Here are the words to the ballad:

Oh Wisconsin, land of beauty,
with your hillsides and your plains
with your jackpine and your birch tree,
and your oak of mighty frame.
Land of rivers, lakes and valleys,
land of warmth and winter snows,
land of birds and beasts and humanity,
Oh Wisconsin, I love you so.
Oh Wisconsin, land of my dreams.
Oh Wisconsin, you'll all I'll ever need.
A little heaven here on earth could you be?
Oh Wisconsin, land of my dreams.
In the summer, golden grain fields;
in the winter, drift of white snow;
in the springtime, robins singing;
in the autumn, flaming colors show.
Oh I wonder who could wander,
or who could want to drift for long,
away from all your beauty, all your sunshine,
all your sweet song?
Oh Wisconsin, land of my dreams.
Oh Wisconsin, you'll all I'll ever need.
A little heaven here on earth could you be?
Oh Wisconsin, land of my dreams.
And when it's time, let my spirit run free
in Wisconsin, land of my dreams.

POPULATION AND PEOPLE

What is the official population of Wisconsin (rural and urban?)

As of 2017—the most recent number at the writing of this book—the population of Wisconsin was 5.795 million people, about two-thirds of whom live in urban areas, while the rest live in rural areas of the state. The gender balance, in both cases, is almost exactly equal between men and women.

There are, at the time of this writing, just over 367,000 veterans living in Wisconsin.

With almost 2.3 million households, the average Wisconsin household statistically consists of 2.45 people; about 700,000 households have children within them but more than twice as many do not. The median age of Wisconsin citizens is 37 years old; about a third of all Wisconsin adults have been single all their lives, while just over half are currently married.

What is the average household income in Wisconsin?

As of the writing of this book, the average household income in Wisconsin is slightly over $66,000 per year. The median household income (which means half of the state's incomes are above and half are below) is nearly $53,000.

Ozaukee and Waukesha Counties are the wealthiest counties in Wisconsin; both boast average household incomes of well over $70,000 per year.

Nearly 60 percent of Wisconsin workers are white collar workers; the rest are blue collar workers, including the states' agriculture workers and farmers.

Rates of home ownership in Wisconsin are higher than the national average and are based, surprisingly, on age. Just 60 percent of citizens ages 37–44 are homeowners, but 80 percent of Wisconsinites age 65 and older own their homes.

Walter Reuther Central High School in Kenosha is an alternative high school housed in a building that is on the National Register of Historic Places. Named after the famous labor leader, the structure was built in the 1920s and is one of the states 2,238 magnet schools.

What is the educational status of Wisconsin schools?

Though Wisconsin has a very good school system and has contributed to education in many ways, some 140,000 adult citizens never attended high school. Thirty-one percent attended high school but didn't graduate. The vast majority of Wisconsinites—roughly half of the state's adults—are college graduates with degrees or post-secondary degrees, however. Today's graduation rate hovers around 90 percent.

The largest public high school in Wisconsin is Indian Trail High School & Academy in Kenosha, with just over 2,200 students; the largest private high school is St. Anthony School of Milwaukee with just under two thousand students.

Wisconsin boasts 2,238 public schools, magnet schools, and charter schools (in 464 school districts) and nearly 1,000 private institutions, serving almost a million scholars.

More than three out of four of the private institutions are faith-based. At the time of this writing, Wisconsin participates in the Common Core State Standards Initiative.

For information on the University of Wisconsin system, see the chapter "Wisconsin History: 1900 to Now."

What are the largest five cities in Wisconsin?

They are, in order, and with 2015 population results:

1. Milwaukee: 957,735
2. Madison: 248,951
3. Green Bay: 100,851
4. Kenosha: 95,730
5. Racine: 78,860

For more information on these, and other top Wisconsin cities, see the chapter "City Life: Milwaukee, Madison, and Beyond."

How ethnically diverse is Wisconsin?

Strictly speaking, if compared to some states, Wisconsin is not very diverse, but there are a few interesting picture-within-a-picture things to know.

- In the nation overall, nearly 63 percent of all Americans identify as "white-only." In Wisconsin, that number is well over 82 percent. People of German ancestry are the largest sub-group in that percentage.

- African Americans make up nearly 10 percent of Wisconsin's population, although nearly 70 percent of Milwaukee County's population is African American, many of whom came (or whose ancestors came) during the Great Migrations in the post-Civil War years and during the early twentieth century. For sure, the vast majority of the state's African American communities are found in the Milwaukee / Kenosha / Racine area and near Madison. African Americans are Wisconsin's largest minority group.

- The Hispanic or Latino population is just under 6 percent, but Wisconsin has a much higher concentration of Spanish-speaking residents than has any other state. Hispanic and Latino individuals make up Wisconsin's second-largest minority group (particularly in the Green Bay area), and its fastest growing one, too.
- Native American population is at about 2 percent. It's also the slowest-growing minority in the state.
- The Asian population is about 3 percent of the entire population. Most of the Asian population are the Hmong people from southeast Asia, who settled here in the years after the Vietnam War.

Which religions are practiced in Wisconsin?

As you might expect in today's world, Wisconsin is quite diverse in its religious practices. Well more than half of all Wisconsinites identify as Christian, with 44 percent of those poll respondents saying they are Protestant and 25 percent as Roman Catholic. A quarter of all Wisconsin residents are agnostic, atheist, or don't claim a religious preference. One percent of Wisconsin residents say they don't know which faith they follow.

Though it doesn't poll as such, you can be sure that just about every religion that can be practiced, is, in Wisconsin.

The state's largest church is Elmbrook Church in Brookfield with a Sunday service attendance of around 7,000 souls a week. Established in 1958, it is one of the nation's top 100 largest churches.

As for the state's smallest church, that's up for argument. There are several tiny churches in Wisconsin that count a handful of congregants and room for just a couple people in their pews.

Which religion was founded in Wisconsin?

In 1848, John Muehlhaeuser, a missionary from Germany, arrived in Wisconsin to serve with the United Rhine Mission Society. In 1850, he met with a group of like-minded people near Milwaukee, helped found the Wisconsin Synod (a council of a church), and became its first president. Eighteen years later, though it retained its strong German heritage at least until modern times, the group broke ties with the church in Germany and moved toward Lutheranism. For the next several years, synods in various nearby states eased toward ties with the Wisconsin Synod; in 1892, the collective group became the Evangelical Joint Synod of Wisconsin and Other States. In 1917, they became known simply as Wisconsin Synod.

In 1959, the organization changed their name again to become officially known as Wisconsin Evangelical Lutheran Synod, or WELS—but just because "Wisconsin" is in the name doesn't mean Wisconsin Synod Lutherans are only in this state. WELS communities are in nearly every state in America, as well as several provinces in Canada. WELS is the third largest Lutheran denomination in this country; doctrines are similar to, but differ sometimes markedly from, that of other Lutheran denominations.

21

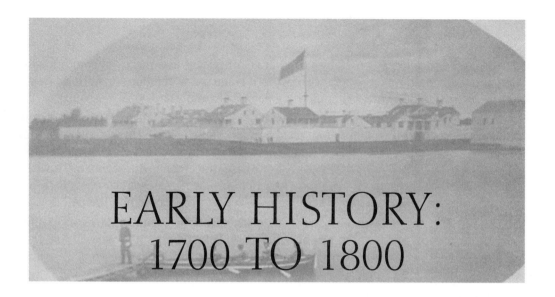

EARLY HISTORY: 1700 TO 1800

Who were the first people to live in Wisconsin?

The earliest people to live in the Great Lakes area are known to archaeologists as the Paleo-Indian People, who arrived in the state, possibly up to 10,000 years ago or so. Sadly, it's hard to pinpoint exactly when they came or where they arrived from; they left no written information and only just a little rock art, a few tools, and some minor possessions, so not much is known about them except that they were hunter / scavengers and were undoubtedly highly mobile.

Even so, scientists think that Wisconsin's earliest citizens arrived from southern and western regions as the glaciers receded. Finding abundant food and shelter, they must have liked what they saw, since they adapted to the area's weather and stayed in small groups as they wandered and foraged. Clues of their lives mostly come from arrowheads and flint they used, as well as rock art and a few intact personal possessions that survived the elements and time.

What is rock art and where can it be found?

Rock art is an overall term to describe three basic methods of etching or leaving symbols on or with rock.

- Pictographs are images left on the surface of rocks; the medium used was generally an ink made of plant extract mixed with animal fat or blood.
- Petroglyphs are images scratched into the surface of a rock with a sharp object.
- It's possible that petroforms may have been used by Wisconsin Native Americans, but petroforms—described as rocks that have been moved to or from something else—were the most-often destroyed of all rock art.

Basically, rock art was used by early Native Americans as a means of communication or documentation in the absence of written language, in religious or spiritual rites, or as a method of documenting something personally important.

Found mostly in southwestern Wisconsin's Driftless Region and dating back at least 1,300 years, rock art is primarily found along rock shelters and in caves. Generally, the art depicts birds, bison, and deer, but humans are also featured, as well as other figures that seem to be merely designs. In at least one case, the etchings (probably made with nut shells, other rocks, or charcoal) are in panel form, which allows scientists to decipher their meanings. Hunting, or stalking prey, seems to be a common theme.

Along with the petroglyphs, archaeologists have discovered remains of cradle boards, moccasins, knives, flint, bits of pottery, and animal bones. It's believed that the creators of southwestern Wisconsin's most well-known rock art formations were ancestors of today's Ho-Chunk.

Wisconsin is filled with caves and rock formations, so it's possible that there is more rock art to be found; certainly, if you ever find a cave with rock art, archaeologists would love to know about it. Alas, it's difficult to visit many of the known sites; they are largely kept secret or are protected with fencing, to keep them from vandals.

How did Wisconsin's first people survive?

Since very little was left to tell us about the daily lives of the Paleo-Indians, researchers have had to piece together what we know from the scant clues they've found in various locations around the state.

What are the most common arrowheads found in Wisconsin?

The two most common kinds of arrowheads from the Paleo-Indian era are the Clovis and Folsom arrowheads, both distinguished by flutes, which are long, shallow grooves on the widest part of the stone, from the base of the arrowhead to its point. Clovis arrowheads have flutes only part-way up both sides, while Folsom arrowheads are grooved nearly to the tip of the point. Both types of arrowheads are used for spears and both are found in Wisconsin, although the Clovis arrowheads are much more common.

You may also find other "points" (what collectors call arrowheads) with different notches and tips, such as the Agate Basin, the Osceola, the Durst Stemmed, the Preston Corner-Notched, or the Madison Triangular. An expert can tell you what you've discovered, if you're ever lucky enough to spot an arrowhead in the wild.

For amateur archaeologists, there's fun to be had here: arrowheads can be found nearly anywhere there's disturbed soil, mostly in Wisconsin's rural areas. Farm kids know that many are turned up in the spring, when farmers begin plowing and planting.

From presumed foraging behavior, we can surmise that early people were willing to move or relocate as needed, not just because of the migration of animals and birds, but because of seasonal plants and, later, crops. At the time when foraging was more common, the Native population of the area was small and group sizes followed suit; researchers believe that individual groups interacted, although we don't know to what extent. Overall, not much is known about these early people's social lives; skirmishes are always a possibility, as are games and cooperation. We just don't know.

Obviously, Wisconsin's earliest people took advantage of the natural resources here, and hunted and fished for their food: Mastodons have been found with Paleo-Indian spear points buried in their ancient bones (most notably, one in Boaz), so we can guess that the Paleo-Indians ate mastodon, at least, and probably venison, bison, mammoth, and ground sloth. It's also almost certain that they took advantage of abundant edible plants such as berries and roots during warmer seasons.

In time, weapons and tools were refined and by about 3000 B.C., Paleo-Indians were using several different kinds of methods of sustaining themselves. While they were still mobile, it appears that they traveled a circuitous route, possibly based on the seasons; edible plants could be preserved for winter meals, and they eventually learned to preserve meats. At that point, they were also burying their dead with artifacts, which researchers say shows a preference for returning to a specific area.

Two thousand years later, Woodland Indians created pottery and began to rely on early methods of agriculture for sustenance. Researchers believe that the Woodland Indians were the makers of burial mounds.

By about 1,000 years ago, the Oneita (at least) largely lived in villages and were known to farm corn, beans, and squash, and possibly other crops. They had also established methods of trade that extended surprisingly far: nearly north to south and coast to coast. For sure, the rich culture of Wisconsin's Native Americans changed when the Europeans arrived.

What are burial mounds?

Found mostly in the southern half of the state, burial mounds (or Effigy Mounds) are literally what they sound like: burial sites in which earth is mounded up higher (some three to five feet [1 to 1.5 meters] higher) than the surrounding ground. It's believed that the deceased were laid on a flat surface and the ground was mounded high around them, in a manner that would leave the mound intact in poor weather. Some burial mounds contain up to two bodies; most contain bodies but not possessions. Using available technology, scientists have discovered that some mounds don't have anything in them at all.

Researchers believe that the Effigy Mound tradition started some eight hundred to sixteen hundred years ago, when Late Woodland Indians began building mounds in the form of animals or birds, conical mounds, or long, loaf-like mounds near water or wetlands. The mounds may have reflected a belief system, social purposes, or they might

25

Man Mound Park in Baraboo is the site of one of the best-preserved Indian burial mounds in the state.

have been used as markers for territory or terrain. The creation of burial mounds may have gone hand-in-hand with the rise of purposeful agricultural practices and the foundation of villages; researchers still aren't quite sure.

Whatever their purpose, it wasn't until 1894 that it was proven by state scientist Increase Lapham that early Native Americans were the creators of the mounds. It's estimated that there were once some 20,000 burial mounds in Wisconsin; today, there are about 4,000 left. Several state and federal statutes protect Wisconsin's Effigy Mounds.

When did the first European residents arrive in Wisconsin?

Although no one can be 100 percent certain, French and English fur traders were the first Europeans to arrive in what eventually became Wisconsin in the early 1600s.

It's possible that Frenchman Étienne Brûlé (1592–1633) was the first European in Wisconsin. He claimed to have traveled to the Wisconsin side of what is now Lake Superior but, since there are no written accounts directly from Brûlé himself (the only reports were written second-hand after Brûlé 's death), trapper Jean Nicolet (1598–1642) is usually given credit for being the "first" European in the state. Nicolet was in search of a fast, easy way to the Pacific; he was disappointed on that hope but he found furs, which were perhaps just as valuable to him, personally—and, in the scheme of things, absolutely more valuable to traders, merchants, and other trappers.

Also arriving in 1634 was Jacques Marquette (1637–1675), who teamed up with Nicolet to explore and document the area, the people they encountered, and the resources they found.

It should also be noted that there's a small possibility that Viking explorers came through the St. Lawrence River into the Great Lakes and to the shores of Wisconsin and Minnesota. If that actually occurred—and it's just speculation for now—they predated Europeans by several hundred years.

What were the first Europeans looking for?

Early French explorers sent from Québec were in search of safe and efficient passage from the Atlantic Ocean to the Pacific Ocean, and they hoped it might be through the St. Lawrence River. Maps of the area, of course, didn't exist then, and they had no idea that that many rivers and a lot of land separated the seas. Their hopes were driven by finances, which shouldn't surprise anyone.

Because plants that yielded spices such as pepper and cinnamon couldn't be grown in Europe, silk worms didn't thrive there, and certain perfumes were only found outside the continent, Europeans had been trading food, materials, and luxury goods with China and Japan for several centuries. That was done by traversing any one of several overland routes, but traveling with a caravan over land took a long time and was often dangerous, not to mention expensive. Traders and merchants hoped that a water route might be faster, so that goods could be delivered in a speedier, simpler manner.

Alas, instead of finding a better way to get to the Orient, they found the Great Lakes, which took them to what would eventually be Wisconsin and other states. By following rivers that flowed from and around the area, they didn't find passage to China, but they found a huge source of furs—which would soon become just as valuable as spices and perfumes.

It wouldn't be until the mid-1600s that fur trappers arrived into Wisconsin en masse, and they didn't get far because of the Iroquois Wars and the danger that came with battle. Even so, they found enough fur to keep them interested in coming back and to keep European entities interested in laying claim to the land on which the beavers were found.

How did the first Europeans get to Wisconsin?

Most traders and explorers arrived in one of three ways: either on foot through Canada from the north, on foot through what is now Illinois and Indiana from the south or southeast, or via canoe down the St. Lawrence River and into the Great Lakes. From there, they spread out in basically the same way, via rivers and over land across what is now the state.

Much later, settlers came from the south or southeast, over land, in wagons, on foot, and on horseback.

What was it like to travel by canoe then?

When you think of a canoe, you likely think of a two-man device and a quiet lake. That couldn't be farther from the truth for Wisconsin's first explorers. Their canoes were considerably larger, and considerably more dangerous to use: canoes could be tippy in rough Great Lakes weather and if river travel was attempted, explorers often didn't know where rapids or shallow areas might be. It's therefore understandable that explorers later took advantage of the availability of French-Canadian voyageurs, men who knew the area's waterways and were skilled at piloting larger canoes that could be loaded with provisions or furs.

Canoes themselves were probably made of flexible cedar or birch and covered with birch bark sewn together with roots or sinew. The whole thing was likely sealed with pine pitch. These materials were abundant along the routes that trappers and traders used, so emergency repairs could easily be made.

Who was Jean Nicolet?

Born in France in the late 1500s, Jean Nicolet (1598–1642) arrived in North America through Canada as a young man in his twenties, brought here by his friend Samuel de Champlain. Champlain, a French explorer, hoped to start a program to teach young men to become fur traders through immersion with the Natives who lived in the territory, and Nicolet was intrigued. Accepting what seems today like an assignment, Nicolet left relative civilization in Québec and moved to a small Indian village near the Ottawa River and learned the Algonquin language and culture.

This 1910 mural painted by Franz Edward Rohrbeck for the Brown County Courthouse in Green Bay is a rather disturbing portrayal of French explorer Jean Nicolet landing in Green Bay and immediately threatening the indigenous people. He is shown wearing a Chinese tunic, symbolizing his quest to find a route to Asia.

In 1634, he and a handful of Huron tribesmen ventured westward through what is now the Great Lakes, in search of what he and Champlain, then governor of New France, believed might be a passage to the Pacific Ocean and, therefore, to the Orient. Instead of finding China, however, Nicolet became the first European to cross Lake Michigan and land on its upper shores near modern-day Green Bay, into Ho-Chunk territory. The Ho-Chunk received him well and Nicolet stayed in the area until the fall of that year, when he returned to Québec to work with Indian tribes there. He died in 1642 when a boat he was riding in capsized.

Who was Jacques Marquette?

Also born in France, Jacques Marquette (1637–1675; sometimes known as Father Marquette) knew from an early age what he wanted to do with his life: in 1654, at age 17, he joined the Society of Jesus and became a Jesuit. Following his training and a dozen years' work as a teacher, he begged for an assignment as a missionary, and was sent by the French to North America, to Québec, in late 1666.

In 1668, he left Montreal for what is now Michigan, where he founded a mission on the western shores of Lake Superior and began working with various Native tribes in the Great Lakes region. In his time in the area, Marquette managed to establish at least two missions, including one in Sault Ste. Marie, in Michigan's first European settlement.

In early May of 1673, Louis Jolliet (see below) arrived at the mission. He and Marquette were chosen to lead an expedition down the Mississippi River on behalf of the French, to explore and document what they found. Marquette also hoped to bring Christianity to the natives they might encounter. Ultimately, it was a trip that excited and inspired other explorers; the discovery of more sumptuous furs didn't hurt, either.

Beginning near Green Bay, the group went down the Fox River and portaged (or, carried their items over ground) to the Wisconsin River. They entered the Mississippi River near Prairie du Chien in mid-June of 1673 and proceeded downstream as far as the Arkansas River. Their trip to the mouth of the Mississippi was aborted, however, when they learned that they were about to enter territory owned by the Spanish, an encounter that they feared could go badly. Returning north, they reached the Illinois River about a month later. After this adventure, Jolliet continued to explore, while Marquette returned to what is now Green Bay in 1673 and died some two years later in Michigan, at age 38.

Who was Louis Jolliet?

Born in Québec, Louis Jolliet (1645–1700; sometimes spelled "Joliet") grew up playing on Ile d'Orleans, an island on which many of Canada's First People lived. It's possible, therefore, that local Native languages were his second languages (French being the first). Later in his life, he became fluent in Spanish and English, too.

Because Québec was a hub for the fur trade, Jolliet also grew up knowing the ins and outs of the industry. After entering school to become a Jesuit priest, he decided, instead, to leave the program and become a fur trader.

In about 1670, Jolliet joined Jacques Marquette for the purpose of exploration. They left what is now Michigan and paddled canoes to northeast Wisconsin. From Green Bay, they paddled on the Fox River, carried their gear to the Wisconsin River and ultimately entered the Mississippi at Prairie du Chien in mid-June. They traveled downriver to the southern half of what is now Arkansas, to the Arkansas River, where they encountered indications of Spanish explorers. Concerned about hostilities from the Spanish, they retraced their route north to explore areas that were much friendlier.

Jolliet married, but does not seem to have left any heirs. Well-known for his expeditions, he left his home near Québec in May 1700 for reasons that are unrecorded, and was never seen again.

Were there any other notable explorers in the early years of Wisconsin history?

Yes!

Étienne Broûlé traveled to the area at about the same time Jean Nicolet was here, possibly to assist de Champlain with mapping. Some say that Broûlé was the first European in Wisconsin but because he left very few details of his trip and his memoirs were written after his death, it's impossible to know for sure. If he did, indeed, beat Nicolet to this area, it was only a year or so earlier than Nicolet's arrival and Broûlé didn't appear to have stayed long.

Médard des Groseilliers (1618–1696) and his brother Pierre Radisson (1636–1710) were fur traders who spent considerable time in the northern and eastern parts of the state. Most of their efforts, however, were spent in the Hudson Bay area; they are credited for helping found the Hudson Bay Company.

Nicolet, Marquette, and most of the other earliest trappers / traders had, by most accounts, very good relationships with the Indians who lived in Wisconsin at the time, which smoothed a path for other explorers who arrived in coming years. Marquette and Jolliet's exploration also inspired the work of others such as Fr. Louis Hennepin (1636–1704); Robert de La Salle (1643–1687); Henri de Tonti (1649–1704); and Daniel Greysolon, Sieur du Lhut (1639–1710; from whom Duluth gets its name).

A 1718 map of Wisconsin created by French cartographer Guillaume de l'Isle is evidence that the area had been quite well explored by that time.

By and large, exploration of Wisconsin went on well past the 1700s and into the time when the settlers arrived. And if you want to get technical and consider caves and underground areas that have yet to be seen and pristine places that rarely see human presence, exploration of Wisconsin still goes on today.

What's the deal about beaver furs, anyhow?

As you can well imagine, life in the mid-1600s was different than it is now.

There were no synthetic fabrics and no central heating. There were no high-tech gloves and no way to know how cold tomorrow would be. People were at the mercy of the weather, especially in winter, and keeping warm could be serious work, especially for the young or the injured. Even for the able-bodied, most work was done outdoors.

Because beavers spend much of their time in the water, beaver fur wicks off water very easily; shaved and felted, beaver skins are also warm and soft. Word spread quickly that beaver pelts made the best hats, and North American beavers were even better. That could make a man mighty rich. For a trapper—someone who only had to put forth effort to acquire the pelt itself—it was worth pursuing.

Undoubtedly, there were trappers who caught their own prey; history has recorded many men who made their livings on the water as such, but most bartered with the Indians instead. Natives had been trapping for generations and they were also expert trappers, perhaps even better than the Europeans. They had the goods and they were willing to trade with white trappers who imported the things they knew the Natives wanted. That included guns and blankets, and so, twice a year—spring and fall—trappers would visit the various tribes to do their trading. Once a deal had been brokered, the trappers picked up the pelts, and stored them in warehouses for later transport north or east through rivers and across lakes to Montreal. From there, the pelts were sent via ship to Europe.

At the beginning of the fur craze in France and England, it's been estimated that there were some 6 million beavers in the Great Lakes region and thereabouts. Around 200,000 pelts were retrieved and exported each year (including those trapped in Canada) and so, by the end of the 1800s, the beaver was near extinction in the area. But because of beaver pelts and the European need for them, explorers set up trading posts all along Wisconsin rivers. Because of beaver pelts, wars were fought over control of territory.

Was it a peaceful transition when the Europeans arrived to Wisconsin on a larger scale?

Not at all!

For the first few years of European presence in Wisconsin, trappers and fur traders, mostly Frenchmen, worked in relative harmony with the Native Americans living here. Shortly after they arrived, they mostly settled near the mouths of main rivers and near Lake Michigan, and interacted peacefully with the Indians; reports were that there were minor problems, but nothing terribly noteworthy, initially. Wars did break out, however (see below).

What happened during the Iroquois Wars?

The Iroquois Wars were also known as the Beaver Wars. Approximately two decades after Jean Nicolet arrived in Wisconsin, the fur industry followed, but few trappers dared to go much further. There was a war out there!

For decades prior to the mid-1600s, Iroquois living near the St. Lawrence Seaway had been trading with explorers and fishermen for beaver robes and pelts. The Iroquois recognized that their territory gave them incredible power, not to mention access to European goods, such as weapons. Beavers were rapidly disappearing from their area, due to overtrapping. It was natural, therefore, that they would want to expand that territory.

Originally a group of five tribal nations—the Mohawk, Oneida, Cayuga, Onondaga, and Seneca—as well as other, smaller groups that joined the battle were led by the Mohawk and supported by Dutch and English traders. The Huron, the group whose territory the Iroquois intended to take, were supported by the French.

The battle, which was particularly vicious and bloody, lasted up to fifty years and totally upended the territory of many tribes from Michigan, Iowa, Illinois, Indiana, Wisconsin, Pennsylvania, up through New York, and all the way down into Ohio. Because of alliances with the Europeans, it also changed the territorial lines of an infant America. Historians say that, because exact written accounts weren't kept by tribal members, we may never know the full story, nor will we ever know the total loss in life.

The Beaver War resonated, later, in the French and Indian Wars.

What is important about the French and Indian Wars?

While it was not fought on Wisconsin soil, the French and Indian Wars are noteworthy in Wisconsin history because of Potawatomi involvement.

Because of their alliances with the French in trading, the Potawatomi sided with French militia in wars with the Chickasaw. From 1746 to 1747, the Potawatomi fought

31

in King George's War, and in the French and Indian Wars (also known as the Seven Years' War) from 1754 to 1763. It should be noted that, in their support, the Potawatomi traveled to Montreal, Pennsylvania, and New York; even so, the British won the wars.

What were the Fox Wars?

In the late seventeenth century, the Fox likewise got involved with disputes over the fur trade and raided French settlements over rights to use the Mississippi River. In 1804, Sauk and Fox tribal representatives had signed a treaty that gave all their land east of the Mississippi River to the U.S. government for the princely sum of $2,500. Sauk Warrior Black Hawk (1767–1838) (known to his people as Ma-ka-tai-me-she-kia-kiak), however, didn't think the treaty was fair or valid; he ultimately signed the treaty, too, but his resentment simmered.

The first Fox war was fought because of problems that began near Detroit; for twenty-three days, the Fox and their allies fought the French and their allies. Although Fox fighters vastly outnumbered French soldiers, the Fox and their supporters lost the battle and around a thousand men. The French and their allies, by contrast, lost fewer than one hundred fighters. Native American survivors, mostly women and children, were captured and taken as slaves.

The freedom of those captives was the basis of the second Fox war in 1727, when a peace treaty between the French and their four Indian allies, and the Fox, was dissolved. The Fox declared war, but they were outnumbered by a large margin of French soldiers, as well as those of their enemy tribes. The French struck with ferocity for four years, but the Fox were equally fierce. Though denied safety with other tribes, they finally were granted sanctuary with the Sauk, who also took up arms against the French. With the help of other western Wisconsin tribes, Sauk / Fox forces overcame the French, causing French officials to offer a pardon and bring back peace.

Even so, the Sauk and Fox never forgot what happened: in the War of 1812, they took up arms with the British.

Slowly, though, as the U.S. government expanded and the nation's population increased, Native Americans were slowly squeezed out. Wisconsin's growing mining and lumbering industries made the rush to settle in the state more urgent, which only exacerbated the problem.

How did the Black Hawk War ignite?

In early 1832, as Sauk leader Black Hawk began to move his people into nearby Illinois, to lands that the U.S. government had gotten in a treaty that was hotly disputed, officials shot at the Sauk band. Sometimes known as the "British Band" because they flew the British flag, Black Hawk and his people gathered other tribes as they moved southward, until they included more than a thousand people.

At that point, General Edmund P. Gaines (1777–1849) tried to intimidate Black Hawk and his followers to leave. The British Band moved to the west side of the Mississippi River, across from Illinois, in June of 1831. Less than a year later, they returned to Illinois; reports differ as to why, when faced with so many government soldiers, Black Hawk returned. Some say his reasoning may not have been clear to Black Hawk himself.

By the first of May, Black Hawk knew he'd made a mistake. Other Wisconsin tribes had turned against him and British supplies had all but dried up. On May 15, government and Sauk forces clashed in what is now known as the Battle of Stillman's Run, where the Sauk soundly defeated the government militia. The British Band then headed north, where they found

Women and children try to escape with their lives in this illustration of the Battle of Bad Axe, which marked the final defeat of Black Hawk.

sanctuary with the Ho-Chunk near the Michigan Territory. Other tribes weren't happy and warned white settlements of impending raids. Government leaders were adamant that Black Hawk and his band be destroyed, as an example to others who might try similar actions.

In July 1832, a reorganization of government forces caught the British Band near present-day Sauk City and, in what's now known as the Battle of Wisconsin Heights, did significant damage to Black Hawk's group. By this time, the British Band was struggling, injured, and starving. It was only a matter of time.

After the Battle of Wisconsin Heights, Black Hawk attempted to surrender, but government forces would not accept it. As some of his followers attempted to flee across the Mississippi one more time, the 150 warriors left fought valiantly at what is now known as the Battle of Bad Axe, on August 2. One week later, after fifteen weeks of hard fighting and with few of the original followers left, the final battle was fought and the Black Hawk Wars were over.

Black Hawk spent the rest of his life under the watch of another Sauk chief who had once been Black Hawk's enemy.

The Treaty of Prairie du Chien of 1825 was also significant. It basically tamped down intertribal warfare that affected the European fur trade, by insisting on peaceful coexistence between Indians and settlers, and between each tribe.

Did the Treaty of Prairie du Chien end the issues between Native Americans and the U.S. government?

No, it didn't. But there was little that any Wisconsin tribes could do; beginning in the late eighteenth century through about 1920, U.S. officials tried to "assimilate" Native American individuals into white society through attempts to eradicate cultural traditions, language, and religious practices. The General Allotment Act of 1887 (also known as the Dawes Act) removed tribal lands and made them into eighty-acre (thirty-two-hectare) farms that were largely sold to white settlers. The Dawes Act was reversed with the Indian Reorganization Act in 1934, which encouraged tribes to return to their lands. The tide turned once again in the 1950s, when attempts were once again made to "relocate" Wisconsin Native Americans off their tribal lands and into larger cities.

Which Native American tribes called Wisconsin home?

While there's no way of positively knowing the full story, researchers and historians think that before European explorers arrived, the Ojibwa, Dakota Sioux, Ho-Chunk (Winnebago), Menominee, Potawatomi, and Fox / Sauk were the main tribes inhabiting Wisconsin. Later, once the Europeans arrived in what is now Illinois, Iowa, and Missouri, the Huron, Cheyenne, Munsee, Illini, Stockbridge, and Oneida moved into the area. Other, smaller tribes may have been in and out of Wisconsin over the years; these are the ones large enough to know about.

Today, the U.S. government recognizes eleven tribes in the state. They are:
- The Bad River Band of Lake Superior Chippewa
- The Forest County Potawatomi
- The Ho-Chunk Nation
- The Lac Courte Oreilles Band of Lake Superior Chippewa
- The Lac du Flambeau Band of Lake Superior Chippewa
- The Menominee Indian Tribe of Wisconsin
- The Oneida Tribe of Indians
- The Red Cliff Band of Lake Superior Chippewa
- The Sokaogan Mole Lake Community
- The St. Croix Chippewa
- The Stockbridge Munsee Band of Mohicans

Most—but not all—of these have designated reservations on which to live.

What notable event nearly made the Menominee tribe disappear?

On August 1, 1953, House Concurrent Resolution 108 was passed. Its intention was, "as rapidly as possible, to make the Indians within the territorial limits of the United States subject to the same laws and entitled to the same privileges and responsibilities as are applicable to other citizens of the United States, to end their status as wards of the United States, and to grant them all of the rights and prerogatives pertaining to American citizenship...."

This, in effect, removed Native Americans from government protection on their rural tribal lands and abolished the federal recognition of many tribes. Targeted tribes were supposed to receive job training and housing assistance while being assimilated and relocated to urban areas. The Menominee was one of the first to go, reportedly because the government felt that they didn't need quite as much assistance; therefore, on April

The Menominee tribal office in Keshena houses administration offices that oversee the now-restored reservation.

30, 1961, the tribe officially was no longer, their lands became a county (rather than a reservation) and the infrastructure they had built started to crumble.

In 1970, a grassroots movement began working to restore federal recognition status of the Menominee and in 1975, fourteen years after the official dissolution of their tribe, the Menominee were restored and the county once again became a reservation.

In 1983, more than two decades after House Concurrent Resolution 108 was passed, treaty revisions were restored that allowed Wisconsin's Native Americans to hunt, fish, and spear on ceded lands.

Why do Native Americans operate Wisconsin's casinos?

In 1987, Wisconsin residents voted in a referendum to allow a state lottery and Class III gambling, which opened the opportunity to establish casinos. Even though it was voted in, the decision to allow gaming was a controversial one but the presence of Class III gambling was an excellent chance for Wisconsin's Native Americans to make up for dwindling funds from budget cuts elsewhere, and several tribes—most notably, the Ho-Chunk, Potawatomi, Ojibwe, and Mohican—opened casinos.

In 1988, Congress passed the Indian Gaming Regulatory Act, which decreed that states and tribes must negotiate regulations concerning Class III gaming, which includes blackjack, slot machines, Keno, roulette, and craps.

A few years back, it was estimated that Indian-owned casinos in Wisconsin collect revenues of over $1 billion a year, nearly half of which is net profit for the casinos themselves.

Why do you sometimes see the Ho-Chunk referred to as the Winnebago?

Although other tribes have known them by different names at other times, the Hoocąągra, or the Ho-Chunk is a Siouan band that is now believed to have come from the East Coast centuries ago, having eventually settled near what is now Lake Winnebago. It's unclear which name came first—the people or the lake—although it's known that the name "Winnebago," meaning something close to "stinky water" and indicating the lake's fishy summertime smell, came from the Algonquins.

In the 1830s, after the Ho-Chunk ceded some of their land to the federal government, the latter tried to move the Ho-Chunk to Iowa territory. Most of the Ho-Chunk moved to Northern Wisconsin instead. Other attempts at removal were made until 1865, when the Ho-Chunk received reservation lands in Nebraska and were relocated; even so, many Ho-Chunk refused all attempts to leave and snuck back into Wisconsin. By the 1880s, the government ended their efforts and allowed the remaining Ho-Chunk to buy forty-acre (sixteen-hectare) farms and stay in Wisconsin.

There are still people of the Winnebago tribe in Nebraska, and the tribe is federally recognized. People of the same lineage are the Ho-Chunk in Wisconsin—also a federally recognized tribe. In 1994, the name "Ho-Chunk" was officially adopted for those who remain in the Badger State.

How have Wisconsin's Native Americans left their mark on the state's cities?

Aside from the name of the state itself, you can see Wisconsin's Indian heritage in the towns people live in.

Milwaukee was reportedly known as "Millioki" by the Algonquins, a word that indicates a place by the water to gather. Oshkosh was a Menominee chief. Mukwonago is said to be a Potawatomi word describing a bend in a river and Oconomowoc is a Potawatomi word for "waterfall." Neenah, Wausau, Mequon, Manitowoc, Fond du Lac, Menominee Falls, Menasha, Waupaca, Waukesha, Waupun—the names for all these cities come from various Wisconsin Native American languages. Even La Crosse is named after a Native American game played next to the Mississippi River (although French settlers were the ones who named the game itself).

Once the Europeans got here, who claimed the state as their territory?

Because they were first in the area, the French made the first attempts at European settlement in Wisconsin with Fort St. Nicholas, possibly near Prairie du Chien, and Fort St. Antoine near Lake Pepin, both constructed in 1686, both founded by Nicholas Perrot. At that time, French outposts rarely served as homes; instead, they were something akin to a modern meeting room and used mostly for doing business.

The state's first recorded black man came to Wisconsin in 1725. A slave to a French man, he was killed in a raid near Green Bay.

During the French and Indian War of 1728–1733, the British were able to gradually take the area and reached total control by 1763. Much like the French were earlier in the century, the British were mostly interested in Wisconsin's rich fur industry; even so, theirs was a symbiotic relationship: within the trade, the British needed the French and vice versa, so the two groups lives amicably.

While Charles Michel de Langlade is generally recognized as Wisconsin's first settler (in the Green Bay area), a real attempt at settlement didn't begin until the late 1700s, in Prairie du Chien. Widespread settlement in the early 1800s was hampered by the Winnebago War of 1827 and the Black Hawk War in 1832.

Were there a lot of forts built in Wisconsin's early years?

There were *dozens* of forts in Wisconsin then!

The first, Ft. St. François, was built by Nicolas Perrot in 1684 near what is now Green Bay, destroyed by Indians in 1728, rebuilt in 1732, abandoned in 1760, and became a British fort in 1761. At that time, it became Ft. Edward Augustus but that was abandoned two years later. You can see a commemorative flagpole today, at the foot of the Dousman Street Bridge near the Fox River.

Other notable forts throughout Wisconsin history were:

- Ft. Howard (Green Bay) and Camp Bragg were used during the Civil War, as were Camp Hamilton (later named Camp Wood, near Fond du Lac); and several smaller camps near what the Milwaukee area is now.

Located on the west bank of the Fox River in Green Bay, Fort Howard was operational from 1812 to 1853.

- Camp Randall (Madison) was used as a Confederate POW camp during the Civil War.
- Ft. Winnebago (Portage) had a stockade built during the Black Hawk War.
- The original Ft. Koshkonong (later named Ft. Atkinson) was dismantled in 1836 by the area's new settlers. They apparently needed the fort for its wood.
- Five camps were located in Milwaukee: Ft. Holton, Ft. Scott, Ft. Sigel, Ft. Trowbridge, and Ft. Washburn.
- In the late 1600s, the French built several smaller forts along the Mississippi River in the Prairie du Chien—mostly to take advantage of the fur trade in the southwest corner of what is now Wisconsin. The Prairie du Chien area is also the site of several forts that protected residents during wars with the British and that served as outposts during the Civil War.
- Ft. McCoy (Sparta) held Japanese POWs during World War II.
- Superior Stockade was built in Superior in 1862 as protection for residents during the Sioux uprising, although there was no such need that far west of any such battles.

THE STATE OF WISCONSIN: 1800 TO 1900

Other than the wars with Native Americans, were there any wars fought on Wisconsin soil?

Yes—but surprisingly just one: a single battle in the War of 1812.

After the war broke out in 1812, Wisconsin's lucrative fur trade abruptly stopped. In order to get the trade jump-started, American forces built Ft. Shelby in Prairie du Chien, halfway between American-held St. Louis, Missouri, and British-held Ft. Mackinac Island, Michigan, a reaction that made the British troops quite unhappy.

Acting upon the American forces' seeming show of force, the British commissioned a militia consisting mostly of local Native Americans; they arrived at Prairie du Chien on July 17, 1814, and asked for a surrender they didn't get. After a nearly three-day battle that was fought on the grounds of what is now the Villa Louis estate, American gunboats were forced to flee, leaving a handful of soldiers behind. Those men were immediately captured.

The British renamed the grounds Ft. McKay, but they didn't get to keep it for long: upon the signing of the Treaty of Ghent in late December of 1814, British troops were forced out of the Midwest by the American troops. Before leaving, they burned Ft. McKay to the ground; American troops returned in 1816 and rebuilt the fort, calling it Ft. Crawford.

Ft. Crawford was closed in 1856.

What important Wisconsin meeting changed national politics?

The Whig Party, a political group formed in 1834 by voters who were against President Andrew Jackson, was struggling with issues of slavery and it became obvious that the party could no longer exist. In February 1854, following the Kansas-Nebraska bill that gave the decision of slave or free over to individual territories, the Whig Party was officially over. Even so, men who had never been pro-Whig had already begun holding meetings at several upper-Midwest places to explore the possibility of a new political party. One of those meetings, held in Ripon March 20, 1854, has long been recognized as the meeting when the Republican Party was officially launched.

In 1860, Abraham Lincoln became the Republican Party's first president.

For more information, see *Wisconsin Politics*.

How did Wisconsin transition from being a territory to being a state?

Once the skirmishes with the Native Americans were largely settled, the area between the Great Lakes and the Mississippi River looked mighty appealing to Americans wishing to expand into new lands. Not only was the area great for farming and fishing, but many settlers were interested in the mining that was available. They'd known for some time that lead was readily available in the southwestern part of the state, so that's where they headed; in fact, that was where most of Wisconsin's early population was centered in the earliest years.

On April 20, 1836, Wisconsin became a territory through an act of the U.S. Congress. The "Wiskonsin" Territory included what is now Wisconsin, Iowa, and Minnesota, as well as the easternmost parts of North and South Dakota. Henry Dodge was the first territorial governor and, after much argument, Madison was built for the sole purpose of being the territory's capital city.

By the mid-1840s, the Wisconsin Territory was home to over 150,000 people, more than enough to qualify for statehood. The territorial legislature applied to the U.S. government for statehood in 1846; a state constitution was drawn up later that year but it was voted down for being too progressive. About a year later, a second constitution was created; it was approved in March of 1848. On May 29 of that year, Wisconsin officially became the thirtieth state in the United States.

Who were the settlers in Wisconsin's early history?

In the earliest time of the settlers' arrival, the French were in the area that eventually became Wisconsin, and they mixed freely with Wisconsin's American Indian tribes; the French were the first to arrive, after all, and they came years after the natives had arrived. Although you can see French influence in some of Wisconsin's

Henry Dodge (1782–1867) served as the Wisconsin territory governor two times (1836–1841 and 1845–1848) and was also a U.S. congressman representing the territory.

oldest cities, the French weren't very populous for very long: after the French and Indian War (1754–1763), they lost control of the area to the British, who quickly moved into the territory. Even well into the twentieth century, there were few French immigrants on record.

Settlers looking for adventure, land, or steady work came to Wisconsin in the first years of its status as territory but towns were few and far between. It wasn't until May of 1849, a year after Wisconsin officially became a state, that U.S. Secretary of the Interior Thomas Ewing declared that land sales were to be advertised in several newspapers in states other than Wisconsin. It was then that Wisconsin began to see an increase in population, beginning in the southeastern portion of the state.

Swiss immigrants arrived. Free Blacks and former slaves applied for Wisconsin land. Welsh miners settled mostly in five counties, two thousand Russian families came in late 1839, and thousands of Norwegians streamed into the state. New Englanders moved west to be here. By far, the largest group to come to Wisconsin were the Germans who first settled on the eastern borders before moving widely to other areas of the state. Just after Wisconsin achieved statehood, it was determined that at least one person from nearly every state in the then-union had moved here to live.

What were the main industries in Wisconsin's early history?

The settlers were initially most interested in mining, specifically lead.

Native Americans had been mining lead in the southwestern part of the state in what is now Grant, Iowa, and Lafayette Counties but after treaties took away the Indians' rights to mine, white settlers were allowed in—and in they came, literally from other territories, states, and from overseas beginning in the early 1830s. Boomtowns sprung up, federal offices were hastily created and by 1840, Wisconsin miners were providing over half the nation's lead.

While lead mining was surely the number one industry for many years, Wisconsin's appeal for agriculture began to grow in the 1830s. Advertisements further enticed immigrants to the area; they brought fruit trees and other crops that Wisconsin land hadn't before seen but which would grow well.

While it wasn't quite the big industry it had once been, fur was still a draw to the state. Lumbermen followed the fur traders and by the mid-1820s, timber was a solid trade near the Black and Chippewa Rivers. Treaties with the Indians opened up lands in the northern part of the territory. It should be noted that neither fur traders nor lumbermen were pleased with the growing agriculture industry; planting crops interfered with trapping and logging.

For more information, check out the chapter "Business and Agriculture."

In what part of Wisconsin's lumber industry did the Mormons play?

After the Mormons moved to Nauvoo, Illinois, and had established a community there, they decided to build a large, grand church to hold their faithful. Knowing that there was plenty of fine wood in Wisconsin, the locals sent a group of men to collect timber for the effort. They purchased mills near the Black River Falls, founded a settlement, hired a large group of workers, and in the summer of 1843, proceeded to float logs, milled timber, and hewn wood down the river to Nauvoo. Needless to say, it was a very large operation that offered many jobs for new immigrants to the area.

Alas, depending on who has written the account, either because of prosecution, internal strife, or minor scandal, there were problems within the community and the mills were sold about a year after their purchase. Whether or not this has any bearing on today's Mormon head count in Wisconsin, a mere 0.4 percent of Wisconsin's population is Mormon.

Why is Wisconsin known as the Badger State?

The nickname of "The Badger State" is an old one: it comes from about the 1820s, when the need for lead and iron ore meant that mining immigrants were flocking to the area for the jobs that were available. Men who worked in Wisconsin's lead and iron ore mines often had no place to live during the cold winters so they hunkered down in holes dug into the sides of hills, or in caves.

Badgers are small black, gray, and white subterranean mammals with claws, fierce teeth and attitude, and they live underground; the similarities were apparently noticed and the wintering miners were dubbed "Badgers."

By the 1840s, the nickname was fast becoming something of which area residents were proud. Steamships, newspapers, and businesses all grabbed onto the badger's popularity. The name eventually stuck and grew to encompass all Wisconsinites—and a certain school's mascot. (And yes, there was once a real badger who stood in as Bucky but it's been said that he escaped one time too many and was eventually replaced).

How were goods and products transported to other areas?

Wisconsin is called "The Badger State," a nickname that developed as a result of the mining days of the nineteenth century, when workers hunkered down in holes like badgers.

- Long before Wisconsin was a territory, furs were transported by canoe or by foot to their ultimate destination, where they would be sold immediately or sold at market elsewhere. The rights to portage goods overland were often purchased from local natives.

- The earliest results of Wisconsin's southwest mining operations were taken south into Illinois by large yokes of oxen and wagons. There, lead was loaded onto ships and taken to St.

Louis. Ore was moved from Ashland, Bayfield, and, in the northernmost part of the state, Superior via ship.

- Early lumbermen used Wisconsin's rivers and lakes to move timber downstream to other places in the United States.

- Other goods left the state via the Mississippi River on steamboats that often had trouble in low waters, or on cargo ships through the Great Lakes or parts inland, which was unwieldy at best. In 1834, the notion was floated to connect the two main waterways, but it proved to be too grand an idea. In 1838, Milwaukeean Byron Kilbourn wanted to build a canal from the southeastern part of the state where lead was mined, to the Milwaukee harbor, but that idea had very little state support. Investors then came up with a plan to connect the Fox and the Wisconsin Rivers in 1839 and Congress granted land to sell to further the project, but the resulting canal turned out to be too long and too winding to be of any use to anyone with serious intentions to use it for shipping.

- Shortly after statehood was achieved, goods were moved by train. The first rail line went from Milwaukee to Waukesha in 1851. A full side-to-side rail line was built in 1857; it went from Lake Michigan to Prairie du Chien. Within a few years, Wisconsin's railroads were connected to others coast-to-coast.

- With the invention of the "horseless carriage," large trucks couldn't be far behind and by 1914, there were around 100,000 trucks on U.S. roads. Today, there are some 15,000 independent trucking companies in Wisconsin. The Wisconsin Motor Carrier's Association says that somewhere near 90 percent of the states' manufactured goods are transported by semi truck.

The Wisconsin Department of Transportation was founded in 1911.

THE U.S. CIVIL WAR

On which side of the war did Wisconsin fight?

In 1860, after several Southern states seceded from the United States and the Confederacy attacked Ft. Sumter in South Carolina, President Abraham Lincoln asked for volunteers and Wisconsinites leaped to fight on the side of the Union. Lincoln only asked for a single regiment but Alexander Randall, who was then the governor of the state, supplied 56 units altogether, in infantry, cavalry, and artillery brigades.

Surely, despite that history shows Wisconsin on the Union side, there were soldiers who served for the Confederacy. Also just as surely, they were few in number.

Did Wisconsin play a large part in the Civil War?

Yes, Wisconsin sent many of its finest young men to war and they played a large part in what happened in the War Between the States, but obviously not as large a part as the states that were closer to the Mason-Dixon line.

Early in the War, volunteerism was as high as the patriotism showed in the state. Some soldiers wished to fight against slavery or they felt strongly about protecting the country's democratic system. Others had more personal reasons to enlist but whatever thoughts spurred them to join the war, more than 91,000 Wisconsinites—or 1 in 9 residents—volunteered to fight in the Civil War. That number included recent immigrants to the state, free Black residents, Native Americans, and people who'd been in the state for generations.

Madison's Camp Randall was the largest Union training center in Wisconsin. Some 70,000 troops trained there during the War years of 1860–1865. Others were trained in the southeastern parts of the state in Fond du Lac, Milwaukee, and Racine; it's also possible that recruits trained unofficially elsewhere in the state.

In the painting *The American Soldier* (1862) by H. Charles McBarron, the artist portrays the 6th Wisconsin attacking Turner's Gap.

Camp Randall, it should be mentioned, was also used to hold Confederate prisoners during the War.

What role did steamboats play in Wisconsin's history?

Though steamboats were invented in the very early 1800s, during the War of 1812, soldiers needing to get supplies to Ft. Crawford in Prairie du Chien used keelboats, which were powered by stout poles and muscle. In 1823, the *Virginia*, a new steamboat, made her way up the Mississippi to Ft. Snelling in St. Paul; later that year, the *Warrior* was used in the Black Hawk War. Surprisingly, the role of the steamboat in the Civil War was minimal, and its use seemed mostly peaceful.

For the immigrant, travel to Wisconsin by steamboat was the way to go: tickets were affordable and the trip was relatively fast, certainly faster than travel across land on foot. Pleasure-seekers could take a trip in the lap of luxury aboard such a craft. Steamboats also ferried lumber, ore, and dairy products from northern parts of Wisconsin down to Illinois and Missouri, stopping at Prairie du Chien, La Crosse, Trempealeau, and other ports north on their way between St. Paul and Galena, Illinois.

Even today, divers continue to find remains of the dozens of steamboats that sank along the Mississippi River. Some of them include the *Quincy*, which sank near Trempealeau, the *Muscatine*, which sank on the Black River, the *Johnny Schmocker* which sank near Arcadia, and several that sunk near La Crosse. It should be noted that diving near some wrecks is prohibited, so check before you go.

And yes, you can still book a ticket on a Wisconsin steamboat. It's a great way to spend an afternoon.

Were there any Wisconsinites who supported the South?

Most certainly, but their names have largely been lost to history.

When the war first broke out, Wisconsinites were largely supporting of the Union, but those who weren't were quite vocal in their feelings: In 1862, when Lincoln first instituted the military draft, riots broke out in protest in Milwaukee, Port Washington, and West Bend. As the war progressed and the number of casualties mounted, however, support for the Union grew.

There is one interesting story that comes from a non-Wisconsinite whose tale is relevant:

Following the Battle at Shiloh, when Confederate forces were captured by the Wisconsin 14th Infantry, those who were captured were given the option of joining the 14th Brigade. Eighteen men joined; of those, nine deserted and four were discharged within thirty days of joining. Five men stayed and continued to fight with the Wisconsin 14th.

Charles Stahl, who joined the Wisconsin14th Infantry upon capture, stayed with the 14th until war's end. Upon his return to civilian life, he was thereby a veteran on both sides of the war.

What was the Iron Brigade?

Also known as the Black Hat Brigade, the Black Hats, and the Iron Brigade of the West, the war's most famous Iron Brigade was composed of the 2nd, 6th, and 7th Wisconsin Infantries, the 24th Michigan Infantry, the 19th Indiana Infantry, and Battery B of the 4th U.S. Light Artillery and was led by Brigadier General John Gibbon.

The Iron Brigade (or Black Hat Brigade) was composed of infantry from Wisconsin, Indiana, and Michigan, including the 7th Wisconsin pictured here. The brigade saw some of the fiercest fighting in the Civil War and suffered more casualties than any other brigade.

While the nickname of "Iron Brigade" was also used to a smaller extent for other brigades during the war, these fierce fighters—known for the black hats they wore (in contrast to the usual blue ones that other units received)—certainly put fear into the hearts of their enemies. The Iron Brigade saw action in the Eastern Theater in several of the War's major battles and, relative to the size of their numbers, suffered the heaviest casualties of nearly any other in the Civil War: 1,131 killed in action, several hundred lost to disease, and countless who returned home, wounded.

According to legend, the Iron Brigade got their nickname when Gen. George McClellan saw them at Turner's Gap and was told who these men were. He supposedly replied, "They must be made of iron."

A monument to the Iron Brigade was erected in Gettysburg; a plaque honoring the men can also be found at Rest Area 9 just off Interstate 90/94 near Mauston.

Were there any major battles fought on Wisconsin soil?

There were no Civil War battles fought on Wisconsin soil at all. Most of the soldiers from Wisconsin fought in the Western theatre, mostly in Tennessee, Kentucky, and northern Mississippi. The most notable exception was the Iron Brigade.

Who was Old Abe?

When Ahgamahwegezhig, a member of the Flambeau band of the Chippewa Tribe, cut down a tree in order to capture two eaglets from a nest there, he decided that he only needed one. He traded the extra baby bird to Daniel McCann, of (believe it or not) Eagle Point, who took the bird to Eau Claire, caged it in a barrel, and tamed it as a family pet. Months later, when the eagle got too big for McCann's tastes, he sold the bird for $2.50 to Capt. John Perkins of the Eau Claire Badgers militia company.

When Capt. Perkins' unit entered federal service and became Company C, 8th Wisconsin Volunteer Infantry Regiment and was sent to Madison, the eagle, who'd become a beloved mascot, was given the name of Old Abe, in honor of President Abraham Lincoln. The 8th Wisconsin—and their mascot, who rode into battle on a shield—fought entirely in the Western Theater. Confederate soldiers often referred to Old Abe as "the Yankee Buzzard," and they tried hard to capture him; at one point, Confederate General Sterling Price even declared that Old Abe's demise needed to happen—and soon!

Old Abe lived well past the war and was donated to the people of Wisconsin at

Old Abe poses for his photograph in this c. 1880 picture.

war's end, on September 26, 1864. In 1865, the Army of the American Eagle was founded, to help wounded veterans, and Old Abe went on tour to veteran's events, special ceremonies, and other events. It's said that he drew large crowds.

After one final tour of the country in celebration of America's Centennial, Old Abe retired to the Capital building in Madison, where he died in 1881. His remains were preserved and displayed, until a 1904 fire destroyed all but a few feathers; they can be seen at the Wisconsin Veteran's Museum in Madison. You can also see likenesses of Abe in Vicksburg, Mississippi; atop Camp Randall in Madison; and on the Screaming Eagle insignia of the 101st Airborne Division.

How was ethnicity a factor in Wisconsin's troops during the Civil War?

While it's true that most troops consisted of a variety of Wisconsin soldiers, the 9th, 26th and 45th regiments were primarily of German immigrants. Norwegian immigrants comprised most of the 15th regiment. Such regiments generally were composed of men who were neighbors, who already knew one another, had grown up together, or came to Wisconsin together. They weren't meant to be segregated as such; it's just that, in the War's early years, regiments were hastily organized locally by men who decided to come together to fight, and they offered themselves up as a ready-made regiment, usually with their own officers already in place.

Following Abraham Lincoln's Emancipation Proclamation on January 1, 1863, African Americans were legally allowed to enlist; overall, Wisconsin had 353 black troops scattered in various units of the Union army.

What part did Wisconsin's lumber industry play in the Civil War?

Because lumber from northern forests was moved into other areas downstream via Wisconsin's rivers and waterways, lumbermen knew all the best methods of getting product downstream quickly and efficiently. When active battle closed roads in war-affected areas during the Civil War, lumbermen-soldiers simply and safely moved supplies down rivers and lakes, just as they'd been taught in the forests of northern Wisconsin.

What role did Wisconsin play in the Underground Railroad?

Though the information is sketchy due to the secretive nature of the work, in the years between 1842 and 1861, it's known that more than 100 slaves were ushered to freedom in Canada with the help of Wisconsinites.

Though it was prohibited through the 1787 Northwest Ordinance for Wisconsin residents to own slaves, it was nonetheless common for slave-owning visitors to pass through the state accompanied by their slaves. In 1850, when the federal government passed the Fugitive Slave Act, which made it legally mandatory for all U.S. citizens to return slaves to their owners no matter the laws in that state, Wisconsin residents had been well aware of the injustices of slavery for quite some time. When abolitionists came to the state, they found plenty of willing helpers.

The first known Underground Railroad escapee in Wisconsin was Caroline Quarlls, a teenager who escaped her owner after having been beaten in St. Louis. She came via steamboat through Illinois and came to Milwaukee in August 1842. She was hidden there for a while, but when her whereabouts were discovered she was spirited away to Waukesha, where residents were known for being vociferously anti-slavery. Later in the month, she was quietly moved from town to town until a local man, Lyman Goodnow, took her via wagon to Chicago, through Indiana and into Detroit, Michigan, where Caroline was able to slip into Canada.

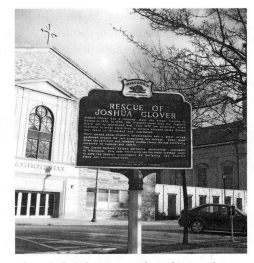

A historical marker sign stands on the spot where the Milwaukee courthouse was from which Joshua Glover was rescued in 1854.

Joshua Glover was rescued from a jail in Milwaukee by abolitionists and was also hidden in Waukesha before being put aboard a steamer in Racine, and sent to Canada in 1854. In early 1861, Janesville residents chased off a slave catcher who believed he'd found a fugitive he was tracking. Even Wisconsin's Native Americans helped: in 1854, a man and his two children passed through Chilton and into Stockbridge land. The Natives got the fugitives to safety in Green Bay, where they were sent to Canada.

Because harboring or assisting an escaping slave was grounds for deep punishment, most of these stories might have been lost to secrecy, were it not for Maximilian Heck and A. P. Dutton, two Racine men who finally admitted how most of the fugitives came into Wisconsin from Chicago or Beloit via local rivers. Once the slaves were on Wisconsin soil, they were hidden as needed (often in the Milton House, a mansion / inn near Janesville) before being taken across land to one of a number of lake ports, where they were entrusted to ship captains who had agreed to see that the fugitives were taken to Canada and safety.

Was slavery ever allowed in Wisconsin?

Although the Northwest Ordinance of 1787 prohibited slavery, slavery was not unheard-of in Wisconsin. The states' first Black resident was a slave who was killed along with his French owner and others near Green Bay in 1725. Over the years, there were a smattering of enslaved people brought to the territory, with an estimated 500 slaves who were included when the French surrendered to the British in 1760.

Slaves weren't the only Black people in Wisconsin, however. Two free Black men established a successful trading post near the mouth of the Menominee River in about 1791, to take advantage of the fur trade. At least one other fur trader followed suit near Chicago.

As Wisconsin was populated with settlers in the early 1800s, many of them brought slaves along. In 1840, censuses show that there were some 200 African American slaves in Wisconsin; at the cusp of the Civil War, that number had grown to just over a thousand slaves brought to the state through immigration or visitation. In 1842, an Anti-Slavery Society formed; later, it merged with the Liberty Party, which was likewise anti-slavery. In 1846, when statehood was imminent, suffrage for Black men was put up for a vote and was squashed; three years later, Black men were given the vote here, although slavery was frowned-upon but technically still in effect in the state.

As the Civil War heated up and abolitionists began moving into Wisconsin, African American men wanted to do their part for the war but it was illegal until January 1, 1863, with President Lincoln's Emancipation Proclamation. By 1865, more than 350 Black men had signed up to fight for the Union in the Civil War.

What roles did Wisconsin women play in the Civil War?

With the men away at war, Wisconsin women who stayed behind were forced to learn to take care of the home front. If the soldier left a farm, that often meant learning to put in crops, harvest, care for a farm's outbuildings, care for livestock, all in addition to their regular house work. Hired hands were often a big help, but because they were generally either very young or very old, the majority of the work and decisions fell to the lady of the house.

Generally, women of the home front also volunteered their time by collecting and sending supplies to the troops: medicine, bandages, shirts and pants, and quilts to keep the men warm. Knitting socks and mittens was considered to be especially patriotic. Many of those homebound women participated in Soldier's Aid Societies or with various Sanitary Commissions in their efforts to raise money on behalf of the soldiers "to obtain comforts and necessaries for the sick and wounded of our army...." In March 1863, a plea went out for vegetables for the prevention of scurvy, and Wisconsin women leapt to action.

For these women who stayed behind in Wisconsin when their menfolk went to war, it was an austere time. Food was often at a premium; prices for basic goods skyrocketed. It was not uncommon for women to seek help from their neighbors, especially if there were children involved. For upper-crust women, to be out of fashion was considered a badge of honor; social events were cancelled or not scheduled, and "keeping the family together" was a noteworthy achievement.

On the battlefield, officer's wives and mothers often accompanied their husbands to the South and, of course, Wisconsin women took care of the wounded. More than one died away from home, near the battlefield, in service of their soldiers.

At least two women served as Daughters of the Regiment, a position recognized by the army: Eliza Wilson went with the 5th regiment and Hannah Ewbank joined the 7th regiment. Both young women cooked, repaired uniforms, did laundry, and cared for the sick and wounded on-site.

History has recorded the names of two Wisconsin women who donned uniforms and served as soldiers: Sarah Collins of Lake Mills, aided by her beloved brother, Mason, cut her hair short, donned a uniform, and followed him to battle. Alas, she was unmasked, supposedly because of the way she put on her shoes. Belle Peterson of Ellenboro had better luck; it's believed that she entered the war in about 1862 and served undetected for some years, possibly as a spy or a scout.

After being widowed when her Wisconsin governor husband died, Cordelia Harvey made it her mission to help wounded soldiers and, later, orphans of the Civil War.

Who was Cordelia A. P. Harvey?

While it's true that Wisconsin wasn't the epicenter of the Civil War, its residents had need of help—and Cordelia A. P. Harvey (1824–1895) came to the rescue.

Cordelia Adelaide Perrine was born in New York and moved to the Kenosha area as a young woman, where her father owned a prosperous farm and young Cordelia found a job as a teacher. She married Louis Harvey in 1845; when he became secretary of state, the couple moved to Madison. He became governor in 1862 but, tragically, drowned some three months after assuming office. He was visiting wounded soldiers when he died, but he gave Cordelia a cause to champion.

For the next several years, she traveled around Wisconsin on behalf of the Western Sanitary Committee of St. Louis, bringing supplies and comfort to the wounded in state hospitals. It was her idea to convince Abraham Lincoln to build more hospitals for the war wounded; the final one was in Madison, named the Harvey Hospital.

At war's end, when the hospital closed, Cordelia thought it would make a fine orphanage. From 1866 to 1875, nearly 700 war orphans called the former hospital home.

Harvey died in February 1870 and is buried in Madison.

Was there a Civil War POW camp in Wisconsin?

Camp Randall isn't just a sports stadium!

Camp Randall began its existence as a training area for volunteer soldiers but for about five weeks in the spring of 1862, the site near Madison temporarily held around 1,400 Confederate soldiers from a battle in Missouri—although most of the captured were from Alabama. Ten days after they arrived, an inspection indicated serious problems with housing the men at Camp Randall, the least of which was that the camp was ill-equipped to handle the sick and wounded among the prisoners. The prisoners were transferred to Camp Douglas in Chicago at the end of May 1862.

How many Wisconsin soldiers were lost in the Civil War?

Of the 91,327 Wisconsin men who enlisted in the Civil War, 3,802 died in battle or of wounds suffered in action. Other war-related reasons—starvation, disease, or accident—were the cause of death for the other 8,499 casualties. Wisconsin soldiers who were captured were often sent to Southern military prisons—Libby in Richmond and Sumter in Georgia, in particular—and it's highly possible that some died there.

Are there any Civil War cemeteries in Wisconsin?

While many—if not most—of Wisconsin's older cemeteries may be the resting places of Civil War soldiers, there are three main places where Civil War-era graves can be found:

- Established in 1857, Forest Hill Cemetery in Madison holds the remains of 240 Union soldiers who died at area hospitals during the Civil War. You'll find them in the Southeast Corner, along with the remains of Spanish-American War soldiers and World War I casualties. Eight children—the orphaned offspring of Civil War dead—are also buried in Forest Hill Cemetery.

- The remains of Confederate soldiers are also found at Forest Hill Cemetery. Most of the 140 unfortunate men had been at Camp Randall in the few weeks it was used as a prison camp. You'll find those graves just north of those of the Union soldiers.

- Twenty-one Union soldiers are buried at Forest Home Cemetery Soldiers' Lot in Milwaukee. They arrived at the cemetery in 1872; most had died while under care at various hospitals in the area.

Did anybody prosper from the Civil War?

Yes: those in the shipping, railroad, and mining industries, mostly. After the lower Mississippi River was closed by Confederate soldiers, it was important that manufacturers figure out other ways to move product. Railroads became especially important and were inundated with goods, which drove shipping costs upwards; railroads were also forced to pay better wages because of a labor shortage, since so many of the states' able-bodied men were at war. Steamboat owners prospered because of the amount of goods that were needed for the war effort and afterward.

Farmers also prospered when wheat, which was then Wisconsin's main crop, was in dire need and prices rose; that also created more of a need for what Wisconsin's farm equipment manufacturers had to offer. And though most farmers' wives had to learn to take care of the farm, hired hands prospered while their employers were away at war.

Wisconsin's lead workers and mine owners prospered because, by the end of the Civil War, the states' mines were producing well more than half the lead needed in the United States.

- The Wood National Cemetery in Milwaukee holds the remains of some 30,000 soldiers, including African Americans and Medal of Honor winners. While the home itself was built in 1867, there was no cemetery until 1871; until then, residents who died were buried in various cemeteries in the Milwaukee area. The first men buried there were residents of the Northwestern Branch of the National Home for Disabled Volunteer Soldiers at the time of their deaths; in later years, rules were relaxed to allow soldiers from any war, anywhere, to be buried in the cemetery. You'll find the cemetery—along with several notable plaques and monuments—on the northwest corner of the home's campus.

POSTWAR WISCONSIN

What were the major industries in the years after the Civil War?

As compared to what the southern states endured, Wisconsin manufacturers were already in a great position to relaunch industry in the post-War years. In addition to the industries that were in place at the beginning of the war and those that were strengthened during the war, these industries thrived in the years after the Civil War:

- While wheat farmers in Wisconsin had enjoyed a time of great prosperity in the war years, wheat as a commodity had fallen off in favor of corn, oats, and hay for cash crops: production for those three crops increased, while production of wheat fell precipitously until nearly 1880. Today, few farmers grow wheat in the Dairy State.

- Immigrants who returned from the Civil War, and those new to the state, had experience with dairy cattle, so production of milk and other dairy products rose. By 1867, nearly a quarter of a million dairy cows called Wisconsin home; in 1869, farmers and their cows produced some three million pounds (1.36 million kilograms) of cheese; in 1872, the Wisconsin Dairymen's Association was founded in Watertown.

- Pre-Civil War, just 124 lumber mills could be found in Wisconsin; by war's end, there were nearly 700 lumber mills in the state with a more than $4 million impact on the economy. At the close of the nineteenth century, that amount would exceed $60 million.

- Mining continued to play a part in Wisconsin industry. The country's largest smelter for zinc ore was found for a short time at Mineral Point. Lead mining continued in various areas until well into the twentieth century. Iron ore, discovered in 1845, was also mined until the twentieth century.

- While there's no doubt that home-brewers had been making beer for their own enjoyment for decades, Wisconsin's first brewery was opened in Mineral Point in 1835. At the beginning of the Civil War, some 200 breweries were in operation in Wisconsin, nearly a quarter of them in Milwaukee. When four of the nation's largest breweries opened in Wisconsin in the post-war years, Wisconsin's presence as a major brewing state was cemented.

What Wisconsin event rivaled the Great Chicago Fire of 1871?

Chances are, you've heard about Mrs. O'Leary's cow and how it kicked over a lantern that started a fire that became the Great Chicago Fire of 1871. But why haven't you ever heard of the Peshtigo Fire, which was bigger and more destructive?

First, the history: it started that summer, and it was a long one: the weather was hot and it was dry all season. The small lumber town of Peshtigo, in the northeastern part of Wisconsin near Door County and Michigan, had gotten just two inches (five centimeters) of rain from the beginning of July through the end of September, which is several inches of rain less than they needed. Farmers fretted about their livestock and crops.

The Peshtigo Fire Museum commemorates the deadly 1871 blaze that killed 2,400 people. It is located in the first church (Congregational) reconstructed after the fire.

They should have worried about something much worse; in fact, the town fathers of Peshtigo had already been stockpiling water for weeks, fearing what nature could have in store.

But it wasn't nature that *caused* the problem: it's true that a cold front and winds were the reason the flames became a "fire tornado," but that wasn't the origin of the fire itself. Some claim that a railroad worker, clearing room for new railroad tracks, set a small brush fire to help make clearing easier. Others said that it was a settler who started it all, but it hardly matters in the end: on October 7, 1871, a small brush fire raged out of control. That night, the small burgh of Sugar Bush was burned to cinders, along with every single house and most residents there.

And the fire raged on.

October 8 was a Sunday and the people of Peshtigo had been battling smaller fires here and there in the area for several weeks. As for day-to-day activities, it was really just like every other Sunday in the small town although the smoke, which had been bad for some time, seemed worse and people were suffering for it, health-wise. Even so, some folks went to church that evening, as they did on every other Sunday.

Ominously, when services were over, some Peshtigo residents might have noticed what looked like snowflakes falling to the ground. It was ash, actually, and that might not have been much of a concern; Peshtigo was a lumber town, through and through: all kinds of hardwoods surrounded Peshtigo and lumbering paid a lot of people's bills. Millionaire William G. Ogden, builder of a wood-ware factory, saw to it that the name of the town was nearly synonymous with wood, including Peshtigo's wooden sidewalks

53

and sawdust floors. You simply didn't have all that wood without an occasional fire or two, but when the dry wood was added to the lack of rain and the methods of clearing that had been done up until then, Peshtigo was a tinderbox in the truest sense.

And then they heard the roar.

That evening, October 8, 1871, the fire that destroyed Sugar Bush raced toward Peshtigo with ferocious flames 200 feet (61 meters) high and temperatures of up to 2,000 degrees Fahrenheit. It was a horror that citizens weren't prepared to see: the heat caused trees and some people to literally explode. Some Peshtigo residents burned to death before they could barely take a few steps toward safety. Some, taking refuge in a water tank, boiled to death. Others, fleeing the flames by jumping into a nearby river, drowned. Still others suffocated from the smoke and ash, or when the flames consumed all available oxygen. Homes and railcars were reported to have been blown into the air by the fire's blast. As the fire burned at those incredibly high temperatures, it got so hot that silica in the very soil liquefied, evaporated, and fell again to the soil as molten liquid from thunderclouds. The few who survived later claimed to have found birds that had been covered by what was basically glass, as they flew.

When it was over, more than a million acres (405,000 hectares) of forest were incinerated and up to 2,400 lives were lost, including some 800 souls in Peshtigo. Parts of Door and Kewaunee Counties were also affected, although not to the extent that Peshtigo was (the disaster was named after Peshtigo because Peshtigo was the area hardest hit). Estimates for damage to property were nearly $170 million in 1871's dollars. That's more than $33 billion at today's currency rate.

And yet, it's been said that the Peshtigo fire—the deadliest wildfire in American history—was just a footnote in many U.S. newspapers. Why? Because October 8, 1871 was the same night that the Great Chicago Fire raged in the Windy City. Chicago was more widely known and had, literally, better press.

Surely, there was heroism shown during the Peshtigo Fire?

Of course there was!

From the Peshtigo Fire Museum:

Fourteen-year-old Joseph La Crosse was said to have saved the life of a baby girl by keeping her from the flames and later, giving her milk from an injured but still living cow that he'd encountered. La Crosse thought the baby's parents had perished in the fire but, miraculously, they also survived the flames.

Henry Bakeman was said to have saved his own life as well as that of his wife, six children, and eight neighbor children by covering them all in dirt from a clearing. Bakeman left their faces uncovered so they could get air, of course, and that was said to have kept them all from perishing.

The four-year-old daughter of J. E. Beebe witnessed her mother, father, and three siblings perish in the fire, but she survived, thanks to the quick-thinking of Fred Guse, who carried the little girl to the river and held her tight. The child was the granddaughter of Henry Baldwin, governor of Michigan, who later gave Guse a handsome reward—enough for Guse to become an entrepreneur himself. It should be noted that, on the same day, Governor Baldwin's state also suffered a large conflagration in which the dead have yet to be counted.

Perhaps because Abram Place had married an Indian woman from the area, Native Americans warned Place that the fire was coming. Though he was somewhat of a pariah in Peshtigo (for his marriage to the Native woman), Place quickly sprang to save his home with wet blankets and landscaping. The house subsequently became a field hospital for injured survivors.

And the Peshtigo Fire Museum has on record a tale of John Cox, who gallantly helped Kate Guillfoyle into the river to save her life. He "noticed Kate was pretty" and she must've felt similarly pleased about him. Within two weeks, the pair was married.

What was life like in Wisconsin at the end of the nineteenth century?

In the years after the Civil War, immigrants poured into Wisconsin from all over the world, particularly those of German, Norwegian, Dutch, and English ancestry but also of Italian and Irish heritage. Many of the new immigrants moved to settlement houses, established in the 1880s, in order to ease into their new lives through classes, clubs, and instruction on how to be an American.

Agriculture, always a major industry, zoomed with the experiment of various crops: cranberries in Waushara County; tobacco in Jefferson, Dane, and Rock Counties rye, barley, and oats everywhere else—not to mention dairy cows. Vegetables also became a major crop in the Dairy State.

If you were one of Wisconsin's Native Americans, you probably already lived on a reservation. Like other states around the nation, Wisconsin established schools expressly for Native American children and was working to assimilate Wisconsin's tribes into white society. The Dawes Act of 1887 removed the ownership of tribal lands in favor of smaller, eighty-acre (thirty-two hectare) parcels, with the excess land sold to white farmers. The Dawes Act lasted until 1934.

If you lived near Milwaukee, you enjoyed a vibrant and growing musical atmosphere, with daily operas in Schlitz Park, music schools, and public recitals. The state's college students were beginning to get used to females among the student body when the UW's South Hall became the first all-female resident hall in 1863.

Though the nation's first hydroelectric plant was established in Appleton in 1882, electricity had not widely reached Wisconsin farms; the Rural Electric Administration (REA) was not made law until 1936.

What part of nineteenth-century Wisconsin history can you visit?

While some of the trade goods needed to survive in Wisconsin were brought overland and up the Mississippi River, much was brought into ports in Wisconsin through Lake

Michigan and Lake Superior. Ships coming through the Great Lakes had to beware of rocks and land where land meets water; fog was often a problem, so visibility was not good—and since electricity wasn't yet widespread, the illumination that lighthouses offered allowed better navigation and kept the ships and their crews safe.

In Wisconsin, there were more than 50 lighthouses to serve ships bringing goods to the shores of Lake Superior and Lake Michigan and each of them required a human who lived in or near the lighthouse itself, in order to keep the light on and operational. Some lighthouse keepers brought their families with them but for some, being a lighthouse keeper was a lonely job, since lighthouses were often remote or even located on an island. It was a good job for an introvert, to be sure.

The North Point Lighthouse in Milwaukee is one of the more beautiful examples of nineteenth-century, Great Lakes lighthouses. It currently houses a museum with docent-led tours.

The oldest lighthouse in the state, Pottawatomie Lighthouse on Rock Island near Green Bay, was finished in December 1837 because, since Green Bay was an early port for goods, there was a dire need for a lighthouse there. Others were built as the years passed; most Wisconsin lighthouses were built in the nineteenth century.

Over time, and because the need for lighthouses has faded with new technology, most of Wisconsin's lighthouses have been deactivated and several were furthermore destroyed. Some of the ones left are privately owned and a few have been made into homes. Though Wisconsin does not have a state-wide lighthouse preservation society, many local organizations are in service to keep lighthouses in good shape and safe to visit each summer.

What were schools like in nineteenth-century Wisconsin?

In the earliest years of Wisconsin history, most of the wealth and resources were focused on industrial growth, so erecting schools was secondary to the establishment of communities and the building of hotels, factories, stores, and places to house workers. Even so, many immigrants were eager to establish schools and churches.

The first public schoolteacher in the state was Electa Quinney (1798–1885), who was a member of the Stockbridge-Munsee band of the Mohicans. She came to Wisconsin from New York in 1826 and, upon hearing of the need for a school, opened the state's first public school a year later. In June of 1845, Michael Frank (1804–1894), publisher of a Kenosha newspaper, abolitionist, and legislator, started a movement for a public school system, thus becoming "The Father of Wisconsin Public Schools."

For public school children in the early years of the state, getting an education would take work. Teachers were in short supply for public schools; those who were hired were often recently out of school themselves and weren't much older than their students. Textbooks were almost nonexistent and generally consisted of whatever books could be found; later, McGuffey Readers were most often found in classrooms.

In most Wisconsin counties, classes were scheduled based on agriculture and weren't held when students were needed for fieldwork; when in session, classrooms were crowded. Rural schools were usually in one- or two-room buildings with an outhouse or two out back; because they were not well-insulated, winters were brutally cold; and furniture and supplies for learning were primitive and scarce because schools operated with tax money and early settlers were against taxation. It took some serious talk to convince them of the need for schools.

The brightest news there was that, at a time when schools in other states charged admission fees, Wisconsin's schools were free, as per the state's Constitution—and that included secondary education.

In the years prior to statehood, the legislature established four private colleges: Beloit College, Carroll College, Lawrence Institute (now Lawrence University), and Sinsinawa Mound College (sold in 1852). In 1848, the state legislature established the University of Wisconsin but, because of the Civil War, classes did not convene until two years later and the university received no state money until after the war.

As for Wisconsin's Native Americans, education wasn't such a rosy picture: in the late 1700s, the U.S. government and several religious groups attempted to force Native American youngsters to attend Missionary School, in which they would be "civilized" with a Christian education and lessons that meshed with white life on farming, keeping house, and raising families. The first two such schools opened around 1830 near Green Bay but the largest number of them operated in Wisconsin's northernmost areas. Though many in power were against these schools and what they were attempting to do, by 1836, 1,300 Native American students were scattered in ten Indian missionary schools throughout the state.

What epidemics swept through Wisconsin at the close of the nineteenth century?

In most places throughout history, the spread of disease went hand-in-hand with the movement of people and Wisconsin was no exception. It started long before the immigrants arrived: between 1539 and 1589, according to the Wisconsin Historical Society, "90 percent of the Indians living in the middle Mississippi Valley" were killed by disease spread by Hernando de Soto's arrival. Those natives traded with Wisconsin's Oneonta nation, and so disease spread northward. Archaeologists further believe that smallpox predated Jean Nicolet's arrival and as more explorers arrived and settled in with the territory's Native villages, disease spread.

Especially for the Native American tribes, smallpox was a killer. Dr. Douglass Houghton, surgeon and explorer with Henry Schoolcraft, administered 2,000 vaccines to Native Americans in the Chippewa area in 1832, and while it seemed to have saved lives, countless other Native Wisconsinites died of the disfiguring disease.

Malaria, carried by incessant swarms of mosquitoes, was a big concern to white soldiers stationed in Wisconsin in the 1820s and 1830s. In Ft. Crawford in 1830, some 75 percent of the soldiers had malaria; most didn't die from it then. Cholera, however, an epidemic at about the same time, was more of a concern.

In the 1840s, a wave of immigrants brought a wave of disease: mumps, measles, and whooping cough were rampant, as was typhoid fever. Alas, cholera and malaria continued to kill because vaccines were hard to get. Several areas created boards of health to combat the illnesses. While doctors most often came to their patients' homes for caregiving, the Sisters of Charity opened the first public hospital in 1848.

What role did Wisconsin play in the Spanish–American War?

When war was declared with Spain in Cuba in 1898, Wisconsin residents responded swiftly but they saw little service. Four regiments were mustered, as well as the first light brigade: The First made it to Jacksonville, Florida, before the war ended. The Second and Third arrived in Cuba late in the war and saw a little action. The Fourth brigade never even left the state because the war was over before they were able to leave.

All brigades were mustered out at the end of the war and returned to Wisconsin; of the 130 dead, most succumbed to illnesses such as typhoid fever and malaria.

It's interesting to note, in the list of soldiers who served in the Spanish-American War, that several men are officially listed as "musicians."

WISCONSIN HISTORY: 1900 TO NOW

What leisure activities did Wisconsinites in the early 1900s enjoy?

At around the turn of the century, nationwide, the working class began to enjoy more leisure time. Factories had set lower hours for the average workweek and new technology allowed for more efficiency: work got done faster, so there was more free time.

While it's true that many early twentieth-century Wisconsin residents had only recently moved to the state in the years before the Roaring Twenties, travel was a regular pastime. In the early 1900s, railroad was a very popular way to travel, and it could be done on a budget or in luxury. Travel by steamboat was a great way to visit river cities, and newfangled automobiles gave travelers more independence in their destination plans—and there were many places to go! Wisconsin Dells was a popular spot to visit, as was Northern Wisconsin and the Green Bay area.

Along with automobiles, camping became all the rage. Campsites began to spring up all over the state, in part because nobody wanted to deal with people sleeping in their cars on the side of the road.

Wisconsinites, like people all over, became sports watchers with the newer games of football, baseball, and basketball. New safety features made bicycling a popular sport for men and ladies alike. Billiards gained popularity, as did bowling and burling, also known as log rolling, a sport beloved by Wisconsin's loggers.

Nationwide pastimes were also surely beloved by Wisconsin residents.

So-called "animal dances" were popular, to a point: the Bunny Hop, the Bunny Hug, the Grizzly Bear, the Turkey Trot, and others scandalized early twentieth-century elders, but teens loved those dances. Ultimately, dancing close made it okay to snuggle in public. For those uptight elders, dancing was still a good way to socialize—just not so close, please, and no touching.

If it wasn't forbidden by church leaders, people played cards and games when they got together. Checkers and chess were widely played by children and adults; kids also played a number of outdoor games similar to those played today. Children, by the way, generally made their own toys out of whatever was on hand, like sticks, rocks, waste paper, scraps of fabric, and the like. Unless the child's parents or relatives were very wealthy, if a toy was "store-bought," it was often too precious for play. The exceptions were marbles, tops, wood hoops, and yo-yos, which were inexpensive enough for the average parental budget to afford.

Of course, with the popularity of sheet music in the early 1900s, families loved to get together and make music. Singing around the piano was an extremely popular pastime and if someone could play a fiddle and maybe a guitar, then it was a good night. Many families had a piano in their homes and it was common to invite the neighbors over for an evening of song.

And if they had the means, attending fairs and expositions were popular with Wisconsin residents, as were vaudeville shows and traveling "Wild West" shows featuring Buffalo Bill Cody and other relatively new legends. Fairs allowed farmers to see new machinery and fine livestock. Finally, lucky was the Wisconsinite who had the chance to travel. They could attend the St. Louis World's Fair in 1904.

How did log rolling become a sport?

In the 1800s and the heyday of logging in Wisconsin forests, logs were moved to lumber mills mostly by water: the logs, stripped of their branches, were dumped into rivers and floated downstream. Naturally, that sometimes resulted in log jams that would have to be dislodged. To do that, someone (specifically, a logger, nearly all of whom were men) would have to walk on the floating logs to gingerly work the jam out. That was easier than it sounds: as a logger would step onto the logs, the logs would roll, thus dumping the man into the water—and with heavy logs on the move, that could be dangerous, as well as unpleasant, so the best loggers developed talents enough to be able to stay on those slippery, rolly logs the longest.

Needless to say, with jobs and lives on the line, loggers got good at staying dry while dislodging the jams and this undoubtedly led to friendly competitions. After a while, logging companies began to hold competitions between their best men. By 1898, log rolling was an official sport; the first unofficial log rolling contest was held in Omaha, Nebraska, that year, and was won by Tom Fleming from Eau Claire.

Back when the sport was not yet a sport, lumberjacks rolled with what they had—namely, logs from pine and fir trees. When the logging industry stopped relying on waterways to move their product, lumberjacks continued teaching new generations to perform their fancy footwork; today's competitors use western red cedar logs that are hewn smooth. Until the early 1980s, spiked shoes were mandatory for competition but the spikes ruined the logs too quickly and were dangerous. In 1981, Judy Scheer Hoeschler of La Crosse came up with the idea of carpeted logs and regular tennis shoes,

Log rolling is a sport still practiced today, although it is somewhat modified. For example, synthetic logs have been created for the competitors to use instead of real wood.

which became the competition standard then. In 2012, Scheer Hoeschler and her daughter, Abby, came up with synthetic log products for their beloved sport and Key Logs are again changing the way log rolling is done.

Since 1960, the Lumberjack World Championships have been held in Hayward, Wisconsin, to showcase twenty-one skills that were everyday jobs for lumberjacks a century ago. One of those skills is log rolling.

What major event was held in Milwaukee in 1905?

Though the Germans brought a bowling-like game to Wisconsin when they came, they didn't invent the pastime; archaeologists found objects that resembled a bowling game in a child's grave in Egypt that dated back to 3200 B.C.E. Throughout British history, games with a ball and pins were popular at times, and it obviously spread throughout Europe: the citizens of many lands love various games that resemble bowling.

The game the German immigrants brought to Wisconsin was called *kegling*, in which a ball was rolled toward pins. Those other European immigrants brought their games, all

61

A photo taken during the 1905 American Bowling Congress tournament in Milwaukee, where the ABC soon moved its headquarters, making it the "Bowling Capital of America."

of which, by the mid-1800s, had morphed into what they called ninepins and we now know generally as bowling. By the late 1800s, ten pins were common in the game.

Bowling was a pretty big thing to Milwaukee's citizens; not only was it associated with bars and beer gardens (of which Milwaukee had many), but it was also perfect for all kinds of gambling and betting. The problem, however, was that there were no standardized regulations for bowling then, so the American Bowling Congress was established in New York, to promote and regulate the sport.

In 1905, the ABC held a major tournament in Milwaukee, which was an astounding success. Because of that, the ABC moved the organization's headquarters to Milwaukee, thus making the city "The Bowling Capital of America," a title it held until 2008, when the ABC moved their offices to Texas.

What are the Wisconsin Idea and the Wisconsin Promise?

In 1905, UW President Charles Van Hise gave an address in which he mentioned something that would revolutionize the entire university system: he declared that "I shall never be content until the beneficent influence of the University reaches every family of the state." In other words, Van Hise envisioned that the university would influence Wisconsin citizens well beyond the classroom and that students would be able to get an education in a town near them, rather than in Madison or another larger Wisconsin city. This notion was later called the Wisconsin Idea.

During his time in office (1903–1918), Van Hise created what is today called the University of Wisconsin-Extension, and he worked with his friend, Robert La Follette, to ensure that university teachers had access to lawmakers and had a seat at the table for lawmaking. Because of Van Hise and his Wisconsin Idea, university professors and experts of the early twentieth century helped craft laws on public regulation of utilities, tax reform, and the nation's first workers' compensation laws.

While not related to the Wisconsin Idea, the Wisconsin Promise works along the same premise: to help youth stay in school and get an education. In conjunction with the U.S. Department of Education, the U.S. Social Security Administration, the U.S. Department of Labor, and the U.S. Department of Health and Human Services, the Wisconsin Promise works with young people to graduate, find and fund higher education, and keep jobs—thus maintaining financial stability to help keep people out of poverty. In this program, Wisconsin is one of six states participating.

What epidemics swept through Wisconsin in the twentieth century?

The answer to that starts with this information: epidemics were not just found in twentieth century Wisconsin. It's been said that one of the first known major plagues happened in 1539 when European traders infected nearly nine out of every ten natives in the mid-Mississippi Valley—and that affected Wisconsin's Oneonta people. Cholera, typhoid fever, and smallpox all came to Wisconsin long before the twentieth century and access to hospitals was a rare thing then.

With all that as background, it might seem that the 1900s might have allowed people to breathe a sigh of relief, since there were more hospitals then and medicine was a bit more "modern." That was all true, but nobody was prepared for the outbreak of the Spanish Flu in the fall of 1918.

It's likely that the flu began in the United States at a World War I training site in Kansas, with a cook who wasn't feeling well. Within hours, he was in sick bay, as were several of his fellow soldiers. Hundreds more boys fell ill in the days to come but before camp doctors could do anything to stop it, the illness spread across the country and, because of the War, across the world. Sufferers complained of headaches, fever, and body aches; they might feel fine in the morning and be dead by dinnertime. The flu often killed entire families with lightning speed.

Overall, in the roughly nine months of the plague, more Americans died of the Spanish Flu than were killed fighting World Wars I and II, the Korean War, and the Vietnam War *combined*. Here at home, little more than 8,400 Wisconsinites died of the disease with more than 100,000 affected.

In the midst of the epidemic, the State Board of Health declared that the Spanish Flu would "forever be remembered as the most disastrous calamity that has ever been visited upon the people of Wisconsin."

Surprisingly, in the end, Milwaukee's death rate was one of the lowest of any larger city in the nation, in part due to efforts by George C. Ruhland, the city's public health commissioner, who closed theatres, saloons, schools, and most other public areas at the height of the flu in the state. That single, sweeping action likely saved many Wisconsin lives.

Other epidemics included tuberculosis, which hit rural residents especially hard in the first decade of the twentieth century; in the very early 1900s, the state legislature explored the establishment of sanitariums for TB patients, with the first being opened in Douglas County in 1903. In the end, money was set aside by the state for counties to have their own sanitariums and / or a health nurse would come and help patients in their homes.

Polio is a disease of the brain and spinal cord that can cause paralysis that can last a lifetime. Since 1955, the disease has been largely preventable, thanks to the Salk and Sabin vaccines, but in the years between the world wars, all the way into the 1950s, it was a disease that was highly feared by Wisconsinites. Like many diseases, victims might feel well one minute, and ill the next. Paralysis might be part of the disease, or it might not (only 1 percent of polio victims suffer paralysis). The number of Wisconsinites to have battled polio is unknown.

As of 1979, the United States was considered polio-free, although there were 22 cases of the disease in 2017.

What odd law was discussed by nearly every farmer in the Dairy State?

Thanks to a product invented by a French chemist, the production of margarine started in the United States in 1875. The product was much cheaper than butter but it wasn't butter—so in 1881, Wisconsin lawmakers took action and passed the Oleomargarine Act, which imposed heavy taxes and fees on the product. About a year later, 23 other states followed suit and passed laws against the use and production of margarine.

But for Wisconsin, that wasn't enough. In 1895, legislators passed a more stringent law that completely banned the production and distribution of margarine that was dyed yellow inside state boundaries (even though butter itself was often dyed, too). It was a contentious law, much discussed throughout the state, and farmers had as much to say about it as did lawmakers and scientists of the time.

In the 1950s, after World War II ended, most states lifted the restrictions because the sale and use of margarine had become common during times of rationing and consumers weren't as uncomfortable using the product. Alas, Wisconsin didn't lift any bans, which resulted in furtive, but now-almost-comic, smuggling of margarine by individuals across state lines. Finally, in 1967, the state repealed the law with one big caveat: restaurants were forbidden to serve margarine instead of butter, unless the customer specifically asks for margarine. Efforts to repeal that law failed in 2011.

Who was Wisconsin's first Wisconsin-born governor?

Born in Primrose, Wisconsin, on June 14, 1855, Robert M. La Follette (1885–1925) was also, coincidentally, the first Wisconsin governor inaugurated in the twentieth century.

Robert M. La Follette (shown here in 1923 with his son Robert Jr.) was the first governor of the state to be born there. He ran unsuccessfully for U.S. president in 1924 as a Progressive.

As a youngster, La Follette worked as a farm hand until entering the University of Wisconsin in 1875. Upon graduation from the university, he entered the bar in 1880. In 1884, he was elected to Congress but was defeated in 1890 and returned to Madison, to practice law.

After a few years of travelling the state and speaking out against big business and corrupt politicians, La Follette was elected as governor of the state in 1900. In 1906, he resigned from office and was elected to the U.S. Senate, where he served until his death in 1925.

While in office, La Follette worked tirelessly against business trusts and business practices of the railroads, and in support of environmental laws, labor unions, and the Seventeenth Amendment (which states that each state is required to have two senators). He was also a big supporter of suffrage and racial equality and he was vociferously against the growing action in Europe, which would become World War II.

La Follette contended for the Republican presidential nomination in 1908 and 1912 but each time lost to William Howard Taft. In 1924, he ran again for president—this time as a third-party candidate—but lost to incumbent president Calvin Coolidge.

Robert La Follette died of cardiovascular disease four days after his birthday in 1925.

What part did Wisconsin play in World War I?

With its sizable immigrant population—roughly 25 percent of Wisconsinites claimed German heritage—it should come as no surprise that many people wanted to avoid war with Germany in 1917, but the fact was that Wisconsin was politically divided: antiwar sentiment came not only from the immigrant community but also from the majority of Wisconsin's congressmen and from Milwaukee Socialists. Senator Robert La Follette strongly opposed American involvement but even so, the majority of Wisconsinites seemed ready for war, out of a sense of patriotism or as a way to promote temperance and suffrage.

After war was declared in 1917, German immigrants particularly struggled: most of them had held onto their heritage and were enormously proud of their lineages. They were absolutely not interested in fighting with what could possibly be kin left overseas. But it had to have dismayed them that suddenly, speaking German in public was frowned upon. Many schools refused to teach German languages and some immigrants with obviously Germanic names were harassed. The problem was particularly keen in Milwaukee, where large numbers of German immigrants had settled in years before the war.

In the end, Wisconsin was the first state to report in the national draft registrations and was the first state to organize a State Council of Defense and a County Council of Defense, which educated citizens on what to expect during the war and how they could survive some of the sacrifices required. Wisconsin National Guard joined forces with the Michigan National Guard, becoming the 32nd Division (see below), which became the division with the highest number of Wisconsin soldiers.

By war's end, nearly 125,000 Wisconsinites went to fight in World War I and almost 4,000 of them died for it.

What was the *Tuscania*?

World War I was the first war to involve most of the major countries of the world and the United States needed soldiers on the ground in Europe to continue the fighting. Two thousand men boarded the *Tuscania,* which was part of a British convoy of ships.

For three years, German submarines had been systemically attacking British ships bringing cargo from Europe to the United States and Canada, and there had been calls for some sort of stop to that. Finally, in May of 1917, it was decided that all British ships traveling across the Atlantic Ocean would travel in a convoy, or a group, and would be accompanied by solid British Naval protection. Up to fifty cargo ships might be accompanied by several British escorts using balloons to keep watch for submarines.

When the United States entered the war in April of 1917, this highly protected way of transporting merchandise worked well with soldiers heading back across the ocean. And so, on January 23, 1918, the *Tuscania* left New Jersey with almost 2,400 American men on their way to war.

Alas, on February 3, 1918, a German U-boat spotted the convoy just a few miles off the coast of Ireland. The U-boat fired two torpedoes; the first missed, but the second hit the *Tuscania* directly. Of the soldiers aboard, the convoy was able to save most—but more than 200 Wisconsin men of the 32nd Division drowned at sea.

Who was Billy Mitchell?

Born in France in late December 1879, William Lendrum Mitchell was the son of Senator John Mitchell and grandson of Alexander Mitchell, who established the Milwaukee Railroad and the Marine Bank of Wisconsin. That's quite a pedigree and yes, young Billy grew up in a wealthy home.

After graduating from college at Columbian College at George Washington University, eighteen-year-old Billy joined Company M of the 1st Wisconsin Infantry Regiment and was sent to fight in the Spanish-American War. Because of his father's influence, he quickly went up in rank and joined the U.S. Army Signal Corps,

Born to a prestigious Wisconsin family, William "Billy" Mitchell was an army officer who saw the potential of airplanes in the military and became the "Father of the U.S. Air Force."

where he stayed for many years. After witnessing the achievement of the Wright Brothers, Mitchell understood that the future of battle was in the air, and he took flight lessons before the beginning of World War I, where his prowess with a plane led him to become one of the greatest airmen of the time.

Though he's considered to be the "Father of the U.S. Air Force" today, Mitchell's career was not without controversy: his plane-versus-ship "tests" rankled the Navy at various times during his career, although he was proven correct during the war. He also tried to further the use of air power in the case of civil disturbances and he was vocal when he didn't think his superiors (or the president) were making good decisions; that kind of outspokenness ultimately got Mitchell into trouble and he was court-martialed in late 1925. Found guilty of the charge of violating the 96th Article of War (bringing "discredit upon the military service") in December of that year, Mitchell resigned his post in February 1926 and moved to Virginia with his wife. For the next ten years—until his death in February 1936—Mitchell spent his hours writing and speaking on behalf of air power in the military.

Billy Mitchell is buried in Forest Home Cemetery in Milwaukee.

What is the Wisconsin National Guard's Red Arrow Division?

The story of the Red Arrow Division doesn't exactly start in the upper Midwest—it begins in Mexico.

In July of 1917, troops were needed to guard the servicemen near the Mexican border to help with the Border War started by Pancho Villa. President Woodrow Wilson had called up several states' National Guards but none of them, even together, had enough soldiers to stop Mexican raiders. It was at Camp Arthur in Waco, Texas, that the Wisconsin and Michigan National Guard joined forces to become the 32nd Division.

In 1917, President Wilson made a request to Congress to send American troops into World War I, and the 32nd Division was one of the first divisions to go. The soldiers arrived on the Western Front in May of 1917. The division later received its "Red Arrow" insignia because of the ability to pierce every single enemy line it encountered during the war. Even the French were impressed with the Red Arrow Division, calling it "Les Terribles."

Right from the beginning, the Red Arrow Division made its mark on history: it was the first unit to deploy overseas as a whole. Though the division only served for a few months, it was the first division to pierce the Hindenberg Line and the Red Arrow Division fought in four major campaigns in France. When the war was over, the division stayed in Germany with the Army of Occupation.

Overall, the division lost more than 13,000 soldiers in World War I; more than 800 individual men were commended for bravery in battle by Belgian, French, and American governments. Later, in World War II, the Red Arrow Division fought for nearly two solid years in New Guinea and the Philippines.

In 1967, the division was reorganized into a battle-ready brigade; today, the 32nd Infantry Combat Team is comprised of more than 3,000 soldiers and is the Wisconsin Army National Guard's largest unit.

How did Wisconsin deal with the laws of Prohibition?

When you consider Wisconsin's history of brewing and distilling, it should come as a huge surprise that Wisconsinites voted for Prohibition! That may have been in part because German immigrants were on the forefront of brewing—it was very important to their culture and their celebrations—and there was a lot of anti-German sentiment following World War I.

When Wisconsin cast its vote in January of 1919, thirty-eight other states had already ratified the proposed Constitutional Amendment to curtail the making and selling of alcoholic beverages so, strictly speaking, the law had already been passed. Almost immediately afterward the voting had finished, thirsty citizens and officials began having second thoughts. No beer? No way!

Many breweries switched gears and began manufacturing near-beer, which was close but not nearly the same; in 1926, Wisconsin voters gave a nod to the Volstead Act, which allowed the production and sale of beer with a 2.75 alcohol content (most beers have 4 to 6 percent alcohol content). Some breweries made products for the home brewer. Other breweries started making products like ice cream and candies—things that had nothing to do with alcohol at all—while some simply shut their doors for good.

Ten short years after the Eighteenth Amendment was passed, Wisconsin beer lovers asked voters if they thought Prohibition should be repealed or altered and more than seven out of ten of them said "yes," thus repealing the Severson Act, which enforced Prohibition. By 1932, state Democrats and Republicans both wanted to see Prohibition end and in December of that year, Senator John James Blaine (who'd once been Governor Blaine), introduced the Twenty-first Amendment, which stated that state constitutional conventions ratify the amendment, rather than the legislatures. In April 1933, Wisconsin delegates to the convention unanimously voted to support the new amendment but, because of opposition in other states, the amendment didn't go into effect until nearly eight months later. By early December 1933, just in time for the holidays, Wisconsinites celebrated with a cold one.

How did Paramount Records change the way we listen to music?

Located in Grafton, the Wisconsin Chair Company was a maker of phonograph cabinets for the Edison Company when they decided to make their own phonographs. The Vista brand phonographs appeared under a subsidiary, Universal Phonograph Company. Sales were not encouraging: Vista record players ultimately failed as a product, but it led to something else: in 1917, Wisconsin Chair Company debuted a line of records on the Paramount label, pressed and recorded by yet another subsidiary.

Paramount struggled and eventually licensed and pressed records for other recording companies under contract. One of those companies was Black Swan label, which was likewise struggling; still, Paramount purchased Black Swan, which initially focused on female African American singers. This so-called "race music" was distributed by mail order and was a hit.

Part of that success can be attributed to J. Mayo "Ink" Williams, a nonmusician with no official ties with Paramount, who was allowed to bring any talent he found to the Paramount studios to record. By the late 1920s, Alberta Hunter, Blind Lemon Jefferson, Jelly Roll Morton, Willie Brown, Ma Rainey, and many others had come north to record their music at the studio in Grafton. By then, Paramount had expanded through agents who scoured the country for talent. Estimates are that Paramount released some 100,000 records or more.

A 1919 advertisement for Paramount Records, a Wisconsin company known for its jazz and blues records that began as a chair company.

Sadly, record-keeping at Paramount was lax, so there's no way to know for sure who came through Grafton to play guitar, drums, or to sing. Some of America's premiere Black talent might have graced a studio for a moment or a day, but no one knows. Paramount Records studio closed in 1932, with sagging sales due to the Great Depression. By the mid-1930s, the factory was completely closed. Today, Paramount records are highly collectible.

How did the Dust Bowl affect Wisconsin?

Partially because of overfarming and largely because of lack of rain in the middle of the United States, the so-called Dust Bowl years—the years between 1930 and 1936—saw high winds, choking-black clouds of dust and dirt, and utter devastation for farmers who'd plowed up the prairie grass that kept the soil from erosion. Many people believe that the Dust Bowl only affected the Great Plains—but the disaster hit Wisconsin residents and farmers, too. Dust rolled into communities and homes, dirtying everything in the cloud's path. Like in the Plains, Wisconsin residents coughed, choked, cleaned, and did the best they could to take care of their families and their livestock.

In a way, in the 1930s, Wisconsin got a little bigger, too: a lot of the soil blowing from the plains states ended up here. It was common for rain showers to bring bits of soil in the form of dust when the wind didn't do it first: on May 10, 1934, according to the *Sheboygan Press*, an engineer noted that dust particles reached a count of 5 million parts per cubic foot. Deland Park in Sheboygan was "covered in an inch of yellowish, (sic) dust blown in from the west."

Long before that, though, Hugh Hammond Bennett, a USDA soil surveyor, had been concerned about soil erosion and he knew that a problem was growing. It was also growing in Coon Valley, Wisconsin, due to overgrazing and water runoff into the Coon Creek. And so, led by Bennett and UW-Madison professor Aldo Leopold, with the help and minds of local farmers, researchers, specialists, technicians, and others, and the physical work of President Roosevelt's Civilian Conservation Corps, the Coon Creek Watershed became the nation's first watershed project in 1933.

Spread across 90,000 acres (36,400 hectares), the project showed how water and soil could be preserved through proper land use, good farming practices, woodland protection, and control of the banks of streams and rivers.

How did Wisconsin fare during the Depression years?

Despite that beer production had returned to Wisconsin, there wasn't much else to celebrate in 1933, due to the worst Depression the nation had ever seen.

Things were looking up, economically, in the state when the stock market crashed in October of 1929. Like it did elsewhere, the crash came as a surprise, and though Wisconsin farmers were better off than, say, their Milwaukee brethren who lost their jobs, everyone in the state suddenly had to deal with economic realities, environmental problems, and they had to tighten their belts.

It was a time of big social change and chaos. Violence broke out in many areas of Wisconsin hardest hit; in Milwaukee, violent strikes "increased sevenfold between 1933 and 1934," according to the Wisconsin Historical Society's website. Farmers, demanding better prices for their milk, held a series of strikes and held milk back from distributors in 1933: the first strike lasted for a week in February, the second strike lasted for almost a week in May and resulted in two deaths, and the third major strike lasted nearly a month in October and November that year, which resulted in even more violence.

Since around the turn of the century, UW economist John R. Commons had been vocal about the need for some sort of protection for out-of-work citizens. Finally, in the midst of the Depression, someone listened to his ideas and the Wisconsin State Legislature passed the United States' first unemployment compensation law in 1932.

After studying what Wisconsin was doing with the law, President Franklin Roosevelt asked UW economists Arthur Altmeyer and Edwin Witte to serve on a committee that ultimately devised a program that would cover a national retirement-age insurance, help for mothers and other citizens who could not work, and unemployment compensation program for state and federal workers. In 1935, the federal government passed the Social Security Act, comprising these protections.

During the Depression, more than 90,000 men worked for the Civilian Conservation Corps (CCC) in planting trees, trail and campground building, and other conservation

What is the Milwaukee Handicraft Project?

Because of the nature of the projects undertaken by the WPA and their construction-heavy nature, Milwaukee State Teacher's College teacher Elsa Ulbricht knew that women needed a way to contribute, too—especially if they were alone in supporting their families. She created the Milwaukee Handicraft Project, a program in which women's handicraft projects were sold at cost and which put unemployed teachers to work when there was no work available in their fields.

With the help of two students serving as director and supervisor, Ulbricht first identified what kinds of things were needed in Milwaukee-area hospitals and schools. Eventually, eleven different "units" were created for tasks such as bookbinding, toy making, sewing, weaving, costume-making, furniture-making, and more. The better a woman got at her job, the more likely she was to be hired for other WPA programs, which had a better pay scale.

On the program's first day, in early November of 1935, two hundred women arrived to work. By the end of the month, the number of workers had more than tripled and included African American workers. First Lady Eleanor Roosevelt was said to have been a big fan of the Milwaukee Handicraft Program.

The program officially ended in 1942, though it still employed older and disabled workers into the beginning of World War II.

efforts. The Works Progress Administration employed another 43,000 people per year from 1935 through the beginning of World War II in construction of roads and other infrastructure. Wisconsinites pulled together during the Depression but, alas, Wisconsin banks didn't fully recover from those years until the beginning of World War II.

What are the glass grottos doing in Wisconsin?

During the Depression, when unemployment was high, people who were used to working with their hands had plenty of time and little to do. That was about when Wisconsin's glass grottos began to spring up.

The largest of these is the Dickeyville Grotto, located in the state's most southwestern corner, on the grounds of the Holy Ghost Catholic parish.

Father Mathias Wernerus was the parish priest from 1918 to 1931, after having come from Germany. With the love of God and his new country in his heart, he began building the grotto with whatever he could find—mostly stones and broken glass, held together with concrete. As the fruits of his efforts grew, so did the support of the people in his community, who brought him things from around the world, such as geodes, sea shells, semi-precious stones, pieces of heirloom dishes, and fossils for his grotto. Father Wernerus worked on his grotto from 1925 to 1930. The Grotto is open year 'round.

Just off Highway 27 between Sparta and Black River Falls, the Paul and Mathilda Wegner Grotto is considerably smaller than its inspiration in Dickeyville, but no less impressive.

The Wegners built their grotto literally in their backyard, beginning after they retired in 1929. Visitors can still see the outlines of the basement of their home, amidst folk art concrete statues of an ocean liner, a wedding cake, a glass star, a fence that's partially crafted of shards of broken glass, and a tiny, three-person nondenominational chapel in which marriages are still occasionally held. Entirely self-taught, the Wegners also crafted tombstones for themselves out of broken glass and concrete.

The Wegner Grotto is open from Memorial Day through Labor Day. Be sure to travel down the nearby side road to see the Wegner Cemetery and its monuments.

The International Chapel on the grounds of the Wegner Grotto is available for weddings and funerals, by prior appointment. But it better be a small wedding: there's room for about three people inside this charming little place.

Through the years, other grottos were constructed from cement, car parts, and scrap metal but they were crafted many years after Father Wernerus and the Wegners built their masterpieces.

WISCONSIN DURING WORLD WAR II

What happened in Wisconsin on and after December 7, 1941?

When the Japanese attacked Pearl Harbor on December 7, 1941, many soldiers and sailors from Wisconsin had already signed up for military service. Fifty-six Wisconsinites were killed at Pearl Harbor, in fact. By war's end, more than 300,000 Wisconsin citizens had enlisted or were drafted into a branch of the military, a number that includes nearly 10,000 women.

Perhaps because unemployment had been so high prior to the war, Wisconsin workers were poised to spring into wartime production: cities that had once been important for ship building—specifically Manitowoc, Superior, and Sturgeon Bay—began building ships again. Ammunition plants and other machinery manufacturers roared back to life. Farmers, who'd lowered productivity during the Depression, quickly made plans to grow more crops and increase dairy, egg, and meat output. This—and increased manufacturing that occurred on behalf of the war effort—meant that the war was an economic boon to Wisconsin.

Aside from the large number of Wisconsinites who joined the war effort via military enlistment, state officials and everyday people also pitched in, in part because they had to: many of the men were away at war. Before the war, for example, women represented just 3 percent of the workforce at the Allis Chalmers plant in Milwaukee; by war's end, almost a quarter of the workforce consisted of women workers. The Allis Chalmers Company even printed brochures and booklets to help its female workforce at what may have been a woman's first for-pay job. The Allis Chalmers Company had several military contracts to manufacture parts for wartime machinery.

UW-Madison scientists and their students worked to isolate and improve penicillin so that the troops had better medicine on the field. Some of the penicillin molds they discovered are still in use today.

By August 9, 1945, at the end of World War II, there were 8,000 Wisconsin casualties and 13,000 wounded. Only one woman—Ellen Ainsworth of Glenwood City—was killed in battle in Italy. She served in the medical corps.

Where were World War II bases and training camps located in Wisconsin?

Wisconsin Air Fields during World War II were located in Milwaukee, at the General Billy Mitchell Field, now known as General Mitchell International Airport and General Mitchell Air National Guard Base; Truax Field in Madison, now known as Dane County

Were there POW camps in Wisconsin?

At the beginning of World War II, when Great Britain was experiencing a housing shortage due to war, British authorities asked the United States to house some of their captured prisoners. Many of the POW camps were in the south, in part because there was no general need for heating the buildings. Some POWs—around 20,000 of them—landed in Wisconsin's camps.

There were thirty-seven branch and base prisoner-of-war camps in Wisconsin during the Second World War. By most reports, the POWs held in Wisconsin were relatively happy to be here. By Geneva Convention rules, they were housed, well-fed, encouraged to participate in extracurricular activities, treated well, and put to work—often on Wisconsin's farms, which were in need of extra hands because of the war, in canning factories, and even in Wisconsin factories. Reports are that many German POWs immigrated to Wisconsin after being repatriated.

Wisconsin did not have any internment camps inside its borders, specifically, but Camp McCoy did hold some Japanese Americans during the war.

Regional Airport and Truax Air Field National Guard Base; and Camp Williams Army Air Field, in Finley, now known as Volk Field Air National Guard Base.

The main training base for the Army was Fort McCoy, in Monroe County, between Sparta and Tomah. In 1938, Ft. McCoy had been expanded to 60,000 acres (24,300 hectares) and an ability to house 35,000 soldiers. During World War II, Ft. McCoy also acted as a POW camp.

What specific population increased in the years following World War II?

It may come as a bit of a shock to learn that when the U.S. Census was taken in 1910, fewer than 3,000 African Americans called Wisconsin home. Twenty years later, that number had barely doubled.

In the two decades between 1940 and 1960, however, Wisconsin's African America population increased by some 600 percent—most of them having arrived in the post-war years. Wisconsin's agricultural industries had few jobs to offer; instead, major opportunities to land jobs in manufacturing drew Black workers primarily from Mississippi, Tennessee, and Arkansas. Those states contributed the most migrants, but workers came from all over the South, primarily to the Milwaukee area. Even though they found good jobs and higher wages here, they still had to endure a certain amount of discrimination in housing and entertainment.

What was life like at the homefront in Wisconsin during World War II?

The soldiers training for war in Europe weren't the only busy ones in Wisconsin! When war was declared and "the boys" deployed, Wisconsinites swung into action on the homefront!

Because the military needed many things to win the war, factories in Sturgeon Bay, Manitowoc, and Superior built ships and submarines, so workers were needed there. The Badger Ordinance Company upped their production, becoming one of the country's largest ammunition makers. Farmers, who had slowed their agricultural output during the Depression, added crops, product, and livestock so they could do their part. All in all, more than $4 billion in orders were filled in the state of Wisconsin during the war years.

Of course, with the menfolk overseas, women were needed to fill many of the factory jobs open in Wisconsin. Prior to the war, the Allis Chalmers Manufacturing Company—makers of tractors and machinery—counted a small handful of women in their factories; shortly after the war began for America, that number had multiplied by nearly seven! Other factories saw the same kinds of leaps in their female workforce, and women stepped up to work around the clock, if that's what it took. They learned to weld, build, wire, plumb, drive, and rivet. On farms, many women took the reins in field and barn, too, keeping farms going for the future.

As with most Americans, Wisconsin families participated in victory gardens, scrap metal drives, and war bond sales. Wisconsin families lived through rations of sugar, coffee, meat, clothing, and gasoline (although farmers were subject to slightly different rules on the latter). For entertainment, one could go to the movies—even better, if there was a drive or an event coinciding with the show.

And if there was a USO nearby, volunteering was a great way to help win the war. USOs offered rest, comfort, and morale boosting for soldiers on their way from one base to another or to war; food might be offered, athletic equipment or competitions may be organized, or it might be dance night. USO centers dotted Wisconsin and, yes, they still exist. Today, the World War II USO Preservation Association is located in Milwaukee.

What important parts did Wisconsin women play during World War II?

Though the vast majority of soldiers during World War II were men, women played a very strong part in winning the war. Some 9,000 women served our country; most served as nurses or doctors but others served as important support staff in various areas.

Women served in four branches of the military:

- WAVES or Women Accepted for Volunteer Emergency Service served in the Navy.
- SPARS or Semper Paratus (which means "Always Ready") served in the Coast Guard.
- WACs or Women's Army Corps served in the U.S. Army.
- WASPs or Womens Airforce Service Pilots served by bringing new airplanes from the factories to the airfields that needed them. (The Air Force didn't exist until 1947).

Like their male counterparts, service women went to boot camp, lived in barracks, and wore uniforms during their deployment.

Other notable Wisconsin women in the war effort:

- Ineva Reilly Baldwin of Madison rose to the rank of U.S. Coast Guard lieutenant commander during the war. At that point in military history, no other woman had risen to such a high rank.

- Mildred Fish-Harnack of Milwaukee was a spy for the Allies. She is the only woman who Hitler specifically condemned to execution.
- Dickey Chapelle of Milwaukee was the first female war correspondent to join American troops via parachute. She died covering the war.
- Ruth Gruber was born in Brooklyn but came to Madison as a teenager. During the war, she worked as a special assistant to the secretary of the interior and was assigned a secret mission to bring a thousand Jewish refugees and wounded American soldiers from Germany to America. Though the vessel on which Gruber was bringing her charges was hunted by German U-boats and planes, the mission was successful.

Born in Milwaukee, Mildred Fish-Harnack was a literary historian and translator who, during World War II, fought with the Resistance against Hitler and served as a spy for the Allies.

- Lt. Ellen Ainsworth of Glenwood City was the only Wisconsin woman to be killed in battle by enemy fire. A nurse at the 56th Evacuation Hospital in Italy, she died of her wounds after a bomb exploded just outside the hospital. Ainsworth died in February 1944.

How did Wisconsin celebrate its centennial year?

Wisconsin knows how to party!

In celebration of the state's one hundredth year, the Wisconsin State Fair in West Allis really put on a show. The Wisconsin Conservation Department built re-creations of pioneer life, including a cabin and a bunkhouse and featuring a water project that gave fair visitors a chance to see what life might have been like in 1848.

Fourteen huge murals were commissioned to tell the story of a century of agriculture. The Century Farm and Home Program was launched to recognize family farms, and the Alice in Dairyland program (once known as the Dairy Queen) was renamed to put a face to the dairy industry. And, of course, fairgoers were encouraged to eat plenty of products from their favorite home state!

Admission to the 1948 Wisconsin State Fair was fifty cents per person, per day. Nearly two million people attended the fair during the course of its twenty-three days.

Who is "Alice in Dairyland"?

Alice in Dairyland officially began in Wisconsin's Centennial Year, to help promote the State Fair. Since 1948, these young women have served as Alice.

Alice in Dairyland is chosen each year in the late spring; modern Alices put their plans on hold in order to serve a one-year term as full-time employees of the Wisconsin Department of Agriculture, Trade, and Consumer Protection. In that year, Alice travels more than 40,000 miles (64,374 kilometers), gives hundreds of radio and television interviews, posts on social media, presents speeches, and writes articles on behalf of Wisconsin's dairy industry. Applicants must be experienced in public relations, female, from Wisconsin, and over age twenty-one. Applications are available online.

What is the Highground?

After having served in the Vietnam War and losing a very close friend, Tom Miller came home to Wisconsin. He began to imagine a memorial of some sort for the war's fallen and, in 1983, he met with a group of Wisconsin Vietnam War veterans that he knew could help him see his dream become a reality.

Located west of Neillsville just off Highway 10, the Highground Veterans Memorial Park honors the fallen from the twentieth-century wars in which Wisconsinites fought, survivors of those wars, their service, and the sacrifices they made.

Visitors to the Highground can pay their respects to WWI and WWII veterans, Korean veterans, Vietnam veterans, women veterans, and Native American Vietnam veterans. The Highground also honors Gold Star families. With just a short walk, you can see the Meditation Garden, the Dove Effigy Mound, a United in Service tribute, and a smaller replica of Washington, D.C.'s Vietnam Veterans memorial ("the Wall"). Paving stones further pay tribute to individuals who died in battle.

At the Highground Project, just past Neillsville on Highway 10, you'll see gardens and monuments to Wisconsin's veterans.

Tours are available, or you can walk the Highground at your own pace. Be sure to visit the museum on the grounds, too.

What role did Wisconsin play in the Korean War?

Sometimes called the "Forgotten War" because it was sandwiched between World War II and the Vietnam War, the Korean War started in June 1950 and ended in July 1953. It was the first war in which many units were integrated; prior to the Korean War, white soldiers and African American soldiers had to serve in separate units.

More than 130,000 Wisconsinites served in the Korean War. More than 800 were killed in action; more than 4,200 were wounded. One-hundred-eleven were captured as prisoners of war; of those, 54 died in POW camps. There are still more than 80 Wisconsinites who are officially listed as missing in action. Five men received the Congressional Medal of Honor.

For more information on the politics surrounding the Korean War, see the Politics chapter, under Joseph McCarthy.

What was the Day the Music Died?

In January 1959, singer Buddy Holly was in the middle of a Wisconsin tour with his friends Ritchie Valens and J. P. Richardson (better known as the Big Bopper). They called it the Winter Dance Party and some 6,000 teens and young adults came out to dance and hear music from Milwaukee to Kenosha, to Eau Claire to Duluth. By all accounts, it was a successful gig but, judging by the amount of travel, it was exhausting.

Heading for their gig in Appleton, the various band members discovered to their chagrin that their rickety bus, complete with a malfunctioning heater, would go no further than Hurley. The Appleton gig was cancelled, but the group managed to make it to their performance in Green Bay, on February 1. That night, they boarded another bus but by then, Holly was disgusted with buses in general and just wanted a warm bed and some rest before their concert in Moorhead, Minnesota, which was after the hastily planned gig in Clear Lake, Iowa. He asked the manager of the venue in Clear Lake to charter a plane from nearby Mason City to Fargo, near the next scheduled performance.

The cost of the charter was $108, and Holly offered seats up to recoup his fee. On Tuesday, February 3, just a little after midnight on a snowy night, Buddy Holly, Ritchie Valens, and a flu-stricken J.P. Richardson boarded a plane to Fargo.

They never made it. The plane went down less than ten miles (sixteen kilometers) from the airport, killing everyone aboard.

One other note: on December 10, 1967, singer Otis Redding's plane crashed in icy Lake Monona. Redding was killed, along with four members of his band, the Bar-Kays.

What is the Menominee Termination Act?

In the years following World War II, the U.S. government badly wanted to cut all relationships with individual Native American tribes. In 1946, Congress passed the Indian

Claims Commission Act, which eliminated all government support to the tribes; even so, in 1951, the Menominee were given over $8 million to settle grievances over timber rights in Northern Wisconsin. They did not receive the money; instead, in 1953, the House passed House Concurrent Resolution 108, which allowed for the termination of U.S. Native American tribes. Five tribes—the Flathead, Klamath, Pottowatomie, Turtle Mountain Chippewa, and Wisconsin's Menominee were to be the first to be "terminated."

For the Menominee, who lost the rights to the timber once again, the deal wasn't good. Tribal governments were no longer recognized and, thus, could no longer control their own lands. All property was transferred to the Menominee Enterprises, Inc. (MEI), a governing board made of Menominee tribesmen and non-Menominee people (heavy on the latter). The reservation became a new Wisconsin county, Menominee County.

Though the termination was to have started in 1958, it wasn't until 1961 that it actually happened and it was obvious from the start that the program was a disaster. Because of the poverty that came from the "termination," there wasn't enough tax money to sustain basic services such as garbage pick-up or a police force. Schools and utilities had to cut back, and the county's lone hospital closed.

Shortly after the Menominee were officially terminated, newly elected Congressmen saw that the program wasn't working and they stopped it. By then, though, the process was complete for the Menominee; the only way they could be restored was by petitioning Congress. In the meantime—in 1967, the MEI had sold some of the tribal lands to developers and there was an immediate outcry over it. The Menominee fought back with an internally organized group called Determination of Rights and Unity for Menominee Stockholders (DRUMS).

On December 22, 1973, President Nixon signed a bill to restore federal recognition of the Menominee People. Full recovery took another six years.

Which Badger Alumni have won Nobel Prizes?

Several faculty, alumni, and former faculty from the university system in Wisconsin have won Nobel Prizes over the years. They are....

Wisconsin Nobel Prize Winners

Name(s)	Year Won	Nobel Prize Category
Joseph Erlanger and Herbert Gasser	1944	Physiology & Medicine
John Bardeen	1956	Physics
Joshua Lederberg	1958	Physiology & Medicine
Edward Tatum	1958	Physiology & Medicine
E. P. Wigner	1963	Physics
Har Gobind Khorana	1968	Physiology & Medicine
Stanford Moore	1972	Chemistry
John Bardeen	1972	Physics
Howard Temin	1975	Physiology & Medicine
Saul Bellow	1976	Literature

Name(s)	Year Won	Nobel Prize Category
John Van Vleck	1977	Physics
Theodore Schultz	1979	Economics
Erwin Neher	1991	Medicine
Paul D. Boyer	1997	Chemistry
Guenter Blobel	1999	Medicine
Alan MacDiarmid	2000	Chemistry
Jack St. Clair Kilby	2000	Physics
Oliver Smithies	2007	Physiology & Medicine
William C. Campbell	2015	Physiology & Medicine

Jonathan Patz and John Magnuson shared a Nobel Peace Prize with Al Gore in 2007. Their names are not on the medal. Note that John Bardeen won two Nobel Prizes.

What happened in Wisconsin during the Vietnam War?

The Vietnam War was America's longest and costliest (in terms of dollars) war from its beginning in 1950 to its end in 1973, when U.S. troops were withdrawn.

During that time, Wisconsin sent 57,000 of its citizens overseas. More than 1,200 young Wisconsin men and women (the average age of a Vietnam soldier was nineteen) didn't come home. Most of those soldiers came from disproportionally rural or blue-collar working class families. As a comparison, the average soldier in World War II was seven years older and came from a financially better-off situation.

It's hard to say whether Wisconsinites gave the same kind of support to the Vietnam War that they did to previous wars. It seems unlikely: by and large, nationally, the Vietnam War was hugely unpopular, especially in the 1960s and following the Tet Offensive, and especially on college campuses.

In the latter years of the war, in fact, UW-Madison gained a reputation as a particular site of unrest and protest. On August 24, 1970, the "New Years Gang," a small group of young male students, set off a bomb near the east wing of UW-Madison's Sterling Hall, where the Mathematics Research Center was housed, funded by the U.S. Army. Physics researcher Robert Fassnacht was killed and four people were

Born in Madison and a University of Wisconsin alumnus, John Bardeen was corecipient of the Nobel Prize in physics for his work on transistors in 1956, and he won again in 1972 for helping to form the theory of superconductivity.

injured. At that time, some were afraid that this act would exacerbate the situation on campus and escalate the protests and the violence that seemed to accompany them. Instead, the seriousness of the detonated bomb seemed to weaken the power of the protests on campus.

What happened in Wisconsin during the civil rights era?

At the dawn of the civil rights era, Milwaukee was one of the most segregated cities in the United States, even though its Black population was relatively sizeable: 15 percent of Milwaukee's citizens were African American, and most of them lived in a small geographical area on the north side. The schools weren't integrated, either: the NAACP discovered, in 1960, that schools on the north side were 90 percent Black, despite the 1954 *Brown v. Board of Education* ruling.

It would naturally follow that tensions simmered. In 1963, Milwaukee's CORE (Congress of Racial Equality) organized a protest for school equality; a year later, there was a boycott of schools.

And then there was the issue with housing.

Legislation was introduced to allow open housing in 1962, but it didn't pass despite repeated attempts to introduce it to the Common Council. Five years later, Milwaukee's NAACP Youth Council marched to protest the Common Council's lack of action on the open housing ordinance; they were met with up to 5,000 white counterprotesters who threw things at the marchers.

But that wasn't the end of the issue: On July 30, 1967, there was an altercation at a Milwaukee hotspot on North Third Street that changed everything.

Reports say that trouble actually started the night before with an argument that drew bystanders. Tensions on the city's north side over lack of jobs, housing, school, and other discriminatory practices simmered the whole next day, and on the evening of July 30, a small group of teenagers started to fight, and the violence spread and escalated when police entered the situation. Though the riots included arson and looting, it only lasted a few hours; even so, when it was over, four people died of gunshot wounds, one died of a heart attack related to the violence, a state of emergency was declared, the National Guard was activated, and more than 1,700 people were arrested.

It was not until spring of 1968, when federal laws were passed, that the Milwaukee Common Council finally acquiesced and passed ordinances prohibiting housing segregation. Not until the late 1970s were Milwaukee's schools fully integrated according to the law.

Who was Father James Groppi?

Born in Bay View to Italian immigrant parents, James Groppi (1930–1985) was the second-to-last child of twelve in the family. He and his siblings helped their parents run their grocery store in Bay View.

81

The James E. Groppi Unity Bridge, named after the priest who was active in the civil rights movement, crosses the Menominee River in Milwaukee.

When Groppi graduated from public high school, he took bus-driving gigs in order to be able to afford seminary school in Mount Calvary, Wisconsin. It was there that he first worked with Black children—work that also took him to summer camp in Milwaukee's "inner core." His first assignment upon graduation from seminary was at St. Veronica's in Milwaukee, but in 1963 he was sent to St. Boniface, which had mostly African American parishioners.

From that point on, Father Groppi became active in the civil rights movement. That same year, he participated in the March on Washington and the Selma to Montgomery march in 1965. Also in 1965, he worked on behalf of the Southern Christian Leadership Conference (SCLC) and voters' rights.

In 1965, Groppi returned to Milwaukee and took up a position of leadership with the NAACP, where he organized a group of African American males that he called the Milwaukee Commandos, who were tasked with helping protect those who marched. For the next few years, he was arrested several times for his work, and he worked wherever he was needed on behalf of civil rights and equality, even though his superiors weren't exactly pleased about it.

In 1976, James Groppi left the priesthood and eventually married Margaret Rozga, an English professor with the university system and they had three children together—but Groppi didn't leave his activism behind: he continued to work on behalf of Volunteers in Service to America (VISTA). He also briefly considered becoming a member of the Episcopalian clergy but decided against it.

At the end of his life, James Groppi was doing what he started out doing—driving buses—but his leadership still ran strong. Two years before he died, he was elected president of his local bus drivers' union.

In the twentieth century, what major immigrant groups settled in Wisconsin?

Wisconsin citizens have always been a diverse bunch, and we welcome immigrants to our borders. That was never truer than during the twentieth century.

- In the years after World War II, Wisconsin welcomed an estimated 1,000 Holocaust survivors. Many of them found new homes in the state's southeast corner.

- Also in the years after World War II, many German immigrants came to Wisconsin—some, after having been prisoners of war in the Badger State; many joined relatives already here.

- Starting in the mid-1970s, the Hmong people from Southeast Asia came to Wisconsin, many after having served with the U.S. military in Laos. In 1980, Hmong citizens in Wisconsin were fewer than 420. Ten years later, the number had increased multiple times. Today, Wisconsin has the third largest population of Hmong people in the nation.

- In the summer of 1980, Ft. McCoy near Sparta became the temporary home of up to 15,000 Cuban refugees who came to the United States via the Freedom Flotilla, also known as the Mariel Boatlift. Preparations were fierce: officials didn't have much advance notice and hastily readied barracks, mess halls, fences, and other buildings for the Cubans. Military support personnel came to Wisconsin to help and hundreds of civilians were hired to make the transition smoother. Although there were reports that the whole situation and interactions with the new settlers seemed positive, as it turned out, many of the refugees had violent backgrounds or a history of mental illness. At least one was later convicted of murdering his sponsor.

What are the Amish and Mennonite communities like in Wisconsin?

In the later 1600s, during Europe's Protestant Reformation, Swissman Jakob Ammann founded a church he called Amish. Several of the Reformation's tenets were rejected by Amish followers, who were subsequently persecuted by local Roman Catholics and other Protestant groups; to escape the trouble, the Amish fled to the mountains and hills in Switzerland and held their meetings in private. In the eighteenth and nineteenth centuries, they fled even further, to North America.

Today, around 20,000 Amish citizens call Wisconsin home. The largest community is in Cashton, which was founded in 1966; other major communities are located in Hillsboro (founded in 1985), the Tomah area (founded in 1969), Medford (founded in 1920), Green Lake County (founded in 1977), and in Clark County (the oldest of which was founded in 1975). Other smaller Amish communities may be found almost anywhere in

83

the state. The Amish bring businesses to the area: buggy-making, clothing stores, cabinet makers, metal workers, and bakeries.

For a time in this century, the Amish population was the fastest-growing population in the state. It has since leveled off; some communities, mostly of the very oldest, can be counted as "extinct." Even so, Wisconsin claims the fourth-largest population of Amish citizens, trailing Ohio, Pennsylvania, and Indiana; most of them are Old Order Amish, which is more conservative than their New Order Amish brethren, who enjoy more lax rules on modern amenities.

Old Order Amish don't generally use cell phones, but they might be granted permission to have them for business (they do not use landlines). They don't have churches, per se; instead, they worship at private homes, sometimes on a rotating basis. Married men have beards; women cover their hair; both wear plain clothing with no embellishments, often black or dark blue. They don't own TVs or computers, automobiles, hot-water indoor plumbing, or electricity, as a whole, but they are not innocent of such conveniences; they are allowed to take advantage of modern things, if given the chance.

Swartzentruber Amish are the largest Wisconsin community of which is found in the Neillsville-Loyal area; they are even more conservative than Old Order Amish. They shun everything that they consider "worldly," including windshields on their buggies,

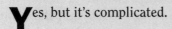

Does Wisconsin allow gambling?

Yes, but it's complicated.

Contests of skill, such as ATV or snowmobile racing, are allowed, as are charitable games such as church bingo. Raffles are also allowed, but only if they are run by charitable organizations.

Horse racing and dog racing are both allowed but off-track betting is prohibited. Bookmaking is illegal. Online gambling, as long as it's with a licensed website, appears to be legal.

Pull tabs are illegal, as are bar gaming machines, but punishment for possession is complicated by the type of establishment in which the items are found.

Indian gaming is legal but casino gambling is illegal. While that doesn't seem to make sense—particularly in light of the fact that Indian casinos dot the state—it basically means that Wisconsin's casinos run by its Native American tribes are legal.

To play bingo in Wisconsin, you must be at least eighteen. To gamble in an Indian casino, you must be at least twenty-one.

The Wisconsin Lottery offers legal gambling with scratch-off tickets and legal pull-tab games. As of this writing, Wisconsin also offers some daily draw games and two jackpot games.

Some Mennonites allow the use of cars, while others, such as the Groffdale Mennonites, demand their members use a different kind of horse power for transportation.

"SMV" signs (orange Slow Moving Vehicle triangles), Velcro, bicycles, and even riding in a car except for an emergency. Swartzentruber Amish generally disallow Rumspringa, which is a period in an Old Order Amish teenager's life when they are allowed to briefly taste modern life.

It's easy to confuse the Amish with Wisconsin's Mennonites—the two share basic roots from centuries past—but there are differences in belief, allowances, and slight differences in dress. Wisconsin's Mennonites can basically be divided into two subgroups: the Groffdale Mennonites and the Weaverland Mennonites.

The Groffdale Mennonites are horse-and-buggy users, and they worship in churches with liturgy written in German. They are allowed to use tractors for fieldwork, as long as the machines don't have rubber tires. The largest order of Groffdale Mennonites is in Clark County.

Weaverland Mennonites allow the use of cars, as long as they are black. They, too, worship in churches, but their liturgy is in English. The largest order of Weaverland Mennonites is also in Clark County.

What part did Wisconsin play in Desert Storm and the Persian Gulf War?

Wisconsin gave up its sons and daughters for war during Desert Storm and the Persian Gulf War.

Ten Wisconsin soldiers lost their lives in Desert Storm.

Seventeen lives were lost in the Persian Gulf War.

What happened to the Dairy State in 1993?

Uh oh. For the first time ever, in 1993, the state of California surpassed Wisconsin in milk production. The truth is, though, that it was a close race and it remains close. And besides, Wisconsin still makes more cheese. So there.

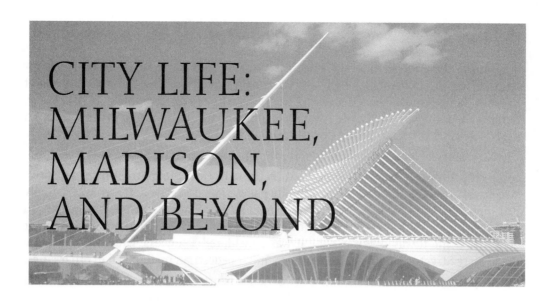

CITY LIFE: MILWAUKEE, MADISON, AND BEYOND

MADISON

What's the history of Madison?

Founded in 1837, Madison actually became the state capital the year before when, in 1836, James Duane Doty (1799–1865), the owner of the land that eventually became Madison, traveled to Belmont to convince the state's territorial legislators to choose Madison for its capital; he'd named his little village after the nation's fourth president, who had died just that summer, and his fast-talking beat out Green Bay, Fond du Lac, and Milwaukee for the honor. Later that year, Eben and Rosalie Peck (1808–1899) became Madison's first white citizens. Later, Rosalie gave birth to Madison's first white child, a girl who was given the mouthful of Wisconsiana Victoria for a name.

Madison's first Black resident arrived in 1839. Alas, her name is lost to history and she appears to have left in about 1845.

For its first two decades, Madison was just a tiny little village. Fewer than fifty-five residents voted in Madison's 1839 election; just a year later, the new capital boasted a whole thirty-five buildings, including three grocery stores. If you were so inclined, you could head down to the capitol square and hunt bears, deer, and game birds any day of the week.

In 1846, Madison became an incorporated village in Dane County, which must have been a signal for growth: a decade later, Madison became a "city" and on March 11, the first city election was held in which Colonel Jarius C. Fairchild (1801–1862) was elected mayor.

Just eight years after Wisconsin achieved statehood, the population of Madison reached a phenomenal 6,800 people, most from the East Coast because city fathers had advertised that land and jobs were available. That, and the fact that Germans, Norwegians, and other immigrants followed, helped boost Wisconsin's population.

During the Civil War years, Madison served as a "hub" for Wisconsin soldiers coming through Camp Randall, which was Wisconsin's main training camp. At the end of the war, Camp Randall became a part of the University of Wisconsin, and in 1917 Camp Randall Stadium was built. Still, military training continued at Camp Randall through ROTC (Reserve Officer Training Corps) training until 2004.

No history of Madison should ignore the influences of State Street.

In the 1970s, Mayor Paul Soglin led an effort to turn State Street from a regular street with vehicles and parking to a totally pedestrian area. The first step was actually just dipping a little toe into the waters: a small part of State Street was blocked off, to see how things went, how much use the area got, and how UW staff and students felt about it. While it was controversial, it was considered a success, which immediately made State Street an anomaly, since other, similar pedestrian malls failed in other cities.

Walk down State Street today, and you'll see apartments, bars, restaurants, and a flow of retail establishments, including the famous University Bookstore, which opened in 1894 and is one of State Street's oldest businesses.

Today, Madison continues to grow: through an agreement reached in 2003, the Town of Madison and the City of Fitchburg will become the City of Madison by 2022.

You'll find Madison in the south central part of Wisconsin.

Where do I go for fun in Madison?

- Olbrich Gardens, established for Michael Olbrich, the founder of Madison's parks system is located on Atwood Avenue.
- Visit the Henry Vilas Zoo on Randall Street. Founded in 1911, the zoo features all kinds of animals, free admission, and free parking.

The State Capital dome is the highlight of the Madison cityscape, which sits on an isthmus between Lake Monona and Lake Mendota.

- Take a tour of the Wisconsin State Capital. Look for it on the Madison skyline—you can't miss it!
- The University of Wisconsin Arboretum always has something fun going on. Take a tour; events are free.
- Take a walk around Lake Mendota. Do a little shopping in Madison's downtown. Enjoy any of the many great parks in the Madison area.
- You're missing out, if you don't take in a Wisconsin Badgers game at the University of Wisconsin Madison! Be sure to stick around for the third quarter, and jump! Jump! Jump around!

What are some fun things to know about Madison?

- In 1836, Madison was named after President James Madison, who died in 1836.
- Madison boasts 10 public beaches and five lakes: Mendota, Monona, Wingra, Waubesa, and Kegonsa.
- Madison's first newspaper, The Enquirer, began printing in 1838. Its first school teacher also arrived that year, to work for a salary of $2.00 a week.
- Even though it's the capital of Wisconsin, Madison, is the second largest city in the state. Milwaukee is larger.
- The World's Largest Brat Fest is held in Madison every Memorial Day weekend. In the last thirty-five years, more than three million brats have been sold at Brat Fest.
- Over 6,000 acres (2,400 hectares) of parkland can be found inside the Madison city limits.
- The formal name of the University of Wisconsin mascot is Buckingham U. Badger
- According to the Visit Madison website, the official bird of Madison is the pink plastic flamingo.
- The dome of the state capital is the largest granite dome on Earth.
- Per-capita, Madison folks buy more books than anyone.

MILWAUKEE

What's the history behind Milwaukee?

Look at the very earliest history of Wisconsin, and you'll find that what is currently Wisconsin's largest city started out as a series of very small settlements on the edge of Lake Michigan. Potawatomi natives called the area Mahn-ah-wauk, which basically meant a gathering place for their counsel. The first Anglicanized version of the name appears in 1761 when a British lieutenant temporarily stationed in Green Bay wrote "Milwacky" in a record book. No matter what it was called then, in 1795, Northwest Fur Company agent Jacques Vieau (also spelled Veau) (1757–1852) moved to the area with his wife and family (French and Canadian fur trappers were the first settlers to the area, by and large). Officially, the Vieaus were the first *seasonal* white settlers to the area but Vieau isn't the guy who gets the recognition for founding Milwaukee.

That honor goes to his son-in-law, Solomon Juneau (1793–1856), who was the area's first *permanent* settler, who also built the area's first log cabin and the area's first frame building. Juneau also set up a trading post on the Menominee River and, along with his partner Morgan Martin (1805–1887), built up a city they called Juneautown; at that time, a few hundred white people lived in the area on either a permanent or a seasonal basis. Not long after, Colonel George Walker (1811–1866) and Byron Kilbourn (1801–1870) stepped in and helped Juneau to develop two other smaller towns; ultimately, all three smaller burghs became Milwaukee in 1845.

In 1846, Milwaukee got its first city charter and Juneau was elected its first mayor. Fifteen aldermen represented the growing area and they did their best to meet, but bad luck beset them: two of the buildings where they met burned over the years and finally, in 1889, $1.25 million was secured through bonds and Milwaukee had its City Hall on Market Street, which is where city hall stands today. In 1929, the new city hall suffered a fire which destroyed a bell tower.

In the earliest years of the twentieth century, German immigrants flocked to Milwaukee, where machinery and foundry jobs were plentiful. The city quickly gained a reputation for political liberalism, art and fine culture, and elegance; its wealthiest got that way through manufacturing and grain exports. City leaders worked hard to keep neighborhoods in peak shape with parks, newfangled sanitation systems, and power and water systems. Education was a top priority for Milwaukee's leaders.

Sadly, that didn't last: the Great Depression hit Milwaukee hard and left a quarter of the city's population without jobs. Labor relations were abysmal and strikes further left Milwaukee reeling in the 1930s; it wasn't until World War II that labor relations were stabilized.

During the war, the face of Milwaukee changed considerably: prior to World War II, the African American population of Milwaukee was very small. In the years during and after the war, great numbers of African Americans from southern states moved to Milwaukee until, by the 1960s, some 15 percent of Milwaukee's citizens were Black. According to the Wisconsin Historical Society, government workers, realtors, and others worked together to keep those newly arriving African Americans "confined" to the inner part of Milwaukee and segregated in both job and education. That changed in the 1960s during the civil rights movement but even today, Milwaukee is considered to be one of America's most racially segregated cities.

If you want to work in Milwaukee today, you're in luck! Milwaukee's city limits have spread considerably more than they were in Solomon Juneau's day. You can work in Milwaukee and live in Waukesha, Oconomowoc, Racine, or one of many cities in the surrounding area. Otherwise, you'll find Milwaukee north of Chicago, on the shores of Lake Michigan.

Where can I go to have fun in the Milwaukee area?

- Take a tour of the Pabst Mansion, built in 1893 for some $225,000 boasts fourteen fireplaces, a dozen bathrooms, and a library filled with secret panels. It's on Wisconsin Avenue.

- The Allen Bradley clock tower is on 2nd Street in downtown Milwaukee and can be seen from the street. On the clock face, each hour hand is nearly 16 feet (4.9 meters) in length and weighs nearly 500 pounds (227 kilograms); the hour markings are four feet (1.2 meters) long. Until just a few years ago, it was the largest four-sided clock in the world (a clock in Saudi Arabia beat it out in 2010).

- Check out the the Milwaukee Art Museum on N. Art Museum Drive, overlooking Lake Michigan. Also, make plans to visit the Milwaukee Public Museum on Wells Street and the Harley Davidson Museum on Canal Street.

- No Milwaukee visit is complete without a trip to the Milwaukee County Zoo. It's open year round, on W. Bluemound Road.

- Shopping! You can't go wrong in Milwaukee if you love to shop! Check out the many boutiques and bookstores, browse local outlet stores, and enjoy lunch at any of the local restaurants. Bring home souvenirs!

- For those who love nostalgia, a visit to the Chudnow Museum of Yesteryear will be a treat. It's filled with memorabilia from Milwaukee's history from 1910 to about

The Shields Building, constructed in 2015 and designed by local architect James Shields, is a $34 million expansion of the Milwaukee Art Museum. The museum houses about 25,000 works of art.

1940, as collected by Abe Chudnow, who was a lawyer. Tours are available; the museum is at 839 North 11th Street.

- Catch the Domes at the Mitchell Park Horticultural Museum on Layton Blvd. Take in a park near Lake Michigan. Be sure to do the RiverWalk. Indulge in some local brews!

What are some fun-to-know things about Milwaukee?

- Throughout its history, the city's name has been spelled several different ways: Millioki, Melwarik, Milwaukie, and its current Milwaukee.
- The first Black resident to vote in Milwaukee was Joe Oliver, who cast his vote in 1835 at the city's first election. Oliver was Solomon Juneau's cook.
- Milwaukee is also known as "Beer Town," The City of Festivals," and "Cream City" (for the color of the bricks on the brewery buildings).
- The U.S. Bank Center is the tallest building in Wisconsin, at forty-two floors and more than a million square feet of floor space.
- Office workers rejoice: the typewriter and the answering machine were both invented in Milwaukee (in 1867 and 1948, respectively).
- Since 1960, just four men have served as mayor of Milwaukee.
- "Bronzie" can be found on Wells Street near the River Walk. It's just what you think it is: it's a bronze, life-size statue of Arthur Fonzarelli of TV's *Happy Days*.
- In 2014, Summerfest-goers ate nearly 170,000 burgers, almost 100,000 mozzarella sticks, and nearly 200,000 miniature donuts.
- Before they came to Milwaukee in 1970, the Brewers were based in Seattle for one year and were known as the Pilots.
- The oldest continuous curling club in the nation calls Milwaukee home.

What's the history of La Crosse, Wisconsin?

You almost can't tell the history of La Crosse without touching upon the history of Prairie du Chien, just down the river.

The first white man to see La Crosse was probably Fr. Louis Hennepin (1626–1704), who traveled down the Mississippi to the area in 1680 on his way to a good exploration of the area. Twenty years later, French fur traders had already decided to name the area after a Native American game with racquets and balls.

Permanent settlement by white people didn't happen until 1841 when nineteen-year-old Nathan Myrick (1822–1903) came from Prairie du Chien, where he'd been trying to work for any one of the traders who did business near there. Alas, he couldn't speak any of the local native languages. Undaunted, and apparently unwilling to return to his New York birthplace, he borrowed a boat and supplies, and moved to La Crosse. There, in late 1841, he built a cabin in what is now Pettibone Park and—in the irony to end all ironies—began successfully trading with the Natives.

By the mid-1800s, Myrick had attained a business, a sawmill on the Black River where he sold firewood to steamers along the Mississippi and logs downstream. In 1848, he acquired the land that would eventually become La Crosse but hard times at the mill forced Myrick to move to Sauk City, Wisconsin, where he eventually retired. Even so, Myrick kept his land interest in La Crosse.

Under Myrick's watch, La Crosse's first post office opened in 1844. Five-hundred forty-three souls called La Crosse home by 1853. In 1856, La Crosse officially became a city. Once that happened, and through the end of the nineteenth century, German immigrants flooded into the city and La Crosse became known as a port city for steamboats, lumber mills, and brewing; in fact, in 1884, more beer was produced in La Crosse than anywhere else in Wisconsin.

Today's La Crosse is home to two hospitals, three colleges, a brewery, and lots of places to visit, hike, and bike. You'll find La Crosse on the west side of the state, right along the Mississippi River and just northeast of Iowa.

Where will I find some fun-to-do things in La Crosse?

- Check out the World's Largest Six Pack on Third Street near City Brewery. While you're down there, cross the street and get a selfie with King Gambrinus.
- Take a drive up Grandad's Bluff and see a panoramic view of the area from the vantage point of nearly 600 feet (183 meters) around the city. There's a small park atop the Bluff, with binoculars, seating areas, and a platform for better viewing. If you're lucky, you can see two other states from atop the bluffs: Minnesota to the west, and Iowa to the southwest.

If you're visiting La Crosse during baseball season, take in a Loggers game at the Lumberyard at Copeland Park.

- Visit the Shrine of Our Lady of Guadalupe on the far south side of the area. It was built to honor the Blessed Virgin Mary and to commemorate the morning when Mary showed herself to a Mexican peasant named Juan Diego in 1531. The Shrine was built from 2001 to 2002 and has since expanded. It's open year 'round; give yourself time to take a nature walk on the grounds.
- Oktoberfest is held in late September / early October each year. It kicks off with a parade and ends with a parade; in between are more parades, music, a beer tent, and plenty of food.
- La Crosse is home to many beautiful historic buildings and houses, so take a drive and keep your eyes peeled. Start in the downtown area, and fan out around the region; you're sure to see some beautiful architecture.
- For a look back at history, take a tour of the Hixon House, near City Hall. The Hixons were one of La Crosse's most influential families, and this house has been remarkably preserved to represent their lives. If you're lucky, you may even meet actors dressed in period clothing. The Hixon House is located on 7th Street North.
- Be sure to take a walk in Riverside Park, where you may glimpse a riverboat. Walk a few blocks to historic downtown La Crosse and visit area craft breweries and unique shops.

What are some fun-to-know things about La Crosse?

- Buffalo Bill Cody loved coming to La Crosse and brought his show to the city's Opera House many times. He owned part of Barron Island at one time.
- George Poage was the first African American to compete in the Olympics in 1904.
- Want to see bald eagles in the wild? Exit off I-90 to the north side of La Crosse; bald eagles like to hunt on the Black River there.
- On a clear day, you can see three different states from the top of Grandad's Bluff.
- In 1930, the La Crosse Rubber Mills was the city's largest employer. Some two-thousand people—a significant percentage of the city's population—worked at the Rubber Mills then.
- The average La Crosse employee takes just fifteen minutes to get to work.
- At the first Oktoberfest in 1961, attendees could participate in a cow-chip throwing contest and a greased-pig contest.
- The first Oktoberfest had no Festmaster. Don Rice was the first Festmaster, for the second 'Fest in 1962.
- You are breaking a law in La Crosse if you "worry" a squirrel.
- Dahl Automotive in La Crosse is the eighth oldest Ford dealer in the nation.

What's the history behind Green Bay, Wisconsin?

Founded in 1634, Green Bay is Wisconsin's oldest settlement. Archaeologists say that Native Americans were in the area for ten thousand years before white explorers arrived, drawn to the abundant game available there.

In 1634, French explorer Jean Nicolet arrived, which is the earliest verifiable date in which white explorers met the territory's natives. Within twenty years, French fur traders and missionaries arrived, the former of which gave the settlement its name: La Baye. La Baye was a major point of entry to the untamed area for decades.

In 1745, the Charles de Langlade family became the area's first white family to move in. Imagine how they felt when the British took control of the area (by then, Green Bay) some eighteen years later—control they had until the American Revolution, when the Americans took over Green Bay once and for all and built Ft. Howard inside what is now the city limits. At that point, skilled workers began to arrive in the state and industry took advantage of the "bay" part of Green Bay. In 1853, some two thousand people lived there and the city was constantly growing.

Not long after that, the railroad had arrived in Green Bay and in the latter part of the nineteenth century, railroads nudged ships out of the way, transportation-wise. That was when Green Bay businessmen and their factories switched gears, and the port city became known for smelting, lumber, and paper products, the latter of which is, today, the most predominant industry in the area.

Oh, and football. Green Bay is big on football.

You'll find Green Bay in the upper western part of Wisconsin, near the peninsula that juts out into Lake Michigan. Go, Pack, Go.

Where are the best places to visit in Green Bay?

- Duh. Lambeau Field, where the Green Bay Packers play football, should be at the top of your list of places to visit. Anybody can point you in the direction of Lambeau Field but just in case, it's on Lombardi Avenue. Curly Lambeau, by the way, was

Green Bay is the oldest city in Wisconsin (founded in 1634) and the state's third largest with about 104,000 residents.

the team's founder and first head coach; Lombardi was perhaps its most beloved coach. Bonus: The Green Bay Packer Hall of Fame is located inside Lambeau Field.

- Open in the summer months, you can't beat Bay Beach Amusement Park, where admission and parking are free, and rides are just twenty-five cents a ticket.

- The National Railroad Museum on S. Broadway is a train aficionado's dream come true. There, you'll find actual, full-size, historic trains that you can tour, inside and out. Train rides are included with your admission. If you're so inclined, you can even book your special event there.

- Check out some of Green Bay's many parks and nature preserves. Do a little shopping while you're there. If you've got time, drive northwest a little and check out the fabulous sites and scenes in Door County.

- Green Bay's maritime history is long and varied: check out any of the several museums based on ships and shipwrecks that happened near Door County. Also be sure to visit the Old Bailey's Harbor Lighthouse, near Green Bay in Door County.

What are some fun-to-know things about Green Bay?

- The oldest house in Wisconsin is in Green Bay; it was originally built by Jacob Roi in 1776 and repeatedly remodeled until Moravian minister Nils Otto Tank and family gave the building to the city.

- Wisconsin's first courthouse is located in Green Bay. So was Wisconsin's first post office. And Green Bay was the home of the state's first newspaper.

- Then-Vice President Richard M. Nixon was at the first Packers game at Lambeau Field. The Pack beat the Bears 21–17 that day.

- The Green Bay Packers are the only NFL team to be owned by its fans. Season tickets are hot commodities and don't often come available; getting season tickets can literally take decades.

- There are two Green Bays in Wisconsin. The city is in Brown County, where the Fox River meets Green Bay on Lake Michigan. The town is located about fifteen miles (twenty-four kilometers) northeast of the city of Green Bay. The population of the city is just over 105,000 people; fewer than 2,000 souls call the town home.

- In addition to earning the nickname of "Title Town," Green Bay is also known as "the Toilet Paper Capital of the World," because the world's first splinter-free TP was developed there.

- The Fox River, which separates Green Bay from its neighboring city, De Pere, is one of the few rivers on the planet to run north.

- Packer Green-and-Gold was not officially adopted until 1950. The first Cheesehead hat appeared in Lambeau Field in 1987.

- In 1880, a devastating fire happened in downtown Green Bay. More than a hundred buildings were destroyed.

- Green Bay's largest employers are the paper industry and the shipping industry.

What's the history behind Eau Claire, Wisconsin?

For years before white settlers arrived, Eau Claire was a hot spot: because of the water and the game that came for it, both the Ojibwe and the Sioux wanted control of the Eau Claire valley.

And then white explorers arrived: Englishman Jonathan Carver (1710–1780) was the first to arrive, and he wrote a description of the area in 1767. He spread the word and by 1784, French fur traders had set up camp and were doing a good business in trading. They called the area "Clearwater," or Eau Claire.

The first white permanent settlers arrived in the area in 1845; just five years later, some one hundred people called it home—and most of them worked in the sawmills. Norwegian and German immigrants flocked to the area in subsequent years, and they brought their skills and culture to the Eau Claire valley.

In the years following the Civil War, Eau Claire's lumber industry boomed, with more than seventy-five sawmills in the area and millions of dollars in total revenue. Furniture, coffins, lumber and other wood products helped the city gain its nickname of "Sawdust City"; other industries made electric motors and other products.

Alas, it wasn't to last: by the early 1930s, Eau Claire's sawdust industry had collapsed due to overcutting of its once-thick, lush forests. Industry was, by then, focused on automobile tires (the Gillette Safety Tire Company began manufacturing tires in 1917) and education (the University of Wisconsin Eau-Claire opened in 1916).

You can find Eau Claire near the western central border of the state, about a ninety-minute drive from Minneapolis.

Where will I find the best fun in Eau Claire?

- Make plans to visit any one of the several wineries and breweries in Eau Claire, including the Leinenkugel Brewery's Leinie's Lodge in Chippewa Falls, just a little north of Eau Claire.

- No matter what the season, Eau Claire is the place for hiking and walking trails, snowmobiling trails, and nature walks. Hint: there are 181 miles (291 kilometers) of snowmobiling trails alone!

- Take a float down the river in Phoenix Park. Take the kids to Carson Park for lots of kid-friendly activities. Take in some shopping. Visit the Paul Bunyan Logging Camp Museum. Or just take five in one of Eau Claire's beautiful parks, and enjoy the scenery!

What are some fun-to-know facts about Eau Claire?

- In the mid-1800s, more than several dozen area sawmills worked 'round the clock to make lumber. At one point, they produced some three million board feet of lumber per hour.

- Each fall, Eau Claire's population swells by about 15 percent when the UW-Eau Claire students return to school.

- The Menard's chain of home improvement stores is based in Eau Claire.

- The words "Eau Claire" mean clear water in French.

- The average household size in Eau Claire is 2 people; just over 34 percent of Eau Claire residents live alone.

- In 2008, Adam Winrich broke a Guinness World Record with 27 stock-whip cracks in one minute. He did it in Stone's Throw Bar in Eau Claire.

- In 2014, NerdWallet ranked Eau Claire as the fourth-best city in the nation for Work-Life Balance.

- Kiplinger's has named Eau Claire as the seventh best city for "cheapskates" because of its free and low-cost amenities and entertainments.

- Residents can bow hunt in certain areas within the city limits of Eau Claire.

- UW-Eau Claire opened in 1916. Raymond Gillette opened his rubber tire plant the following year. For decades, those were the two main employers in the Chippewa Valley area.

What's the history behind the city of Wausau, Wisconsin?

Like most Wisconsin cities, Wausau's history begins before the arrival of white settlers. Long before French traders wandered through the area, the Ojibwe people battled the Sac, Fox, and Ho-Chunk people for control of the Wisconsin River Valley and the waterfall in it. The Ojibwe farmed in the area, too—at least until the U.S. government removed them in the mid-1800s.

Wausau itself was founded in the latter 1830s by George Stevens (1790–1866), who also founded nearby Stevens Point; he called his new town Big Bull Falls because of the nearby waterfall. In 1839, Stevens built a sawmill in the area, acquired rights from the Ojibwe for water power, and began cutting down trees that he floated down the Wis-

Even though it's a small city, Wausau straddles the Wisconsin River, which helped it survive as a center of commerce.

consin River to lumber mills in the southern parts of the state and nearby. By 1850, Wausau had 1,500 residents and more than ten operating sawmills.

That was the same year that Marathon County was founded by local businessman Walter McIndoe (1819–1872) and the settlement became officially known as Wausau. It was incorporated as a village in the spring of 1861 and officially became a city in 1872 (and yes, McIndoe lived long enough to see it happen).

Two years later, the railroad arrived in north central Wisconsin and with it, a better economy for Wausau. The timber surrounding the area had been dwindling slowly for a few years, and lumbering was going with it, so Wausau businessmen set their sights on mining and paper products. By the end of the nineteenth century, nearly 10,000 people called Wausau "home."

You'll find Wausau in the north central part of Wisconsin.

Where is all the fun in Wausau?

- First built in 1899 as the Grand Opera House, the Grand Theatre was the Opera House's replacement in 1927. It was refurbished in 1986–87. See a play, hear a concert, attend a show on North 4th Street.
- If it's winter, grab your skis and head to Granite Peak. Seventy-five runs are waiting for you!
- For something a little quieter, check out the Leigh Yawkey Woodson Art Museum at 12th and Franklin. In addition to a museum, there are lots of activities available there, too. Wausau is a big arts-loving city!
- Look for any of the craft breweries in Wausau. Check out the trails, parks, and playgrounds. Take in a race at State Park Speedway. Visit Wausau's unique shops downtown.

What are some fun-to-know facts about Wausau?

- Legend is that Paul Bunyan is buried beneath Rib Mountain.
- Wausau, along with Marathon County, produces nearly two million pounds (907,000 kilograms) of ginseng each year, which is more than 90 percent of the production of the United States. That's why Marathon County is known as the Ginseng Capital of the World.
- Wausau was first known as "Big Bull Falls." Mosinee, just to the south, was known as "Little Bull Falls."
- The Wausau Curling Facility is one of the largest curling-dedicated facilities in the country.
- As the crow flies, Wausau is 769 miles (1,238 kilometers) from the White House.
- Wausau is home to the Badger State Games, an Olympic-style multiple-sport event for amateurs of all ages and abilities, with no qualification necessary.
- Marathon County is the largest county in Wisconsin.

- Wausau's name is said to mean "far away" in the Chippewa language.
- Until it was incorporated as a village in 1996, Weston was one of the oldest townships in the state. Weston is just east of Wausau but is considered part of the metro.
- Marathon County is second in the state in milk production and in American cheese production.

What's the history behind Superior, Wisconsin?

Much like Green Bay, Superior has a very long history that starts with a Native American settlement. Before white men ever set foot on the area, Ojibwe Indians had set up camp on what we know as Madeline Island. In the very early 1600s, French explorer Étienne Brûlé came across the Ojibwe camp as he was paddling along Lake Superior's shore; he also found copper and furs, which he took back to Québec with him. French traders, missionaries, and explorers arrived in the area soon afterward and they had very good working relationships with the Ojibwe then.

That ended with the American Revolution and treaties would subsequently give more rights to the land to white settlers. By 1847, the U.S. government had control of the entire south shore of Lake Superior.

In 1854, Douglas became a county and Superior its county seat; two years later, some 2,500 people lived in Superior. It would remain roughly so through the post-Civil War years. When the Duluth Ship Canal was built in 1871, financial panic ensued, and the town was nearly crushed in favor of Duluth, which is nearby, in Minnesota.

In 1885, civil engineer and land speculator General John Henry Hammond (1833–1890) and his partner Robert Belknap (1848-1896) founded the Land and River Improvement Company, which did just that: improved the area around Superior by establishing the city of West Superior. They began to hire new immigrants from Great Britain, Croatia, Poland, Germany, and elsewhere to build docks, elevators, railroads, and buildings for new businesses. In 1890, Superior City merged with West Superior, which enjoyed years of boom, followed by times of financial bust throughout the end of the nineteenth century.

Today's Superior is separate from Duluth, but their histories are tied tightly, and Superior is considerably smaller than its sister city. Its main industries are still, regionally, mining, logging, and farming. You'll find Superior way up north, on the edge of Lake Superior.

Where will I find fun stuff to do in or near Superior, Wisconsin?

- Visit Patterson State Park, just off Highway 35. The waterfall is spectacular! And if hiking is your thing, be sure to visit Amnicon Falls State Park, just south of Superior.
- If museums are your thing, Superior has you covered. Visit the Richard I. Bong Veteran's Historical Center or the Fairlawn Mansion and Museum. Take a gander at the Lake Superior Railroad Museum or the beautiful artwork at Canal Park.
- Superior = ships and you can't be in Superior without learning about its maritime history. Stop at the SS *Meteor* Maritime Museum (the *Meteor* is the world's only re-

maining whaleback ship and was built right in Superior) or the Wisconsin Point Lighthouse. Visit the Lake Superior Maritime Visitor's Center, too, of course.

- Take the kids to Lake Superior Zoo. Do a little shopping. And don't forget to go down by Lake Superior itself. It's awe-inspiring. You won't be sorry.

What are some fun-to-know things about Lake Superior?

- Don't get confused: Fond du Lac is also up in the northern part of this area. It's a neighborhood of Duluth.

- Lake Superior has been known by a lot of names in its history: early explorers called it "Grand Lac." Father Marquette called it "Lac Superior de Tracy." French explorers gave it the name that stuck, "Superior," because of its place in the chain of lakes.

- Henry Wadsworth Longfellow said the Chippewa Indians called the lake "Gitche Gumee."

- By surface area, Lake Superior is the largest lake in the world. By volume, it's third largest.

- Lake Superior is 160 miles wide and roughly 350 miles long (257 by 563 kilometers). Its shoreline measures just over 2,700 miles (4,345 kilometers). At its deepest point, Lake Superior is 1,300 feet (396 meters) deep; it rarely freezes that far below the water surface.

- Scientists at the University of Wisconsin say it would take 200 years to refill Lake Superior.

- Yes, The S.S. *Edmund Fitzgerald*, the Great Lakes' largest ship at the time, sunk in Lake Superior. Here's the story:

The *Edmund Fitzgerald* left the Burlington Northern Railroad Dock No. 1 in Superior on the afternoon of November 9, 1975, loaded with taconite pellets, which are unprocessed iron ore. Accompanied by another ship that had come down from Two Harbors, Minnesota, the *Edmund Fitzgerald*'s captain knew that bad weather was coming, so he planned to take a route that went along the north side of Lake Superior, which would, theoretically, afford more protection from winds. The *Edmund Fitzgerald*, piloted by Captain Ernest M. McSorley, went ahead but weather continued to worsen and both ships reported problems. No distress signal was ever sent from the "Fitz," but about 7:10 P.M. on November 10, the *Edmund Fitzgerald* was heard from one last time....

Despite the Navy performing several searches, no survivors were ever found. Twenty-nine men were lost; the wreck itself is still underwater but the ship's bell sits in the Great Lakes Maritime Museum in Whitefish Point, Michigan.

- The city of Superior is bounded by a lake, three bays, and two rivers (respectively, Lake Superior; St. Louis Bay, Allouez Bay, and Superior Bay; and the Nemadji River and St. Louis River.

- Around the turn of the nineteenth century, Superior's catchphrase was "Where Sail Meets Rail."
- During most winters, up to 95 percent of Lake Superior is ice-covered.

POLITICS AND LAW

BALANCE OF POWER

What type of government does Wisconsin have?

The state has a bicameral legislature, with an assembly of ninety-nine representatives and state senate of thirty-three.

Each assemblyman represents more than 57,000 residents and are elected to two-year terms. State senators represent more than 172,000 residents and are elected to four-year terms.

How much do legislators earn in Wisconsin?

The state assembly members are paid just under $51,000 each year, plus a "per-diem" that allows members from outside of Dane County to claim up to another $138 per day when they stay overnight. The position is considered a full-time job.

State senators earn a similar salary just under $51,000, with a maximum "per-diem" of $88.00 for those from districts outside of Dane County. That position is also considered full-time.

Most legislators claim the maximum per-diem regardless of how much they spend while staying in Madison.

How is the governor chosen in Wisconsin?

Originally, terms for the governor's office were only two years. In 1967 the state's constitution was amended to make the 1970 gubernatorial election be for a four-year term. There are no term limits for the office.

The governor is elected by a popular vote every four years during the middle of a presidential term. Under normal circumstances, no governor will be elected during a presidential election. Governor Scott Walker (1967–) took office following the 2010 election, then endured a recall effort. He was reelected in the regular 2014 election with a 52 percent majority. Then, in 2018, he was narrowly defeated by Democrat Tony Evers (1951–).

What is the governor's pay?

The Wisconsin Office of State Employee Relations submits biennial proposals for adjustments to the governor's salary. A committee must approve any changes, which are subject to the governor's veto. In 2015 the salary was raised to $137,328, a 2 percent increase from the previous year.

Which political party held sway in Wisconsin when the state was formed?

Governor Scott Walker, who was elected in 2010, has had a somewhat tumultuous term in office but survived a recall effort to be reelected in 2014.

The Democratic Party controlled the state legislature and governorship when it was admitted into the union in 1848. They held the governor's seat—except for a single two-year term for a Whig Party governor—until the newly formed Republican Party elected their first governor in 1856. Since then only sixteen governors have been non-Republicans.

Of the forty-six office holders from 1848 through 2019, there have been thirty-one Republicans, thirteen Democrats, two Wisconsin Progressives, and one Whig.

Was the 2018 gubernatorial election close?

Yes, quite close. The winner, Democrat Tony Evers, beat incumbent Scott Walker by a mere 3 percent of the vote. A central point of Evers' campaign was health care (he is a cancer survivor), and he has supported the Affordable Care Act and advocated for expanding Medicare for Wisconsin citizens, a strategy that has lowered health insurance premiums in neighboring state Minnesota.

Who controlled the legislature when Wisconsin was admitted into the union?

Of the sixty-six assembly seats in the first session, forty-nine were held by Democrats and seventeen by Whigs. There were nineteen state senators in 1848, sixteen Democrats and three Whigs. This was before the formation of the Republican Party in 1854.

When did Wisconsin's senate shift away from Democratic control?

The balance didn't shift that much through 1853, even after the senate expanded from nineteen to twenty-five seats. Once the Whig Party split apart, Democrats retained sway in the state senate.

In 1854, however, the margin of control dropped to a single senate seat—thirteen to twelve. The following year the margin reversed—thirteen for the Republican Party, twelve for the Democrats.

Apart from a session or two, Republicans held the state senate for decades. The Democratic Party again took the senate for six of seven sessions, 1996 through 2002 (with the Republicans in charge for 1998), then again for 2007 through 2010. Then Republicans swept into power.

Did the Democratic Party hold the state assembly the way they held the senate?

The more volatile assembly had the ratio of power shifting considerably more than the Wisconsin Senate, but Democrats fared only slightly better in the assembly. They held on for another year before the new Republican Party began their dominance in 1856.

As with the state senate, the assembly stayed in Republican hands for two decades with the exception of a session or two. Then various forms of socialists or progressives came on the scene and held brief sway before the Republicans dominated from 1938 through 1956. Democrats and Republicans traded power in the assembly from 1958 through 1968.

In recent years, Republicans have had a firm grip on the assembly. Since 1995, they've controlled the assembly with the exception of 2009 and 2010.

What are the restrictions on a governor's veto power in Wisconsin?

One of the ways a governor can override the legislature is by vetoing a bill. In Wisconsin, the governor has sixty days to sign or veto a bill approved by both the assembly and senate. If he or she does nothing with the bill for those sixty days, the bill fails to become law by way of what's called a "pocket veto." The legislature can attempt to override either a veto or "pocket veto."

What type of vote is required to override a veto?

Two-thirds of the members in each house of the legislature must be present in order to vote in a session after the end of a regular session. Then each chamber must pass the override by a two-thirds majority.

Veto overrides must be voted on outside of a regular session.

Does a Wisconsin governor have "line item veto" power?

Wisconsin has one of the most powerful veto laws in the nation. It's not just a "line item" veto, where specific lines within a law can be stricken. The governor can cross out single words, sentences, paragraphs, and any part of a law in order to change the wording into something the governor finds more favorable.

One of the more famous examples was when in 2005 Governor Jim Doyle struck 752 words from a budget bill to cobble together language that diverted $427 million from the state's transportation fund to education. Some enraged lawmakers called the process a "Frankenstein" veto. The legislature was unable to override that veto, and the budget went into effect.

105

What is a "special session" of the Wisconsin legislature?

A special session is different from a regular session of the legislature in that there are limits to the topics or bills discussed. The special session allows the governor to bring lawmakers back to Madison to address a crisis. Only the topics listed in the governor's call for a special session may be discussed. However, the governor can alter the discussion by issuing new proclamations.

More than seventy special sessions have been called in Wisconsin.

Have there been recent instances when Wisconsin had a unified government?

The state has had a few instances of a "trifecta" government, with the same party holding the governorship and a majority in the assembly and senate. In 1995 that happened when the Republicans had majorities in both houses and had Republican Tommy Thompson as governor. In 1996 and 1997 the Democratic Party held the state senate with Republicans in control of the assembly, but then in 1998 Governor Thompson again enjoyed a trifecta government.

In 2009 and 2010, Democratic governor Jim Doyle held a trifecta state government, but in 2011 the tables turned entirely—Republican governor Scott Walker took the governor's seat, and the GOP swept into the majority in both the assembly and senate.

What is the role of the courts in Wisconsin?

The purpose of the courts is to decide legal disputes based on the constitution of the State of Wisconsin, laws passed by the legislature, and municipal statutes. There are sixty-nine circuit courts in the state, with 249 judges. Sixteen judges serve on the court of appeals, which reviews all appeals in the state's four appellate districts.

Similar to the federal supreme court, Wisconsin has a "court of last resort" called the State Supreme Court. They have the final word on the state's laws. Though nothing explicitly grants the court the authority to strike down laws they view as unconstitutional, that power has been traditionally seen as appropriate because of *The Federalist* No. 78, in which Alexander Hamilton wrote, "Interpretation of the laws is the proper and peculiar province of the courts." In other words, the constitution trumps legislation.

What is an extraordinary session?

Unlike the special session, an extraordinary session may be called by the legislature. This type of session may meet concurrently with a governor's special session, and similar to a special session it may only discuss topics or bills listed in the call for an extraordinary session.

There have been six extraordinary sessions called since the joint rule was adopted in 1977.

In an 1803 decision (*Marbury v. Madison*), the U.S. Supreme Court ruled that courts have the ability to strike down unconstitutional laws. Chief Justice John Marshall reasoned, "A legislative act contrary to the constitution is not law."

How are the courts organized?

The court of final resort is always the U.S. Supreme Court. The level of the judiciary below that is the U.S. Court of Appeals—Wisconsin is in the seventh district. The state's federal district courts are also in the seventh district. There are also courts that deal with specific subject matters such as bankruptcy laws.

At the state level the highest court is the Wisconsin Supreme Court. The state's court of appeals is next in the hierarchy, having a mandatory jurisdiction—they can't pick and choose which cases to hear like the U.S. Supreme Court. The state has ten circuit courts just below the appeals courts.

Municipal courts handle noncriminal traffic cases, as well as ordinance violations. In communities with no municipal court, such cases are heard by circuit courts.

How does the Wisconsin Supreme Court affect the legislature and governor?

Supreme court justices are in theory nonpartisan office holders. In recent years their elections have become contests where partisan organizations have worked for (or against) specific candidates. That does not mean an elected judge will agree with what "his or her" party does in the legislature.

A panel of federal judges ruled two to one in 2011 saying Republicans "gerrymandered" election district boundaries. The courts ruled that maps were so convoluted the voting rights of Democrats were violated. In 2017 the state supreme court agreed to hear an appeal of that case, a clear departure from a legislature controlled by what many would consider the same party.

The same court struck down the lower court ruling to redraw the boundaries by November of 2017 but moved the deadline for new district maps to take effect by the 2018 elections.

How often does the court overturn lower court decisions?

In 2016, the Wisconsin Supreme Court issued almost eight hundred decisions. The percentage of circuit court cases upheld is about 67 percent. When it comes to their support of the appellate courts, that percentage is as high as 93 percent for the first district court of appeals. Those percentages are fairly consistent over the years. Historically, prior to 2016, 86 percent of circuit court cases were upheld.

How do specific judges fare before the state's supreme court?

Of the thirty-seven circuit court judges surveyed by Erika Strebel for 2016, decisions were upheld about two-thirds of the time. Most judges only had one case reviewed by the supreme court. Only five had two, and of those there were three splits concerning "upheld" versus "overturned." One judge had both upheld, another had both overturned.

Is there a difference when Wisconsin's supreme court hears cases about trial judges?

The four trial court judges with the most rulings by the state's supreme court looked a bit different from the appellate courts. All four of those judges were from Milwaukee, and the vast majority of those rulings were upheld. More than fifty cases were reviewed by the supreme court, and only two cases were overturned.

Are Wisconsin judges subject to voters?

Unlike the U.S. Supreme Court, the state's supreme court judges are elected to ten-year terms. Though they can be reelected, they are still under the review of the voter. They can override the state legislature, the governor, but not the voter.

The state supreme court limits its own power as well. The court will not review a legislative action unless there is an actual case or controversy. In 2011 the state passed a voter ID law, and the court would not review the law until at least one voter claimed their ability to vote was impaired.

They also refuse to rule on questions that are purely political and won't rule on the wisdom of statutes or legislation either.

What executive-level offices exist in Wisconsin?

There are eleven officials in Wisconsin with executive-level rankings—four of them are members of the governor's cabinet. There are the governor, lieutenant governor, attorney general, commissioner of insurance, public service commissioner, superintendent of public instruction, and treasurer.

Does the court also have the right to strike down Congressional laws?

Wisconsin played a vital part in deciding when courts can overrule federal legislation. The state Supreme Court asserted they had the power to rule an act of the U.S. Congress unconstitutional, responding to the Fugitive Slave Act of 1850. The act required escaped slaves later captured in free states to be returned to captivity, and the Wisconsin Supreme Court rejected that law.

The U.S. Supreme Court rejected that assertion, reserving for itself the role of judicial review. "If it appears that an act of Congress is not pursuant to and within the limits of the power assigned to the Federal Government, it is the duty of the courts of the United States to declare it unconstitutional and void." Though the Fugitive Slave Act was not overturned, Congress repealed the act in 1864.

The cabinet posts include the secretary of agriculture, trade, and consumer protection, secretary of natural resources, secretary of state, and secretary of workforce development.

What is the size of Wisconsin's state budget?

The total budget for the state is about $37.5 billion for fiscal 2017–2018, and if Governor Walker's recommendations are followed the budget would increase to $38.5 billion the following fiscal year.

The Budget Overview described unemployment at a 15-year low in 2017, with the state ranking in the top ten for labor participation. Median taxes for a family of four will be lowered by an estimated $1,500 across six years, ending in the 2018 tax year. The same document places the state budget deficit at $3.6 billion, the fourth lowest state for long term obligations.

Who are the people most influential in determining state policy?

There are well over a hundred people or organizations that have an impact on setting policy in the state of Wisconsin. They fall into different categories, such as activists, lobbyists, media, individuals, and other organizations.

Ballotpedia lists ten activists, seven influential journalists, seventeen lobbyists, two media companies, six 501(c)(3) nonprofit organizations, and fourteen people listed in the "local influencer" category.

Additionally there are twelve 501(c)(4) organizations who can influence elections. Unlike the (3) designation, the entities with a (4) are not tax deductible for donors and are allowed to engage in political lobbying activities without limit.

Who are the biggest lobbyists in Wisconsin?

Jay Heck, executive director of Common Cause in Wisconsin, is listed first on Ballotpedia. He served on the campaign staff of independent presidential candidate and Illinois congressman John B. Anderson (1922–2017).

Brett Healy is listed second. He is the president of the MacIver Institute for Public Policy.

Third on the list is Ray Cross, president of the University of Wisconsin System.

Ballotpedia does not claim to rank those lobbyists in any particular order.

Who are the top political activists in Wisconsin?

In no specified order, Ballotpedia lists Brad Courtney, Mark Block, Orville Seymer, Chris Kliesmet, and Eric O'Keefe as top activists to the "right" of the political spectrum.

"Left" leaning activists include Scot Ross, Betsy Kippers, Lisa Graves, and Ned Ryun.

The 501(c)(4) Wisconsin Public Interest Group is also on that list. Their focus is on the issue of consumer protection.

Which journalists impact elections in Wisconsin?

The seven listed on Ballotpedia include conservative radio personalities Vicki McKenna and Charlie Sykes.

The print side of media includes Bill Glauber, Dan Bice, Patrick Marley, and Jason Stein from the *Milwaukee Journal/Sentinel*.

Online media puts M. D. Kittle on the list.

What nonprofit organizations sway politics in Wisconsin?

The list of 501(c)(3) groups includes the Wisconsin Institute for Law and Liberty, Wisconsin Democracy Campaign, the Center for Media and Democracy, the Bradley Foundation, the MacIver Institute, and Citizens for Responsible Government.

Those in the 501(c)(4) category include Common Cause in Wisconsin, the Greater Wisconsin Committee, United Wisconsin, Jobs First Coalition, Citizens for a Strong America, Wisconsin Right to Life, Americans for Prosperity Wisconsin, Friends of Scott Walker, Wisconsin Club for Growth, Wisconsin Family Action, and Wisconsin Public Interest Research Group.

The difference between a 501(c)(3) and a 501 (c)(4) is the deductibility of contributions, as well as the type and scope of lobbying.

What does redistricting mean for the balance of power in Wisconsin?

Whichever party controls the legislature is allowed to redraw district maps every ten years. Both houses must agree to the new set of maps, then the governor must sign off—just like any other legislative bill to reach his or her desk. Typically a legislature dominated by a single party will organize legislative districts to favor their party.

If the assembly and state senate cannot agree on district maps, the courts are given the job.

What caused so much controversy in the redistricting of 2010?

In 2010 the Republican Party controlled both the assembly and state senate, as well as the governorship. Leadership rejected a democratically hired firm's assistance, instead hiring an outside firm that had a history of donating to Republicans.

The new maps were unveiled on July 8, 2011, was passed by the legislature on July 19, 2011, and signed by Governor Scott Walker on August 9, 2011. The Wisconsin Government Accountability Board identified errors, and lawsuits resulted in the courts determining that some Milwaukee area maps needed work to enable minorities to be better represented.

The U.S. Supreme Court has been somewhat tolerant of partisan maps in the past, with some justices thinking the courts should not be involved in drawing maps. They heard arguments in October of 2017 in the case of *Gill v. Whitford*, about the issue of equal protection. A similar case in Maryland was taken up by the Court, *Benisek v. Lamone*, on the issue of First Amendment rights. The plaintiff asserted the redrawing of legislative districts was to retaliate against voters for support of past candidates.

Gill v. Whitford was decided unanimously against the plaintiffs because they could not show any harm done to them by redistricting in this case. With *Benisek v. Lamone* the Court also ruled against the plaintiffs.

What committees are there in the Wisconsin legislature?

There are ten standing joint committees in Wisconsin. They include Review of Administrative Rules, Employment Relations, Finance, Information Policy and Technology, Joint Legislative Audit, Joint Legislative Council, Joint Review Committee on Criminal Penalties, Legislative Organization, Retirement Systems, and Tax Exemptions.

THE STATE CAPITOL

Where is the Wisconsin state capitol?

The state capitol is based in Madison, Wisconsin, at 2 East Main Street. The original territorial legislative building was built in Belmont in 1836, sixty-five miles (105 kilometers) southwest of Madison. Lawmakers met in Belmont through December 9, 1836, put forty-two laws on the books and established a judicial system. They also established Madison as the capital city.

When did construction of the capitol building begin?

Stone for the original capitol was ferried across Lake Mendota in 1837. The original cost was about $60,000.

The current capitol building's construction was delayed for years because the requests for bids were penned by committee. In 1906 the wording was finalized, and construction was completed in 1917—one wing at a time. The final project cost was $7.2 million, and the dedication was delayed because of U.S. involvement in what became known as World War I.

The current Wisconsin State Capitol was designed by architect George B. Post and completed in 1917, just before the United States entered World War I.

How many capitol buildings has Wisconsin constructed?

The very first building where lawmakers met in Belmont, Wisconsin, could be counted as the first. It is now a state historical site. The second, mentioned above, had its ceremonial cornerstone laid in 1837. A bill was signed in 1857 authorizing $50,000 to enlarge the capitol, but a year later very little had been accomplished.

Legislators then authorized replacement of the entire building in a multiphase project that lasted a decade. Despite having some of the nation's most advanced firefighting systems, a fire in February of 1904 gutted most of the building. Contractors submitting bids for repairs all agreed—a totally new building would be needed.

After two years of wrangling over wording, a request was finally hammered out to ask for bid proposals for "a complete and harmonious plan . . . including a dome." The selected contractor finished the final details of the state's third capitol building in 1917, though restoration and renovation made minor changes since then.

What caused the 1904 fire that destroyed the Wisconsin capitol building?

When the capitol was shut down at night, a number of gas lamps were left burning so security guards could see while they patrolled. Around 2:45 the morning of February 27, 1904, one of the guards smelled smoke. He traced it to the second floor of the West Wing, and found a small flame above one of those lamps. He threw buckets of water at the ceiling while the other guard ran to the closest fire hose. There was no water.

The tanks on Beacon Hill had been drained the previous day so workmen could repair a boiler at the university. Pressure was too low to force water to the capitol building. The guards dropped their water buckets and called the fire department, which arrived a half-hour later. By that time flames had spread throughout the West Wing. By the time they ran hoses to Lake Monona, the newly varnished ceiling had become engulfed. Fire lit the sky, and by 4:30 that morning Madison crews contacted nearby cities for assistance.

At one point, twenty-six pumper trucks were on the scene. There was little hope of quenching the fire, so students climbed ladders to the second floor and passed out books of records. The flames didn't die out until around 10:00 that morning. Only five offices survived intact.

Was the Wisconsin capitol building designated a historical landmark?

After a $5.3 million renovation, the building was put on the list of national historic landmarks.

A process called "sponge jetting" cleaned the exterior. The granite was repaired, joints were caulked, and the stone was tuckpointed. The process was completed in November of 2001.

What was done to celebrate the hundredth anniversary of the capitol building?

The months-long process was designed to reach people who could not travel to Madison, so a virtual tour was arranged. A temporary museum was placed in the rotunda, and

Were duels ever fought within the legislature?

In the early days, drinking and gambling were rampant during sessions. Madison's first historian, Daniel Durrie, said lawmakers indulged in the worst types of behavior. "Bad whiskey, in large quantities, was said to be consumed, much to the damage of the consumer."

On February 11, 1842, during a debate in the Territorial Council about a political appointment, Charles Arndt disparaged James Vineyard. The legislature took a break to let flaring tempers cool, but it didn't help. Arndt demanded Vineyard withdraw the lies he'd told. Vineyard refused, Arndt struck him, and Vineyard drew a pistol and shot Arendt. Five minutes later Arndt succumbed to the fatal chest wound.

Vineyard was charged with murder but was acquitted. He later served a single term in the Wisconsin Assembly, moved to California, and served in both the assembly and state senate.

a commemorative book was published. Speeches by Governor Scott Walker (1943–) and former governor Tommy Thompson (1941–) kicked off the event on January 31, 2017. During warmer months, visitors could enjoy a centennial flower garden and a special edition of the Wisconsin Chamber Orchestra.

The bipartisan commission was headed by Assembly Speaker Robin Vos (1968–) and Senate president Roger Roth (1978–).

How big is Wisconsin's capitol building?

The volume of the U.S. capitol building's dome is about 850,000 cubic feet (24,000 cubic meters). The Wisconsin dome measures 790,000 cubic feet (22,370 cubic meters). The height to the top of the statuary (284 feet, or 86.56 meters) has the Wisconsin capitol just over sixteen feet (4.9 meters) taller than the nation's capitol.

The building was modeled on the U.S. capitol building, and state laws restrict the height of other buildings within a mile (1.6 kilometers) of the state capitol building. The limit is 1,032.8 feet (314.8 meters) above sea level. The restriction is to preserve the view of and from the capitol.

How is the capitol building laid out?

The central rotunda is bracketed by four wings of the capitol building, each pointing toward the cardinal directions of the compass.

Where is the state's supreme court located?

The supreme court is in the East Wing of the capitol building. In addition to the supreme court hearing cases there, the Fourth District Court of Appeals also uses that room.

There is more marble in that room than any other room in the building, and the furniture and woodwork are the original mahogany.

Four murals illustrate the history of the state and represent events that shaped Wisconsin law. One shows Caesar Augustus (63 BCE–14 CE) presiding over the trial of a Roman soldier, another shows the signing of the Magna Carta, the third is of the signing of the U.S. Constitution, and the fourth shows the trial of Chief Oshkosh in 1830—the first jury trial in Wisconsin history.

What else is in the East Wing?

Also in the East Wing is the Governor's Conference Room. That room is used to hold press conferences, sign bills, and hold receptions and cabinet meetings.

The room is decorated with twenty-two-karat-gold, cherry-wood paneling and wooden floors of teak, mahogany, quarter-sawn oak, and primavera. There is an Italian marble hand-carved fireplace reaching from floor to ceiling, one of five fireplaces in the building. Paintings and murals represent the state's beauty, strength, patriotism, and other aspects and history of the state.

The original French walnut furniture was purchased for just over $4,000 in 1910.

Where does the state senate meet?

The senate chamber is in the South Wing. Above the circular room of Italian Tavernelle marble is a circular skylight. At the front of the room is "The Marriage of the Atlantic and the Pacific," commemorating the opening of the Panama Canal just a year after the chamber opened.

Where is the Assembly Room?

The state assembly meets in the West Wing. With ninety-nine members, an electronic voting board is used. Wisconsin was the first in the world to use some form of electric voting, installing the machines in 1917, with the current system installed in 1999.

The walls are white Dover marble from New York, and the columns made from Italian marble. The thirty-six-foot (eleven-meter) circular skylight in the assembly room is the largest of four in the building. Toward the front of the chamber is a mural, "Wisconsin," showing the past, present, and future of the state.

What is the North Hearing Room?

That chamber is used for public committee hearings and is located on the second floor of the North Wing. The room is different in that it's very colorful when compared with the assembly, senate, or supreme court chambers. The walls are made of yellow Verona marble and panels of Monte Rente Sienna. Black and gold Porte d'Or Italian marble form a border at the edges of the floor and at the base of the walls.

Murals depict the four methods of transportation used in the state early in its history—railroad, horseback, canoe, and stagecoach. Another mural shows more modern forms of travel—steamboat, railroad, automobile, and airplane.

What is unique about Wisconsin's capitol building?

Nestled between Lake Mendota and Lake Monona, the state capitol is the only one built on an isthmus. Additionally, the granite dome is the only one in the United States.

The building—284 feet (86.56 meters) tall from the ground to the tip of the statue "Wisconsin"—is the tallest building in Madison. The "Capitol View Preservation Ordinance" prevents taller buildings from being built within a mile of the capitol.

Does the state capitol have tours?

The building is open to the public on weekdays from 8:00 A.M. to 6:00 P.M. Weekends and holidays they close at 4:00 P.M. Tours start at the information desk and run hourly from 9:00 to 3:00, skipping the noon hour, Monday through Saturday. Each tour lasts nearly an hour.

What other offices are in the capitol building?

In addition to the offices of the governor and lieutenant governor, the legislature, and supreme court, the main building also houses the offices of the attorney general, secretary of state, the state treasurer, capitol police, and the department of the administration. Various staff offices are also on site.

Overall, there is more than a half-million square feet of space. Each wing is five stories high, with the main dome towering over the rest of the facility.

Why did Tommy Thompson overhaul Wisconsin's capitol building?

When completed in 1917, the capitol's grandeur rivaled buildings of more import in the nation's capital and in New York City. The years, however, had taken a toll on the People's House in Wisconsin. More and more state workers meant rooms had to be divided, walls knocked down, fluorescent lighting hung beneath skylights, and acoustic panels covered the more ornate ceiling.

Technological changes had chipped away at the existing structure. Air conditioners appeared in windows, personal computers and more lighting required additional energy, and phone lines were often fixed to the woodworking. The building began to feel so crowded and the employees put up so many personal decorations the original "aura" of the building had faded. The governor had his Department of the Administration hire a firm to draw up plans to restore the building to its previous grandeur.

How were the restoration changes perceived by the public?

The legislature never adopted the guidelines proposed in 1980, but controversy fueled public notice. Some workers proposed aluminum framed windows in place of the original cherry, but eventually appropriateness trumped cost. That trend gained momentum when the Department of the Administration spent extra money to install historically accurate doorknobs.

Then, in 1985, a committee hired consultants to formulate a capitol master plan, which recommended a total renovation project. That plan was approved in 1987, and work began the following year. The facility was restored as it was constructed—one wing at a time.

How long did the capitol restoration take?

Work on the renovation lasted from 1987 to 2001. Shortly after completion the building was designated a National Historic Landmark by the U.S. National Park Service. The reconstruction took more time than the original eleven-year creation of the building. The total cost for the fourteen-year project was more than $140 million.

Are there other uses for the Capitol Square?

The Dane County Farmers Market operates Saturdays from mid-April through early November, ever since their first opening in 1972. Hours are 8:30 to 2:00.

The Wisconsin Chamber Orchestra performs on the square on Wednesdays, from late June through early August. Though the concert starts at 7:00, people can begin staking out territory at 3:00.

The popular Dane County Farmers Market is held on Saturdays at Capitol Square from April to November.

Art Fair on the Square has been running for more than half a century. About five hundred artists from across the country exhibit crafts, paintings, sculptures, and more.

Taste of Madison brings food from restaurants and vendors from the area. Three music stages hold performers, with food items for sale at nominal prices.

What else is in the neighborhood of Wisconsin's capitol building?

There are many shops open year round across from Capitol Square. There are a photography store, a chocolate shop, as well as cheese and clothing shops. So much happens in that area it's impossible to name everything.

There are also museums, a piano bar, a tap house, bicycles, wine, tours, restaurants, comedy club, the civic center, theaters, a convention center, library, an escape room, and more.

What are some of the reasons Madison is ranked as a good place to live?

Business Insider listed seven reasons why people should live in Madison. Their number one reason is because it's a hub of art, music, food, and beer. The city is home to restaurants with top chefs, diverse festivals, and some of the best-valued concert tickets.

Other reasons include a student body that supports the community, plenty of outdoor activities available, accommodation of alternative transportation, and the city was named the "greenest" city in America by Nerd Wallet. They ranked Madison highest in the nation for the number of parks, miles of biking and hiking trails, and more bicycles than automobiles.

What is the demographic breakdown of Wisconsin's capitol city?

Madison is the second-largest in the state, but with less than half the population of Milwaukee. The 2010 census shows Madison with a population of between a quarter-million and a half-million, with 78 percent of those falling into the "white" category. Asian Americans and African Americans are tied for the second-largest segment, each with 7 percent of the population. Hispanic ranks next with 6 percent, then mixed-race at 3 percent.

What other things would attract people to Wisconsin's capitol city?

Madison is home to the largest producer-only farmers market in the nation. That means the freshest produce is available all summer long.

The University of Wisconsin-Madison is one of the best colleges in the Midwest. There are twenty schools in the system, and more than 29,000 undergraduate students study at the UW. Another 8,000 graduate students also attend.

Henry Villas Zoo is free and has been around for more than a century. Extras cost only a dollar, and though it's small, it means there's no rush to finish before the end of the day. They also allow picnic lunches to be brought in.

117

How does Madison rank for economic and ethnic diversity?

Based on a number of factors, Madison ranks an A- from Niche.com. Twenty-four percent hold a master's degree or higher, and another 31 percent have a bachelor's degree—both of those well above the national average. Only 5 percent of residents don't have a high school diploma, compared to the national average of 13 percent.

Demographically, there is a sizable population of minorities. The largest non-white group, Asians, makes up 8 percent of Madison's population. Next is Hispanics at 7 percent, African Americans also at 7 percent, and those with two or more races at 3 percent.

Overall, the web site gives Madison an A+ as a good place to live.

What are the top schools in Madison?

The top five schools in the state capital city rank a grade of A or A+. They are—in order of ranking—West High School, Middleton High School, Memorial High School, Sun Prairie High School, and Verona High School.

Is there a ranking for Madison that's not "better" than the national average?

Crime is ranked as a C+ for the city, with 217 assaults per year for every 100,000 residents. There is an average of three murders (per 100,000), forty-nine rapes, and eighty-nine robberies. All of those statistics are higher than the national average.

Property crimes are likewise higher. The city averages 481 annually (again, per 100,000 residents), nearly 2,200 thefts, and a hundred motor vehicle thefts.

What is the median home value in Madison?

Housing is more expensive than average. Home values are $212,500 on average, more than the national average of $178,600. Rent is eleven dollars over average, at $939 per month. Fifty-two percent of residents rent a place to live; 48 percent own their own home.

How did Madison score in other categories?

Niche.com ranked many other standards for quality of life in Wisconsin's capitol city.

Category	Score
Housing	< B
Good for Families	A+
Night Life	A
Jobs	B+
Weather	C
Cost of Living	B-
Health and Fitness	A
Outdoor Activities	A
Commute	A+

Is the area surrounding Madison a good place to live?

Using the same categories as Wisconsin's capitol city, Niche.com ranked Dane County.

Category	Score
Public Schools	A+
Crime and Safety	B-
Housing	B-
Night Life	A
Good for Families	A+
Diversity	B
Jobs	B+
Weather	C
Cost of Living	B-
Health and Fitness	A
Outdoor Activities	A
Commute	A-

The population of the entire county is just over a half-million, has a median home value of about $230,000, with household income of just under $63,000. The top five cities in the county all score an A+. Those cities are Middleton, Shorewood Hills, Verona, Madison, and Maple Bluffs.

Which employers are the biggest in Madison?

The two largest employers in the Madison area are the state government and the University of Wisconsin system. That could be changing, as many businesses are attracted to the area's skill base and high level of education for residents. Because the city is so attractive to businesses, the unemployment rate remained low—3.5 percent, while the nation's rate lingered just under 10 percent.

Excluding government and the university, other employers in the area include Spectrum Brands, Alliant Energy, the Credit Union National Association, and a broad variety of technology companies.

How does being the center of Wisconsin politics affect wages in Madison?

Having so many lucrative government jobs in Madison helps put Dane County on top when ranking average weekly wages. Dane County wages topped $1,000 per week in the third quarter of 2016. Placing second, Waukesha County is the only other county in Wisconsin with that average above $1,000 per week. Rounding out the top five counties (in order) are Milwaukee, Winnebago, and Brown Counties.

What is the average cost of living?

By itself, average weekly income doesn't mean much. The cost of living in Wisconsin ranks 96.1 percent of the national average. The cost of housing in the state is 85 percent of the national average, with groceries at 97.9 percent. Other items rate higher than average—health, utilities, and transportation.

Dane County, though, ranks above the national average for cost of living at 112.5 percent. The different categories for the county all rank higher than national average—groceries at 100.9 percent, health at 122 percent, housing at 125 percent, utilities at 105 percent, and transportation at 106 percent of the national average.

To put that into perspective, wages in Dane County are less than 1 percent above the national average. Cost of living at 112.5 percent more than offsets the higher pay.

How many political organizations are based in Madison?

There are fifteen lobbyists listed on Ballotpedia. Of those, eleven have verified addresses in Dane County. Of the six 501(c)(3) organizations listed, three have offices in Madison. Of the twelve 501(c)(4)s, seven are based in the Madison area, three others in the Milwaukee area. The listing of local influencers similarly has most based in the vicinity of Madison, with a small number in other major metropolitan areas.

How hard is it to get around in Madison?

There is a wide variety of transportation available in Wisconsin's capitol city. In 2015 the city was awarded a platinum level Bicycle Friendly Community by the League of Amer-

The Dane County Regional Airport in Madison services nearly two million passengers a year.

ican Bicyclists. Only four other cities in America have received that award. There are fifty-five miles (88.5 kilometers) of bike paths, 133 miles (214 kilometers) of streets with marked bike lanes, and 116 miles (187 kilometers) of bike routes within the city.

The Dane County Regional Airport serves 1.8 million passengers annually, county rail service is available for passengers and freight, regional and national bus services have depots, and three interstate highways intersect in Madison. There are also five state highways through the city.

What other bicycle paths are in the Madison area?

Dane County lists six other basic bike paths: the Capitol City Trail, Cannonball Path, Ice Age Junction Trail, Monona Lake Loop, Military Ridge State Trail, and University Avenue. There are also paths for mountain bikers in Badger Prairie County Park, Cam-Rock County Park, and Seminole at Lewis Nine Springs E-Way—part of the Capitol Springs Recreation Area.

How many walking trails are in Madison?

There are nine paths near Madison, most of which have an "easy" rating. Only one—the Curtis Prairie Trail—ranks "moderate." The other eight paths are in the Lake Farm County Park, two trails in the UW Arboretum, The Quarry, Turville Point Trail, Edgewood College Nature Trail, Elver Park Trail, Picnic Point Marsh Loop, and the Capitol City Trail.

What is the draw with Madison's State Street?

No conversation about the state capitol is complete without State Street, which links the Capitol Square with the University of Wisconsin-Madison campus. The street has been a pedestrian mall since the 1970s, which is closed to regular traffic, with extra-wide sidewalks on both sides of the street. Area businesses and official city vehicle traffic is allowed. Other motorized traffic on State Street includes buses, cabs, trolleys, and horse-drawn carriages.

Is Madison a good place for dining?

Madison is definitely a destination for great food. Wisconsin's capitol city has one of the strongest local food scenes in the country. With so many farms surrounding the metro area, farm-to-table dining is common. The plethora of craft brewers also adds to the dining experience.

There is the Dane County Farmers Market, the largest producer-only market in America; the Underground Food Collective; L'Etoile restaurant, flagship location of chef Tory Miller; The Old Fashioned Tavern and Restaurant, with fifty-two taps and a hundred varieties of beer; Fromagination, the so-called chapel of cheese; and so much more.

121

The street is only a twelve-minute walk long, with a variety of shops and dining lining both sides. The standouts are all locally owned, all unique, and some have been there for decades. There are restaurants, shops for vintage kids' toys, aromatherapy supplies, classic and funky hats and handbags, crafting, and kitchen gadgets. Oh, and so much more.

Does Madison have any nicknames?

There are several ways people refer to Wisconsin's capital city, not all of them complimentary. Some pejorative names were embraced by residents, who are proud to have the label of Seventy-Seven Square Miles (199 square kilometers) Surrounded by Reality. In fact, the mayor proposed making the slogan the city motto in 2013.

Other labels include Mad City, Madtown, the Berkeley of the Midwest, Four Lakes City, and the People's Republic of Madison.

POLITICAL PARTIES

What political parties are there in Wisconsin?

There are twelve organized political parties as of 2017 according to votesmart.org. Alphabetically, they are the America First party, America First, Constitution, Democratic, Libertarian, Natural Law, Progressive Dane, Reform, Republican, Socialist, Unity, Wisconsin Green, and Wisconsin Patriot.

Why was the Constitution Party founded?

The Constitution Party was originally the Wisconsin branch of the U.S. Taxpayer's party. Though founded in 1991, they first registered as a political party in 1993 and gained access to the ballot in 1994. They changed their name to the Constitution Party in 1999.

There are fourteen major issues championed by the Constitution Party. The most frequent mentions are based on sanctity of life, freedom from government intervention, and Congressional reform. "Congress must once again be accountable to the people and obedient to the Constitution, repealing all laws that delegate legislative powers to regulatory agencies, bureaucracies, private organizations, the Federal Reserve Board, international agencies, the President, and the judiciary."

There are currently no members of the Constitution Party in the state legislature.

How many counties in Wisconsin have a local Democratic Party office?

Wisconsin has seventy-two counties, and the party has seventy-one "county" offices. Two counties have merged their headquarters. Ashland and Bayfield Counties' offices are called the Chequamegan Democratic Party. Meeting locations vary and might be in either county.

Who are some of the more prominent Wisconsin Democratic politicians?

The list of notable party members from the state could be quite lengthy and somewhat subjective. Narrowing the list to six, Wisconsin has William Proxmire (1915–2005), Gaylord Nelson (1916–2005), Patrick Lucey (1918–2014), Herb Kohl (1935–), Tony Earl (1936–), and Marty Schreiber (1939–).

What is William Proxmire famous for?

William Proxmire was described by the *New York Times* as a "maverick democratic senator" who fought waste in the government.

Senator William Proxmire served in Washington, D.C., longer than any other Wisconsin senator: 1957 to 1989.

After three unsuccessful bids for governor in the 1950s, he won a special election to replace Senator Joseph McCarthy (1908–1957) in 1958. He served until leaving the senate in 1988.

Proxmire was perhaps most famous for his monthly Golden Fleece Award, given to the person or organization he viewed as wasting the most government funding. One such award went to the National Science Foundation, which studied why people fell in love. The 1975 expenditure was $84,000.

Why was Proxmire so respected in Wisconsin?

Voters from Wisconsin saw Proxmire as a true independent, not a party hack. He spent weekends in his home state shaking hands with voters instead of lobbyists. He kept count of the number of people he met, usually in excess of 2,000 per day.

In his last election in 1982. he only spent $145.10—to pay the filing fee and send donations back to those who sent money. Despite that, he won 64 percent of the vote.

What did Gaylord Nelson do to earn respect in Wisconsin?

Nelson founded Earth Day on April 22, 1970. That day is considered the birth of the environmental movement. He witnessed the Santa Barbara oil spill in 1969 and wanted to bring environmental concerns to the national consciousness. Taking a page from the antiwar movement, he sought to tap the energy of a mass consciousness.

When did Nelson serve?

Originally elected to the Wisconsin State Senate in 1948, Nelson served as the floor leader for four years. He was voted as senate governor for the term starting in 1959, serving that position until elected to the U.S. Senate in 1962. He ran an unsuccessful reelection bid in 1980.

When was Patrick Lucey elected governor?

Lucey was originally elected in 1970 and won reelection in 1974. During his second term he left to serve President Jimmy Carter as the U.S. Ambassador to Mexico in 1977. In 1980 he ran for vice president as John Anderson's running mate, seeking to defeat Carter's bid for reelection. Republican Ronald Reagan emerged victorious in that election.

What is Lucey remembered most for?

Lucey fought a hard-won battle to merge the University of Wisconsin-Madison with the state college system. He worked to increase the efficiency of colleges and universities and unify the various boards of regents. Opponents of his plan said the merger would pull money from UW-Madison and erode control from the regents. His plan won state senate approval by one vote in October of 1971. The University of Wisconsin system now has thirteen colleges awarding four-year degrees.

Another notable event for Lucey occurred in 1976 when he appointed the first female to the state's supreme court—Chief Justice Shirley Abrahamson (1933–).

How do Republicans view Patrick Lucey?

Governor Scott Walker remembered Lucey as a dedicated servant of the state. He said it was a joy to be with him.

Despite the domination of Republicans in the state, Lucey was one of the few Democrats to gain election to the legislature in 1948. When elected governor in 1970, one of his first orders of business was to meet with the Republican-controlled state senate to discuss his plan for the merger of the state university system. The senate passed his plan in 1971 by one vote, which required a majority of Republican support. He even appointed Republican Lee Dreyfus (1926–2008) as chancellor of the UW System.

What other Democrats were helped by Patrick Lucey?

When originally elected to the legislature in 1948, he was one of only twenty-six Democrats. He and a small band met to discuss strategies—names that later became prominent include William Proxmire, who became a popular U.S. senator; James E. Doyle Sr., father of Governor Jim Doyle; and Gaylord Nelson, later governor of Wisconsin and eventually U.S. senator.

In 1957 he was elected the party chairman and across six years oversaw three successful Democratic bids for governor, two U.S. Senate races, and an additional Democratic congressional seat. He also oversaw tipping the state's Assembly toward Democrats for the first time since 1933.

Lucey worked on the campaign to elect President John F. Kennedy (1917–1963), eventually becoming part of the president's inner circle. He worked with Robert Kennedy

(1925–1968) and was there moments after his assassination. Lucey also advised Ted Kennedy (1932–2009), Jimmy Carter (1924–), and Walter Mondale (1928–).

How many terms did Herb Kohl serve in the U.S. Senate?

Billionaire Herb Kohl served four terms in the Senate, starting with election in 1988. In 2011 he announced he would not run for reelection. Democrats had hoped—to no avail—to have the popular and proven incumbent in a state with an uncertain balance of Democrats and Republicans. At seventy-six years of age, there were questions about his willingness to invest the time and energy in a hotly contested reelection.

Democrats said the early announcement gave them time to come up with a strong candidate to run for the seat. Possible candidates included Congressmen Ron Kind (1963–), Tammy Baldwin (1962–), Milwaukee mayor Tom Barrett (1953–), and former senator Russ Feingold (1953–), who lost to Senator Ron Johnson (1955–).

What kinds of legislation did Herb Kohl support?

According to a government tracking web site, Kohl supported legislation about health care more than any other types of bills, getting 23 percent of his sponsorships. Commerce came in a reasonably strong second place, followed by crime bills, politics, law, taxation, and housing and education both ranked at 8 percent.

How much money does Herb Kohl's foundation award?

The Herb Kohl Educational Foundation Award Program provides scholarships to one hundred students each year. Each of those students receives $10,000. More than $4,000,000 has been awarded.

The foundation began in 1990, and any school in the state may submit candidates. The number of nominations is based on school attendance, and the nominees are screened regionally for "demonstrated academic potential, outstanding leadership, citizenship, community service, integrity and other special talents." Final selections are chosen by a statewide committee comprised of civic leaders, education professionals, and several other associations in related fields.

Other than students, are there other recipients of Kohl Foundation philanthropy?

The foundation also awards teacher fellowships in the amount of $6,000 for one

Also the former owner of the Milwaukee Bucks and the head of an educational foundation, Herb Kohl was a U.S. senator from 1989 to 2013.

125

hundred teachers each year. So far more than $7,500,000 has been awarded to state educators.

Initiative scholarships are awarded to one hundred dedicated students annually. Each receives $10,000. More than three million of those dollars have been awarded as of 2017.

Sixteen school principals are awarded $6,000 annually, with their schools also receiving a $6,000 grant. The Kohl Foundation began their Leadership Award in 2016 and as of August of 2017 has distributed $384,000.

The Kohl Foundation, in total, has awarded more than $14,000,000 to students, educators, and schools in Wisconsin since the beginning in 1990.

Are there any other Kohl charities?

In addition to the Kohl Foundation, there is the Herb Kohl Charities founded in 1977. Its stated purpose: "Giving primarily for higher and other education, health associations, children, youth and social services, arts and culture, federated giving programs, and community development; some funding also for Christian organizations and churches, and Jewish organizations."

Herb Kohl also funded "Learning Journeys." The program will send four hundred Milwaukee Public Schools ninth-grade students to Washington, D.C., "to have the opportunity to learn about leadership, government, civics and democracy through the invaluable experience of travel that connects the real world to their classrooms." The program is expected to expand to include all Milwaukee Public Schools ninth-grade students.

When did Governor Tony Earl hold political offices?

Tony Earl was elected to the Wisconsin assembly in 1969. From 1970 through 1974 he served as the majority leader, then held the post of secretary of the Department of the Administration in 1975. He also was the secretary of the Department of Natural Resources from 1975 through 1980.

After a stint at the law firm of Foley & Lardner, he was elected governor in 1982, an office he held until January 5, 1987. Governor Tommy Thompson defeated him in 1986.

Governor Tony Earl served a difficult term trying to turn around Wisconsin's economy in the early 1980s.

What was Governor Earl's major achievement?

Earl inherited a deficit of nearly a billion dollars and a 12 percent unemployment rate. He instituted a 10 percent surtax on state income and made Wisconsin's 5 percent sales tax permanent. He ran into trouble with Wisconsin unions over wage freezes, health care reform, and prison staffing. After a single term in office he was defeated (53 percent to 46 percent) by the state's assembly minority leader, Tommy Thompson, in 1986.

Did Governor Martin Schreiber write a book?

The thirty-ninth governor of Wisconsin wrote *My Two Elaines*, published by Book Publishers Network in 2016. "Marty" Schreiber is a long-time crusader for Alzheimer's caregivers and put his personal experience with his wife's disease into the book, which is coauthored by Cathy Breitenbucher.

Schreiber was credited by Governor Scott Walker for the development of the Dementia Friendly Employers toolkit. Schreiber's work with elderly citizens of the state began when when he was a state senator from 1963 to 1971.

What else has Schreiber done since leaving public life?

Schreiber served in the Wisconsin State Senate from 1963 to 1971, when he became lieutenant governor for Patrick Lucey. When Lucey resigned to serve as Jimmy Carter's ambassador to Mexico in 1977, Schreiber served the rest of Lucey's term. He lost to Lee Dreyfus in 1978.

After his defeat, Schreiber formed a public affairs consulting firm, Martin Schreiber & Associates, Inc. His firm "provides tailor-made, specialized government affairs and public relations services." The organization is comprised of an "experienced, bipartisan team of Wisconsin lobbyists and public relations specialists."

Who was the first governor of Wisconsin?

The first Wisconsin governor held office from June 7, 1848, to January 5, 1852. He was Nelson Dewey, a Democrat. In fact, three of the first four governors were Democrats, a party holding sway from 1848 to March of 1856. The only exception was the second governor, Leonard J. Farwell, a Whig, from January 5, 1852, to January 2, 1854.

How many Libertarians have been elected?

As alternate parties go, Libertarians probably rank highest. Nationwide there are more than 150 office holders, from city council members to state legislatures. The only elected Libertarians in Wisconsin are a municipal court judge in Cottage Grove, a county supervisor in Dane County, and the town chair of Erin, Wisconsin.

Some Libertarians performed well in recent elections for major offices. Joe Miller (1967–) polled more than 29 percent in a four-way U.S. Senate election in Alaska. An election for the Supreme Court clerk gave Mike Fellows (1957–2016) 43 percent against the Democratic candidate. In presidential elections, most states have had a Libertarian option since 1976, though only one electoral vote has ever gone to a Libertarian—Ron Paul (1935–), who joined the party in 2015. Gary Johnson (1953–) was the Libertarian candidate that year, so Paul's electoral vote came from a "faithless elector."

Has the Natural Law Party disbanded?

Though the Natural Law Party is still a registered party for the state of Wisconsin, the national office closed in 2004. According to their web site, the U.S. Peace Government is carrying on the work of the Natural Law Party: "Dr. John Hagelin (1954–), the 2000 NLP presidential candidate, is now president of the US Peace Government, and many former NLP candidates and supporters have taken leadership positions."

What is the purpose of NLP and the U.S. Peace Government?

Their stated purpose is to "prevent social violence, terrorism, and war and to promote harmony and peace in the United States and throughout the world." All supporters of the Natural Law Party have been encouraged to back the new organization. Dr. Hagelin, at a press conference in 2000, announced the start of the U.S. Peace Government.

When was the Reform Party formed?

Ross Perot (1930–) founded the Reform Party of America in 1995. He said Americans were disillusioned with the current two-party system of Democrats and Republicans. The Wisconsin Reform Party, originally formed in 1873, was a coalition of various parties who elected Governor William Robert Taylor (1820–1909). He lost his bid for re-election in 1875, and the party's last legislator was listed in 1878. Only one member of the Reform Party holds office in Wisconsin—Jon Winter, chair of the town board in Lakeside, Wisconsin. There is no evidence the party is active in Wisconsin, despite its listing as a political party in the state.

How many field offices does the Republican Party have in Wisconsin?

There are four regional offices in the state, each in a roughly delineated quadrant—Northeast (in Green Bay), Northwest (in Eau Claire), Southeast (in Waukesha), and Southwest (in Fitchburg).

What is "Progressive Dane"?

According to their web site, "Progressive Dane believes that ordinary citizens should control public policies at the community and national levels." They support tax justice, equality in education, affordable housing, and more.

As of 2017 there were six aldermen in Madison from the Progressive Dane Party, and Fitchburg's mayor and four others are from that party.

There are no party members holding state or national office.

There are seventy-two offices—one for each of the counties—throughout the state, as well as another office in each of the eight congressional districts.

Who was the first Republican governor of Wisconsin?

Coles Bashford (1815–1896) began his stint in the governor's seat on March 25, 1856 and held office until January 4, 1858. He was the first Republican governor in a string of seven Republicans. Only two other Democrats were in office from that year through January 2, 1933—William Robert Taylor (1820–1909) for a two-year term from 1874 to 1876, and George W. Peck (1840–1916) for four years, 1891–1895.

The fifth governor of Wisconsin, Coles Bashford, was the first in that office to be a Republican, serving just a few years before the Civil War broke out.

Was former Republican governor Scott Walker recalled?

Scott Walker wasn't the first governor to be recalled, nor was he the first in Wisconsin to be targeted. Republicans sought to recall Democratic governor Jim Doyle (1945–), but the 2009 effort never reached the ballot. Instead it was used as a fundraising tool. Walker's recall did reach the ballot in 2012, the year after he took office.

Measures passed in the Republican legislature and signed into law angered Democrats. The biggest issue was the limiting of collective bargaining for public employee unions. A special primary election was held on May 8, 2012, in which he handily defeated his GOP opponent to face Milwaukee mayor Tom Barrett in the general election. On June 5, 2012, Walker won the election and retained his seat, and was reelected in 2014, but lost the 2018 election.

The Wisconsin Democracy Campaign reported that the total expenditure during the recall effort approached eighty-one million dollars. The previous record for a gubernatorial election in Wisconsin was only $37.4 million during the previous election in 2010.

Who were some other prominent Republicans?

As with the list of prominent Democrats, limiting the Republican list is difficult. Five other noteworthy Republicans are Tommy Thompson, Steve Gunderson (1951–), Ron Johnson, Joe McCarthy (1908–1957), and Paul Ryan (1970–).

Why was Tommy Thompson a notable politician?

Putting Thompson above so many others was the fact he chaired the National Governor's Association, was a senior fellow of the Bipartisan Policy Center, and won a fourth term as Wisconsin's governor in 1998. In addition, he served six years in the National Guard, then four more years in the Army Reserve and achieved the rank of captain, and served in the Wisconsin legislature—eventually serving as the assistant minority leader.

In 2001 Thompson was confirmed as President George W. Bush's (1946–) secretary of Health and Human Services. He led the effort for Medicare prescription drug benefits for senior citizens. Additionally, he encouraged families to lead healthier lifestyles, was chairman of the Global Fund to Fight AIDS, TB, and Malaria, and fought to stem the spread of HIV.

Tommy Thompson served as Wisconsin's forty-second governor from 1987 to 2001 (longer than any other governor of the state), and then he served as President George W. Bush's secretary of health and human services.

When did Steve Gunderson start in politics?

Gunderson served in the Wisconsin State Assembly from 1975 to 1979. In 1981 he began a career as Wisconsin's Third District congressman and held that office until January 3, 1997.

He was appointed by Barack Obama to the President's Commission on White House Fellows in 2010. The purpose of the commission is to "give the Fellows first hand, high-level experience with the workings of the federal government and to increase their sense of participation in national affairs."

What is Steve Gunderson most remembered for?

Gunderson, after already deciding to not seek reelection, was "outed" as gay on the floor of the U.S. House of Representatives. Gunderson said he'd become a target and said right-wing conservatives couldn't allow him to legitimize mainstreaming the issue of homosexuality.

Gunderson became an activist for gay and lesbian issues, was named the president of the Association of Private Sector Colleges and Universities, and was a finalist for the president of the University of Wisconsin System. He wrote *House and Home* with his partner, Rob Morris.

Why did Ron Johnson run for U.S. Senate?

Johnson's stated purpose was that the government was bankrupting America. His background in manufacturing taught him to attack the root cause of a problem instead of symptoms. He believed the root cause was an ever-expanding size of government and that slow job creation, deficit spending, and unemployment are byproducts of huge government.

Who did Ron Johnson unseat when he was elected?

In the 2010 election, Johnson beat three-term incumbent Russ Feingold by a margin of 52 to 47 percent. Both candidates spent a similar amount of money in the election (more than $15,000,000 each), and Johnson carried fifty-seven of the state's seventy-two counties.

The win was historic in that Johnson beat an entrenched opponent and he'd never held elective office. Exit polling clearly indicated a sputtering economy to be the top issue, and Johnson took most of the voters citing that as an issue. Six years later Feingold failed to unseat Johnson, though the margins were much closer.

What is Joe McCarthy famous for?

The term "infamous" might be a better fit for Senator McCarthy. Though a Marine Corps captain who earned the Distinguished Flying Cross in World War II, he is notable mostly for his association with the Un-American Activities Committee—even though he was not a member. He spent five years trying to expose communist infiltration into the United States.

After World War II ended, the "Red Scare" created such a panic that few would speak out against allegations made by McCarthy. He waved a piece of paper, claiming there were over two hundred people listed, employed by the State Department, who were also members of the Communist Party. In 1953 he was put in charge of the Committee on Government Operations, where he was able to conduct hearings on the communist menace within the government. Though no proof was ever found, two thousand workers were discharged because of what became known as "McCarthyism."

Why is Paul Ryan notable?

Ryan was voted into the House of Representatives in 1998 and served his district until January 3, 2019. He also ran as Mitt Romney's (1947–) running mate in the 2012 presidential election, but they lost to Barack Obama's (1961–) reelection team.

The most impressive part of Ryan's career is becoming Speaker of the House in 2015—the first time a Wisconsin representative achieved that office. He also chaired two powerful Congressional committees—the Joint Committee on Taxation and the Ways and Means Committee.

McCarthyism—the witch hunt for Communists within the U.S. government that persecuted many innocent Americans—was named after Wisconsin's Senator Joseph McCarthy (standing at right while questioning U.S. Army counsel Joseph Welch).

How did McCarthyism end?

When McCarthy turned his attention on the U.S. Army, people lost their appetite for the spectacle. McCarthy intimidated and attacked a young Army attorney, whose counsel responded with, "Have you no sense of decency, sir?" A series of court decisions went against those who "blacklisted" suspected communists. Public opinion of McCarthy dropped to a net negative, and the Senate condemned him for "inexcusable," "reprehensible," "vulgar and insulting" conduct "unbecoming a senator." He died in 1957 at the age of forty-eight.

What are Ryan's priority issues?

Ryan explains that Social Security and Medicare need to be made solvent for future generations. Doing that should not be done at the expense of senior citizens, so Congress should not be cutting their benefits.

As a member of the House Ways & Means Committee, he "helped deliver significant tax relief to spur economic growth & create jobs."

What is the stated goal of the Socialist Party in Wisconsin?

There is no specific branch office in Wisconsin, but the national party's web site states, "The Socialist Party strives to establish a radical democracy that places people's lives under their own control—a non-racist, classless, feminist, socialist society in which people cooperate at work, at home, and in the community."

Their platform includes the transformation of the economy away from a need for profit, instead focusing on production. They stand in opposition to America's imperialism and the war on terror, which is another form of that imperialism. They want worker control of industry, free quality education for all ages, universal health coverage, and extensive public transportation.

How many Unity Party offices are there in Wisconsin?

The web site lists two offices—one in Grant County, the other in Waukesha County.

What does the Unity Party support?

Their slogan is "Not Right, Not Left, But Forward."

Founded in 2004 after the presidential election, they have stood for common sense, balanced budgets, and term limits. They say the strength of their party is in unity.

What is the main goal of the Wisconsin Green Party?

That goal is much like the Socialist Party—"We stand for true social, economic, and environmental justice. We are attempting to build a democratic society in which human needs matter more than corporate profits." Their ten key goals include the above statement, as well as personal and collective empowerment, ecological integrity, global responsibility, and nonviolence. Other points can be found on their web site.

Does the American Patriot Party have a Wisconsin office?

Apparently, the Wisconsin branch of this party is still being organized. The values of the national party include strong, smaller states, strong, smaller counties, and limited federal government.

The reason for those goals is to enable greater local control and the advancement of the delegated powers portion of the original Constitution. Their web site lists their platform—"Protect, defend and implement the intents set forth in the Originating Founders Letters which includes The Absolute Rights of the Colonists of 1772 and the Declaration of Independence, the documents which define Freedom."

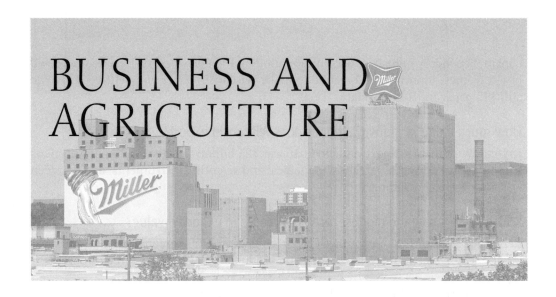

BUSINESS AND AGRICULTURE

MANUFACTURING

What regions are there in Wisconsin for manufacturing?

The Wisconsin Economic Development Corporation (WEDC) divides the state into nine different regions. They are Visions Northwest, Momentum West, 7 Rivers Alliance, Prosperity Southwest, Grow North, Centergy, Madison Region Economic Partnership, The New North, and Milwaukee Seven.

Which manufacturing sectors are biggest in Wisconsin?

The most important industrial sectors for Wisconsin's economy are aerospace manufacturing; biosciences; energy, power, and control; food and beverage; forest products; and water technology.

According to Newsmax, the top five industries are fruit and vegetable preservation, dairy product manufacturing, leather manufacturing, wood product manufacturing, and paper manufacturing.

How big is paper manufacturing in Wisconsin?

The state's paper industry creates 5.3 million tons (4.8 metric tons) of paper, employs more than 31,000 people, and is among the higher-paid manufacturing jobs in Wis-

Which country has seen the largest increase of Wisconsin's products?

In 2016, Japan bought 6 percent more of Wisconsin's output over the previous year. The next largest is Mexico at 2.7 percent. The country with the biggest decline was Saudi Arabia, dropping 22 percent.

consin. Secondary industries account for another 106,000 workers. Despite the growth of electronics, innovations continue to make Wisconsin paper competitive. There are still 115 paper mills in the state.

How much value in industrial goods does Wisconsin export?

In total, Wisconsin's export value in 2016 was $21 billion—a quarter of that was industrial machinery. Eleven percent was medical and scientific instruments, and 9 percent was for electrical machinery.

Which sectors saw the biggest recent increases in exported value?

Aerospace showed the most growth in 2016—almost a 50 percent increase. The next-largest sector was in miscellaneous plastic products, showing an 8 percent increase.

Which sectors saw the biggest decreases in exported value?

Organic chemicals saw a drop-off of almost 30 percent in exports. Industrial machinery, the largest exporter by far, dropped 11 percent. Despite that, industrial machinery remains the largest of Wisconsin's exports.

Which countries receive the majority of Wisconsin industrial exports?

Canada receives 31 percent (or $6.6 billion) of Wisconsin's exports. The next four countries combined don't match Canada's impact.

Those countries are Mexico ($3 billion), China ($1.4 billion), Japan ($865 million), and the United Kingdom ($8.13 million) for a combined $5.27 billion.

How has manufacturing employment changed in Wisconsin?

In 2001, there were twenty-one states in America with the manufacturing sector as the largest employer. By 2013 that dropped to six states—Wisconsin among them. Nearly a half-million residents of the state are employed in that sector. Only Michigan employs more manufacturing workers than Wisconsin.

How do wages in manufacturing compare with other employment in Wisconsin?

Manufacturing pay is much higher than other sectors. The average worker employed in manufacturing earned more than a thousand dollars per week in 2013, while retailers and hospitality workers earn far less—$470 and $259 respectively. The biggest growth in employment, health care, averages $890 per week.

How much does the average salary vary for industrial jobs?

The average annual income for an industrial production manager is nearly $108,000. There were more than 6,700 such people employed in Wisconsin as of May of 2016. That comes to more than $2,000 per week. Industrial truck and tractor operators average just over $35,000 per year, with 12,000 working in that job in Wisconsin. The average weekly wage for that profession is about $680 per week.

How has manufacturing job growth compared with projections?

While expected post-recession job growth has lagged, manufacturing has exceeded estimates. From 2011 to the middle of 2016, total nonfarm employment fell short of forecasts by more than 87,000. In that same period, the manufacturing sector beat projections by nearly 11,000 jobs. Construction jobs were second at 3,000 above estimates.

Professional and business services fell furthest behind forecasts by 22,500.

How many manufacturing companies are there in Wisconsin?

According to the National Association of Manufacturers, the state is home to nearly 8,000 firms that employ nearly a half-million workers. The vast majority of employers are considered "small" companies—those with fewer than 500 workers—with more than three-quarters of them employing fewer than twenty workers.

The manufacturing companies in Wisconsin with the most employees are Kohler (Kohler, WI), Land's End (Dodgeville, WI), Greenheck Fan (Schofield, WI), Ashley Furniture (Arcadia, WI), and Mercury Marine (Fond du Lac, WI).

Which manufacturers still operating are the oldest in Wisconsin?

The oldest manufacturer still in business is Richardson Industries of Sheboygan Falls. In 1848 Joseph Richardson built a sawmill on the Mullet River. The company currently operates three divisions—Richco Structures, Richardson Kitchen and Bath, and Richardson Yacht Interiors.

The second-oldest is Kohler Co. It started in 1873 as Kohler & Silberzahn, specializing in plows and farm implements.

Other long-lasting businesses from Wisconsin include Menasha Corp., Briggs and Stratton, S. C. Johnson, and Harley Davidson.

Why is Wisconsin known as the Dairy State?

Wisconsin has a number of nicknames, from the Badger State to the Copper State. Some are more well-known than others. The most recognized nicknames are Dairy State, America's Dairyland, and the Cheese State.

What is the impact of foreign ownership of industry in Wisconsin?

There are more than 1,500 foreign-owned manufacturers in Wisconsin, employing more than 86,000 people. The countries with the most Wisconsin-based investment are Canada, France, Germany, England, and Japan.

137

The dairy industry in Wisconsin dates back to before statehood when farmers made cheese to help preserve excess milk. Circa 1840, the first cheese "factory" was started by Anne Pickett, who collected milk from neighbors and shared the cheese with contributors.

The industry has a larger impact on Wisconsin's economy ($43.4 billion) than the citrus industry's impact on Florida ($13.9 billion) or the potato industry for Idaho ($6.7 billion). More than 14,000 dairy farmers are Wisconsinites, about 20 percent of the national total, with 1.25 million dairy cows producing 13.9 percent of American milk. Cheese makers produce 2.4 billion pounds (1 billion kilograms) of cheese in 600 varieties every year. California is second in cheese production with only 250 varieties.

How many licensed cheese makers are in Wisconsin?

More than 1,200 cheese makers are licensed in Wisconsin—the only state with a Master Cheesemaker program. In 2007, Wisconsin producers took 60 percent of the Best of Class Awards at the U.S. Championship Cheese Contest.

Thanks to the University of Wisconsin, the state is home to the country's best technology experts, researchers, and scientists in the field of dairy.

How much of Wisconsin's milk is made into cheese?

About 90 percent of all Wisconsin milk becomes cheese. Each pound (0.45 kilograms) of cheese requires about ten pounds (4.5 kilograms) of cow or goat milk. Sheep milk, however, needs only six pounds (2.7 kilograms) to make a pound (0.45 kilograms) of cheese.

What happens to the rest of the milk after cheese is made?

Whey is the leftovers of cheese production. The protein content of whey is high enough that cheesemakers began selling it. Other companies make protein shakes and bars with the whey, and smaller cheese producers save it for soup base.

Some other uses include lowering soil's pH balance, fighting powdery mildew in gardens, animal feed, and some people even bathe in whey. Some cheesemakers use whey to produce "cultured" cheese, and others use it in creating ricotta.

What other products can be made from milk?

The number of things made from milk are nearly endless. Some of the better-known are butter, yogurt, and cheese curds. Some of the lesser-known products include rabri, milk boiled until it forms a viscous fluid, after which sugar and fruit is added; and khoa, milk evaporated until it becomes dough-like.

What are some fun facts about Wisconsin cheese?

Brick cheese was first produced in Dodge County in 1877.

Colby cheese was invented in Colby, Wisconsin, in 1885.

Eating cheese can help prevent tooth decay. Firmer cheeses, such as cheddar, work best.

Cheese craving is the top food craving in the world—beating out even chocolate.

Americans consume thirty-three pounds (fifteen kilograms) of cheese annually—far behind first-place Greece's fifty pounds (22.7 kilograms).

The only American producer of Limburger cheese is Chalet Cheese Cooperative in Monroe, Wisconsin.

Steve Babcock (1843–1931) of the University of Wisconsin developed the first milkfat test in 1890. It's still used today to determine which milk is best for cheese.

Wisconsin is the world's largest producer of cheddar, Limburger, feta, muenster, Parmesan, provolone, and Romano.

Ninety percent of Wisconsin milk is made into cheese, and there are dozens of cheese factories, large and small, in the state, such as the these cheddar blocks from the LaClare Family Creamery.

Wisconsin took home the top prize in the 2016 World Championship Cheese Contest, beating more than 2,900 entries from twenty-three countries and thirty-one states.

Who started the Oshkosh B'Gosh company?

Four men started the company in 1895, but it was originally named Grove after one of the investors. Unable to actually come up with the entire promised amount of $6,250, the other three bought out that investor and named the company after the city in which it was founded—Oshkosh Clothing Manufacturing Company.

To separate their durable overalls from the lower-quality versions made by competitors, they came up with the J & C brand. More convenient than a simple leather apron, their product had stress points reinforced. One retailer called them "tough as a mule's hide."

In 1910, William Pollock from Chicago, Illinois, invested enough to hold half of the company. He already represented two other overall companies so he knew a bit about the business. He renamed it Oshkosh Overall Company. According to legend, Pollock heard a cast member at a theater use the phrase "Oshkosh B'Gosh." He liked the sound, and by the end of 1911 their bib overalls were labeled with the phrase.

Is there another version of how the company picked up "B'Gosh"?

A reporter next to Pollock in a diner in 1928 has another story. An ad for a safety razor depicted Uncle Sam shaving, with the words, "They come off slick as a whistle b'gosh." Pollock thought, "Why not Oshkosh B'Gosh?" Many people believe the story became embellished with the vaudeville angle to add flair to the name.

Why were Oshkosh overalls so popular?

A lot of heavy work happened in Wisconsin—from railroads to carpentry, and farming to factories. All of that required durable clothing. Industrial expansion swept westward, and workers' unions formed. The owners invited the United Garment Workers of America to organize the Oshkosh workforce, and the union was issued a charter. They added "Union Made" to the label, and that became an important part of their marketing.

How did the Oshkosh company fare in the Great Depression?

In the aftermath of World War I, William Pollock saw how the stock market climbed. He offered preferred and common stock for sale in March of 1929. Sales of stock were helped out by record revenue of $1.9 million in 1928, as well as a six-to-one asset-to-liability ratio. Months later the Great Depression struck and markets crashed, ruining many companies.

Employees never took their jobs for granted during the Great Depression, focusing instead on the company's needs. Mostly they worked with one major concern: keeping their jobs. One "temporary" employee worked hard to hone her skills. Her efforts were recognized and she kept her "temp" job for forty-four years.

How long did William Pollock run Oshkosh B'Gosh?

Pollock grew the company from ten employees in 1910 to around 450 at the time of his retirement. He was held in such high regard that the United Garment Workers Local 126 sponsored his retirement party on December 22, 1934.

Who owns the company now?

In 2005 the business was sold to Carters, Inc. for $312 million. While it still produces the Oshkosh brand, they are no longer made in Oshkosh, Wisconsin. The bulk of their manufacturing is done in Mexico and Honduras, with more than 300 stores across America.

The headquarters for the company is in Atlanta, Georgia.

When was Kohler Company founded?

John Michael Kohler (1844–1900), an Austrian immigrant, bought a foundry in 1873. Based near Sheboygan, Wisconsin, Kohler & Siberzahn made farm implements. When minority owner Charles Silberzahn sold his part of the company to two employees—Herman Hayssen (1847–1869) and John Stehn—in 1878, they renamed the business Kohler, Hayssen & Stehn. The factory burned to the ground in 1880, and the company moved to a new location with an enameling shop. In 1883 they put feet on a horse trough, enameled it, and sold it as a bathtub—Kohler's first plumbing product. The purchase price was one cow and fourteen chickens.

In 1899, a new foundry was built four miles (6.4 kilometers) out of Sheboygan in the community of Riverside. When that community incorporated, it was renamed Kohler Village.

Does Kohler manufacture anything besides plumbing products?

Kohler manufactured anchors, projectiles, and shells during World War I. They introduced an engine-powered electric generator in 1920. Kohler Automatic Power & Light was born. Four years later the company started Kohler Stables, which became famous for breeding Morgan horses—one of the first breeds developed in America. To support the nation in World War II, most of Kohler's production shifted to making torpedo tubes, shell fuses, and other military components.

Then, in 1948, Kohler began production of small engines. In 1969, Kohler parts and precision controls were part of the lunar lander during the Apollo moon missions. Ann Sacks Tile & Stone joined the Kohler lineup in 1989, and Kohler began selling ceramic tile, marble, and stone. The following year, the company branched out into furniture.

Delving into food, the company introduced Kohler Original Recipe Chocolates in 2003, then acquired Uninterruptible Power Supplies, Ltd, in 2008.

How many manufacturing sites does Kohler have?

Still headquartered in Kohler, Wisconsin, Kohler has more than fifty sites on six continents with more than 30,000 employees.

How did Land's End begin?

In 1963, Gary Comer (1927–2006) opened a Chicago, Illinois, mail order business for yachting gear. Already a champion sailor and world traveler, he knew more than a little

The Kohler Company headquarters in Kohler, Wisconsin. Kohler is noted for making plumbing fixtures, but it also produces furniture, cabinetry, engines, generators, and tile.

about what equipment yacht enthusiasts would need. Unfortunately, the business only averaged fifteen orders on a good day, and it took three years before the company turned a profit. Their first catalog was eighty-four pages, with apparel appearing on only two or three pages.

Comer wanted to make the business different from other mail order companies. He made returns unconditional, used "real" people as models, and included interesting stories in the catalog. By 1977 the company was a million-dollar business.

The business focus has changed from hardware to apparel over the years, with annual revenue of $350 billion in domestic sales, $1.2 trillion worldwide.

Why did Land's End move to Wisconsin?

Gary Comer liked the look of the scenery of rural Wisconsin and admired the work ethic of the friendly residents. He wanted to expand his operation while helping employees live a healthier life. The move to Dodgeville, Wisconsin, allowed those values to come to fruition. Within a decade of the move, Comer's facility included a fitness center, on-site clinic, day care, and recreational activities.

Where are Land's End products available?

Via the Internet, the company ships to 150 countries around the world. There are custom web sites and catalogs in native languages, with prices listed in sixty different local currencies, including all duties, taxes, and shipping costs.

Who started Greenheck Fan Company?

Greenheck started as a small sheet metal shop in Schofield, Wisconsin, in 1947. Bernie and Bob Greenheck were determined to have their business grow, and it has expanded to a worldwide leader in manufacturing air movement and control equipment. Their brands include Accurex, Airolite, Innovent, Precision Coils, and Valent.

Most of their production is still done at their Schofield factory, though they have additional facilities in three other states, with a minor presence overseas.

What kind of products do they manufacture?

Greenheck Fan produces fans, ventilators, blowers, exhaust systems, energy recovery units, coils, dampers, louvers, and more. Their products are available in more than thirty countries worldwide, and the company won the 2016 Manufacturer of the Year from Wisconsin Manufacturers and Commerce in the category of Mega Corporations—751 or more employees.

What are the origins of Ashley Furniture?

Carlyle Weinberger founded Ashley Furniture Corporation as a sales organization in 1945 with corporate headquarters in Chicago, Illinois. Years later, in 1970, Arcadia Furniture was founded by Ron Wanek (1941–). The two companies merged in 1982, headquartering in Arcadia, Wisconsin, where it's been ever since. As of 2005 they are the world's largest furniture manufacturer, and in 2007 they became the world's largest retailer of furniture.

How much economic impact is there from Ashley Furniture?

Ashley employs more than 22,000 people. Annual sales are nearly four billion dollars.

What kinds of furniture does Ashley manufacture?

Originally the company made wooden occasional furniture. Over the years they've

Wisconsin-based Ashley Furniture has grown into a national chain with sales around $4 billion.

expanded to include bedroom furniture, as well as casual and formal dining furniture. They use glass, steel, marble, leather, and mixed media.

How many stores does Ashley operate?

The organization has expanded to include more than six hundred retail outlets in the United States, Canada, Mexico, Central America, and Japan. Their manufacturing and distribution facilities are in Wisconsin, Mississippi, Pennsylvania, North Carolina, Florida, China, and Viet Nam.

How long has Mercury Marine been in business?

Keikhaefer Mercury was started in 1939 by Carl Kiekhaefer (1906–) as a small machine shop in a converted barn in Cedarburg, Wisconsin. In 1969 Kiekhaefer stepped down as president of the company, and they became known simply as Mercury Marine. Since then the company has grown to the world's largest builder of propulsion systems for boats.

What had been in the converted barn Kiekhaefer bought?

A defunct outboard motor company had produced three hundred engines that Montgomery Ward rejected because of defects. Keikhaefer refurbished the engines instead of selling them for scrap. By April of 1939 he introduced the new line of Thor outboard engines, which Montgomery Ward accepted.

What are some of the "firsts" accomplished by Mercury Marine?

Mercury has a history of "firsts." In 1962 they became the first to sell a hundred-horsepower outboard. In 1976 they were the first to sell a V–6 outboard. They were first to sell a thousand-horsepower outboard in 2004.

143

> ## What is a "splined propeller shaft"?
>
> **S**heer pins were used to prevent damage to the engine when propellers struck underwater objects. The pin would sheer off, saving the system from severe damage. Splines are ridges on the shaft that fit into propeller grooves to provide similar protection, in essence becoming a shock absorber to protect the gears.

They also eliminated the need for a sheer pin by introducing a splined propeller shaft in 1952, and in 1995 sold hub kits to allow their propellers to be used on engines manufactured by competitors. In 1996 they produced a direct fuel injected engine, reducing emissions and making two-stroke engines more efficient.

In 1994 they sold the first three-liter outboard and in 2004 the first supercharged four-stroke outboard. In 2010 they produced the most powerful consumer engine in history–1350 horsepower. Three years later they manufactured the 1650 horsepower QC4v.

How successful is Mercury Marine?

Any business with Mercury's longevity would have to be classified as a success story. Being the world's largest producer of marine engines is another testimony to their accomplishments. On top of that, Wisconsin Manufacturers and Commerce named Mercury Marine their Manufacturer of the Year in 2006, then again in 2013.

How many engines are produced by Mercury Marine?

The company took twenty-four years to sell their first million sterndrive units. Their second million came only ten years later. Across more than seventy-five years, Mercury has sold more than fifteen million marine engines. In 2014, global sales topped $2.2 billion.

How safe are Mercury employees?

Wisconsin Manufacturers and Commerce recently awarded Mercury Racing (a division of Mercury Marine) with their safety award for logging more than 1.6 million consecutive working hours without any lost-time injury. Their steel investment-casting business compiled more than four and a half years without any injury causing time off. Their steel machining operation surpassed four years with a similar record, and their distribution operations accumulated two million hours without such injuries.

Every year the company hosts a Health, Safety, and Environmental summit to conduct planning sessions in an attempt to enhance safety. Employees are involved in design and refinement to company systems in order to reduce manufacturing disruptions.

How "green" is Mercury Marine?

In a 1997 twenty-four-hour race in France, two low-emission Mercury engines placed fourth and fifth overall—right behind three other Mercury entries—and burned half the fuel of the others. In 2000, their OptiMax two-boat team took the two top slots by beating higher horsepower entries—in part because they required fewer stops to take on fuel. The OptiMax system continues to set records for low emissions.

What other steps has Mercury taken to reduce their environmental impact?

The company's energy use is under constant review, and everything that can be effectively reused gets a second use. Water usage has been reduced by 250,000 gallons (746 liters) since 2011 by changes in their painting system, and forty-one billion BTUs have been saved using updated processes.

Engine blocks are created using recycled aluminum and shipping containers are reused. Mercury has received Green Master designations from the Wisconsin Sustainable Business Council, placing it in the top 20 percent of participating companies.

Who started Harley-Davidson Motorcycles?

The world's "first motorcycle" was a three-wheeled mechanism built by Edward Butler (1862–1940) in 1884 and called the "Butler Petrol Cycle." Because of regulations limiting the top speed of self-propelled vehicles, public interest lagged and Butler abandoned the idea, scrapping his project. Many consider the Petrol Cycle to be a car because it sported more than two wheels. Karl Benz could be considered the creator of the first gas-driven motorcycle in 1886. Either way, many steam-powered motorcycles predate either of them.

The grandson of Harley-Davidson cofounder William A. Davidson, Willie G. Davidson, poses on one of the company's motorcycles in front of the museum in Milwaukee that opened in 2008.

In 1901, William Harley (1880–1943) drew a blueprint of an engine that would fit onto a bicycle. He and his friend, Arthur Davidson (1881–1950), loved tinkering with engines. The world's first true gas-powered motorcycle (the Pennington) didn't work very well, so they decided to improve on the machine. They began working on their own version in a shed in Davidson's backyard in Milwaukee. By 1903 the first Harley-Davidson motorcycle was made available to the public. A schoolyard friend of the two bought the first model directly from the founders. By 1907 William and Walter Davidson had joined the project full time.

When did Harley-Davidson incorporate?

On September 17, 1907, the company incorporated with ownership split four ways between William Harley, Arthur, William, and Walter Davidson. The size of their staff grew from six to eighteen workers that year, and their factory size doubled. They also started the search for dealerships in the New England region.

How did the early Harley-Davidson motorcycles rate?

In 1908 the Federation of American Motorcycles held their seventh annual Endurance and Reliability contest. Walter Davidson scored a perfect 1,000 points. Three days later he set a record for economy with 188.234 miles per gallon (80.9 kilometers per liter).

When was the first Harley-Davidson motorcycle sold to a police department?

Detroit, Michigan, put the first Harley-Davidson police motorcycle into service in 1908.

When was the first Harley-Davidson *Enthusiast* magazine published?

Issue #1 appeared in 1916 and featured an article about Effie Hotchkiss and her mother Avis. In 1915 they crossed the continental United States (twice) in a 1915 11-F three-speed cycle with a sidecar. They traveled from Brooklyn, New York, to the Panama-Pacific International Exposition (World's Fair) in San Francisco, California.

They left New York on May 2, 1915, and dipped their front wheel in the Pacific Ocean in August. They returned to Brooklyn in October after logging approximately 9,000 miles (14,484 kilometers).

The *Enthusiast* is still being published.

Who was the first cover girl for a motorcycle magazine?

The first cover shot to feature a female was in May of 1929. The "Enthusiast Girl" was Vivian Bales (1909–2001), who toured the country after her first appearance, logging 5,000 miles (8,000 kilometers) that year.

A dance teacher in Albany, Georgia, Bales wondered why she should travel by horse when motorcycles were so affordable and could cover more ground. She purchased a Model B Single she couldn't kick-start on her own. Nevertheless, she made a three-hundred-mile trip featured in the *Atlanta Journal.*

When she traded in her Single for a 1929 45 Twin D, she wrote to the Enthusiast and made her historic ride of 5,000 miles (8,000 kilometers) in seventy-eight days. At every stop she met dignitaries at Harley-Davidson dealers. Most of the dealership owners voluntarily supported her ride. She even met President Herbert Hoover (1874–1964).

She wrote an article for the *Enthusiast* about her ride, and it appeared in the December 1929 issue.

How is the company viewed by the State of Wisconsin?

Two times Harley-Davidson picked up special awards by Wisconsin Manufacturers and Commerce. In 1988 they were recognized as a "turnaround" company and in 1994 declared a "worldwide leader" in manufacturing.

Worldwide, Harley-Davidson sold more than 250,000 units in fiscal year 2016, with sales more than six billion dollars annually.

How many people work for Harley-Davidson?

According to *Forbes* magazine, Harley-Davidson ranks as the twenty-first best employer in the United States, giving jobs to more than six thousand employees. Salaries vary widely by position, but project managers earn more than $95,000 per year, senior project engineers just over $94,000.

Other than their headquarters in Milwaukee, Wisconsin, where are other Harley-Davidson facilities?

The original site where the wooden shed stood in Milwaukee is on the National Register of Historical Sites. That site is currently the headquarters of the company. There is also a Harley-Davidson museum in Milwaukee and a training and support center that also supplies dealer management software in Valley View, Ohio.

How did the term "HOG" start?

In 1920, a team of farm boys used a hog as a mascot. After winning races—consistently—they would mount the pig on their Harley and take a victory lap. In 1983 the company took advantage of the term by starting a Harley Owners Group—or HOG. When they attempted to trademark "hog," the courts ruled that the term had come to mean "any large motorcycle," not just a Harley-Davidson. However, in 2006 the company changed its ticker symbol on the New York Stock Exchange from HDI to HOG.

A dissenting story is that in the 1960s the bikes were fat and slow and picked up the disparaging name by people who didn't like Harley-Davidson motorcycles. According to that story, the first Harley Owners Group co-opted "HOG" to deflect from the disdain of the day and shed a more favorable light on the motorcycles.

Menomonee Falls, Wisconsin, is home to Powertrain Operations and Wauwatosa, Wisconsin, holds a product development facility. Windshields and plastic and composite parts are manufactured in Tomahawk, Wisconsin, and a second vehicle and powertrain operation center is in Kansas City, Missouri.

Fabrication, painting, and final assembly for some models happens in York, Pennsylvania, and the company's financial services are run from Chicago, Illinois. There are assembly plants in India and Brazil, and they have regional headquarters in Singapore and Oxford, England.

Where did S&S Cycle start out?

George Smith Sr. (1921–1980) built his own motorcycle engine parts to make his cycles go faster. In 1952 he rebuilt cycles in his basement and entered a summer race. When the major sponsor saw his favored racer wouldn't win, the prize money was pulled and Smith won nothing.

Smith teamed with Stanley Stankos to form S&S Cycle Equipment in 1958 in Blue Island, Illinois. A year later, Stankos quit because manufacturing motorcycle parts took too much time away from his upholstering business. Smith retained the S&S name and moved to Viola, Wisconsin, in 1969 and expanded into La Crosse, Wisconsin, in 2004.

Did Wisconsin Manufacturers and Commerce ever give an award to S&S?

In 1998, S&S was recognized by the WMC for "Relentless R&D."

What is FAST Corporation?

FAST is a company that creates fiberglass statues. It's an acronym for Fiberglass Animals, Statues, and Trademarks—FAST.

The company started doing business circa 1970—nobody is exactly certain which year—as Sculptured Advertising. They created larger-than-life fiberglass sculptures of animals for businesses as roadside attractions. For legal reasons the name was changed in the mid-1970s to Creative Display. In 1983 the company incorporated under the name FAST Corporation.

What kind of statues does FAST create?

The first display of a larger-than-life fiberglass figurine was a 145-foot-long musky for Hayward, Wisconsin, in 1978. When they began working toward trade shows, FAST created an eleven-foot-tall (3.35 meters) Viking on a trailer in their parking lot. People asked what it did, and there was no ready answer. The owner decided to make a statue that "did something."

FAST starting making themed water slides and business grew. Sales increased so much that the owner spent too much time running the company and so sold it in January of 2000 in order to keep working with the statues.

What other kinds of animal statues are offered?

There are sixty-nine wild animal options, as well as forty-eight farm animals, fifteen birds, and twenty aquatic creatures. That does not include animals in their other options, such as the Fast Frog water slide or Gorilla Swing.

How many water slides does FAST manufacture?

FAST lists seventy-four options for water slides. Variations include a giant frog, a baby dinosaur, alligators, various birds, dolphins, and elephants. There are also various sprays and rainmakers, as well as pool toys and features such as swings, basketball hoops, and marine animals.

What other kinds of figurines does FAST offer?

In the animal category they have sixty-nine wild animals, fifteen birds, twenty aquatic animals, and forty-eight farm animals.

They also offer statues of fictional and real characters—Abe Lincoln, astronaut Deke Slayton, a clown, Dracula, the three wise men, Robinson Crusoe, Bo Peep, and Miss Muffet. In all, more than eighty "people" are listed on their web site under the category of "Characters." Read more about Deke Slayton in the chapter on Sons and Daughters.

They also create mascots, public art projects, special attractions, and trademarks.

What kinds of trademarks are created by FAST?

Trademarks include the A&W Bear, a Budweiser Bottle, a Mack Dog, and various bottles of Tabasco. The tallest is the Tobasco® bottle at nine feet (2.7 meters) tall, the shortest is a Clydesdale horse on a "stone" base measuring three feet (ninety-one centimeters) tall.

Which food items are available from FAST?

In all, more than two dozen foods are portrayed in fiberglass at FAST. There's a world globe on an apple, a cheeseburger (eight feet or twelve-feet—2.4 meters to 3.66 meters—across), a double-scoop ice cream cone, and even a kitchen sink sundae.

How do FAST's fiberglass figures stand up to weather?

Very little maintenance is required for these items, as they're designed to withstand weather extremes for decades. Automotive cleaning and waxing should be used every six months. Each product is constructed with super strong lightweight fiberglass. There is no foundation required. On water slides, flanges are provided to bolt the slide to a deck or pool. All stainless steel handrails are electrically grounded. Plumbing is common PVC piping and connections, with any worn parts readily available at local stores.

There are no sharp edges, and the products are infused with an antimicrobial permanently bound to prevent fungus, mildew, mold, and bacteria. There are custom sizes for all their products, and they are available in any colors.

The MillerCoors brewery complex is, of course, in Milwaukee. The city is internationally known as a mecca for beer companies. Even the local baseball team is called the Brewers and they play in Miller Park.

FAST made two eagles for the Red Lake Nation, each qualifying as FAST's largest product. They have a wingspan of 360 feet (110 meters). One was placed in the new Tribal Government Center, the other in the new Tribal College.

Their smallest figure is a life-sized cat.

What big breweries are located in Wisconsin?

There are four breweries making more than 100,000 barrels (16.4 million liters) of product annually. The biggest of those four is MillerCoors in Milwaukee (more than seven million barrels or 1.15 billion liters in 2014), Minhas Craft Brewery is in Monroe, New Glarus Brewing is in New Glarus, and the smallest is Stevens Point Brewery in Stevens Point (115,000 barrels or 18.86 million liters).

Did war have an impact on beer production in Milwaukee?

In the years following the Great Chicago Fire, brewers took advantage of their increased production to widen distribution. Pabst tied a blue ribbon to every bottle to make their product more enticing. Their output climbed to a million barrels in 1895.

Schlitz combated the Pabst blue ribbon strategy by sending Commodore George Dewey (1837–1917) 3,600 bottles (1,260 liters) of beer in 1898 to congratulate him on his capture of Manila during the Spanish American War. Dewey ordered a trainload of Schlitz, and in all, 700,000 barrels (111 million liters) of beer from Milwaukee made it to the Philippines.

What caused the decline in Schlitz beer?

In order to meet increasing demand, Schlitz tried a new brewing method in 1967 with a shorter fermenting process. Production time dropped enough to increase output by 25 percent, but word spread about a change in their recipe. Customers didn't want beer not aged long enough and sales sagged. Less than a decade later the brewery produced beer with a slight haze, and ten million bottles (3.5 million liters) had to be dumped.

In 1981 a strike closed down the Milwaukee plant. Legal trouble over sketchy ad campaigns contributed to decreasing demand. Schlitz became known to residents as "the beer that made Milwaukee furious." In 1982 Stroh Brewing purchased Schlitz.

What are some of the other breweries in the area around Milwaukee?

The *Journal-Sentinel* lists several dozen breweries, most of which are now closed. The open businesses include Leinenkugel's 10th Street Brewery, Big Bay Brewing, Buffalo Water Beer Company, C. T. Melms Brewery, MillerCoors, Milwaukee Brewing Company, and Steelhead Ale Works.

Many breweries offer tours and even serve food. Craft brewing is a growing trend across the nation, and Wisconsin is home to many smaller brewers.

How many craft breweries are there in Wisconsin?

Brewingnews.com offers a list of more than a hundred craft breweries in the state. No doubt there are many more. Adding in hobbyists would make that list impossible to keep current. The Wisconsin Brewers Guild lists eighty-seven breweries as members.

The Culture Trip web site has a list of their ten favorite craft breweries. They include 3 Sheeps Brewing Company of Sheboygan, Ale Asylum of Madison, Capital Brew-

---

Was Milwaukee ever known as the "Beer Capital of the World"?

The city of Milwaukee did make that proclamation in 1860 when they exported more beer than any other community. The city has always been a beer town, even before it incorporated into a city. There was a tavern for every forty residents in the 1800s.

By 1880, German immigration had ballooned to the point where 27 percent of the population came from that region of the world. They brought beer yeast and the willingness to brew. Names of those brewers include Joseph Schlitz (1831–1875), Frederick Pabst (1836–1904), Valentin Blatz (1826–1894), and more.

The Great Chicago Fire of 1871 destroyed nearly half of the breweries in Chicago, and Milwaukee producers saw an opportunity. Schlitz shipped free beer to Chicago, thereby becoming known as "The beer that made Milwaukee famous." Other brewers followed their lead. In the years after the fire, more than half of beer production in Milwaukee was sent out of the city.

ery of Middleton, Central Waters Brewing Company of Amherst, Lakefront Brewery of Milwaukee, Lake Louie Brewing of Arena, New Glarus Brewing Company of New Glarus, O'So Brewing Company of Plover, Stevens Point Brewery of Stevens Point, and Tyranena Brewing Company of Lake Mills.

Another top ten list of craft breweries contains many of those same names, with a few exceptions. Matadornetwork.com has a different list. Theirs includes only half of The Culture Trip list, with the additions of Urban Harvest Brewing of Milwaukee taking their top slot, Sand Creek Brewing of Black River Falls, Pearl Street Brewing of La Crosse, Rustic Road Brewing of Kenosha, and Miller Brewing of Milwaukee.

What are the top-rated beers in Wisconsin?

Beeradvocate.com ranks their top hundred favorite beers. The top three (and five of their top six) all come from New Glarus Brewing in New Glarus. They are Serendipity, Wisconsin Belgian Red, and Raspberry Tart. Only two other breweries are listed in their top ten—Central Waters Brewing had a fourth-place ranking with Brewers Reserve Bourbon Barrel Cassian Sunset, and Tyranena Brewing ranked tenth with Devil Over A Barrel Bourbon Barrel-Aged Coffee Imperial Oatmeal Porter.

How widespread is craft beer production in Wisconsin?

The *Journal-Sentinel* lists seven different regions of beer production in Wisconsin, with more than 150 craft brewers across the state. There are fifty-one listed for the Milwaukee area in southeast Wisconsin, thirty-seven in the southern region, ten in the eastern part of the state, another ten in central Wisconsin, twenty-one in the northeast, twenty-two in the northwest, and ten more in the south-central western part of the state.

How many beer festivals are there in Wisconsin?

Every year there are dozens of festivals that feature craft beers, with admission fees ranging from free to sixty dollars. Reddit.com listed more than three dozen for 2015, the earliest in January (Ice Cold Beer Festival in Minoqua), the latest in November (Fall Fest-of-Ale in Janesville).

Six Oktoberfests are hosted in the state.

RETAIL

What is the difference between a retailer and a manufacturer?

A retailer typically sells small quantities of manufactured goods to the ultimate consumer. A manufacturer is the person, group, or company who creates those goods. To use the example from this chapter and the chapter on manufacturing, the difference is Kohler makes the faucets, while Home Depot sells Kohler products.

What is the economic impact of retailers in Wisconsin?

In the United States there are nearly four million retail establishments, employing forty-two million workers, adding $2.6 trillion to the Gross Domestic Product. One in four jobs in America comes from retail businesses.

In Wisconsin, there are nearly 72,000 retail employers supporting more than 800,000 people, for about 16 percent of the state's GDP.

The largest retail subsector for economic impact in the state is food services and drinking establishments, employing more than 200,000 workers, adding $4.7 billion to the economy. To finish out a top five of retail subsectors in Wisconsin, food services is followed by general merchandise (63,000 workers), food and beverage stores (more than 56,000), nonstore retailers (53,900), and motor vehicle and parts dealers (38,700).

The retail industry in Wisconsin employs four times as many workers as the state's dairy industry.

What are the top five retailers based in Wisconsin?

According to the National Retail Federation, only three retailers headquartered in Wisconsin are in the top one hundred in the nation. They are Kohl's (twenty-fifth largest in the nation), Menard's (forty-fifth in the nation), and Roundy's Supermarkets (ninety-eighth in the nation). Their annual income for fiscal 2015 combined for $33.4 billion.

To complete a top five list, the next two are Shopko and Kwik Trip. More details on those later in this chapter.

Beginning as a grocery store in 1927 opened by Polish immigrant Maxwell Kohl, the Milwaukee-based Kohl's opened its first department store in 1962. Now a public company, it commands an annual revenue of about $700 billion.

How big is Kohl's?

For the third year running, Kohl's was named the top workplace in southern Wisconsin for 2017. They operate more than 1,100 stores across America, with more than $19 million in total revenue, and employ more than 140,000 workers. They're headquartered in Menomonee Falls, Wisconsin.

What does Kohl's sell?

Thirty percent of Kohl's sales are in women's clothing. Another 20 percent is men's clothing, 18 percent is home products, with the remainder a combination of children's clothing, accessories, and footwear. More than half of all sales are for national name brands. The rest comes from private and exclusive brand names.

How much of Kohl's sales comes from online purchases?

Most of the store's sales are from "brick and mortar" outlets. Only about 9 percent of sales are from their online presence. The chain's strategy has been to offer free shipping when ordering from in-store kiosks, but a planned focus change will move toward online ordering with free shipping when items are picked up in-store.

Other than Kohl's, are there other retail chains headquartered in Wisconsin?

There are ten total chains based in the state. They include Cousin Subs, Culvers, Erbert & Gerberts, Kopps Frozen Custard, Kwik Trip, Menard's, Roundy's, Streetza Pizza, and Toppers.

What does Menards sell?

Headquartered in Eau Claire, Wisconsin, Menards sells home improvement products. They have 300 stores, with annual revenue of more than $10 million. They're known through the industry as the price leader, and their slogan is "Save BIG Money."

How did the company start?

In 1958, John Menard Jr. (1940–) needed to finance his education. With farms becoming increasingly mechanized, he saw a need for pole buildings. By the summer of 1959 several of his buildings were erected in the Eau Claire area, and his reputation grew. After graduating from college, he went into the construction business full time.

Pole shed customers at the time inquired about purchasing lumber from Menard. He started Menard Cashway Lumber and obliged the demand. In 1969 he added divisions for warehousing and manufacturing for trusses. He began producing steel siding, roofing, doors, composite decking, treated lumber, and more. In 1994 Menard sold his building division to expand his home improvement centers. In 2015, with stores in fourteen states, Menards is a home improvement retail leader with more than ten million dollars in annual sales.

What kinds of home improvement items does Menards sell?

The stores sell building materials for "do-it-yourselfers" as well as experienced contractors, and they carry name-brand tools, gardening supplies, appliances, pet products, and even food. Brands include Mastercraft, Tuscany, Tool Shop, and more. The chain—employing more than 45,000 workers—also prides itself on quality products and services at reasonable prices.

Their staff can help with designing, choosing contractors, estimating prices and materials needed, and assistance along the way with any building or gardening project.

Where is Roundy's headquartered?

The supermarket chain is based in Milwaukee, Wisconsin, with more than four million dollars in worldwide annual sales. They're the leading grocer in the Midwest and they are a subsidiary of Kroger Co. They operate more than 150 stores under the names Pick 'n Save, Copps, Metro Market, and Mariano's.

When was Roundy's founded?

In 1872, Judson Roundy and two partners (Sidney Hauxhurst and William A. Smith) started a wholesale grocery company called Smith, Roundy & Company. When they incorporated in 1902 they took on new partners and the company changed names to Roundy, Peckham & Dexter Co. In the 1970s they pioneered the "warehouse" store concept.

They've expanded to 151 stores, but their distribution centers supply more than 800 supermarkets in more than a dozen states. Roundy's owns the subsidiaries of Shop Rite, Ultra Mart, Mega Mart, Rindt Enterprises, Village Market, and Copps.

What are some of the top name brands that originate in Wisconsin?

In no particular order, ten name brands started in the state include Harley-Davidson Motorcycles, Trek Bicycles, Schneider National, Culvers, Cousins Subs, SC Johnson and Sons, Oshkosh B'Gosh, Carmex, American Family Insurance, *The Onion*, and Miller Brewing. More on Harley-Davidson, Miller Brewing, and Oshkosh B'Gosh can be found in the chapter on manufacturing.

Why did Cousins open a sub sandwich store in Milwaukee?

Bill Specht moved to Milwaukee from Atlantic City, New Jersey, and couldn't find a decent sub sandwich. Since he hated his job, he and his cousin, Jim Sheppard,

The first Cousins Subs was opened in Milwaukee in 1972 at the corner of 60th and Silver Spring Drive.

155

opened Cousins Subs in 1972 to bring a New England taste to the Midwest. They found a baker to help them create the right kind of bread, and the recipe hasn't changed since they opened their first store.

Their motto, "We Believe in Better," exemplifies their point of view. While other chains cut quality to increase profits, Cousins Subs uses superior ingredients. Since the chain is still family owned, their dedication to doing things the right way isn't likely to change.

Isn't there another sub chain in Wisconsin?

The quirky stories of Kevin Schippers were the inspiration of the names of menu items at Erbert & Gerbert's Sandwich Shop. From the Boney Billy (a turkey sandwich) to Tullius (double roast beef), the workers at E & G scrape out part of the bread when making a sandwich. They serve "the guts" to the customer, and created a character based on that part of the bread—"Mr. Guts."

Schippers remembered bedtime stories he heard as a kid, the Adventures of Erbert & Gerbert. They were designed to teach about science and history, and he named his sandwiches to honor the characters his father told him about. The chain started in Eau Claire, Wisconsin, in 1988 and has grown to more than a hundred stores in twelve states.

What can Wisconsinites do about chapped lips?

Winters in Wisconsin can dry out a person's skin, especially lips. Alfred Woelbing whipped up the first batch of Carmex in 1937 to help with his cold sores. Soon he was driving around with boxes of the familiar little jars to sell to others. He started offering his product to pharmacies and drug stores one by one. If the store didn't want any, he gave them a dozen jars for free, along with a postcard to order more. Word spread, and reorders flowed in.

What is *The Onion*?

*T*he Onion started in 1988 as a satirical newspaper created by University of Wisconsin students Tim Keck and Christopher Johnson, though they claim to have been the brainchild of Friedrich Siegfried Zweibel, a 1765 immigrant who traded produce for a printing press and began publishing *The Mercantile-Onion*—named using the only words of English that he knew. The oldest copy of that publication is from 1765.

The motto of the current *Onion* is "Tu Stultus Es," Latin for "You Are Stupid." The company was sold for $20,000 in 1989 and the new owner moved it to New York. The publication is now a multimedia company with videos to their credit. Titles include *The Onion Movie* (2008), *The Onion* (2002), *The Onion II* (2014), and the forthcoming *The Onion*, which was in post-production in 2017. Overall, more than one hundred videos have been produced for *The Onion*.

By 2008 the company had sold more than a billion jars of the salve. The product comes in a squeezable applicator, the traditional "stick" form of other salves, and now is available in different flavors.

As of 1999, Carmex is the most-recommended over-the-counter lip balm.

How many stores does Festival Foods operate?

Festival started in Onalaska, Wisconsin, with a single store attached to the home of Paul and Jane Skogen. They borrowed $500 and opened a 3,000-square-foot (278.7-square-meter) grocery store in 1946. After the family acquired a few small Independent Grocers Alliance (IGA) stores, their son Dave joined the team in 1975. In 1985 Paul was named IGA grocer of the year. There are about 5,000 IGA stores in thirty countries.

After detecting a change in the way his customers shopped, Skogen's IGA opened a Festival Foods in Onalaska, Wisconsin, in 1990. Since then they've expanded to more than two dozen stores in Wisconsin. Festival Foods in Minnesota is owned by Knowlan's Super Markets, Inc. and is not operated by the Skogen family.

What is the motto for Festival Foods?

In 2003, the company began their Boomerang Principle—every business decision they make is based on the question, "Will it bring customers back?" They've pioneered store-brand products like ribs-on-a-stick and Oktoberfest brats, and has produced store brands of many more well-known name brand products.

How has Festival Foods fared against Wal-Mart Superstores?

From 2003 to 2005, five Wal-Mart Superstores opened within two miles (three kilometers) of Festival locations. After a brief down-tick lasting less than six months, the Fes-

Festival Foods has put up a great fight against megastore chain Wal-Mart.

tival stores rebounded. They operated only four stores in 2002, and now run nearly thirty locations.

What businesses has Prophit Marketing helped?

Based in Green Bay, Wisconsin, Prophit has pushed many companies to the "next" level. Recognizable names include Cher-Make Sausages, Dahl Automotive, Great Lakes Foods, and the Community Blood Centers. They stress three key strategies—efficiency, execution, and results. They focus on the business they're helping, not on their own needs.

What has Prophit done to help Cher-Make Sausages?

Prophit helped make a small sausage producer stand out against companies with far deeper pockets. They branded Cher-Make as an authentic sausage maker, and their "Faces in the Cases" labels helped product leap off the shelves. Thanks to Prophit, Cher-Make bridges the gap between a family business and the big players.

Where is Cher-Make based?

Emil Chermak had a set of great old world sausage recipes, and in 1928 he decided to share with his neighbors in Manitowoc, Wisconsin. Emil's son, Art Chermak, remembers personally delivering product to neighbors. The second-generation owner partnered with a family member, Merlyn Hoefner, in 1950, and Cher-Make was eventually named to the Wisconsin Meat Packers Hall of Fame.

How successful was Prophit in helping Dahl Automotive?

In 2005, Dahl had two locations. By 2010 they'd expanded to four stores. Their market ranking improved from fourth to second, employee turnover fell, and the number of brands sold at Dahl climbed from five to nine. A mixture of updated signage, marketing, and employee training went into the Used Car Advantage campaign.

They sold tires in 2005. In 2007 they launched Tire Advantage, which guaranteed matching or beating competitor prices on tires. The number of tires sold by Dahl doubled.

How has Great Lakes Foods improved with the help of Prophit Marketing?

Prophit helped Great Lakes Foods develop their Signature Meat Marketing brand. Strategic marketing gave them—and their clients—more opportunity for growth. The Signature brand provided flavor variations for beef, chicken, and pork products—Meat with a Twist. Fifteen stores feature the Signature brand in Wisconsin and Michigan.

What products are part of the Signature Meat brand?

Beef products include Firehouse Angus Burgers, Love Me Tender Spoon Roasts, and Sizzler Steaks. There is also Sassy Chicken, along with pork products TaleGater Brats and Up Town Pork Roasts, and Sizzler Steaks.

The goal of the Signature brand is to take the work out of creating entrees. The customer can start their grill and have gourmet meals in short order.

What recognizable nonprofits used Prophit Marketing?

The marketing director of media relations has served on the United Way board of directors and executive committee for more than six years. That alone shows their dedication to working with nonprofits. They've helped other organizations such as the Community Blood Center and the American Red Cross.

Groups with less name recognition include The Parent Outlet, Options for Independent Living, The Breastfeeding Alliance of Northwest Wisconsin, and a program to combat childhood obesity called Live 54218.

Where did Shopko's first store open?

While founded in 1961 in Chicago, Illinois, the first Shopko store opened in 1962 in Green Bay, Wisconsin, by a pharmacist named James Ruben. He wanted a company focused on convenience, quality, and value, in locations that combined discount retail items with health care. In 1971 Shopko was the first of the mass retailers to offer pharmacy services inside their stores. In 1978 the chain added optical care centers.

What is "Shopko Hometown"?

Big box retailers are under economic pressure, and Shopko has been responding. The chain hasn't opened a "big box" branch in more than fifteen years, instead focusing on the smaller "hometown" stores. The average size of a typical Shopko location is more than 80,000 square feet (7,432 square meters), so the company has been meeting the needs of smaller communities with Shopko Hometown stores, ranging in size from 15,000 to 35,000 square feet (about 1,400 to 3,250 square meters)—about one-third the size of the larger stores.

CEO Peter McMahon told the National Retail Federation, "The rural population is grossly underserved by retailers, so we're eager to bring Shopko to more communities." They're hoping to compete with dollar stores in the more rural areas of the country. Hometown stores offer widely known name brand products like Nike, Gloria Vanderbilt, and Fisher-Price—items not normally found in dollar stores. Customers usually drive miles to find these names, and Hometown stores can put these brands closer to rural customers. McMahon says they may not be the cheapest, but they offer good value. "We're like a mini department store."

How many Shopko locations are there?

An article in *Stores* magazine from 2016 cites 363 locations in twenty-four states. Those numbers include both the full-sized stores and the Shopko Hometown locations.

The chain employs more than 18,000 people. They're based in Green Bay, Wisconsin, and operate distribution centers in DePere, Wisconsin; Boise, Idaho; Omaha, Nebraska; and Lebanon, Indiana.

How much does Shopko sell in a year?

In 1977 the chain surpassed $100 million in their twenty-one stores. With eighty-seven stores in 1988 they racked up a billion dollars in total sales. When they operated 130 stores in 1997 they topped two billion, and 2001 annual sales exceeded $3.5 billion.

According to *Forbes*, sales for fiscal 2016 was still over three billion but had slipped somewhat from the 2001 numbers.

When did Shopko and Pamida merge?

In 2012 the two chains became one entity, converting more than 170 stores and pharmacies to the Shopko brand.

W. Paul Jones—president, chairman and CEO of Shopko in 2012—said, "Merging Pamida and Shopko is a great move for our businesses and our customers given our complementary strengths, store networks and consumer-centric retail models." Pamida's focus had been on smaller communities, and Shopko's trend toward Shopko Hometown stores was a natural fit—especially since both chains were owned by Sun Capital Partners.

How did Prange's Department Store start?

Henry Carl Prange was the son of a German farmer who immigrated to Sheboygan, Wisconsin. Henry was a frail child who couldn't withstand farm life, so he got a job at a retailer in Sheboygan. After eleven years he asked to buy an interest in the store but was denied.

Founded in 1887 in Sheboygan, Prange's was a successful department store chain for decades, but it later declined and was sold to Younker's in 1992.

Henry quit his job and, with the help of his sister and her husband, opened the original H. C. Prange store on October 4, 1887. The building was two stories with offices and living areas on the second floor, and 3,300 square feet (a bit more than 300 square meters) of retail space on the main level. Other than the three founders, they only employed two people for eighteen months before bringing on a third employee.

What kind of prices did Prange's offer when they opened in 1887?

Prices at Prange's in 1887

Item	Price
A pail of syrup	$1.00
Dried apples, 20 lbs (9 kg)	$1.00
Rice, 15 lbs (6.8 kg)	$1.00
Creamery butter, 1 lb (0.45 kg)	$0.27
Tomatoes, one bushel (35.24 liters)	$0.69

Who were the first customers at Prange's?

Days before the official opening of Prange's, a German couple (William and Otillie Fiebelkorn) knocked on the door and asked if they were open for business. They'd traveled nearly twenty-five miles (forty kilometers) into Sheboygan to shop—quite a distance for 1887. Instead of turning the couple away, Henry sold them quite a list of goods. He conversed the whole time—in German—with the customers.

The couple had been tobacco farmers in Germany and grew sick of being looked down upon for their mere two-acre (0.8-hectare) farm. Having to haul produce ten miles (16 kilometers) to market solidified their decision to move to America. They eventually owned hundreds of acres in Sheboygan County—and two houses in Milwaukee. They were lifelong customers of Prange's.

What was the Prange's slogan?

The customer has always been the center of Prange's efforts. Most people have heard the phrase "The customer is always right." Prange's went a bit further with "It's not yours 'til you like it." Customer service was foundational to the Prange business.

They employed personal shoppers, who would help customers choose items. They'd take orders over the phone (or by mail) and have everything ready at "will call," and workers would carry the packages and load them into cars and wagons for patrons. Floor walkers would point people in the right direction if they couldn't find a specific department, and a delivery service would take filled orders directly to customers' homes within a certain distance from the store.

During the banking crisis in 1933, Prange's accepted checks from customers and issued "due bills," which could be used to buy groceries or pay doctors around town. The company waited to cash the checks until banks reopened after the federally mandated "bank holiday" ended.

In 1937, Prange's installed Wisconsin's very first escalator to help customers get to the second floor of their four-story building. It could accommodate as many as forty-two people at the same time and was capable of moving 6,000 people per hour. Ten years later they added another escalator to reach the third floor, though the basement and the fourth floor still required the staircase or one of the store's elevators.

When did Prange's add a bakery?

The Silver Edge Bakery at Prange's opened in 1942. Their staff expanded over the years, and by 1960 included a bakery superintendent, six full-time bakers, and ten others working in the shop.

They eventually boasted a bread slicer that could cut an entire loaf of bread at one time, they baked more than forty types of bread, and their two ovens could bake more than 250 loaves at the same time.

How many stores did Prange's operate?

In 1991 Prange's owned eighteen stores in Wisconsin, five in Michigan, and two in Illinois. The total square footage of store space topped two million square feet (186,000 square meters). Overall sales ran about $229 million.

They also ran nearly two dozen discount stores, called Prange Way, and a chain of more than a hundred boutique stores.

What kinds of departments did Prange's have?

The departments varied over the years. The company added or liquidated departments based on demand, and Prange's always looked ahead to trends.

When they first opened, the company sold groceries, kitchen gadgets, clothing, hats, hardware, jewelry, furs, and personal items. A 1923 company publication lists drug sundries, notions, stationery and books, leather goods, ribbons and neck wear, hosiery, and footwear. Also sold that year were ice cream sodas, fresh farm produce, yard goods, furniture, carpet, drapery, linoleum, and kitchen equipment. They also operated an art department and gift shop, a toy land, and seasonable displays for the holidays. Eventually they installed a restaurant on the fourth floor.

Did Prange's employ models?

The company frequently used live models in their stores. The increased public interest motivated customers to enter the store, and those same models would appear in their print advertising. Models would provide information to help people make careful decisions on what to purchase from the available selections.

Did Prange's really use an X-ray machine in their shoe department?

From the 1920s into the 1960s, stores used a shoe-fitting fluoroscope to measure feet. A fifteen-second exposure would show foot bones, the outline of the shoe, and the stitching around the edges. The customer could wriggle their toes while remaining on their feet to assure a good fit with plenty of room within the shoe. The machine had steps to allow a child to ascend for fittings.

Customers could look at the images through a portal in the top of the machine.

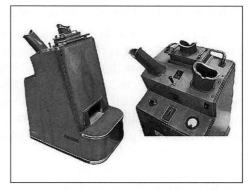

An example of the fluoroscope used at Prange's shoe stores to take X-rays of customers' feet and note bone shapes precisely.

Why did the Prange's chain decline?

On May 4, 1983, a water main burst in the basement of the main store in Sheboygan, undermining the ground beneath the store. Parts of the basement floor dropped more than a foot (thirty centimeters) near support pillars for the escalator system, which shifted. Floors around that system sagged. The building was evacuated, but debris fell from the ceiling throughout the store. One employee described how a customer was nearly struck. A spokesperson would only say the building had structural problems. Utilities were shut off.

By May 26, the company had plans to raze the building. The process was underway when, on October 16, fire broke out. The inferno could be seen from as much as fifteen miles (twenty-four kilometers) away and was later deemed to be arson. Numerous leads were followed, but the case remained unsolved.

The store was rebuilt, but instead of 250,000 square feet (23,000 square meters) with four floors, the new facility only measured 97,000 square feet (9,000 square meters) on one level. When they acquired a specialty store chain in 1989 they took on a massive amount of debt. The recession of the 1990s hit Prange's hard, and they sold the Prange Way discount chain in September 1990. The company was sold to Younkers in 1992.

How is Trek Bicycle unique?

Trek Bicycle manages to make bicycle riding seem as "cool" as riding a Harley. From their web site, "The bicycle is the most efficient form of human transportation. It can combat climate change, ease urban congestion, and build human fitness. It brings us together, yet allows us to escape. And it takes us places we would never see any other way."

Originally, the company manufactured frames for touring bikes in Waterloo, Wisconsin, in the 1970s. Today they have some of the most popular touring and recreational cycles in the world.

163

What kinds of guitars does Dave's offer?

Though they sell a wide variety of instruments, Dave Rogers is obsessed with guitars. He opened his shop in 1982 and has sold guitars to customers around the world to people of all skill levels. Names include ZZ Top's Billy Gibbons, Joe Walsh of the Eagles, and players from Pink Floyd, Night Rangers, and Def Leppard.

The store offers acoustic and electric guitars, both new and used, as well as associated equipment. They have brand names that include Fender, Gibson, Paul Reed Smith, and Rickenbacker—in all, more than three dozen brands are offered.

Dave's Guitar Shop now has stores in the original La Crosse location and in Milwaukee. Founded in 1982, it is a renowned specialty store.

Only about 15 percent of sales come locally; the rest are from around the world. Dave has a personal collection of more than 300 guitars and amps.

Does Dave's repair guitars?

The mission statement at Dave's includes, "We strive to offer our clients the highest level of service in guitar sales, repair and consulting." Yes, that includes repair and restoration services such as a simple restringing all the way to restoring classic instruments.

Past projects include repairing a Guild twelve-string with its headstock broken completely off and the restoration of a flood-damaged Gretch. They offer appraisals and estimates, many times for free.

How did Dave Rogers get into the guitar business?

Dave's brother, Ken, was a guitar player. "It was Ken who got me to pick up the guitar. He was an inspiration." But Ken wasn't very supportive, viewing Dave as the little brother who hung out while the elder brother played in a local band.

The household was always full of music, even after Dave's parents died. He was legally adopted by his older sister, and he taught himself to play on a ten-dollar guitar. His favorite music is rock and blues, but he will buy tickets to any musical performance.

His original store, opened in 1982, was less than 400 square feet (thirty-seven square meters). When he outgrew that in 2000, he moved to the store's current location at the corner of Fourth and Jackson in La Crosse.

Where was the first Kwik Trip store?

According to Steve Wrobel from Kwik Trip public relations, the first store opened in Eau Claire in 1965 at the corner of Fairfax Street and Hastings Way. Their records were not kept up, so the exact date isn't known by the corporation.

That first location was simply a corner grocery store that didn't sell fuel. Gasoline wasn't sold at Kwik Trip until 1970. Their second store opened in 1968 in a strip mall on Birch Street. That mall no longer exists, but there are more than 500 locations in Wisconsin, Minnesota, and Iowa (under the Kwik Star name).

Why is Kwik Trip known as Kwik Star in Iowa?

Another convenience store chain in Iowa already existed under the name Quick Trip. In order to prevent confusion, Kwik Trip decided on Kwik Star.

What kinds of products did Kwik Trip sell?

From the start, the business model focused on "grab and go" food like bread, milk, soda pop, and similar selections. Customers would be between shopping trips and need to pick up one or two items and not want to get bogged down in a full grocery store. Kwik Trip would allow a quick trip.

When did Kwik Trip start selling "real food"?

The chain always sold grocery staples. In 2003 the company rolled out their Hot Spot program that had a focus on ready-to-eat foods. Salads, fresh fruits, and similar foods came out in 2004, and in recent years they've added fresh meats. With their bakery items, Kwik Trip says their stores offer a whole-meal opportunity in one quick stop.

When did Kwik Trip start their own product lines?

The company started what they call "vertical integration" in the 1980s, which helped control costs and allowed them to compete with larger organizations. "We make it, we ship it, we sell it."

They opened their first dairy in 1981, and the bakery in 1985. They now sell their own brands like Nature's Touch, Kitchen Cravings, Kwikery bakery products, Glazer donuts, and Café Karuba.

Where does Kwik Trip produce come from?

Depending on specific items, most of their products come from local sources in Wisconsin, Minnesota, and Iowa. Their eggs are from Reedsburg, milk is from Foremost Farms (world class dairy, master cheesemakers), and they have an exclusive contract for their Ambrosia apples.

Does Kwik Trip control the price of gasoline, like some people claim?

Steve Wrobel emphatically says the chain does not. They purchase fuel from the same vendors as other filling stations, and prices varies from day to day. They need to make some profit, but that margin is minimal. "Each state has different laws pertaining to gas taxes and minimum mark-up requirements." That, and shipping costs, means prices may vary for different store locations. Gasoline is not a loss-leader priced low only to get people to their stores.

Why are there some Kwik Trip stores so close to others?

Generally it's because of traffic flow issues. Some stores can be seen from another location, but with issues of crossing traffic into (and out) of one location, another store is more convenient for shoppers. Their goal is to give customers a quick trip.

Are there plans to have the chain expand nationally?

Steve Wrobel says there is plenty of room to expand in the three-state area of Wisconsin, Minnesota, and Iowa. All their shipping is done out of La Crosse, and all their stores are within 300 miles (483 kilometers) of that city.

Why did Kwik Trip start their own credit card?

Credit cards through other companies cost a percentage of each receipt. As part of their vertical integration business model, Kwik Trip uses their own system to reduce costs, which is passed along to customers as lower prices. This helps the company compete with larger chains and maintain quality and service.

Is Kwik Trip a "green" company?

A lot of "gray" water from their car washes is recycled using reverse osmosis. This saves water, which is then used to wash other cars. Many of their stores are LEED (Leadership in Energy and Environmental Design) certified. They save water and electricity because of efficient building designs.

In addition, they offer compressed natural gas for vehicles using that fuel option, which is safer for the environment. Other alternative fuels include liquefied natural gas, bio-diesel, and propane.

Kwik Trip is based in La Crosse and owns about one thousand convenience stores in Wisconsin, Minnesota, and Iowa.

Also, most stores have recycling containers for customers, and the stores themselves recycle cardboard and shrink wrap.

Do people like working at Kwik Trip?

The normal turnover rate for similar businesses is 77 percent. Kwik Trip enjoys a rate less than half that national average. Their support centers have a turnover rate of less than 1 percent. The company works hard to maintain their workforce, with annual bonuses, profit sharing, and other benefits and incentives.

SHIPPING

How important is the state's transportation network?

The reliability of transportation is a must for Wisconsin's economy. People and businesses need a predictable system of getting to their destination on time. Coordinated systems of travel insure the smooth flow of goods and services, as well as tourism and commerce. The state's freight plan was designed to do just that.

How big is the transportation network in Wisconsin?

There are more than seven million miles (11.25 million kilometers) of roads, railways, navigable water, and pipelines in the state. The components are linked at airports, rail yards, water ports, and other facilities. More than five million residents of the state rely on this network, as well as 230,000 businesses and 109,000 shippers. That system supports an economy of $300 billion.

What are the sectors of the state's economy that depend on shipping freight?

There are six of those identified in a Department of Transportation study. Those sectors are Retail and Wholesale, Manufacturing, Agriculture and Forestry, Construction, Mining, and Transportation, Information, and Utilities/Energy.

Those six sectors are responsible for 40 percent of Wisconsin's employment and 44 percent of the state's GDP. With a slow growth rate of 2 percent compounded, that GDP is expected to be nearly a half-trillion dollars by the year 2040. An overall freight plan was conceived in 2009 to facilitate the needs of getting cargo from one place to another.

When did the interstate highway system originate?

The system was first described in a 1944 publication by President Franklin D. Roosevelt. His pamphlet, sent to Congress, showed routes through Wisconsin that approximate the paths of I-90 and I-94. Route designations were solidified by the State Highway Engineer in 1945 and included the Highway 18 path from Madison to Prairie du Chien, as well as highways 51 (I-94 to Hurley), 53 (Eau Claire to Superior), and routes from Milwaukee to Green Bay and Green Bay to Eau Claire.

The first portion of the system to open was in the Waukesha area, with an I-94 ribbon-cutting ceremony on September 4, 1958.

Which were the first interstate highways to be constructed?

Originally there were two main interstate arteries—I-90 (Milwaukee to La Crosse) and I-94 (Milwaukee to Hudson, Minnesota). The system expanded to eventually include many more miles of interstate highways.

How many interstate highways are there in Wisconsin?

The web site wisconsinhighways.org lists eight: I-39, I-41, I-43, I-90, I-94, I-535, I-794, and I-894. The first miles of interstate highway were begun in 1956 in Waukesha County. By 1969 the state's system was three-quarters completed.

The term "completed" might exaggerate the reality. The moment pavement is laid deterioration begins. By 1983, with many of the interstate miles aged twenty-five to thirty years, reconstruction was needed. As with the original construction, reconstruction began in Waukesha County.

How many state patrol officers enforce weight limits?

Across Wisconsin, fewer than one hundred officers work on enforcing the limits. The freeze/thaw cycles in winter do damage to interstate highways, but nothing like an overloaded semi.

There are thirteen weight stations in the state, but numerous "weigh in motion" sites, which have scales built into the highway. Cameras monitor those locations to allow enforcement. There are also portable scales for immediate enforcement.

What percent of statewide traffic uses the interstate system in Wisconsin?

Wisconsin has one of the lowest rates of interstate usage—17 percent. Only the states of Vermont and Delaware have lower rates, and Washington, D.C., has the lowest of all at 12 percent.

The states with the highest rates are Utah (36 percent) and Connecticut (33 percent).

How can a highway be called an "interstate" if it's all within one state?

It's a myth that interstate highways were designed only to move traffic from one state to another. Many interstate highways (beltways and spurs) are completely within one

Wisconsin's major freeways and highways. There are about 750 miles (1,200 kilometers) of interstate freeways in Wisconsin and more than 100,000 miles (161,000 kilometers) of other roads and highways.

state. Their original design was specified to serve "interstate, regional, and intra-state" traffic.

Even Hawaii has three interstate highways. They're designated H1, H2, and H3, and all of them connect Pearl Harbor with other military installations on Oahu.

How many miles of highways are in Wisconsin?

The Wisconsin Department of Transportation lists 115,454 miles (nearly 186,000 kilometers) of roads in the state according to a 2016 publication. They're broken down into "State Trunk Highways"—which includes interstate highways, U.S. highways, and the

169

state highway system. There are 11,787 miles (nearly 19,000 kilometers) of those. That's 10.2 percent of all roads in the state, and that handles 58.5 percent of all the vehicular miles traveled.

The interstate highway system itself measures only 876 miles (1,410 kilometers). That's less than 1 percent of all roadways in the state, handling 21.8 percent of miles driven.

How has the number of road miles grown over the years?

The interstate hasn't grown a great deal since 2009, nor has the number of miles of other roadways. The 2009 number of miles of all roads was 114,910 (nearly 185,000 kilometers)—only 544 additional miles (875 kilometers) of all roads. The interstate highway system has grown only 153 miles (246 kilometers) since 2009.

Since 1970 the total miles traveled on Wisconsin roads have increased from just under twenty-six million miles to nearly sixty-four million miles (forty-two million kilometers to 103 million kilometers)—about 2.5 times the number of miles driven in 1970.

How many trucking companies are based in Wisconsin?

According to fleetdirectory.com, there are one hundred trucking companies in the state. Not surprisingly, most are clustered around large metropolitan areas—Milwaukee, Madison, and Green Bay. None of those are among the eleven "intermodal" companies in America.

How much freight is hauled on the road through Wisconsin?

According to a study, 576 million tons (522 million metric tons) of freight moved in or through Wisconsin during 2013. Trucking carried about 60 percent of that total—341.1 million tons (309.4 million metric tons). In terms of dollars, the percentage is almost 70 percent—just under a half-billion dollars.

What commodities are trucks hauling on Wisconsin roads?

By weight, most of the cargo on state roads is farm products, nonmetallic minerals like sand and gravel, petroleum, and coal.

What kinds of roadways are listed in the National Highway System?

The NHS lists five important highway assets for the economy, national defense, and mobility. They are broken down into Interstates, Other Principle Arterials, Strategic Highway Network, Major Strategic Highway Network Connectors, and Intermodal Connectors. The goal of these routes is to connect all communities in Wisconsin with populations higher than five thousand.

These are broken down into backbone routes and connector routes. The backbones are principally interstates and multilane divided highways connecting major economic centers. Connectors are mostly two-lane highways giving access to significant economic centers from the backbone routes.

How do overweight and oversize loads fit into Wisconsin shipping?

The number of roads capable of handling such loads is limited. When constructed, the highway system wasn't designed for bearing up under such weights and sizes. The state is widening interchange loops to more easily accommodate larger loads. This gives oversize shipping more ability to reach their destination.

Bridges also hamper the movement of large loads, and updating infrastructure will enhance the ability of loads to move about. The typical maximum load for Wisconsin trucking is 80,000 pounds (36,287 kilograms), seventy-five feet (22.86 meters) long (includes truck/tractor and trailer), thirteen feet and six inches (four meters) high, and eight feet six inches (2.6 meters) wide. Permits and special routing are required to exceed those dimensions.

How do local roads fit into the freight plan?

Roads owned by municipal and county governments provide critical linkages to economic business centers such as rail yards, shipping ports, and airfields. Though the DOT doesn't have direct control of the usage, maintenance, or construction of such roads, funding for local road projects is funneled toward higher priority issues.

The 100,000 miles (161,000 kilometers) of such roads and nearly 9,000 bridges are utilized mostly by the general public. They are, however, very important in getting produce and other cargo to their final destination.

How many miles of railroads are in Wisconsin?

The state contains more than 3,300 miles (5,311 kilometers) of railroads, with more than 1,300 miles (2,092 kilometers) publicly supported or owned. There are 360 publicly

---

How many miles of state and U.S. highway are in Wisconsin?

The Wisconsin Department of Transportation lists about 10,100 miles (16,254 kilometers) of state and U.S. highways in a 2016 publication. They carry 36.7 percent of traffic, with more than 23.4 million miles (37.7 million kilometers) traveled annually.

owned bridges in the system. Ten private railroad businesses own and operate the remainder of the system in Wisconsin.

How much freight is transported by rail?

The 2013 number indicates 207 million tons (188 metric tons) of freight are sent via railroads in Wisconsin. The total value is nearly $180 billion. In terms of tonnage, 36 percent of freight is sent by rail. Forecasts predict the tonnage will double by the year 2030.

What are the principle commodities sent by rail in Wisconsin?

The most freight (by tonnage) consists of coal, crude oil, natural gas, chemicals, and nonmetallic minerals such as gravel and sand. Farm produce is also a major factor in tonnage sent.

Which private rail companies operate in Wisconsin?

Common freight carriers include Burlington Northern, Canadian National, Canadian Pacific, Union Pacific, and others. The principle passenger rail carrier is Amtrak, though a few others operate. There are seven other industrial carriers, which include Wisconsin Public Service, Domtar Paper, Badger Mining, the U.S. Army, and Port of Milwaukee.

BNSF is responsible for delivering about 8 percent of rail freight, Canadian National carries the most at 43 percent, and Union Pacific accounts for another 18 percent. Carriers not ranked as Class I generally have much smaller percentages of overall freight delivered. The exception is Wisconsin and Southern Railroad Company, which takes care of an additional 18 percent of the total.

How many counties are served by rail service in Wisconsin?

Of the seventy-two counties, fifty-nine have active rail service. Many railroad miles have been abandoned or inactive over the years and have been transformed into recreational trails. The Rails to Trails program preserves those areas for future transportation needs. Read more about recreational trails in the chapters dealing with tourism.

Since 1987, 70 percent of decommissioned rail miles have been preserved or are in negotiations to be preserved. Those rail beds retain their characteristics as rail lines and may be reactivated in the future.

Where are the major rail yards in Wisconsin?

There are eleven major rail yards in the state. They include Milwaukee, Madison, Butler, Janesville, Neenah, Green Bay, North Fond du Lac, Stevens Point, La Crosse, Superior, and Portage.

How are railroads classified in Wisconsin?

There are three different levels, based on usage and revenue. The highest level is Class I, with operating revenue of more than $467 million (in 2013 dollars) annually. Regional lines must be at least 350 miles (563 kilometers) with annual revenue between $37 mil-

This new Amtrak station in Sturtevant was completed in 2012. Fourteen trains connecting Milwaukee and Chicago pass by here daily.

lion and $467 million. Short line rails are less than 350 miles (563 kilometers) and less than $37 million.

How important are pipelines for moving commodities in Wisconsin?

The state is crisscrossed with nearly 75,000 miles (120,700 kilometers) of pipelines. In 2012 they moved twenty-nine million tons (26.3 million metric tons) of natural gas and petroleum products with a total value of almost $16 billion. Most of that system (97 percent) is used for natural gas. The remaining 3 percent is used for various petroleum liquids.

The importance of pipelines is evident in that 70 percent of Wisconsin residents rely on them to provide heating. Residential heating consumes more than 130 trillion BTUs sent via pipeline.

Are there crude oil pipelines in Wisconsin?

Wisconsin is a "pass through" state for crude oil. Crude enters the state and flows through without stopping. The only operator of crude oil pipelines in Wisconsin is Enbridge Energy.

Wisconsin has just over a thousand miles of pipeline devoted to the movement of crude oil.

Where are the nearest oil refineries?

Wisconsin is fortunate to have a number of nearby refineries that have a direct pipeline connection. The only refinery in the state is in Superior, Wisconsin. There are two in Minnesota—Rosemount and St. Paul. Three other refineries are nearby—Whiting, Indiana; Joliet, Illinois; and Lemont, Illinois.

How many commercial water ports are in Wisconsin?

The DOT lists twenty-nine such ports in the state, breaking them down into categories. There are six gateway ports, three diversified cargo ports, six limited cargo ports, and many other smaller facilities. Many ports are equipped for intermodal connections.

What types of cargo are sent by water?

The primary commodities sent through commercial ports are coal, metallic ore, non-metallic minerals, clay, concrete, glass, and stone. Other freight includes petroleum, heavy machinery, bagged and canned cargo, and components for wind turbines.

What is another important waterway in the state?

The upper Mississippi River averaged 107 million tons (ninety-seven metric tons) of cargo in 2013. That waterway connects Wisconsin to Minnesota, Iowa, Illinois, and Missouri, and links to the lower Mississippi. The U.S. Army Corps of Engineers maintains the system to a depth of nine feet (2.7 meters) and operates the system of twenty-nine locks and dams between St. Paul, Minnesota, and the mouth of the Ohio River.

When was the lock and dam system built?

Originally built in the 1930s, the facilities were designed to operate for fifty years. They continue to operate, with occasional renovations, far beyond their expected lifetime.

The dams create pools along the course of the river, which help maintain a navigable depth of 9 feet (2.7 meters). Pools also create recreational opportunities for private watercraft, as well as nesting grounds for migratory birds. Several communities utilize the pools for drinking water. For more on recreational uses, see the chapters dealing with tourism.

Which waterway is most important to Wisconsin?

Waterways are access. Businesses can use water routes to deliver cargo regionally, nationally, and internationally. The biggest is the Great Lakes Navigation System, which provides a continuous route for watercraft with a twenty-seven-foot (8.23 meters) draft all the way from the western point of Lake Superior to the Atlantic Ocean. That's a distance of more than 2,400 miles (3,800 kilometers).

The U.S. portion of this waterway contains sixty commercial harbors, two operating locks, and more than 600 miles (960 kilometers) of maintained navigable channel. It's connected to several lower-draft channels—the Illinois Waterway, the New York State Barge Channel, and others. They all form a network of water transportation reaching deep into the continental United States.

A lock on the Fox River opens to let a freight ship through in De Pere.

The locks are used by commercial or private watercraft to "step up" or "step down" from one pool to the next. They facilitate boat traffic of all kinds, providing the opportunity for efficient movement of cargo and pleasure craft.

What is the typical delay at a Wisconsin lock?

The ten locks on the Upper Mississippi River system all have an average delay of less than two hours. Most of the ten are in the neighborhood of one hour, with the longest being Alma, Wisconsin, with an average delay of ninety-six minutes. The lock with the shortest average delay is at La Crescent (across the river from La Crosse) at 38.4 minutes.

The percentage of vessels delayed varies, not in proportion to the delay time. At Dubuque, Iowa, 43 percent of watercraft experience delays—the most in the Upper Mississippi lock system. The facility with the fewest number of delays is Alma, Wisconsin, with only 12 percent of vessels delayed.

How much freight is sent via waterway?

In 2013, about 5 percent of cargo moving in or through the state did so using Wisconsin waterways or ports. That amounts to more than twenty-eight million tons (25.4 million metric tons) worth an estimated two billion dollars.

175

Water transport is a very efficient way of moving commodities, with a ton of freight moving on average about 607 miles (977 kilometers) on a single gallon (3.78 liters) of fuel. Though rail is also effective, that average is only 202 miles per gallon (86.86 kilometers per liter) of fuel for each ton. Trucking can only move a ton of freight 59 miles (95 kilometers) on a single gallon (3.8 liters).

How many Wisconsin airports provide regular freight services?

There are six such airports, and in 2013 they handled 105,000 tons (95,254 metric tons) of freight worth ten billion dollars. Those six facilities are in Green Bay, Mosinee, Madison, Milwaukee, Appleton, and Rhinelander.

Freight sent by air is typically high-value and low-bulk, time sensitive, or highly specialized. The most common such cargo is electrical equipment, photographic or optical equipment, and fresh products with a short shelf life.

Which airport handles most of the state's air cargo?

General Mitchell International Airport handles about 70 percent of all air freight in Wisconsin. That facility is a hub for air cargo heading to other airports in the state. Nearly all other air traffic carrying cargo is handled by Madison and Appleton.

Are there other airports that handle air cargo when there's demand?

There are seven other "feeder" airports that are available for cargo contracts during high demand. Cities with that service available are in Baraboo, Eau Claire, Mineral Point, La Crosse, Menomonie, Cameron, and Janesville.

How many international airports are in Wisconsin?

There is just one—Mitchell International in Milwaukee—with international flights listed. Chicago, Illinois, is near enough to limit the number of international flights. The only flights to outside the United States are to Mexico, Canada, and the Caribbean. International travelers typically connecting to longer flights travel to O'Hare in Chicago.

Austin Straubel International Airport in Green Bay is technically an international airport. They list no international flights to or from Green Bay.

How many other airports are in Wisconsin?

There are seventeen airports listed on mapsoftheworld.com, but there are hundreds—perhaps thousands—of smaller and private airstrips scattered throughout the state. Wikipedia categorizes facilities and lists eight commercial airports and six "reliever" airports to ease congestion at larger facilities. The list includes seventy-three general aviation airports, forty-five for "other public use," and five more military or private facilities.

THINGS TO SEE AND DO

HISTORIC TOURISM

How can people learn what Wisconsin had been like in the early days?

The Wisconsin Historical Museum in Madison would be a great place to start, though it would only be a start. Learn about the politics of the state, how people lived and worked when the state was on the frontier, and which immigrants settled the state.

The People of the Woodlands exhibits show homes of the native people, artwork, food, and much more. There is clothing, a trading post, and much to learn about the fur trade of early Wisconsin.

Where is the only battle that took place within the current borders of Wisconsin?

The battle took place in 1814, when British-Canadian militia helped secure a victory at Prairie du Chien. Every year a reenactment of the battle is staged, complete with what women and children would be doing during a battle. The American forces defended against a British army ten times their size and surrendered after two and a half days.

Hercules Louis Dousman (1800–1868) earned quite a fortune in his various trades. He was a fur trader, lumberman, land speculator, and frontier entrepreneur. In the mid-1840s his family developed a property on the Mississippi at Prairie du Chien that evolved into the historic site called Villa Louis.

What are some of the programs featured at the Villa Louis?

Prairie du Chien is the oldest European settlement on the upper Mississippi River. Field trips to the Villa Louis include a scavenger hunt for historic facts, a fur trade museum tour, and a "minds on" tour of the villa grounds, mansion, and outbuildings.

Tours are on the hour from 10:00 to 3:00 Monday through Thursday and from 10:00 to 4:00 Friday through Sunday. The villa's ground floor is wheelchair accessible, as are the fur trade museum and restrooms.

Where can visitors to the Villa Louis stay?

There are hotels in the area, cabins, B & Bs, and campgrounds. Restaurants and retail stores are nearby to compliment the atmosphere.

What is Old World Wisconsin like?

The historic site opened in 1976 in time for America's bicentennial. There are more than sixty structures collected from across the state. They were documented, dismantled, and relocated to Eagle, Wisconsin, in Waukesha County.

The museum is modeled on Wisconsin of the 1880s and very little is different from what a settlement would look like at that time. The Old World Wisconsin Foundation is a nonprofit organization set up to support the site, which is owned and operated by the Wisconsin Historical Society.

What kinds of activities are there at Old World Wisconsin?

Every aspect of rural life is recreated at Old World Wisconsin. The village has everything from a blacksmith to an inn, a church to a shoemaker. Hands-on activities include basic daily chores like laundering, seasonal food preparation, caring for traditional domestic animals, and gardening with heritage crops using tools appropriate for the era.

Where is Wade House, and what is it?

The land between Fond du Lac, Wisconsin, and Sheboygan (a trip of nearly forty miles, or sixty-four kilometers) was untamed forestland. In 1844 Sylvanus and Betsey Wade purchased land along a stagecoach route where coaches crossed the Mullet River. They didn't want to merely have a homestead, but to found a community. They sold much of their land to settlers with a similar vision, and Greenbush, Wisconsin, became a regular stopping point on the coach route. By the time Wisconsin became a state in 1848, Greenbush had expanded considerably.

The Wade House has a visitors center that opened in 2013, sixty years after the historic site opened to the public. It's LEED (Leadership in Energy and Environmental Design) certified and contains orientation exhibits. Within the site itself is a carriage collection, a sawmill, blacksmith shop, and "period" rooms throughout the Wade House itself.

Is Reed School worth a visit?

Located near Neillsville in Clark County, Reed School is a restored one-room schoolhouse. Built in 1915, much of rural Wisconsin education was done in such schools. The educational model was that older students would help younger students—a difficult model to attain.

If you travel to Pendarvis, you will find a scattering of historic homes constructed by Cornish immigrants in the early nineteenth century. Several of the houses host tours.

The school remained in use through 1951 and is typical of more than 6,000 such schools in the state. Tours are held on weekends, none on weekdays.

Where is Pendarvis, and what is it?

Pendarvis House is near Mineral Point, Wisconsin, and is a house built by Cornish immigrants settling to mine zinc and lead in the early 1800s. By 1935 the homes and culture had all but vanished from the area. Restorers traveled to Cornwall to learn how the deteriorating limestone homes had been built.

Eventually several structures were rehabilitated. The Cornish tradition was to give houses a name, and the first was called Pendarvis. Gardens were added, other homes (Polperro and Trelawny) as well, and by 1988 a total of forty-three acres (17.4 hectares) formed the historic site.

What is there to see at Pendarvis?

The three houses already mentioned are available for tours. See how the immigrants from Cornwall lived, worked, and cooked. There's a pub on site and a store in the visitors center with gifts of Cornish culture.

Is there really a Paul Bunyan Museum?

The museum is located on Half Moon Drive in Eau Claire. Logging in Wisconsin was a big industry in the middle of the 1800s. From 1843 to 1855, annual output grew from

179

5.5 million board feet (1.7 million board meters) to 75 million (22.9 million board meters). But by 1910 the forests that supplied America had been decimated. Mark Wyman wrote, "Giant stumps like bleached skeletons littered the landscape, which supported no trees beyond a few inches in diameter. With much of the forest destroyed and ground cover burned, floods became frequent and large."

The grand opening of the Paul Bunyan Museum was in 1934 with a simple logging camp. Over the years other features have been added—a tool shed, blacksmith shop, heavy equipment shed, and more. They're open daily from May through September.

Was Paul Bunyan a real person?

The average lumberjack of the time was probably around sixty-four inches (163 centimeters) tall and weighed 140 pounds (63.5 kilograms). Historians believe a French Canadian lumberjack of about seventy-eight inches (198 centimeters) tall is the source of the Paul Bunyan "myth."

Lumberjacks were prone to telling tales, and one of the best ones is Paul Bunyan digging watering troughs for Babe the Blue Ox, which became the Great Lakes. Another has a tired Bunyan dragging his ax behind him, creating the Grand Canyon. The first documented legend of Paul Bunyan is credited to James Rockwell for a collection of tall tales.

What is there to see at Madeline Island?

The American Fur Company built a complex on Madeline Island in 1835. Native Ojibwe coexisted with fur traders and explorers on the island just off the northern shore of Wisconsin. The blend of French, British, American, and native people produced a thriving culture on the frontier.

Visitors can view tools and other artifacts from an old jail, a lighthouse, the Old Sailor's Home, and much more. An on-site store offers crafts from the Ojibwe, books, and other items related to the history of the island.

Who lived at Stonefield?

Stonefield is a historic site where Nelson Dewey (1813–1889)—first governor of Wisconsin—lived. The 2,000-acre (809-hectare) site is the culmination of Dewey's dream of a home, which included a three-story Gothic Revival mansion near the Mississippi River. That building burned to the foundations in 1873 and was rebuilt in a more modest style in the 1890s. The state purchased the site in 1936, and it was placed on the National Register of Historic Places in 1954.

The current facility features an agricultural museum with farming equipment from circa 1900, a farmstead from the same era, and a rural farming village. Learn how Wisconsin became the "Dairy State," more about Governor Dewey, and how people lived and worked in the early part of the twentieth century.

Who built Black Point Estates?

In the wake of the Great Chicago Fire of 1871, many wealthy people from the city had summer homes constructed. In 1887 Conrad Seipp (1825–1890), a beer baron from Chicago, had Black Point developed. The Queen Anne-style "cottage" boasted twenty rooms—thirteen of them bedrooms—and only a single bathroom. The site is about eight acres (3.24 hectares) and includes 620 feet (189 meters) of Geneva Lake shoreline.

Four generations of Seipp's family enjoyed the home, though Conrad Seipp died two years after construction was completed. The building and grounds were donated to Wisconsin in 2005 and after a $1.9 million renovation was opened for tours. In 2013 the state's historical society assumed responsibility of the site.

Where is the Pabst Mansion located?

Beer baron and sea captain Frederick Pabst (1836–1904) built this mansion on Milwaukee's historic Grand Avenue. The Flemish Renaissance home was completed in 1892 after two years of construction.

Where was the first capital of Wisconsin?

The state capital has always been in Madison, but the first capital of the territory of Wisconsin was in Belmont, Wisconsin. Between October 25, 1836, and December 9, 1836, the legislature of the territory passed forty-two laws for what would become a state twelve years later.

There are two buildings on the site—the Council House and the lodging house where legislators spent their nights. In 1924 the Council House was restored, with the lodging house restoration waiting until 1956. Tours of the historic site are available "in season."

The Council House and lodging house became part of the Wisconsin Historical Society in 1994.

Tours of the mansion are Monday through Saturday and from 10:00 to 3:00, Sundays from noon until 3:00. During the holiday season (which runs from the middle of November to the middle of January), the tours are self-guided.

Completed in 1892 by beer company founder Frederick Pabst, the Pabst Mansion was designed by architect George Bowman Ferry. Today, it is open to public tours.

Why is there a shrine of Our Lady of Guadalupe in La Crosse, Wisconsin?

In 1531 a man had a vision of the Virgin Mary on a hillside near Mexico City. Over the years he saw Mary a number of times, and his cloak was miraculously imprinted with the image of Mary. The event became a powerful sign to people in the Americas, and the Catholic Church constructed the Basilica of Our Lady of Guadalupe in Mexico City.

After Raymond Burke (1948–) was installed as the eighth bishop of the Diocese of La Crosse, he wanted to do something about the increasing violence in American culture. When a family donated seventy acres (twenty-eight hectares) of wooded hills near La Crosse, Burke decided to construct a shrine to honor the Virgin Mary. He wanted to recall the appearances of 1531 and proclaim Mary's message of God's mercy and love.

What is there to see at the Guadalupe shrine?

Admission is free, and after passing through the visitor's center there's a winding path up the country hillside. Along the way is a brick Votive Candle Chapel, many memorials, and at the top is the main church constructed in a seventeenth-century style of Italianate Renaissance. Nearby is an outdoors Stations of the Cross and a rosary walk.

Golf carts are available for those unable to hike the whole path.

Where is Surgeons Quarters?

Surgeons Quarters is where the surgeons were quartered for Fort Winnebago near Portage, Wisconsin. The site overlooks where Louis Joliet (1645–1700) and Father Marquette (1637–1675) left the Fox River to portage to the Wisconsin River.

Originally a residential home for a mixed French/native man who ran a portaging business, the log home became the home of Fort Winnebago's surgeon. When the army sent soldiers to the Mexican American War, the surgeons quarters became the home of a local physician. Later the building was converted to an apartment.

Learn more about Joliet and Marquette in the chapter on early American history.

What is there to see at Surgeons Quarters?

In 1938 the Wisconsin Society Daughters of the American Revolution bought the property, which was the only remaining structure of Fort Winnebago. The historic site opened for tourists in 1954 and showcases medical equipment from the early 1800s, period books, and blacksmith tools, as well as children's toys and implements used in the course of daily life by frontier residents.

Also on the site is the Garrison School—a one-room schoolhouse. Nearby is the Old Fort Winnebago Cemetery, the historic Indian Agency House, and a marker for the 234-mile (377-kilometer) military road connecting the old fort with Fort Howard (116 miles or 187 kilometers away) and Fort Crawford (115 miles or 185 kilometers away).

How many historical markers are there in Wisconsin?

The first marker was erected at the Peshtigo Fire Cemetery. A total of 566 "official" markers have gone up throughout the state. The latest listed by wisconsinhistory.org is the East Park Historic District in Stoughton. Each tells a story about historic people, places, or events. Many of these markers are found at roadsides.

Is there a list of historical markers?

A list can be found at hmdb.org. Each marker includes the marker number, name and location, and a map index to find the general area on an official state highway map. If information is incomplete or incorrect, an email link at the web site is available to file an application for correction.

Official markers all have a badger emblem at the top. Markers could cost as much as $4,440 plus installation. Someone wanting to add a marker must pay for the marker, installation and upkeep, and must have permission from the landowner where the marker will be installed.

How many sites in Wisconsin are on the National Register of Historic Places?

Across the nation there are more than 85,000. Each of Wisconsin's seventy-two counties has at least one, and the state has more than 2,300. The only county with just one is Menominee, counties with only two include Pepin and Washburn, and four others have only three sites.

What is the Indian Agency House?

The house was built by the U.S. government for John Kinzie (1803–1865) in 1832. He was the agent to the Ho Chunk (Winnebago) tribe, and the house stands at the original site of the portage from the Fox River to the Wisconsin River.

Located at the strategic site between watersheds of the Great Lakes and the Mississippi River, the Federal-style house is outfitted with furnishings and artifacts of the period. The building was placed on the National Register of Historic Places in 1972.

The counties with the most properties on the Register are Milwaukee (254), Dane (237), Waukesha (152), and Rock (139).

What are some other historic sites to visit in Wisconsin?

The opportunities are nearly endless. There is a round barn in Dell, Wisconsin, and many scattered through the state. In the 1880s a Norwegian immigrant became the largest tobacco retailer in the area. His warehouse is listed on the National Register of Historic Places. Historic markers trace the Trail of Tears through Crawford and Vernon Counties. Norskedalen Nature and Heritage Center in Coon Valley is dedicated to preserving the cultural heritage of the area. Those few mentioned are a small fraction of what is available.

What museum is the best to visit?

Tripadvisor.com has listed the top destinations for museums. The top of their specialty museums includes the Harley-Davidson Museum, the EAA Aviation Museum, the Green Bay Packers Hall of Fame, and the Circus World Museum.

Of those, the Aviation Museum hasn't been covered in other chapters. Located in Oshkosh, the facility contains more than two hundred historic aircraft. This museum is the most extensive aviation museum attraction in the world.

In Oshkosh you will find the EAA Aviation Museum, one of the finest air museums in the United States, where you will see such things as the Eagle Hangar.

What are the top history museums in Wisconsin?

The top four listed by Tripadvisor.com include the Wisconsin Maritime Museum in Manitowoc, the H. H. Bennett Studio in Wisconsin Dells, the WWII History Museum in Portage, and the Door County Historical Museum in Sturgeon Bay.

Why is there a maritime museum in Wisconsin?

Founded in 1970, the museum covers the vast history of sailing on the Great Lakes, the shipbuilders, sailors, and submariners. There are tours of WWII submarines built in the area, a re-creation of a nineteenth-century shipbuilding town, and hands-on experiences for kids of all ages.

There is a simulator to give visitors a taste of what submarine crew experienced during a depth charge attack, a 1911 steam engine used on an icebreaker, and an exhibit of the wide variety of ships built at the shipyard. The aquatic species lab will let people wade through details of invasive aquatic species.

Are there good art galleries in Wisconsin?

Sturgeon Bay is home to Popelka Trenchard Glass, Marshfield features Jurassic Park—detailing the work of amateur paleontologist Clyde Wynia—Ellison Bay Pottery Studios, Frykman Studio Gallery in Sister Bay, and the Francis Hardy Gallery in Ephraim.

What art museums are in Wisconsin?

The museum ranked first in the state by Tripadvisor.com is the Milwaukee Art Museum. They collect and preserve art, then present it to the community. There are more than 30,000 pieces of art. They have been operating since 1888.

With more than forty galleries, artwork is rotated regularly. Featured are the War Memorial Center, the Kahler Building, and the Quadracci Pavilion. In all, more than 341,000 square feet (31,700 square meters) of space receives nearly a half-million visitors annually.

Are there museums suitable for children?

TripAdvisor ranks ten such museums, the most popular in Madison, Milwaukee, and Eau Claire. The Madison Children's Museum wants to promote imagination and curiosity, and encourage children to play.

The museum has won multiple awards annually since 2007. Those include Best Museum, Most Loved Place to Go, Top Family Attraction for Wisconsin, and Best Kids' Entertainment.

What is the top ranked science museum in Wisconsin?

Discovery World Science and Technology Center in Milwaukee is suitable for all ages. The Reiman Aquarium features aquatic species from the Great Lakes to the Caribbean Sea. Experience impossible environments, game playing, and a new kind of storytelling in the Virtual Explorer. Discover the fundamentals of physics, explore engines and motors, explore a nineteenth-century schooner replica, and much more.

What notable planetariums does Wisconsin have?

The state is home to three distinguished planetariums. Those are the Yerkes Observatory in Williams Bay (near Lake Geneva), the Kovak Planetarium in Rhinelander, and the Barlow Planetarium in Menasha.

The Yerkes Observatory was established in 1897 and is considered the birthplace of modern astrophysics. Founded by the University of Chicago, the observatory was once home to the world's largest refracting telescope.

Was a Wisconsinite one of the men who raised the American flag on Iwo Jima?

John Bradley (1923–1994) of Antigo, Wisconsin, was one of the six men who raised that flag in World War II. However, some say he was not one of the six who were in the iconic photograph taken ninety minutes later. The first flag was smaller, and some theorize Bradley witnessed the Pulitzer Prize picture but was not in it.

The prize-winning picture was used to create the Marine Corps memorial dedicated in 1954.

Who was Jim Flatley?

Flatley (1906–1958) was a Green Bay native who flew air combat in World War II. After the Battle of the Coral Sea he received the Navy Cross for "extraordinary heroism and conspicuous courage." After the war he trained other pilots and eventually earned the rank of vice admiral.

Awards he earned include the Distinguished Flying Cross, Bronze Star, Navy Distinguished Service Medal, and a Presidential Unit Citation. A guided missile frigate was named after Admiral Flatley, and annually a ship is given the Admiral Flatley Memorial Award for safety.

A memorial statue was erected in Admiral Flatley Park in Green Bay.

Who is Fort McCoy named after?

Major General Robert McCoy (1867–1926) was born in Kenosha, moved to Sparta, and became the mayor. Though he was nominated for governor, he lost that race.

McCoy fought in the Spanish American War and World War I, commanding the 4th Wisconsin Infantry Regiment. After

One of the soldiers who raised that famous flag over Iwo Jima in World War II was John Bradley of Antigo, Wisconsin.

WWI he began purchasing land outside Sparta, Wisconsin, to create an artillery training center. After his death in 1926 the facility was renamed for McCoy, and the fort covers more than 60,000 acres (24,000 hectares).

Who was the most influential military veteran from Wisconsin?

Fleet Admiral William Daniel Leahy (1875–1959) eventually served as the chairman of the Joint Chiefs of Staff during World War II. He was the first sailor and only Wisconsinite to achieve the five-star rank. A close friend of President Franklin Roosevelt (1882–1945), he was tasked with diverting the attention of possible German spies prior to the D-Day invasion. He "went on vacation" to visit his hometown in Iowa. The idea was to allay any suspicions of a possible invasion.

After the war Leahy continued to serve as the chair of the Joint Chiefs of Staff into the Truman administration. He was appointed governor of Puerto Rico and became an ambassador to France.

A historical marker (#304) was erected in 1991 in Ashland, Wisconsin, where he graduated from high school.

Were any Wisconsin natives distinguished in the Civil War?

Perhaps the most notable is the tenth governor of the state, Lucius Fairchild (1831–1896). As a general, he led the 2nd Wisconsin Infantry during the Battle of Antietam and the Battle of Gettysburg.

In the first day of fighting at Gettysburg his men became the first to capture a Confederate general officer, but almost immediately afterward they were ambushed. More than three-quarters of the men were killed. Later in the battle General Fairchild was shot in the arm, which had to be amputated. Read more about Fairchild in his biography, *The Empty Sleeve.*

The town of Fairchild was named for the Civil War general, whose father, Jairus Fairchild (1801–1862), was the first mayor of Madison.

Which Wisconsin soldier said he would "come out a dead sergeant or a live lieutenant"?

Military records misspelled Denis (as Dennis) Murphy (1830–1901) from Green Bay. He joined the 14th Wisconsin in 1861 and distinguished himself in the second Battle of Corinth. Wave after wave of Confederate soldiers assaulted the position where Murphy carried the regimental colors. Sergeant Murphy stated his intent to "come out a dead sergeant or a live lieutenant."

The cool efficiency of the Union forces pushed the Confederates into retreat, but the Confederate forces of the 1st Missouri and 33rd Mississippi combined to put the Union position in a crossfire. Men fell left and right, and Murphy, though wounded multiple times, maintained his hold on his colors. The Union, however, was forced to retreat.

Murphy was crippled for life and discharged, but the following month he received a lieutenancy in Company B of the 24th Wisconsin. Nearly thirty years later he received the Medal of Honor. The flags he held are on display in the Wisconsin Veterans Museum in Madison.

Are there other recipients of the Medal of Honor from Wisconsin?

The rules were rather broad when the Medal of Honor was first instituted in 1861, and many awards were later rescinded. A board was established in 1911 to review all past awards, and that review board pulled 911 of the 2,625 medals awarded by that time. Only one of those rescinded was from a Wisconsin soldier.

There were twenty-two recipients of that medal from the Civil War, though the one was later removed. Seven more were awarded for action during the Frontier Wars of 1865 to 1891. Only one award was given to a Wisconsin soldier during the Spanish American War, another during the Philippine American War, one more during the Boxer Rebellion in China, two during the Mexican Border Campaign, two more during World War I, and sixteen in World War II. Eleven Medals of Honor were awarded during the Korean and Viet Nam Wars, bringing the total to sixty-three—one of which was later rescinded. Of those, seventeen were awarded posthumously.

Is Wisconsin the home of Flag Day?

In 1885, a teacher in a one-room schoolhouse in Waubeka, Wisconsin, had his students write essays about what the American flag meant to them. He called June 14 the flag's birthday, since that was the day in 1777 when Congress "resolved that the flag of the thirteen United States be Thirteen stripes alternate red and white: that the union be thirteen stars, white in a blue field, representing a new constellation."

Bernard J. Cigrand (1866–1932) inspired his students, and America, of the meaning and majesty of the flag. That schoolhouse, Stony Hill School, is now a historical site.

Does Wisconsin have a Civil War museum that focuses on the event from a local perspective?

That is exactly what the Civil War Museum in Kenosha is designed to do. More than a

Born in Waubeka and originally a dentist, Bernard Cigrand was a dentist and educator with a love for the American flag. His promotion of the flag and patriotism helped pass a Congressional resolution to create Flag Day on June 14.

Did Abraham Lincoln ever visit Wisconsin?

The year before he was elected president, Lincoln (1809–1865) delivered a speech at the Wisconsin Agricultural Society fair in Milwaukee. He was paid $150 to speak—a rather hefty sum for 1859—and kept his comments confined to the topic of agriculture.

Lincoln was then elected president in 1860. After a war to keep the United States united, he was shot and killed in 1865. A small memorial marker was placed to commemorate the site of his 1859 speech.

million Union soldiers in that conflict came from the states of Illinois, Indiana, Iowa, Michigan, Minnesota, Ohio, and Wisconsin. Personal stories connect events in the upper Midwest of prewar America to postwar effects.

Permanent exhibits include:

- The Fiery Trial—the home front as seen by people from the area who fought and returned.
- Seeing the Elephant—a phrase used by Civil War soldiers to describe their first combat experience.
- Veterans Memorial Gallery—a group of Civil War soldiers is depicted, huddling around a campfire. Surrounding them are displays of artifacts and memorabilia from other wars.

Are there any Civil War memorials to the Confederacy in Wisconsin?

The "Northernmost Confederate Cemetery" is in the Madison area with 140 soldiers who fought for the South. A stone marker lists all the names, erected by the United Daughters of the Confederacy. A short distance away is a cemetery for 240 Union soldiers who died at the Camp Randall training center.

As debate continues about the removal of Confederate monuments, a professor of history at the University of Wisconsin-Stout would rather keep the monuments and contextualize them. "History is messy, and while American history shows the greatness of the nation, it also shows some of the problematic sides," Robert Zeidel said. "Do we start to whitewash history? Ignore the parts of history we don't like? I would say, add to the narrative." He believes the proximity of the Confederate and Union graves provides a context of what the Civil War was like.

What are some of the more strange galleries and museums?

Wisconsin is home to a number of odd places to view eclectic art and historic items. There are far too many to list them all, but here are some notable ones:

189

- A World of Accordions in Superior
- 319 Gallery and Bistro in Wausau
- Fred Smith's Wisconsin Concrete Park
- Against the Grain (carved hardwood and sewing antiquities) in Mineral Point
- Abler Art Glass Gallery (hand blown glass, metal art, oil paintings, and more) in Keil
- The Angel Museum in Beloit
- The Aztalan Museum in Lake Mills
- The C. J. Conner Studio (specializing in artwork of Wisconsin flora and fauna) in Chetek
- Cabin Fever Pottery (clay wall art) in Danbury
- The Chocolate Experience Museum in Burlington
- Curious Antiquities (the Midwest's largest collection of swords, armor, and artifacts) in Oconomowoc
- The Fennimore Doll and Toy Museum in Fennimore
- The International Clown Hall of Fame in Baraboo
- Mr. Marvel's Wondertorium (living history of shrunken heads, two-headed turtles, and more) in Wisconsin Dells

What is the Day the Duck Hunters Died?

In 1940, a perfect combination of cold Canadian air mixed with moist Gulf air stirred up a blizzard in the upper Midwest. Mild conditions persisted into the first part of November, and forecasters predicted colder temperatures for November 11, Armistice Day—later called Veterans Day. Cooler weather meant better duck hunting. Many hunters had the holiday off, and they made plans to hunt. A cold front dropped across Wisconsin and Minnesota, pushing temperatures from above freezing to deadly cold. Snow fell. Winds picked up. Blizzard.

Motorists were buried alive as drifts "three times as tall as a man" made driving impossible. Barometric pressure sank to all-time lows. Farmers would check on livestock and lose their way walking from their barn back to the house. Though nobody knows for sure, *Time* put the death toll at 159. Gordon MacQuarrie, outdoors editor for the *Milwaukee Journal*, wrote, "The winds of hell were loose on the Mississippi Armistice day and night. They came across the prairie, from the south and west, a mighty freezing force. They charged down from the high river bluffs to the placid stream below and reached with deathly fingers for the life that beat beneath the canvas jackets of hundreds of duck hunters."

To sportsmen, that day became known as the Day the Duck Hunters Died.

Is there a shipwreck museum in Wisconsin?

There is a shipwreck museum, but it's located in Michigan. The most famous display is about the *Edmund Fitzgerald*, which sank in 1975 on Lake Superior. The twenty-nine crew were all lost. At the time, the *Edmund Fitzgerald* was the largest ship on the Great Lakes.

Wisconsin has more shipwrecks on the National Register of Historic Places than any other state. There are fifty-five such wrecks, among them the *Appomattox*, the *Christina Nilsson*, the *Continental*, and too many more.

Which wreck is the most strange?

For twenty years Captain Herman Schuenemann (1865–1912) hauled Christmas trees and sold them from his deck to celebrants along the Lake Michigan shore. On November 22, 1912, he sailed the *Rouse Simmons* from Thompson, Michigan. On his second day out he sailed into the teeth of a northwest gale-force wind. He hoisted a distress flag, but the ship sank before rescuers could arrive.

For years afterward Christmas trees washed ashore, and the *Rouse Simmons* became known as the Christmas Tree Ship. The wreck is about twelve miles (19.3 kilometers) from Two Rivers, Wisconsin, 165 feet (50 meters) below the waves.

ATTRACTIONS

How important is tourism for the Wisconsin economy?

Tourism brought $20 billion into the state in 2016—a substantial increase over the previous year. More than 107 million visitors came to Wisconsin for the purpose of tourism, and international tourism brought $100 million into the state.

The state ranks first in the Midwest for fun, family atmosphere, affordability, and outdoor recreation. Wisconsin has won eighty-eight international, national, and regional awards.

Which counties bring in the most visitors?

The three counties ranked highest for direct visitor spending are Milwaukee, Dane, and Sauk Counties. Each of those counties had more than a billion dollars in tourism dollars. The top five counties for tourism-related employment include those three, with Brown and Walworth Counties added in, each employing more than ten thousand workers.

What is the most popular event in the state?

AirVenture, put on by the Experimental Aircraft Association every year near the first weekend in August, is an airshow featuring more than 15,000 planes of varying makes and models, from home-built, fixed-wing craft to the latest military hardware.

The 2017 show was attended by nearly 600,000 people. Whitman Field alone averaged 123 takeoffs and landings per hour over the ten days of the show. They hosted more than 1,100 home-built planes, nearly 1,200 vintage aircraft, 351 warbirds, and included ultralights, rotorcraft, and aerobatic demonstrations, including the Blue Angels.

How many rest areas are there in Wisconsin?

These facilities are scattered across the state along highways with at least four lanes. The thirty such sites are maintained by the Department of Transportation and open year-round. Waysides, on the other hand, have fewer amenities and are open seasonally—late May through early September.

Many times both rest areas and waysides have historical markers to commemorate a person, place or event. These are maintained by the Wisconsin State Historical Society.

Are there famous architectural attractions in Wisconsin?

Ranked second for popular attractions is Taliesin East in Spring Green. Frank Lloyd Wright's perfect country home was started in 1911 and was a work in progress until his death in 1959. The 600 acres (243 hectares) also feature the Monona Terrace Community and Convention Center.

Wright's work can be seen scattered throughout the state where he lived much of his life. Guided tours for Taliesin East run from May through October, though limited tours are available in April and November. The private estate is available only through these tours.

Taliesin East in Spring Green is one of the more famous works by architect Frank Lloyd Wright in Wisconsin.

Is House on the Rock another Frank Lloyd Wright project?

Close, but Alex Jordan only mimicked Wright's style. Also located in Spring Green, the House on the Rock is ranked twelfth on the Planetware web site.

Jordan wanted a retreat as awe inspiring as the scenery on Deer Shelter Rock. The facility has grown beyond Jordan's original vision to include many buildings, exhibits, and collections. Tours differ through the year, with a winter tour, a regular season tour, The Dark Side tours in the Halloween season, and the Christmas tours.

Is the Wisconsin capitol building an attraction?

Completed in 1971, the state capitol building is only 3 feet (0.9 meters) shorter than the U.S. Capitol in Washington, D.C. After a multimillion dollar renovation was completed in 2001, the building was put on the list of national historic landmarks.

Ranked the #3 attraction, the building is open to the public on weekdays from 8:00 A.M. to 6:00 P.M. Weekends and holidays they close at 4:00 P.M. Tours start at the information desk and run hourly from 9:00 to 3:00, skipping the noon hour, Monday through Saturday. Each tour lasts nearly an hour.

Read more about the Wisconsin capitol building in the chapter on the state capitol.

Where is the Harley Davidson Museum?

The museum is located in Milwaukee, the original home of the first Harley-Davidson motorcycle. The facility features more than 400 motorcycles, displays, and exhibits. Tours are year-round, with extended hours on Thursdays.

This museum is ranked #4 on the Planetware list. Read more about Harley-Davidson in the chapter on Manufacturing.

Are circuses on the list of attractions?

Circus World Museum in Baraboo ranks fifth and is a tribute to the circuses of Wisconsin. Formerly a leading national entertainment, circuses were appropriate for all ages. During the summer Circus World holds a Big Top show with traditional circus acts, complete with live animals.

Baraboo was once the home of the Ringling Brothers Circus.

What are "dells"?

A dell is a small hollow or valley, usually wooded. Ranking number six on the list of attractions in Wisconsin is the Dells on the Wisconsin River. This should not be confused with the city of Wisconsin Dells, though they're in the same area.

For five miles the state's largest river, the Wisconsin River, wanders through a gorge of sandstone cliffs with natural beauty along the way. Some of the flora and fauna is unique to the area, such as cudweed and six species of dragonfly. Tours of the area are conducted by boat; most famous are the duck boats.

The Dells are a series of sandstone cliffs surrounding the Wisconsin River in the middle of the state. They have become a popular spot for boating and nature lovers.

Are there other outdoor attractions in Wisconsin?

Ranked eighth on the Planetware list is the Land O' Lakes region. A great place for water sports, the area contains hundreds of lakes of all sizes. The area is perfect for camping or backpacking, and enthusiasts can also explore by boat or kayak.

For someone interested in bird watching, Land O' Lakes has some of the last remaining white-tailed eagles. The fishing is excellent, and during the winter visitors can use cross country skis or snowshoes.

Is Lambeau Field on the list of attractions in Wisconsin?

Ranked seventh, the home of the Green Bay Packers could hold nearly the entire population of the city of Green Bay. It's the only NFL team operated as a nonprofit, and is owned by more than 360,000 individual stockholders. There are self-guided tours for a behind-the-scenes look at how a professional football team operates.

Also on site is the Walk of Legends, a walkway showing two dozen "greats" from the team. Green Bay also boasts the Packers Heritage Trail, a walking tour of the city to view landmarks associated with the team.

For more on the Green Bay Packers, read the "Sports" chapter.

Why is Door County so popular?

At number ten, Door County is billed as the prettiest corner of Wisconsin. Not far from Green Bay, the peninsula juts out into Lake Michigan and forms the "thumb" of the state. There is trout fishing, sailing, diving, and more.

A lighthouse graces Sturgeon Bay—one of many such constructions in Wisconsin. Not far from that is Washington Island, home of the country's oldest Icelandic settlement.

Are there any good hiking trails in Wisconsin?

The state's myriad nature trails rank #11 on the list of Wisconsin attractions. The longest of the lot is the Ice Age National Scenic Trail, stretching more than a thousand miles (1,609 kilometers) from Potawatomi State Park to St. Croix Dalles.

Nature trails crisscross the state. A memorable one includes 117 miles (188 kilometers) of the North Country National Scenic Trail, which runs from the state of New York to North Dakota. An easier path for beginners is the Geneva Lake Shore Path, twenty-one miles (33.8 kilometers) of trail through country estates.

What is the driftless area?

During the ice age, glaciers missed scouring the landscape in parts of Wisconsin. Located about halfway between Chicago, Illinois, and Minneapolis, Minnesota, the scenery is within easy reach of many Wisconsin cities.

Scenic drives along the Mississippi River, as well as the Kickapoo and Wisconsin Rivers, will take a visitor through steep limestone bluffs, orchards, rolling farmland, and vineyards.

Hundreds of artists have made the driftless area their home. Historic sites are scattered throughout the regions. There is prime fishing, camping, and mountain biking, and when the leaves change color in the fall the scenery is breathtaking.

Where is Glacial Lake Wisconsin?

A glacial lake was formed during the ice age when a lobe of ice blocked the Wisconsin River, because the melting Laurentide Ice Sheet had no outlet. Lake depth reached perhaps 160 feet (48.8 meters) deep, and covered about a million acres (405,000 hectares). When the ice dam broke, the lake drained in less than a week, causing erosion and leaving behind steep cliffs and grass-topped spires where islands had been.

The Dells of the Wisconsin River are part of where the prehistoric lake had been.

Does Wisconsin have any tributes to their history of railroads?

The National Railroad Museum in Green Bay remembers the history of rail in Wisconsin. Steam engines, artifacts, and memorabilia are on display. The highlight of the museum is the Eisenhower Collection, which includes the streamlined engine used to pull the future president's military train across Europe in World War II.

Events, train rides, and tours are all available.

Is Glacial Lake Wisconsin a tourist attraction?

More than 550,000 acres (223,000 hectares) of public land and waterways are available for sightseeing, camping, water sports, and other outdoor activities. The Necedah National Wildlife Refuge is part of that whole.

There are wetlands, woodlands, lakes, bluffs, and some of the rarest Wisconsin wildlife. Portions of the National Ice Age Trail pass through Glacial Lake Wisconsin.

Which are the best places to visit in Wisconsin?

The website Vacationidea.com lists some of the best vacation spots in the state and gives several reasons to go to each. Those cities are Milwaukee, Madison, Lake Geneva, Spring Green, Green Bay, La Crosse, Kenosha, Eau Claire, the Bayfield Peninsula, Wausau, Oshkosh, and more.

Why is Milwaukee a vacation destination?

Milwaukee is home to many different museums, such as the Milwaukee Public Museum, Museum of Wisconsin Art, the Harley-Davidson Museum, and the Betty Brinn Children's Museum. They also have the forty-acre (16.2 hectare) Lynden Sculpture Garden, Marcus Center for the Performing Arts, the Milwaukee Ballet, a symphony orchestra, trails, kayaking, and Bradford Beach.

Other than being Wisconsin's capital city, what's special about Madison?

As with Milwaukee, Madison has museums scattered throughout the city. There is also a lively culture of performing arts. Included within the city are tours of the University of Wisconsin-Madison campus, Olbrich Botanical Gardens, and a huge array of hiking and cycling trails.

Keep in mind that's in addition to the historic capitol building, which is on the list of national historic landmarks.

Where is Lake Geneva, and why visit that city?

Just a few miles north of the border with Illinois, halfway from Lake Michigan to Beloit, Lake Geneva has year-round opportunities for vacationing, such as water sports, beaches, hiking and biking, even zip-lining or rides on hot air balloons.

The city has a historic downtown to explore, tours of the Black Point Estate and Gardens, and plenty of shopping and dining. During winter, there are sledding, skiing, skating, and other related activities.

Does Green Bay have anything other than a professional football team?

Green Bay is the oldest city in Wisconsin, dating back to the 1600s. They have a narrated trolley tour of the city so visitors can get familiarized with the city. They also have an amusement park, a wildlife sanctuary, zoo, recreational trails, the historic Meyer Theatre, and sightseeing on a riverboat.

Why is La Crosse listed as a vacation destination?

Nestled alongside the Mississippi River on the West coast of Wisconsin, La Crosse has a myriad of diverse activities available. One attraction is City Brewery, which holds tours across from the World's Largest Six Pack. Three large rivers in the state converge in the area—the Mississippi River, the Black River, and the La Crosse River. The La Crosse River Marsh is home to a very diverse grouping of wildlife.

There are six golf courses nearby, two historic districts in the city, water sports, and regular festivals throughout the year—the most famous is Oktoberfest. The city also hosts Riverfest, Irishfest, and Airfest.

Grandad Bluff Park is an excellent place to view the city of La Crosse. The Mississippi River separates Wisconsin from Minnesota, with two "big blue bridges" crossing the waterway.

Visible from the park at the far left is the (formerly nuclear) power plant in Genoa, and at the far right—in the distance—one can see the town of Trempealeau. The trip would take an hour by car and is forty miles (sixty-four kilometers) distant. In the middle of the left panorama is the Northeast corner of Iowa.

What notable beer attraction is found in La Crosse?

The "World's Largest Six Pack" is found across from City Brewery (formerly Heileman Brewing Company) in La Crosse, Wisconsin. There is enough beer within to fill more than seven million cans (2.5 million liters). If the entire stock were canned and placed end-to-end, the line of beer cans would stretch 565 miles (909 kilometers). There's enough beer for a person to have a six pack (2.13 liters) every day for 3,351 years.

Where is Grandad Bluff Park?

The park tops a large bluff 600 feet (183 meters) above the city of La Crosse. There is a picnic area, hiking trails, and at times a great place to watch fireworks put on by the La Crosse Skyrockers. That nonprofit organization has been in existence since 1929.

What can visitors do on the Apostle Islands?

Just off shore of Wisconsin in Lake Superior, the twenty-one Apostle Islands are only accessible by boat. The scenery is breathtaking, and the area provides a perfect opportunity for sailing, fishing, boating, or island hopping. Visiting the Sea Caves is a must for anyone taking a trip there, as are the Ice Caves in the winter.

On land, there are trails for hiking, camping, and lighthouses—the oldest built in 1856—to tour. Also on the Apostle Islands is the Hokenson Brothers Fishery complex, maintained by the National Park Service. The family retired in the mid-1960s, but the facility exists as a museum for people to explore the past.

The "World's Largest Six Pack" is found at the La Crosse plant for City Brewery. It packages fifty million cases of beverages a year.

Were there farms on the Apostle Islands?

The moderating influence of Lake Superior gave the islands a growing season forty days longer than on the mainland. However, the isolation never allowed farms there to compete with ventures that didn't need boats to move produce.

The soil was indeed great for fruits and vegetables. Imagine a four-foot (1.2 meter) cucumber, or a seventy-pound (31.8 kilogram) squash, even potatoes eight inches (20.3 centimeters) around. Though produce thrived, the farms didn't. As early as 1895, farms disappeared into second-growth forest. By the end of World War II, the last farm was gone.

What are some of the events held in Wisconsin?

Escapetowisconsin.com has a page filled with more than a thousand events held in the state. They range from plays at a history museum in Appleton to an exhibit in Outagamie County focusing on the people who lived and worked at the County Asylum.

Learn to dance, take rides in horse drawn carriages, take in an opera, or visit any of a number of light shows during the Christmas season. Take in a winery tour, listen as authors read their own poetry, or attend free concerts in the park.

What are some of the hidden attractions in Wisconsin?

Some of the out-of-the-way things to visit have already been mentioned, here and in other chapters. For instance, read about House on the Rock earlier here. FAST (Fiberglass Animals, Shapes and Trademarks) is in the chapter on Manufacturing. They have a fiberglass mold graveyard, where they place unusable sculptures. Below is a list of some of the more memorable attractions.

- Dr. Evermore's Forevertron—the world's largest scrap metal sculpture.
- Cave of the Mounds—a cave of colorful geological oddities.
- The Mustard Museum—a display of thousands of mustards from around the world.
- Al Johnson's Swedish Restaurant—complete with a grassy roof where goats graze.
- The Rock in the House—a mirror treatment of House on the Rock, but here the rock is in the house.
- Mount Horeb Trollway—a highway decorated with wooden troll sculptures.
- Sputnik Crash Site—a spot marked with a metal ring is the landing site of the Soviet satellite.
- Dead Pals of Sam Sanfillippo—amateur taxidermy museum with a large collection of white squirrels.

What are some of the more beautiful destinations in Wisconsin?

- Door County has already been mentioned, but there are many more attractions to lure visitors to Wisconsin.
- Boynton Chapel—modeled after twelfth-century Nordic style, just south of Baileys Harbor.

Gigantic fish, life-size elephants, and massive long-horn bulls are just some of the things you'll see in the "Fiberglass Graveyard" at FAST Corporation on the northeast side of Sparta.

- Amnicon Falls State Park—a covered bridge from which to view the Amnicon Falls.
- Parfrey's Glen—a cool and damp ravine ready for some creepy photo opportunities.
- Dells Mill—a five-story mill built in 1864, now a museum.
- Pewits Nest—glaciers created Skillet Creek, and its caverns. The scene is reminiscent of a pewit's nest.

What are some of the more scenic drives in Wisconsin?

Ranked the top scenic drive in the state by discoverwisconsin.com is Barron County in Northern Wisconsin. Here Rustic Road 83 in the town of Bear Lake winds through 4,100 acres (1,659 hectares) of forested land and intersects with the Ice Age National Scenic Trail.

How many other scenic drives are listed?

There are seven others, and ranked second is the Door County Coastal Byway. As the name suggests it's in Door county, and follows along sixty-six miles (106 kilometers) of Highway 42/57.

What scenic drive is ranked number three?

More than 33 miles (53 kilometers) of Highway 14 and Highway 33 wind through the Driftless Area. Hardwoods populate the ridges and valleys where the Amish keep their farms. Trout streams can be found, along with limestone bluffs, plenty of local diners, as well as a collection of family shops.

What are good places to watch leaves change in the fall?

Marinette County's Waterfall Tour is a great place to see fall color. The 125 miles (201 kilometers) of the loop feature more than a dozen waterfalls and cataracts. There are footbridges, picnic areas, and county parks to enjoy all along the way.

What is another area for fall color?

The Hayward Lakes area in Northern Wisconsin's Sawyer County has six fall color tours. The shortest is forty-five miles (72.4 kilometers), and the longest is seventy miles (113

What is the most recognizable scenic drive in the state?

The Great River Road follows the Mississippi along the Western edge of the state. For 250 miles (402 kilometers) Highway 35 runs from Prescott in the North to Kieler in the South. The drive features bluff top views, nature trails, and dozens of river towns along the way.

Nearly two-thirds of the drive is through protected habitat. Bird watching opportunities abound, and there are plenty of places for biking, boating, and other outdoor activities.

kilometers). Most of the driving routes are through the Chequamegon Nicolet National Forest, the Lac Courte Oreilles Indian Reservation, and the Blue Hills. The routes are well-marked, and the area is a prime vacation spot any time of year.

Are there other fall colors drives in Wisconsin?

There are still many other places to drive to watch trees change color in the fall. There is the Lake Superior Scenic Byway, the Kettle Moraine Scenic Drive, the Hilltop Color Tour, rustic roads in the Lake Geneva area, the Black River State Forest, the Wisconsin River/Baraboo Hills Tour, and an eighteen-mile (twenty-nine-kilometer) stretch of Highway 23 from Dodgeville to Spring Green.

Are there a lot of water parks in Wisconsin?

There are enough water parks in the state to have a "ten best" list for Wisconsin Dells alone. However, Travelwisconsin.com has a list of the best indoor water parks for the state.

Water Parks

Rank	Park Name	Location
1	Kalahari Resort & Convention Center	Wisconsin Dells
2	Chaos Waterpark	Eau Claire
3	Tundra Lodge Resort & Waterpark	Green Bay
4	Grand Lodge by Stoney Creek	Rothschild
5	The Waters of Minocqua	Minocqua
6	Blue Harbor Resort & Spa	Sheboygan
7	Timber Ridge Lodge	Lake Geneva

Each of these water parks is a perfect place to escape the cold, harsh winter. The whole family will have a lot of fun. It's a great way to escape cabin fever.

Other than water parks, what other kinds of resorts are available?

Pampering and relaxation come immediately to mind. The top resort for that is in Kohler, Wisconsin. The American Club was built in 1918 to be a home-away-from-home for immigrants employed by the Kohler Company. In 1978 it was placed on the National Register of Historic Places and underwent a transformation into a world-class resort.

The hotel features four champion-level golf courses and nine restaurants. The Kohler Waters Spa was given a five-star rating by Forbes. Only thirty-five spas in the world have that rating. Each of the 241 rooms pays homage to a famous American, with portraits and memorabilia.

What kind of resort is there for someone who doesn't want a spa?

The Osthoff Resort in Elkhart Lake is on 500 acres (202 hectares) overlooking a scenic lakefront. Recreational options include tennis, volleyball, various water sports, or even a cooking class.

Every day (Memorial Day through Labor Day) the resort hosts a lakeside bonfire, complete with s'mores. If a member of your party does want a spa, the Aspira Spa—on site—ranks among the top 100 in the nation.

What other great resorts are available in Wisconsin?

There are two other luxury resorts listed at Travelwisconsin.com:

1. The Blue Harbor Resort in Sheboygan, featuring a full service spa, a Jack Nicklaus Signature Golf Course, and the Beacon Bay indoor waterpark.
2. The Heidel House Resort and Spa in Green Lake is a popular destination for honeymoons. Acres of woodland surround the resort on Green Lake, the deepest inland lake in the state. There is plenty to do year round, from tennis to ice skating.

Are there great places for fishing in Wisconsin?

While Minnesota is listed as the state of 10,000 lakes (probably an understatement), Wisconsin has "one of the largest concentrations of natural lakes in the world." Vilas County alone has more than 1,300 lakes. There are thousands of places for great fishing opportunities across the state.

One of the best is Big Saint Germain Lake in Northern Wisconsin. The 1,600-acre (647-hectare) lake is large enough to allow huge muskies to grow. A professional guide said, "This is a trophy lake. It has big fish in high numbers. The population, food, and habitat are all bigger here."

What other kinds of fishing are good in Wisconsin?

What Big Saint Germain Lake is for muskies, Lake Winnebago is for sturgeon. The self-sustaining population is rated as one of the best in North America. Though the success rate is only around 13 percent, those fortunate enough to land a fish will find a giant in the neighborhood of 200 pounds (91 kilograms).

In addition to sturgeon, the lake boasts walleye, northern pike, largemouth bass, perch, and bluegill.

Where is a good spot for trout in Wisconsin?

Black Earth Creek has been protected from urban sprawl by conservation groups, so it is a prime spot for good trout fishing. Though Cross Plains and Black Earth are located right on the waterway, most people prefer to stay in Madison, twenty minutes away.

There is no end to the number of places one can fish in Wisconsin, such as Castle Rock Lake, where these friends have decided to relax.

The twenty-seven mile (forty-three-kilometer) creek runs through woodlands, and prairies, and has a good amount of brown, rainbow, and brook trout.

What other destinations have different varieties of fishing?

Lake Wisconsin and the Wisconsin River have a wide selection of fishing opportunities. Try Baraboo, Portage, Prairie du Sac, and Sauk City. There are walleye, crappie, largemouth bass, and even white bass.

The river and lake have a lot of sandbars and islands in choice locations. Nearby are accommodations for those not willing to camp.

Where are good places to hunt in Wisconsin?

The Department of Natural Resources has four hunting zones in the state: Central Farmland, Central Forest, Northern Forest, and Southern Farmland. The best time of year for bow (and crossbow) hunting runs from September into October.

The counties with the biggest yields are in the Central Farmland management zone—Waupaca, Marathon, and Shawano counties topping the list. In Southern Farmland hunters found the best luck in Sauk and Columbia Counties. Others have found luck in the other zones in Taylor and Adams Counties.

Has Wisconsin produced any trophy whitetails?

The state's highest scoring whitetail came from Buffalo County, which is ranked by Boone & Crockett as America's best county for trophies.

In 1973 the highest scored whitetail was taken from that county and scored 253 points. As of 2012 eighty-six deer from Buffalo County were registered in the Boone & Crockett record books.

What other counties have yielded trophies in Wisconsin?

Pope and Young has a list of ten of the best counties in the country, and Wisconsin has eight of them. In order of the most trophies, those counties are Buffalo (1,134), Trempealeau (481), Dane (417), Columbia (365), Sauk (340), Waupaca (334), Waukesha (288), and Polk (272).

If limiting the time frame to 2010 and beyond, all ten of the best counties are in Wisconsin.

What else is there to do in Wisconsin?

The opportunities are nearly endless. Thousands of destinations are available for every interest in every season. There are listings for festivals, natural wonders, and fun for the whole family.

SPORTS

BASEBALL

How many major league baseball teams are in Wisconsin?

There is only one team in Wisconsin currently in the Major League Baseball organization—the Milwaukee Brewers. Historically, quite a few professional ball clubs were based in Wisconsin. Limiting that list to MLB teams, there were only two others—the Milwaukee Braves (which moved from Boston, Massachusetts, in 1953, then to Atlanta, Georgia, for the 1966 season), and the Milwaukee Grays (which were in the National League). The Grays team lasted only one season—1878.

Was there another team known as the Milwaukee Brewers?

In the late 1800s a team known as the Milwaukee Brewers played in the Western League. In 1900 that league renamed itself the American League and the following year declared itself a major league. The franchise leadership of the Brewers intended to move the team to St. Louis but couldn't find an owner. They operated in Milwaukee for a "lame duck" season in 1901.

In 1902 the team moved to St. Louis and changed their name to the Browns. In 1953 the team moved to Baltimore and became the Orioles.

How did Milwaukee get the current Brewers baseball team?

The team began in Seattle, Washington, when the American League granted an expansion franchise originally called the Pilots. The organization lasted only the one season of 1969 before falling into bankruptcy.

In 1970, Brewers, Inc., bought the franchise for more than ten million dollars and moved it to Milwaukee.

205

Who headed the Milwaukee Brewers when they moved to Wisconsin?

The driving force for the Brewers came from Allan "Bud" Selig (1934–). His company bought the team less than a week before the start of the 1970 season.

Which baseball teams called County Stadium home?

The Milwaukee Braves played the first baseball games in County Stadium when it was completed in 1953. They played their last game there in 1965 before moving to Atlanta.

The Seattle Pilots became the Milwaukee Brewers in 1970 and played there until the new Miller Park was ready for the 2001 season.

The original cost of County Stadium was five million dollars, and the facility was demolished on February 1, 2001.

Who announced the first radio broadcasts for the Brewers?

Jimmy Dudley (1909–1999) announced for the Pilots while they played in Seattle, but when the team was bought he didn't make the move to Milwaukee. Another announcer, Bill Schonely (1929–2012), also stayed in Seattle.

The first announcer for the team in Milwaukee was Merle Harmon (1926–2009), who started with the team in 1970. He partnered with Bob Uecker (1935–) when he started in 1971. Over the decades there have been more than a dozen radio announcers, with Uecker still in the broadcast booth for many games.

Did Bob Uecker ever play professional baseball?

Uecker signed with the Milwaukee Braves in 1956 but didn't play in his first major league game until 1962. Even he wasn't impressed with himself, later poking fun at his undistinguished career.

He played for the St. Louis Cardinals and Philadelphia Phillies for a time before returning to the Atlanta Braves, where he retired in 1967.

His career stats across six years in the major leagues gives him a batting average of .200, scoring only sixty-five times in 297 games. His best years were his first two, when he hit .250.

A former Milwaukee Braves player, Bob Uecker (shown here in 2011) became best known for being a sportscaster for the Brewers.

What awards has Bob Uecker won?

Across more than six decades in professional baseball, Uecker has won the Ford Frick award (2003), was inducted into the National Sportscasters and Sportswriters Association (now known as the National

Sports Media Association) Hall of Fame (2011), and is a five-time honoree of that organization for Wisconsin Sportscaster of the Year (1977, 1979, 1981, 1982, 1987). He was inducted into the National Radio Hall of Fame in 2001, and in 2005—his fiftieth year in baseball—the team put a "50" in their Ring of Honor near the retired numbers of Robin Yount (1955–) and Paul Molitor (1956–).

On April 10, 2000, Uecker threw out the first pitch to celebrate thirty years as the voice of the Brewers. That day the team beat the Florida Marlins 4–3.

In 2012 the Brewers erected a Uecker Monument outside Miller Park near the statues of Hank Aaron (1934–), Robin Yount, and Bud Selig.

Did Bob Uecker ever act?

Uecker appeared as a sportswriter on the television show *Mr. Belvedere* (1985–1990), a series of Miller Lite commercials in the 1980s, movies such as *O. C. and Stiggs, Fatal Instinct,* and the *Major League* movie trilogy.

Uecker also had small parts in the television shows *Who's the Boss, D. C. Follies, Lateline* voiced a part in an episode of the animated series *Futurama*.

In what division did the Brewers originally play?

The team began in the American League West. In 1972 the team was placed in the AL East until they moved to the National League Central division in 1998. They currently play in the NL Central.

How did the Brewers play in their first game?

The Brewers drew more than 37,000 fans in their first game. They lost to the California Angels 12–0 on April 7, 1970, less than a week after the Pilots moved to Milwaukee and became the Brewers.

When did the team score their first win?

Four days after their first game, on April 11, 1970, the Brewers doubled up the White Sox 8–4 in Comiskey Park.

When was the team's first home win?

More than three weeks passed between the Brewers' first win and their first win at home. May 6, 1970, the Brewers shaded the Boston Red Sox 4–3. They'd already won five road games at that point.

Has snow ever interfered with a Brewers game on opening day?

Opening day at County Stadium was canceled because more than thirteen inches (thirty-three centimeters) of snow had fallen in Milwaukee on April 8, 1973, and into the following day. The groundskeeper told the *Milwaukee Journal*, "Nothing like this in the eighteen years that I've been with the Braves and Brewers."

Snow was knee deep in some areas, with the wind swirling snow up as far as the thirty-fifth row. Upper box seats were filled with snow, the mezzanine had big drifts, and unlike a football game it couldn't simply be pushed aside. The stadium manager said, "What if a guy hit a line drive and it landed in a snow pile?"

As many as two hundred people—including Bud Selig—helped shovel. Though a tarp had covered the field, the ground was still so soggy a helicopter was brought in to hover over the field to help dry the field.

On the rescheduled opening day, April 13, there were still drifts along the outfield fence and some snow lingered in the stands. The field was clear and dry as the Brewers shut out the Baltimore Orioles 2–0.

Were any other opening days snowed out for the Brewers?

On April 6, 1982, eight inches (20.3 centimeters) of snow pushed back another opening day at County Stadium. That one was delayed until April 16.

Rain has forced a reschedule of opening day a few times; sometimes it just delayed the start of a game. Even cold weather has forced alterations in their home opener. Since the current facility of Miller Park has a roof, it's unlikely there will be other weather-related issues for opening day.

Who was the first Brewers pitcher to win twenty games in one season?

On September 26, 1973, Jim Colborn (1946–) won his twentieth game, beating the New York Yankees 5–2. That same game, George Scott (1944–2013) drove in his hundredth run—another first for the franchise.

The following year Colborn won only ten games and lost thirteen.

How did Mike Caldwell earn his nickname?

"Iron Mike" earned his nickname for the sheer number of innings pitched. Across fourteen years he pitched 2,408.2 innings. In five of those fourteen seasons he hurled more than 200 innings.

In 1978 he pitched twenty-three complete games—six of those shutouts. On days when Caldwell took the mound in 1978, the bullpen was typically given the day off. That year he racked up a 22–9 record with an ERA of 2.36. He shut out the New York Yankees three times and pitched 293 innings.

When did the Brewers first draw a million fans in one season?

The Brewers sold their one-millionth ticket for the first time for the game on September 1, 1973. The Red Sox beat the Brewers that day 5–0. They finished the season with 1,092,158 tickets sold.

Only one other MLB pitcher has twenty-plus wins and twenty-plus complete games since Caldwell's 1978 season: Phil Niekro (1939–) with the Atlanta Braves, who had twenty-one wins and twenty-three complete games in 1979.

Who was the first Brewers pitcher to lose twenty games?

On September 22, 1974, Clyde Wright (1941–) lost his twentieth game, 6–5 to the Detroit Tigers.

Who were the three infielders to pitch on August 19, 1979?

Manager George Bamberger (1923–2004) couldn't find a good relief pitcher while playing the Texas Rangers. He ended up bringing in three infielders, Sal Bando (1944–), Jim Gantner (1953–), and Buck Martinez (1948–). They did the trick. The Brewers won the game 4–3 after a 7–3 loss to the Rangers the previous day.

When did the Brewers record their first winning season?

The first few years were tough, with their first year the worst. As the Seattle Pilots they racked up ninety-eight losses. The next year, their first in Milwaukee as the Brewers, they only improved by one game. In 1978 they finally registered a winning season at 93–69, finishing third in the AL East.

When did the team first play in the World Series?

In 1982, manager Harvey Kuenn (1930–1988) led the Brewers to win the ALDS in Game 5 and advance to the World Series. They lost to the Cardinals 4 games to 3.

Which player from the Brewers was the first to hit the cycle?

On September 3, 1976, Mike Hegan (1942–2013) hit a single, double, triple, and home run in the same game, making him the first member of the team to complete the cycle. They beat the Detroit Tigers 11–2.

He also held the record for the most error-free games (178) until that record was broken in 2007 by Kevin Youkilis (1979–) of the Boston Red Sox. That record of 238 games, started in 2007, went into the 2008 season.

When did Hank Aaron start with the Brewers?

Hank Aaron (1934–) originally signed with the Milwaukee Braves, and played his first game with that team on April 13, 1954. He stayed with the Braves when they moved to Atlanta, Georgia, in 1966.

He was traded to the Milwaukee Brewers on November 2, 1974, after recording his lowest season's batting average of .268. Over the next two years, he wrapped up his career with twenty-two home runs and ninety-five RBIs in 222 games. He hit his final home run on July 20, 1976, against the California Angels in Milwaukee. The Brewers won the game 6–2.

When did Hank Aaron wrap up his baseball career?

Hank Aaron's final at-bat came October 3, 1976, in County Stadium. He hit an RBI single against the Detroit Tigers, but Milwaukee lost 5–2.

How good was Hank Aaron?

Hank Aaron's #44 was the first Brewer number to be retired, which happened in 1976.

From 1964 through 1976, Aaron collected more RBI and extra-base hits than any other player in baseball. He was named an All-Star for twenty-one straight years, and for twenty consecutive seasons slugged at least twenty home runs. He hit better than .300 in fourteen seasons, and eight seasons he registered more than forty home runs.

Across his career he had a batting average of .305, hit 755 home runs, had 7,771 hits, and 2,297 RBI. He was awarded the Gold Glove in three consecutive seasons (1958–1960), helped win a World Series (1957), and held the home run record until broken by Barry Bonds (1964–) in 2007. Aaron is one of only three players to have more than 700 home runs along with Babe Ruth (1895–1948) and Barry Bonds.

Which player from the Brewers was the first to lead the American League in home runs?

Gorman Thomas (1950–) was picked up by the Brewers in time for him to have a breakout season in 1978 with thirty-two home runs and 86 RBI. The following year he led the American League with forty-five home runs and 123 RBI. In 1981 he was selected for the AL All-Star Team.

Despite rotator cuff surgery late in 1981, he led the league in home runs (thirty-nine) again in 1982 and had 112 RBI—fifth in the league.

In 1983 he was traded to the Cleveland Indians but returned to the Brewers in 1986 and finished his career in Milwaukee.

When did the Brewers get their first postseason berth?

Major League Baseball had a work stoppage in 1981. The first half of the season ended on June 12, and a strike by the players lasted for fifty days and wiped out a full one-third of the regular season.

The Brewers were able to win the second half of the season and ended up atop the American League East with a record of 62–47. This was their first ever postseason appearance. They played the Yankees and lost the ALDS in Game Five by a score of 7–3.

When did Rollie Fingers come to the Brewers?

Fingers (1946–) signed with the Kansas City Athletics in 1964 and stayed with the team when they moved to Oakland in 1968. After the 1976 season he moved to San Diego and played with the Padres through the 1980 season.

In 1981, the Padres traded Fingers to the Brewers. He won the Relief Man of the Year award, the AL MVP, and AL Cy Young award that year. He's the first relief pitcher in the major leagues to win the Cy Young award and MVP in the same season.

Were there any other Cy Young winners on the Milwaukee Brewers?

In 1982, Pete Vuckovich (1952–) won the Cy Young. His record was 18–6 that year, with an ERA of 3.34. He tied with Jim Palmer (1945–) of the Baltimore Orioles for the leading percentage of wins.

The following two years he pitched in pain, then discovered he'd torn a rotator cuff. He skipped surgery in favor of rehab therapy and despite attempts at a comeback was released by the Brewers in 1986.

Did the Brewers ever sweep the MVP and Cy Young award in consecutive years?

Rollie Fingers took both MVP and Cy Young for the American League in 1981. In 1982 Pete Vuckovich won the Cy Young with Robin Yount taking MVP honors. The Brewers were the first American League team to win both awards in consecutive seasons.

Did the Brewers ever play in the World Series?

Rollie Fingers' pitching went a long way to putting the Brewers into the postseason in 1982. They won the American League with a record of 95–67. Unfortunately, they lost the World Series in Game 7 by a score of 6–3.

Did Rollie Fingers pitch for the Brewers in the World Series?

Fingers was too injured to play in the World Series. On August 21, 1982, he be-

After successful stints with the Oakland A's and San Diego Padres, Roland "Rollie" Fingers finished off his MLB career with the Brewers, winning the MVP and Cy Young Awards in 1981.

came the first pitcher to record 300 saves. Less than two weeks later, he sustained a torn muscle in his pitching arm that left him in the dugout the rest of that season, including the World Series.

The ball club left his name on the roster, but he was unable to pitch. Manager Harvey Kuenn had hoped to use him in Game 7 of the World Series, but just prior to the game Fingers told him it was a no-go. "Up until that last day, he thought he could pitch," Kuenn said. "But if I had used him even once, that would have been it."

The injury was so bad Fingers missed the entire 1983 season as well.

Did Rollie Fingers ever pitch after missing the 1983 season?

Fingers came back to pitch again in 1984 and 1985, with his worst pitching his last season. He registered an ERA of 5.04, compared with his career ERA of 2.90. He was credited with twenty-three saves in 1984 and seventeen saves in 1985.

What was Rollie Fingers' injury?

A number of different publications have conflicting stories. According to the Milwaukee Brewers Media Guides, Fingers missed the final month of the 1982 season because of a torn muscle in his right (pitching) arm. On March 27, 1983, he was placed on the twenty-one-day disabled list with tendinitis, and on June 10 he had surgery to remove bone spurs from his right elbow and reattach a muscle that had pulled away from the bone. On August 15 he was placed on the sixty-day emergency disabled list.

Doctors had determined the initial muscle injury healed itself and Fingers had tendinitis. By May the diagnosis changed to bone spurs. Fingers claimed he felt the muscle tear near his elbow.

Is Rollie Fingers in the National Baseball Hall of Fame?

In all, Fingers pitched 1,701 innings across 944 games, and overall has 114 career wins. He recorded 341 saves and 1,299 strikeouts.

In 1992 he was inducted into the Hall of Fame, receiving 349 out of 430 votes by the Baseball Writers of America. His number of 34 was retired by the Brewers on August 9, 1992.

Which other Brewers players were inducted into the National Baseball Hall of Fame?

There are six players from the team in the National Baseball Hall of Fame. They are Hank Aaron (inducted in 1982), Rollie Fingers (inducted in 1992), Don Sutton (inducted in 1998), Robin Yount (inducted in 1999), Paul Molitor (inducted in 2004), and Trevor Hoffman (inducted in 2018).

Why was Paul Molitor inducted to the National Baseball Hall of Fame?

Third baseman Paul Molitor (1956–) was described by Hall of Famer Ted Williams (1918–2002) as another Joe DiMaggio (1914–1999). Across 10,835 at bats he racked up 3,319 hits, drove in 1,307, hit 234 home runs, and stole 504 bases. His career batting average came to .306.

In his fifteen years with the Milwaukee Brewers he played 1,856 games, hit .303, and drove in 790 runs. He played in the 1981 ALDS and helped the team advance to the World Series in 1982. His batting average that year of .302 went a long way to pushing the Brewers into the World Series.

He played for the Brewers from 1978 until he was sent to the Toronto Blue Jays (1993–1995) and was voted the World Series MVP in 1993, then moved to the Minnesota Twins (1996–1998).

What awards were won by Molitor?

Molitor won too many awards to list them all, but the major awards include the Silver Slugger four times, being named to the AL's All-Star Game team seven times, the Hutch Award, Babe Ruth Award, Edgar Martinez Award (twice), World Series MVP, Lou Gehrig Memorial Award, and the Branch Rickey Award.

Why was Don Sutton named to the National Baseball Hall of Fame?

Pitcher Don Sutton (1945–) had a winning record of .559 across 774 games—178 of those complete games and fifty-eight shutouts. His twenty-three-year career gave him an ERA of 3.09 with more than 5,000 innings pitched.

His three years with the Brewers gave him a record of .500. He pitched 486.2 innings and had an ERA of 3.86.

What awards did Don Sutton earn?

Sutton played in the All-Star Game four times, won the Lou Gehrig Memorial Award, was the All Star MVP in 1977, and won the National League ERA title.

Did Don Sutton make any other notable accomplishments?

On June 28, 1983, Sutton (1945–) struck out his 3000th batter. He became only the eighth pitcher to hit that milestone. The following year he became the first MLB pitcher to strike out at least a hundred batters in nineteen consecutive seasons.

Did Cecil Cooper set any franchise records for the Brewers?

In 1983, Cooper (1949–) set a franchise record with 126 RBI. The record stood until 2009, when Prince Fielder (1984–) racked up 141 RBI.

Pitcher Don Sutton played with several MLB teams, including the Brewers from 1982 to 1984.

213

What was the longest game the Brewers played?

On May 9, 1984, the Brewers lost to the Chicago White Sox 7–6 in twenty-five innings. The game started on May 8, and was suspended in the top of the twenty-first inning when a 1:00 curfew halted action. The score was tied at 3–3. The game resumed on the 9th, with Ben Oglivie (1949–) hitting a three-run homer for the Brewers in the twenty-first inning. The White Sox scored three times in the bottom of the inning to keep the action going. A solo homer in the twenty-fifth put the White Sox ahead for good.

The entire game lasted eight hours and six minutes, setting a record for the longest game in major league baseball. Even that didn't break the record for the number of innings. The Brooklyn Robins (later called the Dodgers) and Boston Braves played to a 1–1 tie on May 1, 1920, when the game was called due to darkness after twenty-six innings.

What is the longest nine-inning game played by the Brewers?

On July 10, 1983, the Brewers played the longest nine-inning game to that point in the American League. After four hours and eleven minutes, the Brewers beat the Chicago White Sox 12–9. The record was broken in 2006 by the New York Yankees and the Boston Red Sox.

What is the all-time record for attendance in Milwaukee for a single season?

The most fans to watch the Brewers came in 1983—the year after their World Series run—when 2,397,131 fans attended games in County Stadium.

When did Robin Yount collect his 2000th hit?

On September 6, 1986, Yount hit number 2,000. The Brewers lost the game 17–9 to the Cleveland Indians at County Stadium.

When did Robin Yount record his 3,000th hit?

On September 9, 1992, Yount became the seventeenth player in the majors to hit number 3,000. The hit came in the seventh inning of a game against the Cleveland Indians at County Stadium. The Brewers lost by a score of 5–4.

He was the third-youngest to achieve that milestone, behind only Ty Cobb (1886–1961) and Hank Aaron.

Across his career he racked up 3,142 hits.

Hall of Famer Robin Yount played shortstop and center field for the Brewers from 1974 to 1993.

When was Robin Yount inducted into the National Baseball Hall of Fame?

Robin Yount was drafted by the Brewers when he was 18. In his twenty-year career with the Brewers he played 2,856 games, registered 3,142 hits, 251 home runs, and drove in 1,406. He retired with a batting average of .285 in 1993 and was inducted into the National Baseball Hall of Fame in 1999—his first year of eligibility.

How many times did Yount earn the MVP?

Before Yount, only three shortstops had won the MVP in the American League. Yount was number four in 1982 in a near-unanimous vote. Injuries forced him into the out-field in 1985, and in 1989 he picked up a second MVP award, making him only the third player in MLB history to earn the award for two different positions.

What other awards did Yount earn?

Yount was an All-Star in 1980, 1982, and 1983. He received the Gold Glove in 1982, and three times earned the Silver Slugger—1982, 1983, and 1989. His number 19 was retired by the Brewers on May 24, 1994.

Who was the first of the modern Brewers to be inducted into the National Baseball Hall of Fame?

Robin Yount became the first player wearing a Brewers cap to be honored, July 25, 1999.

Officially, however, Hugh Duffy of the 1901 Milwaukee Brewers was the first overall.

Which newspaper named Robin Yount their Player of the Decade?

USA Today proclaimed Yount their Player of the Decade for the 1980s. Baseballanalysts.com lists him among baseball's greatest players for that decade, along with Wade Boggs (1958–), George Brett (1953–), Rickey Henderson (1958–), Dale Murphy (1956–), Tim Raines (1959–), Cal Ripken Jr. (1960–), and Mike Schmidt (1949–).

When did the Brewers record their first no-hitter?

On April 15, 1987, Juan Nieves (1965–) recorded the first no-hitter for the team. They beat the Orioles in Baltimore 7–0. That also made him the first player from Puerto Rico to accomplish the feat.

What was the best start to a season for the Brewers?

In 1987, the Brewers tied a major league record with thirteen wins to kick off the season. Across their first eighteen games, they lost once—an American League record.

Starting on May 12 that year they dropped twelve straight games and finished the season 91–71—third in the American League East.

215

What is the franchise record for the most runs scored in an inning?

On July 8, 1990, the team set a franchise record with thirteen runs in the fifth inning. They beat the Angels 20–7.

When did Paul Molitor record his 2,000th hit?

Molitor became the fourth Milwaukee player to hit for the cycle on May 15, 1991, and on June 30 got his 2,000th hit. The team retired his #4 on July 11, 1999.

Did any other Milwaukee player ever have 2,000 hits?

On June 12, 1983, Ted Simmons (1949–) hit number 2,000. The Brewers edged the New York Yankees 6–5. He retired from the Atlanta Braves in 1988 with 2,472 career hits.

Robin Yount totaled more than 3,000 in his career.

Who was the first Brewers player to win Rookie of the Year?

In 1992, Pat Listach (1967–) recorded 168 hits across 149 games—twenty-six of them extra-base hits. He stole fifty-four bases and had a batting average of .290. He was voted the American League Rookie of the Year.

Two years later, in 1994, his batting average peaked at .294 across only sixteen games. He was traded to Houston before the 1997 season, his last in the major leagues, where he hit .182.

When did the Brewers acquire a new stadium?

On August 19, 1995, the Brewers unveiled plans to build a new stadium with an estimated cost to the taxpayer of $250 million. The Wisconsin State Assembly passed the financing package on September 28 by a vote of 52–47. The State Senate approved the plan on October 6 by a vote of 16–15 after failing to pass twice the previous night. Governor Tommy Thompson (1941–) signed the bill into law on October 12.

Groundbreaking for the new stadium came on November 9. Their first game took place on April 6, 2001, when the Brewers beat the Cincinnati Reds 5–4. President George W. Bush (1946–) and Commissioner Bud Selig attended.

When was the final game at County Stadium?

The last game at County Stadium came on September 28, 2000. Olympic gold medalist and Brewer farmhand Ben Sheets appeared, as did Hall of Famers Hank Aaron and Warren Spahn (1921–2003) of the Milwaukee Braves, Willie Davis (1940–2010) and Jim Taylor (1981–) from the Green Bay Packers, as well as Rollie Fingers and Robin Yount from the Brewers.

Milwaukee lost the game to the Cincinnati Reds 8–1.

When was Miller Park opened?

A crane lifting a section of roof into place collapsed on a windy day, killing three workers on July 14, 1999. A camera crew caught the event on video. Originally scheduled to

Completed in 2001 and home of the Brewers, Miller Park is both architecturally beautiful and functionally well designed. In 2012 it was awarded the best ballpark by MLB.

open in 2000, the deaths resulted in an investigation and repair work, pushing completion into 2001. The first game played was on April 6, with the Brewers beating the Cincinnati Reds 5–4.

Has Miller Park won any awards?

In 2012, ESPN.com ranked Miller Park as Major League Baseball's best ballpark in fan voting. In 2013, they ranked Miller Park as third in the "stadium experience" category and eighth in "affordability."

The Brewers continue to make updates to the facility, including a state-of-the-art high definition scoreboard, stores, party suite, and outdoor Plaza Pavilion. When the team is on the road, the stadium hosts major musical concerts and has been used for on-site filming of movies (such as *Mr. 3000* in 2004). The facility has also hosted the Professional Bowlers Association finals and the Midwest's largest youth chess tournament.

When did the Brewers play their first interleague game?

On June 13, 1997, the Brewers became the first American League team to play a regulation game at Wrigley Field in Chicago since the 1945 World Series. They beat the Cubs 4–2.

Did the Brewers ever lose more than a hundred games in the same season?

On September 21, 2002, the Brewers registered their hundredth loss. The San Francisco Giants took the game 3–1. Milwaukee finished the season 56–106.

They started the season at 3–12 and fired manager Davey Lopes (1945–), but Jerry Royster (1952–) didn't improve things. The team averaged only 3.87 runs per game that season, the worst in MLB. Their pitching wasn't much better—second worst in the NL with a 4.73 ERA.

Did Milwaukee ever host the All-Star Game?

Milwaukee hosted three All-Star Games for MLB. The first came in 1955 where the National League won 6–5 at County Stadium. The second came in 1975, with the National League winning again, this time 6–3 at County Stadium. The third All-Star game—the first in Miller Park—came in 2002.

The final score of that game came to a 7–7 tie, as both teams exhausted their rosters after eleven innings.

When did the Brewers move to the National League?

In the 1990s, Major League Baseball wanted to even out the number of teams in the American League and National League. At the time, there were fourteen teams in the AL, sixteen in the NL. The Brewers moved to the NL Central when the Tampa Bay Devil Rays joined the AL East in a 1998 expansion and Houston moved to the AL West.

After all the realignment was finished, there were three divisions in each of the two leagues. The Brewers played their first NL game on March 31, 1998, losing to the Atlanta Braves 2–1.

When did the team get their first NL win?

On April 2, 1998, Jeromy Burnitz (1969–) hit a grand slam in the eleventh inning, and the Brewers beat the Braves in Atlanta 8–6.

Did Manager Phil Garner ever reach 500 wins?

On August 26, 1998, Garner (1949–) earned his five hundredth victory against the Rockies in Colorado. The Brewers won the game 6–5.

Garner is the only Brewers manager to hit that milestone. Across eight years with the team he racked up 563 wins, but lost 617. In his entire fifteen-year career he had a record of 985–1054.

When did Brewers owner "Bud" Selig become commissioner of MLB?

Allan "Bud" Selig was unanimously elected commissioner by baseball owners on July 9, 1998. He set aside his interest in the Milwaukee Brewers and relinquished all involvement.

He retired from the office of commissioner on January 14, 2015, and was elected to the National Baseball Hall of Fame on December 4, 2016. He had the second-longest tenure as commissioner after Judge Kenesaw Mountain Landis (1866–1944), the first to hold the office as commissioner, from 1920 to 1944.

What were some of Selig's accomplishments while commissioner?

His most significant contribution to baseball was a historic labor agreement with the Players Association on August 31, 2002. He avoided a work stoppage and gave major concessions to the baseball clubs. That was the first time in thirty years a new contract was agreed upon without a strike by the players.

He instituted interleague play, oversaw significant revenue sharing among the clubs, started an extra tier of playoffs called the Wild Card, and gave home field advantage for the World Series to the league winning the annual All-Star Game.

Another historic achievement was instituting a tougher drug-testing policy on

Bud Selig is a former owner of the Brewers who served as the ninth commissioner of the MLB.

November 15, 2005. First offenders would be suspended for fifty games, a second offense resulted in a suspension of one hundred games, and a third offense required a lifetime ban.

What was the biggest comeback win for the Brewers?

The team was losing big to the Cincinnati Reds on April 28, 2004. Down by a score of 9–0, they came back for a 10–9 win in Miller Park.

When were the Brewers sold?

On January 16, 2004, Wendy Selig-Prieb (Bud Selig's daughter) and the board of directors announced the team was up for sale. On October 6, Mark Attanasio (1957–) was introduced as a prospective buyer. On January 13, 2005, the owners unanimously approved the sale of the team to Attanasio.

What is the longest streak of losing seasons for the Brewers?

A number of teams have lost twenty or more games in a row in a single season. The Brewers, widely considered a sub-par team, never lost that many in a row in one season. They have, however, put together an impressive record of losing seasons.

In 2005, Milwaukee broke a twelve-season streak of losing seasons by finishing 81–81—a fourteen-game improvement over the previous year. In the 2007 season they posted a winning season, finishing 83–79 to place second in the NL Central.

What is the greatest number of home runs the Brewers hit in a single inning?

The major league record for home runs in a single inning is five. The Brewers tied that on April 22, 2006, in an 11–0 win against the Cincinnati Reds. The home runs were hit by Bill Hall (1979–), Damian Miller (1969–), Brady Clark (1973–), J. J. Hardy (1982–), and Prince Fielder—all in the fourth inning.

The other teams to hit five homers in the same inning are the Minnesota Twins on June 9, 1966, against the Kansas City Royals, the New York Giants on June 6, 1939, against the Cincinnati Reds, the Philadelphia Phillies on June 2, 1949, against the Cincinnati Reds, and the San Francisco Giants on August 23, 1961, also against the Cincinnati Reds.

Since their appearance in the World Series in 1982, have the Brewers ever clinched a postseason berth?

On September 28, 2008, the last day of the regular season, the team clinched a wild card position, beating the Chicago Cubs 3–1. They finished the season 90–72, but fell to the Pirates 3–1 in the NLDS. That was their first postseason appearance since moving to the National League in 1998.

In 2011 they qualified again for the postseason. They beat the Arizona Diamondbacks three games to two in the NLDS, but lost to the St. Louis Cardinals in the NLCS in Game Six of the series. They reached the postseason in 2018 as well.

How was attendance in 2008?

With the team doing so well, attendance was way up. The stadium sold out forty-four times that season, including twenty-two games straight from July 10 through September 1. That season overall ticket sales topped three million for the first time in team history.

The team reached the three million attendance mark in 2009 for the second time.

How did the Brewers acquire CC Sabathia?

On July 7, 2008, Cy Young winner Sabathia (1980–) was traded to Milwaukee from the Cleveland Indians. In return, the Indians received an outfielder, two pitchers, and a player to be named later.

Sabathia posted a record that season of 11–2 with a 1.65 ERA for the Brewers.

When was the first no-hitter pitched at Miller Park?

That first no-hitter didn't involve the Brewers. Because of Hurricane Ike, two games scheduled for September 14 and 15 of 2008 between the Houston Astros and the Chicago

---

Who was the first Brewers pitcher to start in an All Star Game?

In 2008, Ben Sheets (1978–) threw a pair of scoreless innings in Yankee Stadium. That was the final season for the old Yankee Stadium.

Cubs were played in Miller Park. The Cubs won both games (5–0 and 6–1), with the no-hitter by Carlos Zambrano (1981–) on the 14th.

Who won the NL MVP in 2011?

Ryan Braun (1983–) was named MVP on November 22. He was the first Brewers player since 1989 to take home the honor. That was only the fourth time in franchise history for a Brewers player, but only the third Brewers player.

The others were Rollie Fingers (1981) and Robin Yount, who picked up the award twice (1982 and 1989).

Was Ryan Braun ever suspended for violations of the league's drug policy?

On July 22, 2013, Braun was handed a sixty-five-game suspension. Since the suspension stipulated "without pay," he lost more than three million dollars.

Brewers left fielder Ryan Braun received the MVP award in 2011. As of the end of 2018, he has a batting average of .299, 1,802 hits, and 322 home runs.

The suspension was for involvement with a Florida company, Biogenesis, which distributed performance-enhancing drugs. Commissioner Bud Selig's statement of Braun's suspension used the phrase "unspecified violations" of baseball's drug program and labor contract.

Has a catcher ever had two seven-RBI games in the same season?

Jonathan Lucroy (1986–) is the first in Major League Baseball to produce two such games in the same season. The first game came on May 20, 2012, with a 16–4 win over the Minnesota Twins. On August 30, Lucroy repeated the performance during a 12–11 loss to the Chicago Cubs.

What is the longest time the Brewers spent with the best record in baseball?

In 2014, *Sports Illustrated* asked the question, "Is this the best Milwaukee Brewers team ever?" They started the season 49–32, two games better than the 1979 team and tied by the 2007 squad. They were on pace to a franchise record of 96 wins. They spent 150 days with the best record in all of baseball.

Instead, they melted down and finished the season at 82–80, failing to make a postseason appearance. In July they lost sixteen of twenty-five games.

How good was the team in 2018?

The Milwaukee Brewers finished the season at 96–67 after a one-game, tie-breaking playoff with the Chicago Cubs, winning 3–1. They advanced through the NLDS by sweeping the Colorado Rockies in three games.

The Brewers took the NLCS into Game 7 but missed out on the World Series after falling to the Los Angeles Dodgers 5–1.

Did Christian Yelich win any major awards in 2018?

Outfielder Christian Yelich (1991–) was certainly a big contributor to the Brewers' success in the 2018 postseason. He was the National League Batting Champion and received his second Silver Slugger Award, as well as the Hank Aaron Award. On November 15, 2018, he won the National League MVP award.

Yelich also played in the All-Star Game in 2018 and ranked quite highly in many categories in MLB. For the 2018 season, he played 147 games, drove in 110, and had a batting average of .326. He was also named Player of the Month for September of 2018 and was named Player of the Week three separate times.

Yelich ranked as second in the NL for runs (118) and hits (187) and tied for third in home runs (36) in the regular season.

Did a Brewers pitcher start two consecutive games in the 2018 postseason?

Left-handed pitcher Wade Miley (1986–) started in both Game 5 and Game 6 in the NLCS, but after Miley pitched to only one batter in Game 5—a walk on five pitches—manager Craig Counsell (1970–) changed pitchers to put a right-hander on the mound.

Miley became the first pitcher to start consecutive games in the postseason since George Earnshaw (1900–1976) started in Game 5 and Game 6 of the 1930 World Series.

Which numbers have been retired by the Milwaukee Brewers?

Retired Brewers Numbers

Number	Player	Position	Years in Milwaukee	Year No. Retired
4	Paul Molitor	Infield	1978–92	1999
19	Robin Yount	Shortstop/Outfield	1974–93	1994
34	Rollie Fingers	Pitcher	1981–85	1992
42	Jackie Robinson	Second Base	–	1997
44	Hank Aaron	Outfield	1954–65, 1975–76	1976
50	Bob Uecker	Catcher/Announcer	1971–	2005

Jackie Robinson's (1919–1972) number was retired by Major League Baseball in 1997, and the Brewers held a ceremony at County Stadium on July 18 of that year to formally retire the number from the Brewers organization, even though Robinson never played for Milwaukee. However, pitcher Scott Karl (1971–) already wore that number

---

What did the Brewers hope to gain by pulling Miley after one batter?

The move was representative of a new trend in baseball in which the manager uses a relief pitcher to start the game and then almost immediately switches to another pitcher. The move is designed to take advantage of matchups (for example, using a right-handed pitcher against a right-handed batter).

The Brewers lost that game 5–2.

---

and continued to do so until he was traded to the Colorado Rockies in December of 1999. The Rockies gave him #19.

Mariano Rivera (1969–) was the last player in Major League Baseball to wear #42, and he did so until the New York Yankees retired the number in 2013.

Bob Uecker never used #50, but as part of a ceremony celebrating his fiftieth year in baseball, the team retired the number in his honor.

BASKETBALL

When did professional basketball begin in Wisconsin?

The Sheboygan Red Skins were founded in 1933. They played in the National Basketball League (NBL) and were a charter member of the National Basketball Association (NBA), and then played in the National Professional Basketball League (NPBL).

When the National Basketball League and the Basketball Association of America (BAA) merged in 1949 to form the National Basketball Association, the small market of Sheboygan, Wisconsin, couldn't compete with larger, better-funded, teams. They left the NBA for the NPBL and played there for a single season before that league folded.

The Red Skins played independently for another season before hanging it up in 1952.

Were there other professional teams in Wisconsin?

The Buffalo Bisons were established in 1946. After only thirty-eight days in Buffalo, New York, the team moved to Moline, Illinois, and changed their name to the Tri-Cities Blackhawks. Originally a member of the NBL, that league and the BAA merged to become the NBA in 1949.

In 1951 the team moved to Milwaukee and became the Hawks. They moved to St. Louis in 1955, then to Atlanta in 1968.

The Oshkosh All-Stars, founded in 1929, played in the NBL until the team dissolved in 1949—another casualty of the trend toward bigger markets in the NBA.

There were also three teams in the Continental Basketball Association, a team in the International Basketball League, and another in the Women's Professional Basketball League. The teams, as well as the leagues, no longer exist under those names.

Who was the Bucks' first head coach?

Larry Costello (1931–2001) played in the NBA for most of the years from 1954 to 1968 as a point guard. His career field goal percentage was .438 across twelve seasons. He made the All-Star team in six seasons, the last in the 1964–1965 season.

In 1968 he was named the Milwaukee Bucks' first head coach.

What was Costello's record with the Bucks?

From his first game in 1968 to his last game in 1976, Costello's record was 674–410. In five of his nine full seasons with the Bucks franchise, he earned a winning record. In his first season he went 27–55, then he came out ahead in the next five. In the two full seasons starting in 1974 and 1975, he registered 38–44 losing seasons.

In 1976 he coached only eighteen games, winning only three, before resigning on November 22. He was hired by the Chicago Bulls in 1978 but was fired after fifty-six games with a record of 20–36. That ended his coaching career with a total of 430–300, a winning average of .589.

How did the team become known as the Bucks?

The organization held a contest to name the new team. More than 14,000 fans participated, and forty-five of them voted for the name "Bucks."

One fan indicated that the name suggested spirit, good jumping, speed, and agility. The name was confirmed on May 22, 1968.

How did the Bucks raise money?

The organization issued 300,000 common shares that sold at five dollars each to Wisconsin residents. They were so popular the franchise later sold another 125,000.

The team was bought by millionaire Herb Kohl (1935–) in 1985 for $18 million, assuring the team would have adequate funding and blocking a movement to move the team to California. He owned the team and served as president of the organization for twenty-nine seasons.

Who started the Milwaukee Bucks?

A group of investors—headed by Wesley D. Pavalon (1933–2009) and Marvin L. Fishman (1925–2009)—was awarded an NBA franchise on January 22, 1968. Milwaukee Professional Sports and Services was incorporated on February 5, with Pavalon named president Fishman named vice president.

How did the Bucks perform under Herb Kohl?

Kohl owned the team for twenty-nine seasons, and under his tenure the Bucks compiled a record of 1,084–1,268. There were twelve coaches, and the team earned fourteen postseason appearances.

When did Herb Kohl sell the Bucks?

After weeks of rumors, Herb Kohl announced the sale of the Milwaukee Bucks on April 17, 2014, to Marc Lasry (1959–) and Wesley Edens (1961–), two hedge fund investors. The expected sale price of $550 million topped the $535 million for the Sacramento Kings the previous year. The prospective owners pledged $100 million for a new multipurpose arena.

In January of that year, *Forbes* Magazine had listed the Milwaukee Bucks as the least valued team in the NBA, estimating its worth at $405 million. The magazine also listed Lasry's net worth at $1.5 billion, placing him among the 400 wealthiest Americans.

When was the Bucks' NBA debut?

A crowd of less than 5,000 watched the Bucks in their first game, October 16, 1968. They lost to the Chicago Bulls 89–84 in the Milwaukee Arena. Jon McGlocklin (1943–) scored the first points in team history on a jumper only thirteen seconds into the game. Guy Rodgers (1935–2001) led the team with sixteen points.

Which team did they beat in their first victory?

Wayne Embry (1937–) led the Bucks in scoring with thirty points, becoming the first player on the team to reach that milestone. After losing five straight, they beat the Detroit Pistons in Milwaukee 134–118 for their first win, October 31, 1968.

Did Embry get selected to the Hall of Fame?

Embry was inducted into the Hall of Fame in 1999, though he only played one season for the Bucks. Across his career he shot a .440 and averaged 12.5 points per game. He played in six consecutive All-Star Games and ranked in the top ten in field goal percentage.

When did the Bucks have their first sellout game?

The Bucks beat the Baltimore Bullets 126–117 in front of a capacity crowd of 10,746 on February 27, 1969. Flynn Robinson (1941–2013) led the team with thirty-five points.

Center Wayne Embry played for Cincinnati and Boston before finishing out his stellar career with the Bucks.

Who was Jonny Mac?

Jon McGlocklin (1943–) was known as the "Original Buck," having been with the organization since they formed in 1968. "Jonny Mac" averaged 19.6 points per game in that inaugural season. He played for eight years for Milwaukee, and his name appears in five categories on the team's all-time career leader's list.

After retiring from play in 1976, McGlocklin joined the front office at the Bucks. That same year he and Eddie Doucette (the original "Voice of the Bucks") founded the Midwest Athletes Against Childhood Cancer. The organization has raised more than forty-five million dollars (U.S.) to fight childhood cancer.

Jon McGlocklin is a longtime broadcaster, providing color commentary on television for the Bucks.

Why was Bob Lanier elected to the Hall of Fame?

Lanier (1948–) was the first overall pick in the 1970 draft, chosen by the Detroit Pistons. He played there until traded on February 4, 1980, shooting a whopping .508 with 22.7 points per game.

After moving to Milwaukee, his field goal percentage improvedto .541, but he only produced 13.5 points per game.

Across his career he appeared in eight All-Star Games, earning MVP honors in 1974. For the four seasons running 1971–1972 through 1974–1975, he ranked in the top ten in field goals. He retired from the Bucks in 1984.

When did Hall of Famer Guy Rodgers play for the Bucks?

Guy Rodgers Jr. was one of a number of Hall of Fame players who played in Milwaukee at the same time. From 1968 to 1970 he played with the Bucks, Oscar Robertson (1938–) started with the team in 1970, Wayne Embry played in the 1968–1969 season, and Kareem Abdul-Jabbar (1947–) played from 1969 to 1975.

Rodgers played for Milwaukee in 145 games, shot .373, and averaged 7.2 points per game. Across his career, from 1958 to 1970, he played 892 games, shot .378, and averaged 11.7 points per game.

Four times in five seasons he played in the All-Star Game, twice ranked first in the NBA for games played, and ranked first in assists. Rodgers was inducted into the Hall of Fame in 2014.

Kareem Abdul-Jabbar played with the Bucks from 1969 to 1975 before being traded to the L.A. Lakers.

When did the Bucks acquire Kareem Abdul-Jabbar?

Lew Alcindor, who later changed his name to Kareem Abdul-Jabbar, was the first round draft pick of the Milwaukee Bucks in the 1969 draft.

How did the Bucks end up with the number one draft pick?

The teams that finished last in each division were awarded the chance to pick first. A coin toss on March 19, 1969, determined which team—Bucks or Phoenix Suns—would pick first. The name of the draft pick was a foregone conclusion. Lew Alcindor from UCLA, at seven feet one inch (216 centimeters) tall, literally stood out of the available picks.

In New York, then-commissioner J. Walter Kennedy (1912–1977) tossed a 1964 Kennedy half-dollar coin into the air. The Suns called "heads" based on a fan vote and lost the pick. The Bucks chose Lew Alcindor. Jerry Colangelo (1939–), general manager of the Suns, said he was shell-shocked. He drove around Phoenix, Arizona, for hours trying to shake the mood.

In Milwaukee, the principle owner of the Bucks, Wes Pavalon, and his vice president/general manager, John Erickson, hugged. Pavalon was so excited he forgot he had a lit cigarette in his mouth and jammed it into Erickson's ear. Erickson said, "It stung a little bit, but I didn't notice it. I didn't care, once we had Lew."

When did the Bucks first enter the postseason?

The Bucks picked up two rookies for the 1969–1970 season who improved the team enough to put them in the playoffs: Kareem Abdul-Jabbar and Bob Dandridge (1947–). Both players earned "All Rookie" status.

Abdul-Jabbar finished the season as the NBA's second-leading scorer with 28.8 points and 14.5 rebounds. The Bucks improved by twenty-nine games over the previous season. They beat the Philadelphia 76ers in the Division Semifinals 4–1 and fell to the New York Knicks in the Division Finals by the same record, 4–1.

What notable achievements did the Bucks rack up in the 1969–1970 season?

On March 8, 1970, Kareem Abdul-Jabbar set a single-game franchise record with twenty-five free throw attempts against the Boston Celtics. The entire team set a franchise record for forty-eight free throws and sixty-two attempts during that game. For the entire season Abdul-Jabbar set another record with 743 attempts.

Flynn Robinson (1941–2013) scored an NBA record .898 for successful free throws.

On March 30, 1970, the Bucks set a club record for points in a single game, beating the 76ers 156–120 in Game Three of the Division Semifinals.

Did Kareem Abdul-Jabbar set records in the 1970 postseason?

Abdul-Jabbar set two postseason records for the Bucks. On April 30, he scored forty-six points against the 76ers, and on April 17 he grabbed thirty-one rebounds against the Knicks.   **227**

In what ways did Abdul-Jabbar change the game of basketball?

Because Wilt Chamberlain (1936–1999) and Bill Russell (1934–) had already changed the way pro basketball was played, Abdul-Jabbar's inclusion wasn't as drastic as it could have been. Chamberlain's sheer size and Russell's skill had already caused the NBA to push out the restraining line beneath the basket where no offensive charges can be taken by defenders. Offensive goal tending was also forbidden.

College basketball, however, was substantially changed by Abdul-Jabbar. The NCAA made it illegal to dunk because he could dunk without leaving his feet. The professional leagues, however, didn't have that rule.

How did the the Bucks change because of Abdul-Jabbar?

The Bucks went from the basement to the playoffs, thanks largely to Kareem Abdul-Jabbar. The season before the Abdul-Jabbar era, the Bucks won only twenty-seven games, then went to the playoffs once he joined the team. Since he left the team the Bucks have not been back to the NBA finals.

When did Hall of Famer Oscar Robertson play for the Bucks?

Robertson started his career in 1960 with the Cincinnati Royals. Across his ten years with that team he averaged 29.3 points per game with 752 points and a field goal percentage of .489. In 1970 he started with the Bucks, and in four seasons scored 288 points with a field goal percentage of .468. He played his last game for Milwaukee in 1974.

According to the Naismith Memorial Basketball Hall of Fame, Robertson could score from anywhere on the court, any way he saw fit. He was named an NBA All-Star twelve times and received three single-game MVP awards, six if the All-Star Game awards are included. He was inducted into the Hall of Fame in 1980.

When did Lew Alcindor change his name to Kareem Abdul-Jabbar?

After reading Malcolm X's (1925–1965) autobiography in the mid-1960s, Lew Alcindor converted to Islam and changed his name. Though still known for years as Lew Alcindor, he saw that name as a burden. "'Alcindor' was the name of a slave owner," he explained—the name of the family who owned his ancestors when brought from what is now Nigeria. "I've always felt that I had the right to be who I am."

On May 1, 1971, the day after the Bucks won the NBA Championship, he adopted the name of Kareem Abdul-Jabbar. Roughly translated, it means "generous noble servant of the mighty stern one."

How good was Moses Malone?

Malone (1955–2015) played for the Bucks 1991–1993. In those two seasons he had a field goal percentage of .467, averaged 14.3 points per game, and played in ninety-three games—seventy-seven of those he started.

In his twenty-two seasons he played for nine teams, had a field goal percentage of .495, and scored 20.3 points per game. He won the NBA MVP award three times, played in the All-Star Game thirteen times—twelve of those consecutively from 1978 to 1989. In three seasons he ranked in the top ten for field goals, seven times he ranked top ten in points scored, and eight times he ranked first in offensive rebound percentage. He was inducted into the Hall of Fame in 2001.

When was Dave Cowens inducted into the Hall of Fame?

Cowens (1948–) and Nate Archibald (1948–) were both inducted into the Hall of Fame in 1991. Both players were in Milwaukee only a single year, with Cowens playing for the Bucks in the 1982–1983 season.

Cowens played for the Boston Celtics most of his career, from 1970 through 1980. He registered a field goal percentage of .460 and averaged 18.2 points per game.

After a two-year hiatus (retired, according to basketball-reference.com), he played for the Bucks for his single season. He averaged .444 with 8.1 points per game.

Across his career he played in eight All-Star Games, earning MVP status in the 1973 All-Star Game. In 1972 he earned the NBA MVP outright.

Did Cowens ever coach?

In the 1978–1979 season Cowens coached for the Boston Celtics and earned a record of 27–41. He then was assistant coach for the San Antonio Spurs the following two years before leading the Charlotte Hornets for more than two years. He spent time as a Golden State Warriors' assistant coach before taking over the helm in 2000, then moved to Detroit as an assistant once again.

Across his career as a head coach, he directed 352 games with a record of 161–191. He never coached the Bucks.

Why was "Tiny" Archibald inducted into the Hall of Fame?

Nate Archibald only played the 1983–1984 season in Milwaukee but racked up his best shooting that season, .487. Across his thirteen-year career he had a field goal percentage of .467, played in the All-Star Game six times, and was the NBA's All-Star Game MVP in 1981.

In the 1972–1973 season he topped the NBA with 1,028 points and ranked fourth the following two years. For three seasons (1971–1972, 1972–1973, 1974–1975) he topped the NBA in free throws, pulling in second in the 1975–1976 season.

Archibald was inducted into the Hall of Fame in 1991.

When did the Bucks earn their first championship?

Coach Larry Costello posted a record of 66–16 in the team's third year in existence, earning a postseason slot. No expansion team in any professional sport has won a championship so quickly as the 1971–1972 Milwaukee Bucks.

In the 1971–1972 season the Bucks beat the Golden State Warriors in five games in the semifinals, then lost in the finals to the Los Angeles Lakers in six games. The year after that the Bucks lost to the Warriors in the semifinals in six games. The 1973–1974 season they advanced to the finals and fell to the Boston Celtics in seven games.

When did the Bucks trade away Kareem Abdul-Jabbar?

Abdul-Jabbar wasn't ever really happy in Milwaukee. The Muslim community was almost non-existent, there wasn't enough sun, and he was too far away from family. He told the Bucks he wanted out in October of 1974 and didn't announce it to the press. That allowed the Bucks to make the best possible trade.

After getting poked in the eye in a preseason game in 1974, Abdul-Jabbar punched a stanchion and broke a hand. He missed sixteen games, and the Bucks only won three of them. Even after Abdul-Jabbar returned the team didn't perform as well as before.

On June 16, 1975, he was traded to Los Angles along with Walt Wesley (1945–). In return the Bucks received two younger players (which is what they wanted) and second- and eighth-round draft picks. The trade could be considered a foolish idea, but what they picked up in return could be credited for keeping the team viable.

Who did the Bucks get in return for Abdul-Jabbar?

The Bucks were trying to keep their team young, and Los Angeles had young players to trade. In addition to the two draft picks, Milwaukee received Elmore Smith (1949–) and Brian Winters (1952–). While Smith was already twenty-five years old, Winters was in his rookie season. With the draft picks the franchise took Dave Meyers (1953–2015) and Junior Bridgeman (1953–).

Winters and Bridgeman went on to have their numbers retired, so in all the trade wasn't as bad as it could have been. "It is not immodest to say we saved our franchise with our deal," said William Alverson, the team president. "But it was not a good deal for Milwaukee, it was an absolutely sensational deal for Milwaukee."

Have the Bucks been back to the playoffs since trading Kareem Abdul-Jabbar?

In the 1974–1975 season the Bucks didn't qualify for the playoffs. However, the following season they qualified. The Bucks were eliminated by the Detroit Pistons in the first round, getting swept in two games.

230   Below is a list of all the appearances in the postseason by the Milwaukee Bucks.

Post-Season Bucks Appearances

Season	Coach	Result
1969–1970	Larry Costello	Lost the Eastern Division Finals
1970–1971	Larry Costello	Won the NBA Finals
1971–1972	Larry Costello	Lost the Western Conference Finals
1972–1973	Larry Costello	Lost the Western Conference Semifinals
1973–1974	Larry Costello	Lost the NBA Finals
1975–1976	Larry Costello	Lost the Western Conference first round
1977–1978	Don Nelson	Lost the Western Conference Semifinals
1979–1980	Don Nelson	Lost the Western Conference Semifinals
1980–1981	Don Nelson	Lost the Eastern Conference Semifinals
1981–1982	Don Nelson	Lost the Eastern Conference Semifinals
1982–1983	Don Nelson	Lost the Eastern Conference Finals
1983–1984	Don Nelson	Lost the Eastern Conference Finals
1984–1985	Don Nelson	Lost the Eastern Conference Semifinals
1985–1986	Don Nelson	Lost the Eastern Conference Finals
1986–1987	Don Nelson	Lost the Eastern Conference Semifinals
1987–1988	Don Nelson	Lost the Eastern Conference first round
1988–1989	Don Nelson	Lost the Eastern Conference Semifinals
1989–1990	Don Nelson	Lost the Eastern Conference first round
1990–1991	Don Nelson	Lost the Eastern Conference first round
1998–1999	George Karl	Lost the Eastern Conference first round
1999–2000	George Karl	Lost the Eastern Conference first round
2000–2001	George Karl	Lost the Eastern Conference Finals
2002–2003	George Karl	Lost the Eastern Conference first round
2003–2004	Terry Porter	Lost the Eastern Conference first round
2005–2006	Terry Stotts	Lost the Eastern Conference first round
2009–2010	Scott Skiles	Lost the Eastern Conference first round
2012–2013	Scott Skiles	Lost the Eastern Conference first round
2014–2015	Jason Kidd	Lost the Eastern Conference first round
2016–2017	Jason Kidd	Lost the Eastern Conference first round

Where did the Bucks originally play?

The first arena to host the Milwaukee Bucks was the University of Wisconsin Milwaukee Panther Arena. Dedicated in 1950, the arena hosted Marquette University's Warriors (now called Golden Eagles) and the Bucks when they came into existence in 1968.

The Milwaukee Arena held 11,000, the smallest crowd of any NBA facility. The Bucks used it until the Bradley Center opened in 1988. In their first game there on November 5, 1988, they lost to the Atlanta Hawks 107–94 in front of more than 18,000 fans.

How did the Bradley Center get its name?

Local philanthropist Jane Bradley Pettit (1918–2001) named the facility in honor of Harry Lynde Bradley (1885–1965), her father. The Center was built using only money donated from the family and is the only public arena in North America underwritten by a single family.

In 2012, the naming rights were sold to BMO Harris Bank for a financial shot in the arm for the facility and was renamed the BMO Harris Bradley Center. The arena wasn't up to NBA standards, and a new facility was in the works, but the infusion of cash helped the Bucks remain in Milwaukee until a new arena could be built.

Did the team get a new arena?

Groundbreaking for the new home of the Milwaukee Bucks began in June of 2016. On June 5, 2018, the new facility was given a certificate of occupancy. Fiserv Forum is now the home of the Bucks, as well as Marquette's Golden Eagles basketball team.

The new facility seats more than 17,000, covers 714,000 square feet (66,000 square meters), and cost more than a half-billion dollars. Herb Kohl contributed $100 mil-

Fiserv Forum opened as the new home of the Milwaukee Bucks in 2018. It also hosts Marquette's Golden Eagles basketball team.

lion from the sale of the team to assist in the construction costs. The new ownership group also gave $100 million. Additional funds were approved by the legislature and the bill was signed by Governor Walker on August 12, 2015. The Bucks opened their 2018 season in Fiserv Forum in downtown Milwaukee.

When was Alex English drafted by the Bucks?

Milwaukee picked English (1954–) in the second round of the 1976 draft, and he only played two seasons for the Bucks. He was picked up as a free agent by the Indiana Pacers on June 8, 1978.

In his time in Milwaukee, English shot an average of .522 and scored 7.7 points per game. Across his career he averaged 21.5 points per game with a shooting percentage of .507.

English played in eight consecutive All-Star Games, was first in field goals in three seasons, and first in points for two seasons. He was released by the Dallas Mavericks on May 1, 1991, and inducted into the Hall of Fame in 1997.

Why was the 1978–1979 season special for the Milwaukee Bucks?

The Bucks didn't qualify for the playoffs—partly because they lost Dave Meyers (1953–2015) for the whole season because of a back injury—but they did set records. They shattered the NBA's record with 2,562 assists in a single season. On December 26 they set a single-game assist record with fifty-three, and for a single quarter with nineteen assists.

They also set a team record with their widest victory, beating the Detroit Pistons by fifty-nine points, 143–84.

On March 14, 1979, the Bucks scored eighty-seven points in the second half—another team record—and set a record for most points in a non-overtime game, beating the New Orleans Jazz 158–102.

How did the Bucks do in the 1979–1980 season?

The Bucks won their sixth Midwest Division title. In a February 4 trade, they acquired Bob Lanier from Detroit and went 20–6 afterward. The final thirty-eight games were sellouts, and the Conference Semifinals set an NBA record with a crowd of 40,172 for Game Five at the Kingdome. The Bucks won that game 108–97 over the Seattle Super-Sonics, but lost in Game Seven 98–94.

The following year the Bucks lost the Conference Semifinals to Philadelphia 4–3, and the year after that 4–2—also to Philadelphia.

Did the Bucks ever play a triple-overtime game?

On March 6, 1982, the Bucks lost to the Spurs in San Antonio 171–166. Though they lost, they set a team record for overall points scored, including another team record for ninety-seven points in the first half of the game.

How well did the Bucks perform in the 1984 playoffs?

The Bucks won their division for a fifth consecutive season. They led the league in defense, allowing only 101.5 points per game.

They beat Atlanta 3–2 in the first round of the playoffs, then topped New Jersey 4–2 in the Conference Semifinals, racking up a single playoff game record with fifty-five free throw attempts on May 3, 1984.

They lost to Boston in five games in the Conference Finals.

What team records did the Bucks set in the 1985–1986 season?

The team racked up their sixth straight Central Division title and set records for free throws attempted (2,701) and free throws made (2,063). On December 15, 1985, they set a single-game record of .667 for field goal percentage on their way to crushing the Sacramento Kings 140–82.

Craig Hodges (1960–) racked up seventy-three three-pointers that season on 162 attempts. The team advanced to the Eastern Conference Finals for the third time in four years.

On May 7, 1986, Paul Pressey (1958–) set a single-game playoff record with fifteen free throws on a record seventeen free throws attempted against the Philadelphia 76ers. Two days later Craig Hodges (1960–) set the single-game playoff record for steals—eight, against Philadelphia. The entire team set another record for steals during that game, taking the ball away nineteen times.

They beat the 76ers 4–3 in the semifinals, but fell to the Boston Celtics in the finals 4–0.

Also, the team racked up their seventh consecutive season winning fifty games or more, and extended their streak of .500+ to fifty straight months. The following season that streak ended at fifty-two consecutive months.

Did the team ever set attendance records?

For the 1986–1987 season, the Bucks set an attendance record of an average of 11,000 fans, including thirty-six sellouts. For the entire season the arena had only 2,145 empty seats.

The following year was their last in the Milwaukee Arena before moving to the Bradley Center. They drew 452,057 fans that year.

When did the Bucks record their thousandth win?

The Franchise beat the Pistons 109–84 in Detroit for win number 1,000 on December 6, 1988. They qualified for the postseason for the tenth straight year, and seventeenth time across twenty-one seasons. The team beat the Atlanta Hawks in the first round of the playoffs 3–2, but were shut out in the conference semifinals in four games.

When did Hall of Famer Adrian Dantley play for Milwaukee?

Dantley (1956–) played the last of his seventeen seasons with the Bucks in 1990–1991, and by far that season was his worst. He scored only 5.7 points per game in ten games on .380 shooting. His career averages were much higher, .540 shooting with 24.3 points per game.

Across seven years he played in six All-Star Games, ranked in the top ten in field goals (ranking first in the 1980–1981 season), five times was first in free throws, twice topped the list in points, and was inducted into the Hall of Fame in 2008.

Have the Bucks ever been listed as a top team?

The Bucks entered the 1990–1991 season as the "winningest" team in the history of the NBA. Since joining the league in 1968, they averaged 49.31 wins per season. That season Milwaukee started with eighteen straight home wins, racked up a record of 48–34, and posted their twelfth consecutive winning season.

What is the longest game the Bucks ever played?

On November 9, 1989, the team went into a fifth overtime before they beat the Seattle SuperSonics 155–154. The game lasted four hours, seventeen minutes.

The longest NBA game ever went into six overtimes before the Indianapolis Olympians beat the Rochester Royals 75–73 on January 6, 1951.

They also made their twelfth consecutive postseason appearance, but were shut out by Philadelphia in the first round of the playoffs. The following season they did not qualify.

How did the Bucks perform in the 1991–1992 season?

After twelve consecutive winning seasons, the Bucks started the season winning ten of their first thirteen games. They promptly melted down, losing fifty-one of their last sixty-nine games.

The team finished the season 28–54 and did not qualify for the postseason for the second consecutive season.

What was the team's biggest loss?

On February 20, 1995, the Bucks lost to Orlando 152–54—the biggest defeat in franchise history.

The following season the team suffered a franchise-record losing streak, dropping fifteen straight from March 4 to March 30, 1996.

When did the Bucks allow the fewest average points per game?

In the lockout-shortened season of 1998–1999, the Bucks only allowed 90.0 points per game. The fewest for a full eighty-two game season came in 2010–2011 season, when they allowed 92.7 points per game.

When did the Bucks next qualify for the postseason?

The Bucks played in the postseason in 1999, their first appearance since 1991. They finished the lockout-shortened regular season with a record of .560.

They were shut out in the first round of the playoffs 3–0 by Indiana. The Bucks made it to the playoffs again in 2000, losing again in the first round. In 2001 they advanced to the finals, losing to Philadelphia 4–3.

How well did George Karl coach the Bucks?

Karl (1952–) coached the team from 1999 through 2003. Across that time he went 205–173 for a winning record of .542, and

George Karl coached the Bucks from 1999 to 2003. Over his career, he led his teams to over a thousand wins.

235

was the coach reaching fifty wins in the shortest time on January 17, 2000—only eighty-nine games into his tenure. At the time he was considered one of the most beloved sports figures in the state of Wisconsin—perhaps second only to Brett Favre (1969–). (Read more about Brett Favre in the section on the Green Bay Packers.)

Then Karl demanded the team trade one of their three best players or fire him as coach. They traded Glenn Robinson (1973–) in 2002, and Karl became involved in a feud with another of the team's top players, Ray Allen (1975–), who was promptly traded away.

Karl is credited with the biggest regular-season collapse in team history. The Bucks won only six games between March 8 and April 17, 2002, finishing the season with a record of 41–41 after being ten games above .500 on March 6.

How long did Hall of Famer Gary Payton play for the Bucks?

Payton (1968–) only played in Milwaukee for a few months. He was traded to the Bucks on February 20, 2003, then signed with the Los Angeles Lakers as a free agent on July 16, 2003. In his time with the Bucks he played in twenty-eight games, shot .466, and averaged 19.6 points per game.

Across his seventeen-year career he shot .466 and scored 16.3 points per game. He played in nine All-Star Games in ten seasons, ranked in the top ten in field goals six times, and four times was in the top ten in points—three times in the top ten in points per game.

Payton was inducted into the Hall of Fame in 2013.

Did Milwaukee ever set a record for fewest turnovers?

On April 1, 2003, the Bucks only committed two turnovers—an NBA record that has since been matched seven times. The previous NBA record was three; the previous franchise record was four.

The Bucks beat Indiana 96–89.

How many players from the Bucks were inducted into the Hall of Fame?

Eleven members of the Bucks organization were selected for the Naismith Memorial Hall of Fame. The first was Oscar Robertson, the most recent Guy Rodgers in 2014.

Bucks Hall of Famers

Name	Years in Milwaukee	Year Inducted	Nickname
Oscar Robertson	1970–1974	1980	Big O
Dave Cowens	1982–1983	1991	Big Red
Tiny Archibald	1983–1984	1991	Nate the Skate
Bob Lanier	1979–1984	1992	Dobber
Kareem Abdul-Jabbar	1969–1975	1995	Lew, Cap, Murdock, Big Fella
Alex English	1976–1978	1997	The Blade

Name	Years in Milwaukee	Year Inducted	Nickname
Wayne Embry	1968–1969	1999	Goose, The Wall
Moses Malone	1991–1993	2001	Chairman of the Boards, Big Mo
Adrian Dantley	1990–1991	2008	A. D., Teach, The Teacher
Gary Payton	2003	2013	The Glove, GP
Guy Rodgers Jr.	1968–1970	2014	

Which numbers have the Milwaukee Bucks retired?

Retired Bucks Numbers

Number	Player	Years in Milwaukee	Date Retired
1	Oscar Robertson	1970–1974	October 18, 1974
2	Junior Bridgeman	1975–1984, 1986–1987	January 17, 1988
4	Sidney Moncrief	1979–1989	January 6, 1990
10	Bob Dandridge	1969–1977, 1981–1982	March 7, 2015
14	Jon McGlocklin	1968–1976	December 10, 1976
16	Bob Lanier	1979–1984	December 4, 1984
32	Brian Winters	1975–1983	October 28, 1983
33	Kareem Abdul-Jabbar	1969–1975	April 24, 1993

FOOTBALL

Which major sports teams call Wisconsin home?

There are few major sports teams in Wisconsin. One of the teams, the Green Bay Packers, part of the National Football Conference's North Division, might be the only name readily known and respected nationwide. In baseball, the Milwaukee Brewers have been contenders from time to time, but have languished much of the time. The Milwaukee Bucks are Wisconsin's only NBA team.

Why is the NFC North called the "Black and Blue" division?

The term was coined by the Vikings' public relations director, Bill McGrane (1933–2015), in the 1960s. The philosophy of "run first" resulted in hard-nosed running backs, and the teams in the NFC North produced quite a few famous running backs as a result. The names include the Detroit Lions' Barry Sanders (1968–), the Chicago Bears' Walter Payton (1954–1999), Green Bay Packers' Jim Taylor (1935–), and the Minnesota Vikings' Adrian Peterson (1985–).

Where did the Green Bay Packers get their name?

In August of 1919, the *Green Bay Press-Gazette* held a pair of meetings to form a football team. Earl "Curly" Lambeau (1898–1965) asked his employer, the Indian Meat Packing Company, to provide funding for equipment and uniforms. They agreed, provided the team be named for the company.

The Indian Packing Company was later bought by Acme Packing, and their name appears on the first printed material in the NFL. The sale didn't become final until January of 1920, so the first money—and the name—comes from Indian Packing.

Who was Curly Lambeau?

Earl "Curly" Lambeau was the driving force behind the founding of the Green Bay Packers. He was the first star of the

The founder of the Packers, Curly Lambeau, played with the team for ten seasons and then coached them until 1949. The Packers' home stadium is named after him.

team and coached the Packers for thirty-one years. Using the forward pass more than any other team at the time, he led the Packers to national championships in 1929, 1930, and 1931. He resigned from the Packers after the 1949 season, and his 229 career victories ranked second only to George Halas's (1895–1983) 324 career wins. Halas coached the Chicago Bears from 1920 through 1967.

What was Curly Lambeau's job at the packing plant?

Lambeau's position as foreman at the loading dock earned him $250 per month.

How much was the Green Bay team worth?

According to a document displayed at the Green Bay Packers Hall of Fame, the team's value was $50.

What was the team's record their first season?

The Packers lost only one game in 1919—6–0 to a team fielded by Fairbanks-Morse Co. from Beloit. Overall they outscored opponents 565–12 and had a record of 10–1.

Did Lambeau play on the team?

Lambeau was the team's first coach and also played at the halfback position. He was both the primary runner and passer for the seventy-seven games he played. He threw twenty-four touchdown passes, rushed for eight touchdowns, and caught three touchdown passes. He even kicked a field goal and was the first on the team to do so. He hung up his cleats after the 1929 season.

When did professional football begin in Wisconsin?

In August of 1921, the Green Bay Packers were granted a franchise in the American Professional Football Association (APFA) in the name of the Acme Packing Company.

Why were the Packers removed from their league?

The APFA removed the Packers from the league in January of 1922 for using college players with assumed names on their roster. On June 24 of that year an executive meeting readmitted the team. At that same meeting the APFA changed the name of their association to the National Football League.

In which game did Lambeau use college players?

Some say the team they played was the Racine Legion, others the Chicago Staleys. According to the Packers website, the opposing team was the Legion.

How many college players were used?

Three players from Notre Dame played in the game that resulted in the team being removed from the APFA. The most famous was Heartly "Hunk" Anderson (1898–1978) from Michigan's Upper Peninsula. The other two were Buck Shaw (1899–1977) and Fred Larson (1897–1977). Eight days later their names were published in the *South Bend Tribune*. When Notre Dame found out, all three players were stripped of their football letters.

Why didn't the Packers' insurance policy cover a rained-out game in 1922?

The total rainfall was one one-hundredth of an inch (0.25 millimeters) short of what the policy covered. The insurance company wouldn't pay.

How did the Packers normally earn money?

The Packers "passed the hat" among spectators to raise revenue. No admission was charged, no seats were available, the team had no cheerleaders, and no public address systems were used. Without any protection from weather, rain would hurt income.

How did the Packers become owned by stockholders?

Bad weather in 1922 hurt income, and the Packers were in danger of insolvency. On December 7, football boosters met at a local Elks Club to raise money. A stock sale brought in the $5,000 needed to keep the team operating.

When were the first bleachers installed?

Before bleachers, fans would cluster at the sidelines and follow the action up and down the field. In 1920 a small set of seats were installed—only a couple-hundred. A small fee was charged to sit there.

The following year a canvas fence was erected around the field so the team could charge admission.

Which player is considered the first star on the team from outside the Green Bay area?

In 1921, Howard "Cub" Buck (1892–1966), formerly a Wisconsin tackle, moved to Appleton. The year before he'd played for the Canton Bulldogs. He'd also played for the Lapham Athletic Club in Milwaukee. When they'd played the Packers, Buck had so impressed Curly Lambeau, the coach wanted him as a core element in his team.

With which team does the Packers have the longest rivalry?

The Packers/Bears rivalry began in 1921, with the Packers losing to the Decatur Staleys by a score of 20–0. The Staleys changed their name to the Chicago Bears after the 1921–1922 season. By the end of the 2017 season the two teams had met 196 times. The Packers lead the rivalry 96–94–6.

Why doesn't the NFL recognize the first Packers' win over the Bears?

That game was played before the official start of the 1924 season, which is listed as beginning on September 28. The Packers won 5–0 on September 21, 1924—a week before the season officially started.

Are there any other long-standing rivalries for the Packers?

In 1930 the Packers played their first game against the Portsmouth Spartans. Green Bay won the game 47–13. The Spartans were founded in 1929 in Portsmouth, Ohio. They moved to Detroit and became the Lions in 1934. Across 177 games through the 2017 season the Packers lead 100–70–7.

Another team that evokes strong feelings in Packers fans is the Minnesota Vikings. Founded in 1961, the Vikings trail the Packers with an overall record of 60–53–2 at the end of the 2017 season.

Which other pro football teams called Wisconsin home?

The NFL lists three professional football teams in Wisconsin from 1922 through 1924. Other than the Packers, there were the Milwaukee Badgers and the Racine Legion. The Legion didn't play in 1925, and in 1926 the team was called the Tornadoes. Neither of those teams played after 1926.

240

Was Blood's name change legal?

The state of Wisconsin allowed a change of that sort as long as it wasn't intended for fraudulent purposes. Johnny Blood always insisted his last name was "Blood," and it was not a nickname. He claimed his nickname was "The Vagabond Halfback."

There is a Johnny Blood Legends Room in the Packers' Atrium.

When did the Packers win their first title?

On November 18, 1928, the Packers beat the New York Giants 7–0, creating enough buzz to sign three veteran players: Robert Calvin Hubbard (1900–1977), John "Johnny Blood" McNally (1903–1985), and Mike Michalske (1903–1983). They finished the 1929 season at 12–0–1, claiming their first NFL title. They won their second NFL title the following year. In 1930 they became the first NFL team to win three consecutive titles.

Which player for the Packers is in both the Pro Football Hall of Fame and the Baseball Hall of Fame?

Robert Calvin Hubbard was inducted to the Pro Football Hall of Fame in 1963 as a player and the Baseball Hall of Fame in 1976 as an umpire. In addition, he was inducted into the College Football Hall of Fame in 1962.

His name is listed in eight separate halls of fame.

How did Johnny Blood get his nickname?

In football, John McNally was Johnny Blood from his first day of semi-pro play. He used "Johnny Blood" to remain eligible for college ball.

The NFL's first official guide in 1935 listed him as Johnny Blood, and all his contracts were signed using that name. In the Pro Football Hall of Fame, however, he is listed as "Johnny (Blood) McNally."

The "Blood" moniker was taken from a popular film of the era, *Blood and Sand*.

When did the Packers file for incorporation?

The original articles of incorporation were filed in the state of Wisconsin in 1923, using a now-defunct nonprofit tax law. In 1931 during a bleacher collapse, a fan was injured and awarded nearly $5,000 in a judgment. The team was put in receivership, then reorganized with new articles of incorporation on January 26, 1935.

When was the first commercial broadcast of a Green Bay Game?

On November 24, 1929, Russ Winnie (1907–1956) re-created a play-by-play game broadcast from ticker tape news releases on WTMJ in Milwaukee. The game was held in New York against the Giants, and the Packers won the game 20–6.

241

When was the first live game broadcast for the Packers?

In the 1930 season, Green Bay radio station WHBY carried live play-by-play by Ted Moore (1926–2014) from 1958 through 1969. WTMJ didn't have an exclusive contract at the time.

When did the first stock sale happen for the Packers?

In 1923 the first set of stock was sold to raise $5,000. One thousand shares were sold for five dollars each, and every buyer was required to purchase six season tickets. A second wave of stock was sold in 1935 to raise $15,000. There have been three subsequent stock sales, raising more than $88 million in total.

Why are the Packers the only publicly owned team?

The NFL's current ownership policy mandates no more than thirty-two owners per team, with at least one person owning 30 percent or more. Those rules were implemented in the 1980s, but the league grandfathered in the Packers' ownership structure.

With so many stockholders, who actually runs the Green Bay Packers?

An annual stockholders meeting is held in July every year. A board of directors is elected by the stockholders, and the board then elects a seven-member executive committee for the corporation. There is a president, vice president, treasurer, secretary, and three members-at-large. Only the president has a paid position.

What happens if the team is ever sold or moves out of state?

According to the articles of incorporation filed in 1923, after all expenses are paid, the remaining revenue would go to the Sullivan-Wallen Post of the American Legion in Green Bay to build a "proper soldier's memorial." The rationale was to remove financial incentive to move or sell, thus keeping the club in Green Bay. In 1997 a shareholder vote changed the beneficiary of any sale to the Green Bay Packers Foundation.

What is the home field for the Green Bay Packers?

The Packers originally played in a field owned by the Hagemeister Brewery starting in 1919. In 1923, because of prohibition, the name of the corporation that owned the brew-

Can stock in the Packers be sold by shareholders?

Shares can only be sold back to the nonprofit corporation. No dividends are ever paid, and the value of shares never increases in value. No individual may own more than 200,000 shares, so no single person can gain control of the corporation. There are more than five million shares.

Originally called City Field when it opened in 1957, Lambeau Field was renamed in 1965 and is the oldest operating NFL field. Last renovated in 2013, it has a standing room capacity of 81,442 now.

ery became Bellevue Products Co. The field's name was changed to reflect that new name.

In 1925 the team moved to City Stadium, closer to town and with a facility that had more of the infrastructure required for a professional football team. In 1957 the team moved to a newer stadium, informally known as New City Stadium. On September 11, 1965, that facility was renamed Lambeau Field in honor of Curly Lambeau, who had died on June 1, 1965.

Who did the Packers play in their last game at the old City Stadium?

On November 28, 1956, the San Francisco 49ers used three Green Bay fumbles in the last quarter to polish off the Packers 17–16.

What world-famous politician spoke at the dedication of New City Stadium?

Richard Nixon (1913–1994), then vice president, helped inaugurate the new facility on September 29, 1957. The Packers beat the Chicago Bears 21–17.

What was the original capacity of Lambeau Field?

New City Stadium held 32,500 fans. In 1963 seating was expanded to 42,327. For the 1965 season, when renamed Lambeau Field, the stadium could hold 50,837.

Which other players were also head coaches?

Bart Starr (1934–) coached from 1975 through 1983 (52–76–3), and Forrest Gregg (1933–) coached from 1984 through 1987 (25–37–1). Neither of them was head coach while playing for the team.

Who were the best coaches of the Packers?

The top five coaches are listed as Mike Sherman (59–43), who coached from 2000 through 2005, Mike McCarthy (121–70) from 2006 to 2018, Mike Holmgren (1948–) with a record of 84–42 from 1992 through 1998, Curly Lambeau (212–106–21) from 1921 through 1949, with Vince Lombardi (1913–1970) with a record of 98–30–4, ranking him as the number one coach of the team.

How successful was Coach Curly Lambeau?

Lambeau, like every other coach, had good years and bad. His overall record has him 212–106–21. The worst year was 1949, only winning twice the entire season. His best season was 1929, with not a single loss. In 1941 he lost once, in 1936 he lost once and tied once. He led the Packers to six championships during his tenure as coach.

How did Lambeau get the nickname of Curly?

Lambeau had very curly black hair.

Why did the Packers play some home games in Milwaukee?

Starting in 1933, the Packers played a few of their scheduled home games in Milwaukee to attract more fans in order to boost revenue. Four Milwaukee-area stadiums were used—Borchert Field, then State Fair Park, Marquette Stadium, and County Stadium.

The last Milwaukee game was in 1994.

Who played against the Packers in their last game at County Stadium?

In 1955, the NFL threatened to move the Packers from Green Bay to Milwaukee if they didn't build a new facility in the team's listed city of origin. Bonding for what eventually became Lambeau Field progressed slowly, and games continued in Milwaukee.

The final home game at County Stadium pitted the Packers against the Atlanta Falcons on December 19, 1994. Green Bay beat Atlanta 21–17 in front of nearly 55,000 fans.

The Packers Hall of Fame was the first such hall dedicated to a single football team. Inside, you will see lots of memorabilia, including a reproduction of Vince Lombardi's office.

When was the Green Bay Packers Hall of Fame dedicated?

The Packers Hall of Fame was dedicated in 1967 and was the first built to house a single professional football team. The "hall"

Who replaced Mike McCarthy?

In his thirteen years with the Green Bay Packers, Mike McCarthy (1963–) went 125–77 with a Super Bowl championship in 2010. However, after only four wins in the first twelve games of the 2018 season, he was fired.

Joe Philbin (1961–), offensive coordinator for the Packers and former head coach of the Miami Dolphins, took over as interim coach.

was literally a hall where exhibits were displayed in the Brown County Veterans Memorial Arena.

When did the Packers Hall of Fame have their first permanent facility?

On April 3, 1967, President Gerald Ford (1913–2006) dedicated an addition to the Veterans Memorial Arena, which would be the official home of the team's Hall of Fame.

When were the first inductees honored at the Packers Hall of Fame?

Since 1970, 157 players have been inducted into the Packers Hall of Fame. Eight were inducted that first year. They include Bernard "Boob" Darling (1903–1968), LaVern "Lavvie" Dilweg (1903–1968), Francis "Jug" Earp (1897–1969), Robert "Cal" Hubbard* (1900–1977), Earl "Curly" Lambeau* (head coach/back/cofounder), Verne Lewellen (1901–1980), John "Blood" McNally*, and August "Mike" Michalske* (1903–1983).

*These players were also inducted into the Pro Football Hall of Fame.

Where is the Packers Hall of Fame housed now?

The Hall of Fame was moved to the Lambeau Field Atrium on September 4, 2003. On August 21, 2015, a new Hall of Fame was opened on the first floor of the Atrium with interactive displays using the latest technology.

Who was the first African American player for the Packers?

Bob Mann (1924–1906) played from 1950 to 1954 and was inducted into the Packers Hall of Fame in 1988.

Which team gained the most yards against the Packers in a single game?

The Los Angeles Rams gained 611 yards against the Packers on December 16, 1956. They beat the Packers 49–21.

What was the biggest loss suffered by the Packers?

The Baltimore Colts stomped the Packers 56–0 on November 2, 1958.

Which season was the worst for the Packers?

In January of 1958 the Packers fired head coach Lisle Blackbourn (1899–1983) and hired Ray "Scooter" McLean (1915–1964). That was the worst year in Packers history, as they finished with a record of 1–10–1. McLean resigned on December 17.

When was the Packers first losing season?

In 1933 the Packers recorded their first losing season, 5–7–1, under Coach Curly Lambeau.

What happened to make the Packers lose so many games in 1933?

Quarterback Red Dunn (1901–1957), who led the Packers to three NFL titles, retired after the 1931 season. The following year another star player, Verne Lewellen, retired. The loss of those two players contributed greatly to the first losing season for the Packers.

Which team with two different names did the Packers play in the same season?

In 1934 the Packers played a game against the Cincinnati Reds, winning 41–0 on October 14. The Reds moved to St. Louis and played their final three games as the Gunners. They played the Packers on December 12, and Green Bay won that game 21–14.

Did any team beat the Packers more than twice in a single regular season?

The Chicago Cardinals beat the Packers three times in 1935—7–6 on September 15, 3–0 on October 13, and 9–7 on November 28. In 1960 the Cardinals moved to St. Louis, and in 1988 they moved to Arizona.

Who was the first player for the Packers to rush for 1,000 yards?

Halfback Tony Canadeo (1919–2003) rushed for 1,052 yards on 208 carries in 1949. He played in twelve games and was only the third in the league to run for 1,000 yards or more.

Which quarterback for the Packers was the first to throw for 2,000 yards in a single season?

Cecil Isbell (1915–1985) set an NFL record throwing for 2,021 yards in 1942. His twenty-four touchdown passes also set an NFL record. He was the first Packers quarterback to

---

How good a coach was Vince Lombardi?

Lombardi posted the first winning season in twelve years immediately following the Packers' worst season. In 1959 the team finished 7–5. He led the team to five championships and never had a losing season. His best season was 1962 with a 13–1 record. The worst season for Lombardi was his last, 1969, with a record of 7–5–2 with the Washington Redskins.

complete more than a hundred passes in a single season—117 passes in 1941.

What is the highest Packers score in a single game?

The Packers beat the Detroit Lions 57–21 on October 7, 1945. That score of fifty-seven points continues to stand as a team record.

When did the Packers play their first overtime game?

On December 26, 1965, the Packers beat the Colts 13–10 on a twenty-five-yard field goal kicked by Don Chandler (1934–2011). That won the team the Western Conference Playoff game.

Who was the oldest player to ever play a regular season game for the Packers?

In 1961, kicker Paul Hornung (1935–) was drafted into the army. His backup, Jerry Kramer (1936–), was injured. The Packers acquired forty-two-year-old Ben Agajanian (1919–). Across three games he kicked a field goal and eight extra points for a total of eleven points.

A statue of Vince Lombardi was unveiled in front of Lambeau Field in 2003.

Which defensive player was the first to score in Super Bowl history?

In Super Bowl II, Packers cornerback Herb Adderley (1939–) intercepted a pass thrown by Oakland Raiders quarterback Daryle Lamonica (1941–). He returned it sixty yards for a touchdown.

What was the shortest game the Packers ever played?

On November 17, 1946, the Packers beat the Detroit Lions 9–0 in one hour, forty-five minutes.

Did the Packers play any other games lasting less than two hours?

Two other games were less than two hours, both played against the Detroit Lions. On October 25, 1942, the Packers beat the Lions 28–7 in Detroit in one hour, fifty minutes. The second, also in Detroit, ended with the Packers winning 14–3 in one hour, fifty-two minutes.

Which Packers game was the longest?

The Packers played the Detroit Lions on October 11, 1987. The Packers lost in overtime 19–16 after four hours and nine minutes.

The longest game in regulation play was also against the Lions on November 27, 1986. After three hours and forty-three minutes, the Packers came out on top 44–40.

Who did the Packers play when they set an NFL record for the most games decided by a single point in one season?

There were four such games in 1989 for the Packers. They beat the New Orleans Saints 35–34, the Chicago Bears 14–13, the Minnesota Vikings 20–19, and the Tampa Bay Buccaneers 17–16. The Packers ended the season with a record of 10–6.

What is the shortest completed touchdown pass in Packers history?

On October 18, 1942, Cecil Isbell threw a pass to Don Hutson (1913–1997) in a 45–28 win over the Cleveland Rams. The total distance recorded was four inches (10.16 centimeters).

When was the first televised game for the Packers?

The Packers lost to the Steelers in Pittsburgh on Saturday, October 24, 1953, 31–14.

In what year was the first complete season televised for the Packers?

Ray Scott (1919–1998) was the first television announcer for the Packers during their 1956 season. He announced for CBS for the Ice Bowl, Super Bowl I, and Super Bowl II as well. In 1968 the network ended the practice of having dedicated announcers for specific teams.

When was the "Ice Bowl" played?

On December 31, 1967, the Packers played the Dallas Cowboys in what later became known as the Ice Bowl. The official game-time temperature was thirteen degrees below (–25 Celsius), with a wind chill of forty-eight below (–44.4 Celsius). That game was the coldest in NFL history. One reporter in the press box said, "Dallas won the toss and elected to go home." The cold weather gave Lambeau Field the nickname of "frozen tundra." Bart Starr's (1934–) quarterback sneak won the game for the Packers, 21–17, with thirty seconds on the clock. More than 50,000 were there watching.

This was Vince Lombardi's last game as coach of the Green Bay Packers.

Did Vince Lombardi really say, "Winning isn't everything, it's the only thing"?

The best answer is "yes" and "no." The quote was originally spoken by John Wayne (1907–1979) in the 1953 movie, *Trouble along the Way*. Lombardi may have borrowed the phrase, but he didn't come up with it on his own.

Who was Bart Starr?

The Packers picked Starr in the seventeenth round in the 1956 draft. Only four years later he led the Packers to the West Division championship. He played for the Packers for fifteen years and is considered one of the team's best players. He held seven passing records while with the Packers and took the team to five NFL titles and two Super Bowl Championships. He earned MVP three times, including Super Bowl I and Super Bowl II. He was inducted into the Pro Football Hall of Fame in 1977.

What was Bart Starr's real name?

His full name was Bryan Bartlett Starr.

Did Bart Starr ever coach the team?

After his last season as a player, Starr was quarterback coach in 1972. He was hired

Bart Starr (kneeling) is shown here with coach Vince Lombardi. Starr played for the Packers from 1956 to 1971 and was twice chosen as Super Bowl MVP.

as head coach on Christmas Eve of 1974. After nine seasons, five of those as general manager as well as head coach, he posted a record of 52–76–2.

After Bart Starr retired from play in 1972, who replaced him as starting quarterback?

Sixth round draft pick Scott Hunter (1947–) took over for three years following Starr's tenure at quarterback. He accumulated a record of 15–11–3 with the Packers, with a total of 2,904 passing yards, and a 43.9 percent pass completion percentage.

In 1974, Dan Devine gave up draft picks to obtain what player?

Dan Devine (1924–2002), the team's coach and general manager, gave up two first-round picks, two second-round picks, and a third-round pick to get Los Angeles Rams quarterback John Hadl (1940–). In seven games that year he threw three touchdown passes.

What were ticket prices for Super Bowl I?

Prices ranged from $6 to $12. Even at that price there were 30,000 seats left empty in Memorial Coliseum in Los Angeles.

What was the final score for Super Bowl I?

The Packers beat the Kansas City Chiefs 35–10 on January 17, 1961.

How much did each winning player make for playing in Super Bowl I?

Each player received $15,000 for winning.

What one-time only media event happened at Super Bowl I?

The game was televised by CBS and NBC. The big game has only been on one network following that day.

In which season did the Packers fumble most?

In 1988 the team fumbled forty-four times.

What is the team record for the most fumbles in a single game?

The Packers fumbled eight times in a 34–14 loss to the Philadelphia Eagles on December 1, 1974.

Which Packers quarterback was sacked the most during his career?

Lynn Dickey (1949–) was sacked 268 times in his career as a Green Bay Packer.

Lynn Dickey was forced into retirement because of what injury?

With three games left in the 1985 season, just days after the Snow Bowl, Dickey injured his neck while weight lifting. He never played again.

What was the Snow Bowl?

On December 1, 1985, Green Bay had the biggest snowfall ever on game day. Sixteen inches (40.6 centimeters) of snow fell on the city, and the wind registered thirty mph (48.3 kph). The stands were mostly empty, and many who arrived did so on snowmobiles.

The game went well for the Packers. Despite four turnovers, Lynn Dickey completed twenty-two of thirty-six passes for 299 yards. Eddie Lee Ivery (1957–) and Gerry Ellis (1957–) each topped a hundred yards rushing. Total offense for the Pack was 512 yards, compared to sixty-five yards for the Tampa Bay Buccaneers.

Packers Hall of Famer Greg Koch (1955–) said about Lynn Dickey, "He played best in mud games and snow games."

The final score of the Snow Bowl: Packers 21, Tampa Bay Buccaneers 0.

Have the Packers ever lost a Super Bowl?

In 1998, when the Packers faced the Denver Broncos, the team came up short by a score of 31–24. Nearly 69,000 watched in San Diego, California. If the Packers had won, they would have earned back-to-back Super Bowl wins. A last-ditch drive at the end of the game ended with an incomplete pass and a Packers loss. A frustrated Bob Harlan (1936–), president of the Packers, said, "[The players] were walking, instead of running."

Why is Green Bay called Title Town?

No team in the history of the NFL has more championships than the Green Bay Packers. Since the team formed in 1919, twice they've won three consecutive league crowns–1929 thru 1931, and 1965 thru 1967. The Packers have thirteen championships, including four Super Bowl titles— I, II, XXXI, and XLV.

Who received Brett Favre's first completion?

Favre (1969–) played two games with the Atlanta Falcons before being traded to Green Bay. In those two games he threw four times with no completions. The Packers traded a first-round pick to get the rights to Favre.

A 2010 photo of Brett Favre. He played in the NFL from 1991 to 2010, most of that time (1992–2007) with the Packers.

In the second game of the 1992 season, Don Majkowski (1964–) was sidelined against the Tampa Bay Buccaneers. In his first play, Favre threw a pass that bounced off the helmet of Ray Seals (1965–). The ball flew right back at Favre, who caught it. He was tackled for a loss of seven yards.

The Buccaneers won the game 31–3.

What was Brett Favre's first win in Green Bay?

Brett Favre (1969–) took over for the injured Don Majkowski (1964–) in the first quarter on September 13, 1992, against the Cincinnati Bengals. Majkowski limped to the sideline and said he heard something pop. Head coach Mike Sherman (1954–) told Favre, "You're in."

Midway through the fourth, the Packers hadn't gained many yards with Favre. He'd completed less than half his passes, fumbled four times, and was sacked five times. An eighty-eight-yard drive put the Packers within three points, then the Bengals kicked a field goal to make it a six-point game.

The Packers took over on their eight with just over a minute to play and no time-outs. With thirteen seconds left on the clock, Kitrick Taylor (1964–) caught a pass from Favre as he crossed the goal line.

The Packers came from behind to beat the Bengals 24–23.

Was Brett Favre really that good?

Quarterback Brett Favre started his pro football career with the Atlanta Falcons in 1991, then joined the Packers in 1992. He was traded to the New York Jets for the 2008 season, then went to the Minnesota Vikings for 2009 and 2010. Across his twenty years he played in 302 games, participated in the Pro Bowl eleven times, and was voted the NFL's MVP in three consecutive years (1995–1997). He recorded six seasons with at least 4,000 yards passing and retired as the league's all-time leading passer with 6,300 completions on 10,169 attempts. He racked up 71,838 yards and 508 touchdowns.

Linebacker Ray Nitschke was the backbone of the Packers' defense during the Vince Lombardi years.

Why is Ray Nitschke's name displayed at Lambeau Field?

For Nitschke's (1936–1998) entire fifteen-year career he played for the Packers. As middle linebacker he grabbed twenty-five interceptions. He was the first defensive player from the team's "dynasty years" to be enshrined in the Pro Football Hall of Fame, and he intercepted a pass for a touchdown in the 1964 Pro Bowl.

Sportswriters of the time ranked him among the best of linebackers, citing his strength, speed, and leadership.

When were the Packers' dynasty years?

According to the Pro Football Hall of Fame, the dynasty years for Green Bay are the decade of the 1960s. With Vince Lombardi at the helm, the Packers won five championships, including two Super Bowls.

Who invented the Lambeau Leap?

The Lambeau Leap is when a player leaps into the arms of adoring fans in the stands behind the end zone following a touchdown. The first-ever leap was by LeRoy Butler (1968–), a defensive player.

Which player for Green Bay had a tower fall on him?

In a practice game on September 1, 1960, a half-ton tower, used by photographers and coaches, blew over and landed on Ray Nitschke. He wiggled his fingers and toes to show he was still alive and the iron tower was lifted off him. He stood up, pulled a bolt out of his plastic helmet, and returned to practice.

The helmet is on display at the Green Bay Packers Hall of Fame.

In 1993, Butler caused a fumble, and the ball landed in the hands of Reggie White (1961–2004). Heading for the end zone, White looked over his shoulder and saw he was about to be tackled. He flipped the ball to Butler, who ran it in for the score while pointing at a fan.

The excited Butler jumped up the fence but failed to get his hips over the top. Several fans hauled him into the stands, and the Lambeau Leap was born.

Who made the Lambeau Leap famous?

Nobody mentioned that leap in any of the six stories written about that game the next day. Butler says people kept talking about it, and Robert Brooks (1970–) made it famous the following season. Every time he scored he would leap, and fans loved it. The first few rows in the end zones became more coveted than seats mid-field.

LeRoy Butler, who was a Packer from 1990 to 2001, performed the first Lambeau Leap while playing against the Los Angeles Raiders in 1993.

Why is the Lambeau Leap still allowed?

One of the complaints about end zone celebrations is the mocking tone against the opposing team. The Lambeau Leap is seen as an appreciation of the fans. Commissioner Paul Tagliabue (1940–) grandfathered the Lambeau Leap because fans could be sitting in sub-zero weather, and, as Butler said, "The least we could do is jump up and give you a hug."

What was so special about Reggie White?

Reggie White, in his Hall of Fame career, chalked up 198 sacks in fifteen years. Nicknamed the "Minister of Defense," White was a thirteen-time Pro Bowler and awarded the NFL Defensive Player of the Year three times. His number, 92, was retired by both the Packers and the Philadelphia Eagles in 2005.

In his eight years with the Eagles, he had more sacks (124) than games played (121).

Who was the first player to wear #4?

Most football fans know Brett Favre wore #4 for the Packers. In the entire NFL, more than 130 players have worn #4. The first for the Packers was Chuck Fusina (1957–) for

What did the fan whisper to Butler during his Lambeau Leap?

Butler has no idea who the fan was, but the man was holding a beer when Butler jumped for the stands. The beer spilled all over Butler, and he told his teammates the man whispered, "You owe me a beer."

the 1986 season, then Dale Dawson (1964–), also for a single season. Brett Favre picked up #4 in 1992 and wore it until 2007. That number was retired by the Packers in 2015.

Which other numbers have been retired by the Packers?

Only four other numbers were retired by the Packers. The first was Don Hutson's #14, which was retired in 1951. Then came Tony Canedeo (1919–2003), who wore #3, retired in 1952. Bart Starr's #15 was retired in 1973, and Ray Nitschke's #66 was retired in 1983.

In 1995, Brett Favre completed his thousandth pass. How many of Green Bay's quarterbacks had done that before?

Bart Starr completed 1,808 in his career, and Lynn Dickey completed 1,592. Across his career, Favre completed 6,300 passes.

How did Brett Favre perform the day his father died?

The Packers were scheduled to play the Oakland Raiders on Monday Night Football on December 22, 2003. With a few hours of down-time, Favre began a round of golf with Doug Pederson (1968–) and a few other players. Then Doug's cell phone rang.

Irvin Favre (1935–2003) had died of a massive heart attack while driving near the Favre home. Head coach Mike Sherman (1954–) told Brett he'd support his quarterback whether he played or decided to go home. Brett played.

Warming up before the game, Favre's hands shook. Fans in Oakland, obviously aware of the situation, applauded Favre when he ran onto the field. That was the first time they'd ever given a standing ovation to an opposing player. When he stepped into the huddle, Favre said, "Hey, we need this game. Here we go."

The Packers crushed the Oakland Raiders 41–7. Favre threw four first-half touchdowns and claimed that as the greatest half he'd ever played. By the end of the game he'd completed twenty-two of thirty passes for 399 yards and racked up a passer rating of 154.9—just about off the charts.

What was so special about the 1996 season?

Led by Mike Holmgren (1948–), the Packers ended a decades-long Super Bowl drought. They were the top-scoring team (456 points), and they led the league with fewest points allowed (210), fewest yards allowed (4,156), and fewest touchdowns allowed (nineteen).

Brett Favre set a National Football Conference record for throwing thirty-nine touchdown passes in the regular season, breaking his own record of thirty-eight set the year before. He won the NFL's MVP award both of those years.

Did any other Green Bay players win the NFL MVP?

Quarterback Aaron Rodgers (1983–) won the NFL MVP award twice after the Favre era—2011 and 2014. Quarterback Bart Starr claimed the award in 1966, fullback Jim Taylor in 1962, and running back Paul Hornung in 1961.

Quarterback Aaron Rodgers made his NFL/Packers debut in 2005, was Super Bowl XLV MVP, and was twice chosen as NFL MVP (2011 and 2014).

In 1996, the Packers set a record with fifty-six touchdowns in the regular season. What was the previous record?

In 1962 the team racked up fifty-three touchdowns in the regular season.

Head coach Phil Bengtson (1913–1994) resigned two days after the 1970 season. Who replaced him?

Dan Devine coached from 1971 to 1973. In his first game he was run over by a group of players and suffered a broken leg.

Did the Packers defense perform well in 1996?

In 1996, eleven defensive players sacked opposing quarterbacks seventy-seven times. Reggie White led the way with 8.5 sacks. Ten players picked off passes, Eugene Robinson (1963–) taking six of the twenty-six interceptions that year.

Three interceptions were run back for touchdowns, by LeRoy Butler, Doug Evans (1970–), and George Koonce (1968–). Butler ran his interception back for ninety yards against the San Diego Chargers.

In all, the defense took away the ball from opponents thirty-nine times that season: twenty-six interceptions, thirteen fumbles.

How many sacks did Reggie White register in his first season with the Packers?

In 1993 White lead the team with thirteen sacks.

Which player led the Packers in sacks the following year?

Sean Jones (1962–) registered 10.5 sacks in 1994. Reggie White had eight.

Who is the all-time leading scorer for the Packers?

Kicker Mason Crosby (1984–) leads the team in total points with 1,345 by the end of the 2017 season. He started for the team in 2007.

The second leading scorer was also a kicker—Ryan Longwell (1974–)—who played from 1997 through 2005. He racked up 1,054 points.

Third goes to Don Hutson with 823 points in 117 games as a split end for the Packers from 1935 through 1945.

What is the longest field goal scored by the Packers?

Mason Crosby has set a lot of records over the years, including the franchise's top scorer. He's racked up more than a thousand points and has nine consecutive seasons with 100 points or more. Only three players in NFL history have registered more than 140 points in three or more seasons—Stephen Gostkowski (1984–) while kicking for the New England Patriots, David Akers (1974–) while kicking for the San Francisco 49ers and the Philadelphia Eagles, and Crosby.

He's also kicked the seven longest field goals in franchise history, with the longest being fifty-eight yards on October 13, 2011. That kick at the end of the third quarter put the Packers ahead of the Vikings 33–17, and Green Bay went on to win 33–27.

Why is Don Hutson considered a legend?

Hutson played for eleven years—all with the Packers. He had 488 career receptions, 7,991 yards, and ninety-nine touchdowns. He was the NFL's receiving champ for eight years, twice voted MVP, and held eighteen NFL records when he retired in 1945.

Why did the Packers set up two accounts to pay Don Hutson's salary?

In 1935, Hutson's salary was so large the team wanted to hide how much he was paid. His Depression-era salary was $175 per game.

Split end Don Hutson played for the Packers from 1935 to 1945 and served as the team's assistant coach for three years after that.

Which member of the Packers was voted the Toughest Guy in America?

In the March 2004 issue of *Men's Journal*, a panel of a hundred experts in various professions voted Brett Favre as the toughest. They based their vote on perseverance, fearlessness, pain threshold, and modesty.

The article credits Favre for playing with a broken thumb and starting more than two hundred (as of voting day) consecutive games—including playoff games.

A list of other injuries sustained include a first-degree separation of his left shoulder, a deep thigh bruise, a severely bruised left hip, elbow tendonitis, foot sprains, and a sprained lateral collateral ligament. Favre said he's not sure it makes him the toughest, but might make him the most beaten up. He added, "The older a player gets, the more the injuries seem to hurt, and the longer they take to heal."

Did family members ever play for the Packers at the same time?

George Svendsen (1913–1995) played for the Packers from 1935 through 1937, then again in 1940 and 1941. His brother Earl "Bud" Svendsen (1915–1996) played in 1937 and 1939. George played for the championship team in 1936, Bud with the championship team of 1939.

Which father and son both played for the Packers?

Elijah Pitts (1938–1998) was a halfback from 1961 through 1969 (and again in 1971), and his son, Ron Pitts (1962–), was a defensive back 1988 through 1990. Elijah played in 126 games, Ron in forty-four.

The Packers have a reputation as a passing team. What is the fewest passes attempted in a single game?

On October 8, 1933, the Packers beat the Portsmouth Spartans 17–0 with not a single attempted pass.

What is the biggest point-deficit the Packers overcame for a win?

On September 12, 1982, the Los Angeles Rams lead by 23–0. The Packers came back to win the game 35–23.

Who were the Gold Dust Twins?

In 1966 Donny Anderson (1943–) and Jim Grabowski (1944–) were both All-American running backs. During a bidding war between the AFL and NFL, the Packers gave them a combined $1,000,000 signing bonus. The huge (for the time) bonus earned them the nickname.

257

In 1992, the Packers had their first six-game winning streak since when?

The Packers started that season 6–0, the first time they put together six wins in a row since 1965.

What is the longest winning streak in Green Bay history?

Nineteen. On December 6, 2010, the Packers crushed the New York Giants 45–17. They won the next 18 games, culminating with a 46–16 win over the Oakland Raiders on December 11, 2011. The streak ended the following week when they lost to the Kansas City Chiefs on December 18, 2011.

The only team with a longer winning streak is the New England Patriots, who won twenty-one straight games 2003 into 2004.

How does Mike Holmgren's record compare with Vince Lombardi's?

It's hard to compare the two since they coached a different number of games, but in Holmgren's first thirty-four games he went 30–4. Lombardi was 28–6.

What subject did Mike Holmgren teach while a high school coach?

While coaching football, Holmgren taught history at Lincoln High School in San Francisco, California, in 1971. The following year he moved to Sacred Heart Cathedral Prep, then Oak Grove High School in San Jose.

Who has the Packers' team record for the most completed passes in a single game?

Aaron Rodgers completed thirty-nine passes in the contest against the Chicago Bears October 20, 2016. The Packers won 26–10.

Who provides cheerleaders at Green Bay games?

Cheerleaders from the University of Wisconsin-Green Bay have led cheers at Lambeau Field since the 1990s.

Which member of the Packers went to medical school?

Tackle Malcolm Snider (1947–) attended the University of Wisconsin-Madison off-and-on during playing seasons, full time during the off season. Eventually he became an orthopedic surgeon.

Which team have the Packers dominated in the most NFL title games?

The Packers have beaten the New York Giants in four championship games. In 1939 they won 27–0, in 1944 the score was 14–7, in 1961 the margin was 37–0, and in 1962 it was 16–7.

What did the Giants quarterback say after the 37–0 loss to the Packers?

Quarterback Yelberton Abraham "Y. A." Tittle (1926–) said the Packers were so dominant in that game he doubted the Giants could have won with twenty-two men on the field.

Which NFL game first had gross ticket receipts of more than a million dollars?

The Packers and New York Giants faced off on December 31, 1961. The Packers blasted the Giants 37–0. This was the first of five NFL title games won by Vince Lombardi.

How much did the players earn for that game?

Each player on the Packers team picked up $5,195. Players for the Giants earned $3,340.

What Packers notables were on leave from the army for that game?

Ray Nitschke, Boyd Dowler (1937–), and Paul Hornung played while on leave. Hornung was awarded the MVP of the game for scoring nineteen points—a touchdown, three field goals, and four extra points. *Sport* magazine gave him a 1962 Chevy Corvette.

Who arranged to have Paul Hornung put on leave for that game?

Hornung's captain refused to grant leave to the private. Hornung called Lombardi, who said he'd handle the situation. Twenty minutes later the captain received a phone call from President John F. Kennedy (1917–1963). "Paul Hornung isn't going to win the war on Sunday," he said, "but the football fans of this country deserve the two best teams on the field that day."

Why are Green Bay fans known as "cheeseheads"?

When the Bears won the 1985 Super Bowl, Chicago fans began mocking Green Bay fans by calling them "cheeseheads," because Wisconsin is known as the "dairy state." Packers fans embraced the insult.

In 1987, Ralph Bruno (1961–) was refurbishing his mother's couch and had the idea of carving the cushion into a wedge shape as a hat. He wore it to a Brewers game, and other fans wanted hats like his. He started making Styrofoam hats and selling them at baseball games. He sold so many he started a company, Foamation, Inc.

259

Did the first "cheesehead hat" really appear at a Milwaukee Brewers game?

The creator of the foam hat seen at Green Bay Packers games saw someone wearing a cardboard hat at a Milwaukee Brewers game at County Stadium in 1987. Ralph Bruno (1961–), founder of Foamation, Inc., doesn't recall which game, or even who played.

While working on his mother's sofa he carved the first foam hat from a seat cushion and wore it to another Brewers game. Other fans fell in love with the hat and requested he make hats for them. He began selling them, and capitalized the idea into a company that sells tens of thousands of cheese-related apparel every year.

Packers fans are very proud of the fact that their football team is owned by the public and not a private corporation, which is why this cheesehead has "NFL Owner" printed on his hat.

Circa 2014, Bruno's company sold enough cheesehead hats to reach across America.

What are the divots in cheesehead hats called?

Ralph Bruno has dubbed each of those indentations as a "schmivitz." The typical cheesehead hat sports twenty-five of them.

According to Bruno, there is no yellow cheese with indentations like his hats contain. He's published a book about his company, "Where There's a Wedge, There's a Whey."

RACING

How many NASCAR tracks are in Wisconsin?

Of the sixty-seven tracks in the United States, National Association of Stock Car Auto Racing (NASCAR) lists four of them in Wisconsin—Cedar Lake Speedway, La Crosse Fairgrounds Speedway, Madison International Speedway, and Spring Lake Speedway. Tracks are in thirty-one states, as well as thirteen tracks in Canada, ten in Mexico, and six in Europe.

Only three states have more tracks than Wisconsin—California (five tracks), New York (six tracks), and North Carolina (seven tracks). Virginia is tied with Wisconsin at four tracks.

Why is the Milwaukee Mile Speedway not on the list?

The Milwaukee Mile Speedway is the oldest operating race track in the world. There has been at least one race every year (except during WWII) since it opened in 1903. The 1.8 miles (2.9 kilometers) of dirt track was paved in 1954.

In 2010, Wisconsin State Park officials confirmed that the Milwaukee Mile would no longer host NASCAR or IndyCar races. There was a promoter turnover, and in the post-season of 2009, officials were forced to terminate promotional contracts. The sanctioning bodies waited months for the Mile to find a new promoter, but eventually decisions needed to be made for the 2010 season and races were scheduled elsewhere. Races are still scheduled, but no NASCAR or IndyCar races have been at the Mile since.

What type of tracks are in Wisconsin?

The Cedar Lake Speedway is a high-banked oval dirt track in New Richmond, Wisconsin. The track is under a half-mile (0.375 miles or 805 meters), with a clay surface. The Cedar Lake schedule listed more than sixty races during the 2017–2018 racing season.

The La Crosse Fairgrounds Speedway is a semi-banked oval in West Salem, Wisconsin. The track is more than a half-mile long (0.545 miles or 877 meters) with an asphalt surface. Their schedule listed twenty-nine races for the 2017–2018 season.

The Madison International Speedway is an oval track in Oregon, Wisconsin. The facility has both a quarter-mile (402 meters) and a half-mile (805 meters) track with an asphalt surface. The schedule included twenty-four races for the 2017–2018 season.

The Spring Lake Speedway is an oval dirt track in Unity, Wisconsin. There were twelve races for the 2017–2018 season.

Are there any Wisconsin racers in the NASCAR Hall of Fame?

The NASCAR Hall of Fame opened in 2010 in Charlotte, North Carolina. Since then, five people have been inducted annually. As of the class of 2018, nobody born in Wisconsin has been inducted.

Are there any race car drivers from Wisconsin?

There are nearly three hundred racers from the state. Eighteen were active in the 2017–2018 season.

Located at the Wisconsin State Fair Park in the suburb of West Allis, the Milwaukee Mile Speedway opened in 1903 and wasn't paved until 1954. The oldest operating race track in America, the track's infield hosted Packers games from 1934 to 1953.

261

Active Wisconsin Racers

Name	Born	Home Town
John Beale	?	Madison
Dexter Bean	1987	Westby
Tom Berte	1943	New Berlin
Josh Bilicki	1995	Menominee Falls
Natalie Decker	1997	Eagle River
James French	1992	Sheboygan
Nicolas Hammann	1993	Elkhart Lake
Max Hanratty	1993	Milwaukee
Dick Karth	1952	Grafton
Matt Kenseth	1972	Cambridge
Derek Kraus	2001	Stratford
Travis Kvapil	1976	Janesville
Ty Majeski	1994	Seymore
Scott Mayer	1964	Franklin
Paul Menard	1980	Eau Claire
Johnny Sauter	1978	Necedah
Rick Tackman	1975	Waukesha
Aaron Telitz	1991	Birchwood

Why isn't Danica Patrick on the above list?

Danica Patrick was born in Beloit, Wisconsin, but currently resides in Roscoe, Illinois. She announced in November of 2017 that she would retire after racing in the Daytona 500 and Indianapolis 500 in 2018, which she did.

What significant events does NASCAR host?

There are seven nationally sanctioned series by NASCAR. They are the Monster Energy Cup Series, Xfinity Series, Camping World Truck Series, Pinty's Series, PEAK Mexico Series, Whelen Euro Series, and the iRacing.com Series—a "sim" racing series.

In addition to those are four regional series: Whelen All-American Series, Whelen Modified Tour, K&N Pro Series, and the AutoZone Elite Series.

Have active Wisconsin drivers done well in NASCAR?

The racers from Wisconsin who have the most wins—in NASCAR and affiliated organizations—include Matt Kenseth, Tom Berte, James French, Travis Kvapil, and Johnny Sauter. Each has at least thirty wins in a specific series.

Which NASCAR event is the most popular?

The Daytona 500 is the premiere NASCAR racing event in America. This takes place on the last weekend in February at Daytona International Speedway in Florida.

Matt Kenseth is one of only eleven racers who have won the Daytona 500 more than once. He took the race in 2009 and 2012. No other Wisconsin driver has won that race more than once, and only one Wisconsinite has picked up a single Daytona win.

Daytona 500 Winners from Wisconsin

Name	Year	Time
Marvin Panch	1961	3:20:32
Matt Kenseth	2009	2:51:40
2012	3:36:02	

Which Wisconsin native holds the record for the most starts at Daytona?

Wausau native Dave Marcis (1941–) started his NASCAR career at the Daytona 500 in 1968—he finished twentieth. After thirty-five years of racing, his last race was also at Daytona. In all, he holds the record for thirty-three starts at Daytona—thirty-two of them consecutively. He appeared in 883 races in his career.

What was the CWRA?

The Central Wisconsin Racing Association was a racing circuit that produced some of the best racers from Wisconsin. Some names are nationally known, others obscure even to racing fans. People who have followed stock car racing will recognize names like Dick Trickle (1941–2013), Tom Reffner, Jimmy Back, Augie Winkleman, and more. Many of their names are now merely recorded on lists, but at the time they were larger than life.

The total number of programs run in the 1960s and 1970s topped a hundred. Racers of the day had one car and one engine. Wrecks were common, cars repaired, and racing continued—often within days. Dick Trickle said, "I remember one Saturday night they hauled half my car off the track with one wrecker and the other half off with another wrecker. Sunday afternoon I raced again."

Father Dale Grubba, a CWRA fan, wrote, "Wednesday night was La Crosse, Thursday night Wausau, Friday night Madison or Adams-Friendship, Saturday night Wisconsin Dells and Sunday night Griffith Park. Tuesday nights became a night for specials." More recent drivers seldom race more than two or three times each week.

How many racetracks—overall—are in Wisconsin?

The number of tracks varies greatly depending on who is counting and their definition of what qualifies as a "race track." Dirtfan.com lists twenty-five dirt tracks alone.

The Travel Wisconsin web site lists five "exciting" tracks. They are—in no particular order—La Crosse Interstate Speedway in West Salem, Road America in Elkhart Lake, Plymouth Dirt Track Racing in Plymouth, Great Lakes Dragaway in Union Grove, and Sugar River Raceway in Brodhead.

What makes the La Crosse track so exciting?

The paved oval at the La Crosse Fairgrounds Speedway is the only NASCAR-sanctioned asphalt track with weekly racing. There are two tracks—a quarter-mile (402 meters) oval and a five-eighths mile (one kilometer) oval. Every Saturday night from April to September is a NASCAR race.

The main attraction, however, is the Oktoberfest Race Weekend, which began in 1970. This is one of the oldest and largest racing events in the Midwest.

Who are some of the big name racers who drove in La Crosse?

In 1959, future Indy star Parnelli Jones (1933–) competed at the La Crosse Interstate Speedway. Two more IndyCar drivers drove the following year—Johnny Rutherford (1938–) and Jim McElreath (1928–2017). More IndyCar future stars include Tom Bigelow (1939–) in 1964 and Ken Petrie in 1999.

Stock car racers who were—or became—well known include Dick Trickle, Jim Sauter, Jay Sauter, Tim Sauter, Tom Reffner, Marv Marzofka, Joe Shear, Jim Back, Dave Marcis, Bobby Allison, Larry Detjens, Mark Martin, Darrell Waltrip, Ted Musgrave, Dale Earnhardt, Matt Kenseth, Bill Niles, and Paul Menard.

Why did Waltrip race in La Crosse?

Darrell Waltrip (1947–) wanted to try his skills against some of the best in Wisconsin. He came to La Crosse Speedway but didn't have a car to race. Mark Martin (1959–) said, "No problem. You can borrow mine. I'll even lend you my crew." Waltrip raced in the ARTGO Summer Nationals on July 20, 1980, setting a new track record of 19.393 sec-

The La Crosse Fairgrounds Speedway in West Salem is a 5/8-mile track that opened in 1957. It hosts weekly stock car races, including NASCAR-sanctioned races.

What is unique about Great Lakes Dragaway?

Not only is Great Lakes a drag racing strip, it's also open to the public. Anyone with a car can race there. While the season is on, there's a race on most nights. Then there's the Nitrous Street Car Brawl, if you want something else to supercharge your evening.

onds on the five-eighths mile (one kilometer) oval. That topped none other than Mark Martin's previous track record of 19.480 set the month before.

Waltrip—reviled for years—was voted NASCAR's Most Popular Driver in 1989 after Rusty Wallace hit the rear of his car and spun him out on May 21. Wallace went on to claim the prize, and Waltrip stated, "I hope he chokes on that $200,000." Hall of Famer Darrell Waltrip's career includes eighty-four Winston Cup wins, and across his career he's won nearly $20 million.

What is racing like at the Plymouth track?

The quarter-mile (402-meter) dirt track in Sheboygan County is less predictable than paved tracks. Vehicle classes include grand nationals, wingless super mods, four cylinders, and more. They also offer demolition derbies, always exciting on dirt.

Which NASCAR driver started at Sugar River Raceway?

Danica Patrick (1982–) started her career at this asphalt go-kart track. No need to have your own equipment at Sugar River—everything you need is available right there. Some of their go-karts can achieve speeds of seventy miles per hour (113 kph).

Patrick drove IndyCar races for years before moving to NASCAR. She raced in the Indianapolis 500 seven times—2005 through 2011—with her best finish in 2009 when she finished third.

What was racing like in the early years of Wisconsin racing?

Jere O'Day said, "It was like a sickness." He recalled a pregnant woman with a small boy giving her racing husband an ultimatum to give up racing. The man had just smashed his car for the second time and told his wife he'd give up her before the car."

O'Day equated the era's racing style to barnstorming. Race, drive all night to another track, and race again the next day. "I wasn't trying to prove anything. The pay wasn't great. I just loved doing it."

What was Augie Winkleman like?

Winkleman had to wear glasses—thick glasses—which were always covered with welding specks. Walking around he'd trip over equipment, and on the track he'd drive right into another car and claim he'd never seen it.

Dick Trickle said he drove like he was crazy, or in a rage, "banging and bumping everyone." But he was willing to help off the track. Marlin Walbeck recounts a story of being stuck on the side of the road when his tow car broke down, but Winkleman came along, hooked on, and Walbeck made the next race.

Which racer is known as "America's Winningest Driver"?

Though he never won a points-earning race, Dick Trickle (1941–2013) has that moniker because of his very successful career on the short track. Born in Wisconsin Rapids, he started racing at the age of thirteen in 1954 and appeared in his last race in 2001.

Trickle is credited with more than 2,000 races, a million laps, and has won more than 1,200 races. He started in thirteen Daytona 500 races, with a best finish in 1992 in fifth place.

Is Dick Trickle really his name?

There are a number of racers with strange names—Will Power (Australian IndyCar), Duck Waddle (Sports Car Club of America, fifty-year veteran racer), and Fonty Flock (Hall of Fame NASCAR racer) just to name a few. Richard Trickle is really the racer's name.

Why did Dick Trickle limp?

Many people would think his limp was because of a racing accident, but in truth it's because he shattered his hip playing when he was eight years old. He and his brother were in an under-construction home, and Dick fell from above the first floor, through the floor joists, and landed on the concrete basement floor. He spent three years in a cast.

While still in that cast he climbed a tree and fell out—shattering the cast. Doctors wondered if he'd ever walk again. Not only did he walk, but he ran, played "BB tag," and eventually raced.

Once, while doing hot laps to warm up, he told the owner of his 1946 Dodge that it didn't feel right. The owner told him they're supposed to feel like that. During the race he flipped it. The following week he flipped again during hot laps, then bought his own car to race.

How many races did Dick Trickle race in a year?

Trickle worked many jobs over the years in an effort to earn enough money to race. He

Born in Wisconsin Rapids, Dick Trickle (left, with track announcer Todd Behling in 2012) won over 1,200 races over the course of his career.

swept floors at his uncle's shop, worked for farmers, and eventually earned enough money for his first car. While working for a local telephone company he decided to call it quits and race full time.

As a full-time racer he'd drive in more than a hundred races per year—a pace he continued for fifteen years. The turning point for his career came in 1966 when he entered the first National Short Track Championship. The other racers laughed at him and anyone who drove "rat cars," but after two days of racing he'd earned some respect. He ended up winning and pocketed $1,645.

In 1971 Trickle picked up forty-one wins, and in 1972, set a record by winning sixty-seven races. In 1983 he won the World Crown 300 and picked up his biggest purse to-date—$50,000. That day he was dubbed the king of short trackers.

Who was Jimmy Back?

Back has been referred to as the Willie Nelson of central Wisconsin Racing. His motto was "do or die and let the parts fly," both on the track and off. He began his career in 1960 driving a 1952 Mercury. A fellow racer, Tom Reffner, said, "When Back is running, nobody can touch him."

His team won seventeen feature races in 1973 and nineteen the following year. He held track records at four different tracks. People joked that Back's best driving was when he got a new pair of glasses—one without welding specks blocking his view.

When did Tom Reffner start his racing career?

Rudolph, Wisconsin, native Tom Reffner's first race was in 1959. Over the years he picked up numerous feature wins—sixty-seven in 1975 alone—and Elko Speedway in Minnesota inducted him into their Hall of Fame in 2012. Dubbed "The Blue Knight," Reffner was known throughout the Midwest racing community.

Reffner was so fast, that during the 1970s he was the target of various "bounties," payable to anyone who would beat him. Despite being targeted, Reffner was named the Golden Sands Speedway track champion in 1975 and again in 1977.

What were some of Jim Sauter's accomplishments?

The Necedah, Wisconsin, native won the National Short Track championship in 1980 and earned the ARTGO Challenge Series championship in 1981 and 1982. The following year he won the All American 400. He won seventy-six races over fourteen years in what is now the Monster Energy Cup Series. He also tested IROC cars along with Dick Trickle and Dave Marcis, and he raced in the Daytona 500 seven times.

Sauter's sons followed his lead and made a career of racing—Tim, Jay, Johnny, and Jim Jr., as well as a grandson, Travis. Jim Sr.'s last NASCAR Nationwide Series also featured Tim, Jay, and Johnny. His seven daughters and another son, Joe, never raced.

Did a racer really drive with a rooster in his car?

Lyle Nabbefeldt drove a six-cylinder 1933 Chevy coupe they called a "chicken coop." One day someone decided it would be funny to have a chicken in the chicken coop. Nabbefeldt tied a rooster to the roll bar. The rooster would even go along to bars after races, where he'd eat peanuts and drink from a shot glass filled with beer. Eventually the "Legendary Leghorn" would doze off.

One time the rooster was along when Nabbefeldt flipped his car end-for-end. "I found my lighter where I flipped the first time, my cigarettes where I flipped the second, and [the rooster] where I landed the third time. He hung on for dear life after that."

"Roho" the rooster survived the racing but eventually died of pneumonia.

What reactions did fans have to a rooster riding in a race car?

Lyle Nabbefeldt conducted an interview on a Wisconsin Rapids morning radio show. One caller said the chicken should be turned over to the Humane Society instead of being forced to ride in a race car. Nabbefeldt replied, "Lady, you are worried about the chicken. What about me? I ride in the same car!"

Often "Roho" would be the first to emerge after a crash. A cloud of dust and smoke would block everyone's view, and then a chicken would fly out of the haze. Spectators would cheer as the bird emerged.

Roho's career lasted only a single summer.

Was there much drinking in early Wisconsin racing?

Life wasn't all a grind, according to what Father Grubba wrote. "You know the difference between northern racing and southern racing? In the north they get their racing done by 10:30 so they can start their partying. In the south they just mess around at the track all night." In that era, everyone who rolled his car at the track would get a case of beer. Sometimes, because cars were so inexpensive, a driver would roll on purpose to collect that "prize."

When did Alan Kulwicki break into NASCAR?

Kulwicki (1954–1993) was an American Speed Association (ASA) racer, staying on short tracks. He said moving to NASCAR involved financial risks and depended on timing. After five NASCAR races at the end of 1985, he was broke. "I went to Daytona and didn't make the show. I could have failed." But he took a look at the up-and-coming drivers and knew it was time. "Timing is critical."

In 1986 Kulwicki was named NASCAR rookie of the year. In 1992 he won the Winston Cup championship. He died in a plane crash in 1993 and is buried in Milwaukee, Wisconsin.

What has Paul Menard accomplished in racing?

The son of the founder of the Wisconsin-based lumberyard chain, Menards, Paul Menard (1980–) has a career in racing that started in go-karts at the age of eight. He began ice racing at age fifteen and won ten international ice racing events in his career.

In 2000 Menard began a limited NASCAR schedule, and in 2003 he entered what is now the Monster Energy Cup Series. Across fourteen years he has only a single win but placed in the top five nineteen times. Since 2003 he's picked up three wins in the Xfinity Series.

Read more about the Menards lumberyard chain in the chapter on Retail Business.

Greenfield native Alan "Special K" Kulwicki was a NASCAR Rookie of the Year (1986) and won the Winston Cup (1992) before dying tragically in a 1993 airplane crash in Tennessee.

Was Kvapil's #44 ever recovered?

About twenty-four hours after first stolen, police received a call about a suspicious vehicle along a suburban road. Kvapil's race car had apparently been abandoned by thieves. Though recovered on Saturday, there wasn't time for Kvapil to prepare for his race the next day. The team's owner said there was no damage to the car. The truck and trailer were not at the scene, but the car—worth about $250,000—was there.

A few hours later Kvapil's truck was spotted not far from where the theft took place. The truck received some minor damage—a broken door handle and ignition switch.

Did Travis Kvapil have his race car stolen?

At the end of February of 2015, Kvapil's trailer, along with his number 44 stock car, was stolen from an Atlanta, Georgia, hotel parking lot on an early Friday morning. He was to race Sunday afternoon, and was forced to withdraw from the NASCAR Sprint Cup race. Kvapil said, "I just can't believe it. I'm sure that whoever stole it had no idea they were getting a Cup car and a spare engine."

Police say a video shows Kvapil's black pickup towing the trailer as it pulled out of the lot. In addition to the truck, trailer, and car, a spare engine worth $100,000 was also lost. Additional parts and equipment was also lost, all of which would cost $17,000.

The trailer, parts, and spare engine were not at that scene. Crew chief Peter Sospenzo (1956–) said, "I've been doing this since 1979. I've probably been in 1,200 hotels and 1,200 race tracks. Never once has this happened."

What has Kvapil accomplished on the track?

Kvapil has raced in 271 Monster Energy Cup races, started at pole only once, and has never placed in the top five. In the Camping World Truck Series he picked up nine wins in 195 races and raced in the Daytona 500 seven times. His best placing there was nineteenth.

What could be considered the worst luck a racing team has had?

Furniture Row Racing had a horrible 2017 on a personal level. Jim Watson texted his wife about what a wonderful time he was having with teammates at a go-kart track, then suffered a fatal heart attack in November of 2017. The girlfriend of Martin Truex Jr. had a recurrence of ovarian cancer and another round of chemo. A close friend of Cole Pearn died after a small cut became infected, and Pearn had to put down a dog they'd owned for thirteen years.

On the track, however, Furniture Row fared well. Truex rallied to win a Cup race the Sunday after Watson died, won at Watkins Glen, Charlotte, and dominated all season.

Do any Wisconsin drivers have memorials?

Alan Kulwicki—who started on Wisconsin short tracks—eventually won the 1992 Winston Cup. He has a memorial in Greenfield, Wisconsin, where he grew up. In fact, the twenty-eight-acre (eleven-hectare) park that contains the memorial is named Alan Kulwicki Memorial Park. University of Wisconsin-Milwaukee and the University of North Carolina-Charlotte both offer scholarships in his name.

Dick Trickle was born in Wisconsin Rapids and spent a lot of time in Rudolph, Wisconsin. He has a memorial in Rudolph. An eight-foot bronze statue of Trickle waving to fans is amid displays of many of the cars he drove.

How do racers advance into NASCAR racing?

Drivers have many different career paths. Some start as dirt track racers—or even go-kart racers, like Danica Patrick—but all move on to paved tracks if they want to

Born in Beloit, Danica Patrick is the most successful female racer in history, including her victory at the 2008 Indy Japan 300.

move toward a NASCAR career. They advance through different levels of local racing before moving to a regional and national touring series.

COLLEGE SPORTS

Which organizations have a presence in Wisconsin college sports?

There are a number of different associations with member colleges in the state. They are the National Collegiate Athletic Association (NCAA), the National Association of Intercollegiate Athletics (NAIA), the National Junior College Athletic Association (NJCAA), the Wisconsin Junior College Athletic Association (WJCAA), the National Christian College Athletic Association (NCCAA), and the United States Collegiate Athletic Association (USCAA).

How many divisions of the NCAA are represented in Wisconsin?

All three divisions of the NCAA have schools in Wisconsin. Four schools qualify as Division I schools: Marquette, UW-Milwaukee, UW-Green Bay, and UW-Madison.

What is the team name for Marquette University?

Marquette has a variety of varsity sports programs at the university, all of which are called the Golden Eagles. They include men's (and women's) basketball, cross country and track, football, men's golf, lacrosse, and soccer. Only the men's basketball team has ever won the NCAA National Championship, and that happened in 1977.

Did Marquette ever have another mascot?

The mascot for Marquette has changed a number of times over the years. Unofficially, the team was known as the Blue and Gold (still their team colors) in 1892. In 1917 the student body wanted something with more of a name instead of colors. Since the college's first building stood on a hill, they named their teams the Hilltoppers. That was their first official nickname.

The football team was known by another name, though. The Golden Avalanche was very popular, and that name appeared in school yearbooks. In 1954 the Golden Avalanche and Hilltopper nicknames faded, and the student senate chose to have their school teams known as the Warriors. In 1961 they held a contest to name their mascot, and the contest's winning name was Willie Wampum. That name lasted until 1971 when outrage over the degrading representation of Native Americans brought an end to Willie.

After debate and discussion, the school settled on the First Warrior. The mascot's outfit was designed to reflect authentic native dress. The representation wasn't particularly popular, and in 1984 the vote came back with Bleuteaux, a muppet-like animal with blue fur and a stumpy trunk. That mascot was retired in 1991.

271

In 1994, after continued controversy, the school became known as the Golden Eagles. In 2004 a survey of student opinion showed a strong support to the previous Warrior name. Trustees instead scrapped the Golden Eagles in favor of the Golds. Protests ensued, hundreds of letters were received objecting to the change, and another survey resulted in a return to the Golden Eagles. The team colors have never changed. They're still blue and gold.

In what conference does Marquette basketball compete?

From 1916 through the 1988–1989 season, Marquette competed as an independent school. Starting with the 1989–1990 season the school played in what is now the Horizon League. For the 1991–1992 season through the 1994–1995 season they were in the Great Midwest Conference, then Conference USA from 1995–1996 through 2004–2005.

Currently Marquette University plays in the Big East.

How many basketball players from Marquette played professionally?

Thirty-nine players moved on to the NBA or ABA. The first was Bill Downey (1923–), who played in three games for the Providence Steamrollers in 1948. He scored no points. Numerous players from Marquette played in the NBA into the 2000s.

Three players and coaches from the school were part of the Milwaukee Bucks organization: Jim Boylan (assistant coach, 2008–2013), Steve Novak (forward, 2016–2017), and George Thompson (point guard, 1974–1975).

Were any Marquette football players drafted by NFL teams?

According to pro-football-reference.com, seventy players from Marquette played in the NFL, many of those drafted. There were six who were members of the Chicago Cardinals, three each for the Pittsburgh Steelers, New York Giants, and Chicago Bears. Two were picked up by the Detroit Lions, and one each drafted by the Dallas Cowboys, Washington Redskins, Cleveland Rams, and Green Bay Packers.

Which Marquette players were members of the Green Bay Packers?

LaVern "Lavvie" Dilweg (1903–1968) played in three sports in college—football, basketball, and track. He played for the Milwaukee Badgers their last season in the NFL, then played with the Packers as an end from 1927 through 1934. He scored twelve receiving touchdowns and averaged twelve yards (eleven meters) per reception.

Red Dunn (1901–1957) played running back for the Milwaukee Badgers, Chicago Cardinals, and the Green Bay Packers 1927–1931. He played in fifty-eight games for Green Bay, starting forty of them. Overall he scored fifty-four points, forty-eight of them on extra points, two field goals for six points.

Gene Ronzani (1909–1975) was the second head coach of the Green Bay Packers, 1950–1953. In 1950 and 1951 he led the team to records of 3–9, but in 1952 the Packers finished at .500 with three straight losses to finish the season. In 1953, Ronzani resigned the day after a disastrous Thanksgiving Day to the Detroit Lions, 34–15, on national television.

Have any Marquette student athletes won Olympic medals?

Ralph Metcalfe (1910–1978) was a two-time silver medalist in the 100-meter dash, once each in the 1932 and 1936 games. In the 1936 Olympic games he brought home a gold medal in the 4 × 100-meter relay.

John Bennett (1930–) also did well in the Olympics, bringing home a silver medal in the long jump in 1956.

Frank McCabe (1927–) earned gold in the 1952 Olympics in basketball.

In addition to those players, a multitude of alumni from Marquette have played in the Olympic games, for the United States and against.

Marquette University alumnus Ralph Metcalfe won two silver medals in the 100-meter dash at the 1932 and 1936 Olympics. He later served as a U.S. congressman for Illinois's first district.

What is the team name for UW-Milwaukee?

Milwaukee started as the Green Gulls in 1927, changed to the Cardinals in 1956, then switched to the Panthers in 1964. Prior to 1990 the university competed mostly in the D-2 or D-3 levels of the NCAA.

The Milwaukee Panthers have thirteen teams now competing at the D-1 level of the NCAA in the Horizon League. There are teams for basketball, baseball, cross country, soccer, swimming & diving, track & field, tennis, and volleyball. Some of those have both men's and women's programs, others only men's or women's.

Are there any Panthers alum who played in the pros?

Von McDade (1970–) was selected in the second round of the NBA draft by the New Jersey Nets, though he never played in any NBA games.

Bill Carollo (1951–) played quarterback for the Panthers from 1970–1973. He officiated NFL games from 1989 through 2008, including eight conference championship games and two Super Bowls (XXX and XXXVII). Afterward he became the director of officiating for the Big Ten Conference.

Mike Reinfeldt (1953–) was captain of the Panthers varsity football team in 1974. He played as a safety in the NFL for the Oakland Raiders and Houston Oilers. He served in various nonplayer roles for the Los Angeles Raiders, Green Bay Packers, and Seattle Seahawks.

Demetrius Harris (1991–), despite playing only club football at Milwaukee (they had no varsity program), was signed by the Kansas City Chiefs as an undrafted free agent in 2013.

Were any Panthers players drafted by the NFL?

While six Milwaukee players played in the NFL, only one—Ken Kranz (1923–)—was drafted. Green Bay took him in 1949. He played in seven games as a defensive back, scored no points, but recovered a fumble for seven yards.

The undrafted players were Demetrius Harris (1991–), Paul Meyers (1895–1966), Clem Neacy (1898–1968), Mike Reinfeldt (1953–), and Whitey Wolter (1899–1947).

Where do the Panthers play at home?

The men's basketball program competes at Panther Arena for the most part. Some of their games are at the J. Martin Klotchke Center, which hosts the women's basketball program, as well as volleyball, swimming and diving, and indoor track and field. Englemann Field is home for men's and women's soccer.

Henry Aaron Field hosts the baseball program, and women's tennis is played at the Paley Tennis Center.

What is the McCafferty Trophy, and how many times have the Panthers won it?

James J. McCafferty (1916–2006) was the Midwestern City Conference's first commissioner. Later that conference was renamed the Horizon League. Each year a trophy is awarded to overall athletic performance. Points are earned in each of nineteen sports, based on regular season or championship finishes.

Milwaukee has earned the McCafferty Trophy seven times (along with Notre Dame and Oral Roberts), second to Butler who has won eight times.

What is the name of UW-Green Bay's teams?

From the start the University of Wisconsin-Green Bay fielded the Phoenix, though the school's name has been slightly altered over time. The UW-Green Bay Phoenix became the UWGB Phoenix, and are now simply the Green Bay Phoenix.

The school has fifteen varsity teams: basketball, cross country, golf, soccer, sofball, swimming and diving, tennis, volleyball, and skiing. Softball and volleyball are programs fielding only women's teams, with skiing a co-ed team.

The school does not have a varsity football program.

Have any members of Green Bay athletics become notable sports figures?

Logan Vander Velden (1971–) went undrafted in the 1994 NBA draft but went on to play small forward for the Los Angeles Clippers for fifteen games in 1995. He played a total of thirty-one minutes, scoring only nine total points. He was released by the Clippers on January 4, 1996.

Jeff Wallace Nordgaard (1973–) also played in the NBA. He was selected by the Milwaukee Bucks in the second round of the NBA draft in 1996. He played in thirteen games for a total of forty-eight minutes, scoring only eighteen points. He was released by the Bucks in 1997 and served two ten-day contracts in 1998.

Tony Bennett (1969–) was drafted in 1992 and played in 152 games for the Charlotte Hornets from 1992 to 1995. He scored 538 points those three seasons.

What is the mascot and name for the UW-Madison sports teams?

"Bucky" Badger is the mascot for all the University of Wisconsin teams. A human-like cartoon of a badger first appeared in college publications in the 1930s. At that point the mascot had no name. The portrayal of the badger wearing a sweater with the iconic "W" was drawn by Art Evans in

Designed by artist Art Evans, "Bucky" Badger debuted as the University of Wisconsin's mascot in 1940.

1940. An actual live badger was used as a mascot at some football games but was retired to a zoo when he proved too difficult—and dangerous. The mascot was replaced with a raccoon named Regdab ("badger" spelled backwards).

An art student produced a paper-mache headpiece in the shape of a badger's head, and it was worn by a gymnast/cheerleader at the 1948 homecoming game. A contest was started to name the mascot, and the winning suggestion was "Buckingham U. Badger"—Bucky.

What varsity sports are played by the Badgers?

There are twenty-three varsity sports played at the University of Wisconsin-Madison. They include football, men's and women's basketball, wrestling, men's and women's ice hockey, softball, boxing, cross country, track and field, and more.

Were any Badgers football players in the NFL?

More than three hundred players from the Badgers played in the NFL or AFL. Nearly two hundred were drafted. Twenty were taken by the Green Bay Packers. Four Badgers went on to be listed in the Pro Football Hall of Fame.

For more on professional football, see the chapter on the Green Bay Packers.

What championships have been won by the Badgers?

The University of Wisconsin is ranked seventeenth in the nation for the most Division I championships in the NCAA. The Badgers have won twenty-eight NCAA national championships, with eight in boxing—though half of those are unofficial, earned before 1948.

The men's program has championships in six different sports—basketball, boxing, cross country, ice hockey, track and field, and soccer. The women have been tops in cross country and ice hockey.

Did any Badgers play professional basketball?

Dick Schultz (1917–1968) was the first of the Badgers. From 1946 through 1950 he played for six teams, starting with the Cleveland Rebels and finishing with the Sheboygan Red Skins. He played in 205 games, and averaged 5.6 points per game.

Twenty-five players from the Badgers appeared in the NBA or ABA, with several playing into the 2017 season and beyond.

How many bowl games has the Badger football program participated in?

The Badgers have appeared in twenty-nine bowl games, starting with the Rose Bowl in 1952. They lost to USC 7–0. Their first win didn't come until 1982, when they beat Kansas State in the Independence Bowl 14–3.

In all, Wisconsin has appeared in the Rose Bowl nine times. They were in the following seasons: 1952, 1959, 1962, 1993, 1998, 1999, 2010, 2011, and 2012.

What is the longest streak of bowl appearances for the Badgers?

Wisconsin has appeared in seventeen straight bowl straight Bowl games, from 2002 (the Alamo Bowl, where they beat Colorado 31–28) through 2016 (another win, beating Western Michigan 24–16). Of those, three were the Rose Bowl, three were the Outback Bowl, three were the Capitol One Bowl, two were the Champs Sports Bowl, and one each for the Holiday Bowl, Cotton Bowl, Alamo Bowl, Orange Bowl, Music City Bowl, and Pinstripe Bowl.

Have the Badgers ever won back-to-back Rose Bowl games?

Wisconsin won the Rose Bowl two years running in 1998 and 1999. Over the years the Badgers have a 3–6 losing record in the Rose Bowl, only winning in 1993 (beating UCLA 21–16), 1998 (beating UCLA 38–31), and 1999 (beating Stanford 21–9).

Across all bowl games, the Badgers have a record of 16–14.

What is the longest streak of consecutive-year Bowl game wins for the Badgers?

In addition to back-to-back Rose Bowl wins, Wisconsin won bowl games in consecutive years in 1993 (beating UCLA in the Rose Bowl 21–16) and 1994 (beating Duke in the Hall of Fame

Bowl 34–20). Another back-to-back bowl win happened in 2005 (beating Auburn in the Capitol One Bowl 24–10) and 2006 (beating Arkansas in the Capitol One Bowl 17–14).

However, the Badgers have won bowl games in four consecutive seasons, though not in consecutive years. In the 2014 season they beat Auburn in the Outback Bowl (34–31) on January 1, 2015. The following season (2015) the Badgers beat Southern California (23–21) on December 30, 2015—the same year as their previous bowl win. The same thing happened—consecutive season wins in the same year—when they beat Western Michigan (24–16) in the Cotton Bowl on January 2, 2017 (2016 season), topped Miami of Florida (34–24) on December 30, 2017 (2017 season), and defeated the Miami Hurricanes (35–3) on December 27, 2018.

How much money does the University of Wisconsin bring in from sports?

ESPN looked at six years of revenue available from public records and ranked the University of Wisconsin as number two nationwide in bringing cash into the system. They trailed only Texas. Revenue generated by sports in the UW system reached a staggering $149 million in the 2012–2013 academic year. Of course, expenses were ranked second again only to Texas in the nation as well—$146.7 million.

The study's authors were amazed that more than half of the money brought in came from sources other than football and basketball. Other sports, conference payouts, and donations accounted for more than half. Donations and contributions alone reached

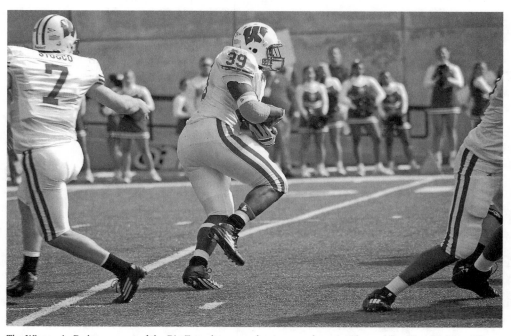

The Wisconsin Badgers—part of the Big Ten—have won fourteen conference titles and five West Division titles.

$58.9 million. A dip in the popularity of any one sport couldn't possibly spell doom to the University of Wisconsin, which has a well-rounded revenue stream.

How much revenue do other colleges pull in?

Another study, this one by Business Insider, ranks the Badgers at number eight nationwide, earning $127.9 million in 2015. The top earning school was Oregon at $196 million, with donations of $124.9 million their top source of cash. Tickets brought in only $26.6 million. Rounding out the top five schools were Texas ($161 million), Michigan ($157.9 million), Alabama ($153.2 million), and Ohio State ($145.2 million).

According to the study, twenty schools earn more than a hundred million dollars annually from their sports programs. The top revenue source in all those programs is donations and contributions.

Who are the most notable athletes who came from Wisconsin?

An article by si.com lists fifty men and women who were educated in Wisconsin. They include Olympians, football players, basketball, baseball, and more. The most famous, arguably or not, would be Curly Lambeau—who ranked number four on the list.

Notable Wisconsin Athletes

Name	City	Sport	Notes
Eric Heiden	Madison	Speed Skating	Gold in 1980 Olympics Ten world championships
Ernie Nevers	Superior	Football	All-Pro five NFL seasons
Al Simmons	Milwaukee	Baseball	100+ RBI twelve times in MLB 200+ hits six times in MLB
Curley Lambeau	Green Bay	Football	Founded Green Bay Packers Coached Packers to six NFL titles
Dan Jansen	West Allis	Speed skating	World record 1,000 m 1994 Olympics
Bud Grant	Superior	Basketball	Guard for LA Lakers in 1949–50 championship. Head coach for the Minnesota Vikings 1967–85
Addie Joss	Woodland	Baseball	Career ERA of 1.89 One-hitter for the Indians in 1902
Mike Webster	Tomahawk	Football	Won four Super Bowls with Steelers Nine-time Pro Bowl
Dave Casper	Chilton	Football	Two Super Bowls, Pro Bowl five times
Helene Kapphahu	Madison	Swimming	World records twenty events Olympic records in two events 1932 games

Rounding out the top twenty notable athletes from Wisconsin includes Jim Otto (Oakland Raiders center), D. Wayne Lukas (U.S. Racing Hall of Fame horse trainer), Alan Ameche (Heisman Trophy winner and Baltimore Colts player), Jim Montgomery (Olympic medal swimmer), Alvin Kraenzlein (1900 Olympic medal track and field star),

Elroy "Crazy Legs" Hirsch (Hall of Famer who played for the L.A. Rams), Harvey Kuenn (MLB player and manager), Dave Krieg (NFL star), Frank Parker (pro tennis player), and Tony Kubek (Yankees shortstop and TV broadcaster).

How many soccer programs exist in Wisconsin colleges?

There are twenty-nine men's soccer programs in the state, with eighty-four coaches. Most of those are clustered in the southeast portion of the state, inside a rough triangle from Milwaukee to Madison to Green Bay and back. Those outside that area are Beloit, Platteville, Viterbo, Northland, and Superior.

Women's soccer has more programs and more coaches. There are thirty-five programs with ninety-seven coaches in the Badger state, most of them again clustered in the same triangle as for the men.

How is college rugby organized in Wisconsin?

There are three divisions of men's rugby in the state: Division 1, Division 2, and NSCRO (National Small College Rugby Organization). Only the University of Wisconsin ranks in the D1, seven schools rank as D2, and seven more rank as NSCRO. Note: Michigan's Upper Peninsula is organized into the Wisconsin system for rugby.

The D2 schools include Marquette, Northern Michigan, UW-La Crosse, UW-Stout, UW-Milwaukee, UW-Platteville, and UW-Whitewater. The NSCRO schools include Michigan Tech, MSOE (Milwaukee School of Engineering), Ripon College, UW-Stevens Point, UW-Eau Claire, UW-Madison, and UW-Parkside.

How many hockey programs are there in Wisconsin college athletics?

The NCAA lists only one hockey program for men, another for women, for Division One schools. Both of those are at UW-Madison. The men's team joined D-1 in 1947 and have six national championships. The women joined D-1 in 2000 and have picked up four national titles.

The men's D-3 schools in Wisconsin include Concordia, Lawrence, Marian, MSOE, Northland, St. Norbert, UW-Eau Claire, UW-River Falls, UW-Stevens Point, UW-Stout, and UW-Superior. Schools with women's programs include Concordia, Marian, St. Norbert, UW-Eau Claire, UW-River Falls, UW-Stevens Point, and UW-Superior.

Wisconsin has no D-2 ice hockey in the NCAA.

When did the UW hockey program start?

The Badgers started out playing hockey on Lake Mendota in the late 1800s. Their informal hockey program began in the 1910s, and their first scheduled games were played in 1921.

The program ended in 1934 but restarted in 1962. They advanced into the NCAA playoffs and took third place in 1970. Three years later they won the tournament. By 1990 they they'd won their fifth national title.

279

How many professional hockey players came from Wisconsin?

According to Quanthockey.com, thirty-seven Wisconsinites have become professional hockey players. The first was Roger Jenkins (1911–) who played for the Chicago Blackhawks and Toronto Maple Leafs in the 1930 season. Overall he played 324 games in the NHL, scored fifteen goals—three of them game-winners—and played for the Blackhawks during Stanley Cup championships in 1934 and 1938.

How many NCAA Division One schools in the state have a tennis program?

Of the four D-1 schools in Wisconsin, all four have a tennis program. Those schools are Marquette, UW-Green Bay, UW-Madison, and UW-Green Bay.

What other college sports are played in Wisconsin?

On the men's side, other sports include cross country, golf, rowing, soccer, swimming and diving, track and field, and wrestling. The women have all those as well as rowing lightweight and softball.

Which teams in University of Wisconsin athletics scored the highest cumulative GPA?

Data from the university system as of the fall of 2013 ranked grade point averages for a number of different sports. Cumulative GPAs for men and women were a bit different, with the top five listed.

GPA among Wisconsin College Teams

Ranking	Men's Sport	GPA	Women's Sport	GPA
#1	Tennis	3.18	Cross Country	3.28
#2	Cross Country	3.09	Swimming	3.22
#3	Soccer	3.00	Track	3.21
#4	Rowing	2.99	Golf	3.19
#5	Hockey	2.93	Rowing	3.11
		2.92 overall average		3.11 overall average

OLYMPIC ATHLETES

How many Olympic athletes has Wisconsin produced?

Sports-reference.com lists nearly 10,000 American participants since the first Olympic Games of the modern era. Of those, citizens have brought home more than a thousand gold medals, more than nine hundred silver medals, and nearly eight hundred bronze medals.

Ranker.com lists sixty Wisconsin athletes participating in the Olympic Games. All totaled, eighty-one medals were brought back to the Badger State—forty-four of them gold, twenty-five silver, twelve bronze.

In the book *Going for Wisconsin Gold*, Jessie Garcia lists nearly two hundred Olympic athletes with connections to Wisconsin.

Are there Wisconsin Olympians not on the ranker.com list?

Yes. And no. The web page lists only Olympians who were born in Wisconsin, as opposed to every person who resided in the state at the time they won Olympic contests.

Erin Jackson (1992–), who resides in Milwaukee, Wisconsin, competed as a speed skater in the 2018 Olympics (see below).

Another notable name missing from the ranker list is George Pogue (1880–1962). He was a sprinter and hurdler for the University of Wisconsin-Milwaukee, and on August 31, 1904, he became the world's first African American Olympic medal winner. He placed third in the 400-meter hurdles in the St. Louis Games that day, and the following day placed third in 200-meter hurdles.

Is there an Olympic speed skater from Wisconsin who'd only been on the ice for a few months?

Erin Jackson qualified for the 2018 Olympics as a speed skater after only four months of training on actual ice. The long-time speed skater usually competed on in-line skates and has won multiple medals on the track. Just not on the ice.

She has three World Champion gold medals on in-line skates, two for the 500 meter and another for the 1,000 meter. In addition Jackson has two other golds—2014 Pan American Championships 500 meter, and 2014 Pan American Olympic Festival 500 meter.

She also holds multiple silver and bronze medals, and she joined Team USA in the 2018 Winter Olympics.

Which Wisconsinite has won the most Olympic gold in one year?

In the 1980 Winter Olympic Games in Lake Placid, New York, Eric Heiden (1958–) of Madison, Wisconsin, accomplished what no other Olympian had done before. He won five individual gold medals in a single Olympics. At the age of twenty-one he became known as The Man of Gold.

His first win was February 15, when he won the 500-meter speed skate with a time of 38.03 seconds. The next day he took his second gold in the 5,000 meters, then won again in the 1,000 meters on the 19th, again on the 21st in the 1,500 meters, then took the 10,000-meter race the day after the Americans beat the Soviet Union in the "Miracle on Ice" hockey game.

After all his wins, thrilled as he was, he said, "I'd rather get a nice warmup suit. That's something I can use. Gold medals just sit there."

Eric Heiden, who hails from Madison, won five gold medals in the 1980 Olympics, setting four Olympics that year, in speed skating.

Did Eric Heiden's sister ever win in the Olympics?

Beth (1959–) and Eric Heiden trained together as teenagers, and both participated in the 1976 Olympic Games. Neither won recognition that year, though they did make enough waves to get noticed during training for the 1980 Olympic Games. While Beth never reached the same heights of fame as her brother, she was a world-class speed skater.

Beth won four gold medals at the 1979 World Championships. In the Olympic Games the following year she earned the bronze medal in the 3,000 meters. Perhaps her biggest accomplishment is doing so well considering her size—five feet two inches, 105 pounds (157 centimeters, 47.6 kilos). "At my size, skating outdoors was tough. Cutting through the wind made things harder for me."

Has any other Wisconsin native won five gold medals?

Speed skater Bonnie Blair of Milwaukee participated in four Olympic Games. A nineteen-year-old Blair qualified for the 1984 Olympics under the tutelage of Eric Heiden's former coach. Though she didn't

Speed skater Bonnie Blair of Milwaukee won five gold medals and a bronze medal in the 1988, 1992, and 1994 Olympics, as well as three gold, four silver, and two bronze medals in the World Championships.

medal—she finished eighth—she was ecstatic. "If you had seen me cross the finish line, you probably would have thought I had won." It was a learning experience that served her for the following Games.

In 1988, one of Blair's competitors was the gold medal winner from the 1984 Games, who promptly set a world record and a very high bar. Blair ended up with a gold after beating that new world record by two one-hundredths of a second in the 500 meters. Four days later she earned bronze in the 1,000.

Two Winter Games later, after 1992 and 1994, she'd earned four more gold medals. She was the first Olympic athlete to win gold in the same event—500 meters—in three consecutive Olympic Games. She was also the first woman to win five gold medals.

Who are the most prominent Wisconsin Olympians?

In her book, *Going for Wisconsin Gold*, Jessie Garcia lists twenty-two of the most prominent gold medalists from the state of Wisconsin. They ranged from the very first to bring home gold (Alvin Kraenzlein), the first African American medalist (George Poage), and the first Olympian (Eric Jansen) to win five gold medals in a single year.

Who was the first gold medalist from Wisconsin?

Alvin Kraenzlein (1876–1928) of Milwaukee, Wisconsin, not only won the first gold medal to come back to the state but also helped revolutionize hurdling. His coach pioneered the "crouching start" position, which is now widely used for sprinting starts. Together they developed a lead-leg technique for clearing hurdles.

Before Kraenzlein, the usual way of hurdling involved sprinting to the barrier, slowing, and hopping over with legs tucked. Kraenzlein was the first to master the technique of extending one leg straight over the hurdle to glide naturally through the course.

On his way to the 1900 Olympic Games, Kraenzlein and his fellow athletes from America competed in the UK Track and Field Championships. They cleaned up.

In Paris, France, Kraenzlein competed in four events. He became the first athlete to win four individual events in a single day.

What did Alvin Kraenzlein win in Paris?

Instead of medals, the French gave out pieces of art, including paintings across a range of values. The tradition of handing out medals wouldn't come into practice until 1904 at the Summer Games in St. Louis.

After the 1900 Olympic Games Kraenzlein gave up his career in dentistry to become a coach. He led teams in Pennsylvania, Michigan, and was even invited by Kaiser Wilhelm (1859–1941) of Germany in 1913 to coach their track and field team for the 1916 Olympic Games in Berlin. He signed a five-year contract, but prior to a declaration of war, the kaiser warned Kraenzlein to leave while he still could. World War I broke out shortly after Kraenzlein and his family left the country.

Track and field athlete George Poage of La Crosse (shown here at the 1904 Olympics 60-meter sprint) was the first African American to medal in the games.

Who was the first African American Olympic medalist?

George Poage (1880–1962), whose family moved to La Crosse, Wisconsin, when he was four years old, was the first black person to medal in the Olympic Games. After graduating from what is now La Crosse Central High School, Poage became the first black varsity runner for the University of Wisconsin and the first black person to fill in for the track coach when he left town.

The black community called for a boycott of the 1904 Olympic Games in protest of racial segregation in the host city of St. Louis. Poage refused and entered four events. He raced into the history books on August 31, 1904, taking bronze in the 400-meter hurdles. Hours later another African American medaled—Joseph Stadler (1880–1950) took silver in the high jump. The next day Poage scored another bronze in the 200-meter hurdles.

In 1998 Poage was inducted into the Wisconsin Athletic Hall of Fame. In 2013 La Crosse, Wisconsin, named a park in his honor.

Were any of the 1980 "Miracle on Ice" hockey players from Wisconsin?

Two of the twenty members of that team were from the Badger State. Both were smaller players, both were raised in Madison, Wisconsin, and both were twenty-two that winter.

Mark Johnson (1957–), who had skated from time to time with Eric Heiden, feared he'd be cut from the team. Instead he became a starter and went on to be the team's top scorer.

What is the Wisconsin Olympic Oval?

The Olympic Oval is an outdoor skating rink built in the late 1960s outside West Allis, Wisconsin. The refrigerated 400-meter oval was the first refrigerated outdoor rink in North America, and could keep ice for half a year at a time. It quickly became a draw for ice skating athletes throughout the Midwestern states of America.

That track was replaced by the Pettit National Ice Center, which opened in 1993.

Bob Suter (1957–2014) picked up two nicknames—"Woody," because of his resiliency similar to a wood duck, and "Bam Bam," for the hits he dished out on the ice. He set records at the University of Wisconsin for number of penalties (177) and penalty minutes (377).

Nobody expected much from the American hockey team, which had to fight for every dollar of funding. An exhibition game prior to the 1980 Games resulted in a massive 10–3 loss to the Soviet team. At that point even a silver medal seemed a long shot. But after an initial tie with Sweden, the Americans won game after game in convincing fashion. In the third period of their game with the heavily favored Soviets, America scored twice for the win. They clinched the gold by beating Finland, leaving the Soviet team to take silver.

Did any mother-daughter pairs from Wisconsin ever compete in the Olympic Games?

Nancy Swider-Pelz (1956–) competed in four separate Games—1976, 1980, 1984, and 1988. Though she never earned Olympic medals, she held the world record for the 3,000-meter speed skate in 1976 and another world record in the 10,000 meters in 1980. She is a member of the Speed Skating Hall of Fame.

Her daughter, also named Nancy (1987–), also skated in the Olympics. In 2010 she finished fourth in the team pursuit event.

Neither of them called Wisconsin "home," but they both trained at the Pettit National Ice Center near West Allis, Wisconsin.

How did Dan Jansen become an Olympic skater?

Jansen's (1965–) answer sounds like a joke, but really isn't. "It was literally and honestly so they didn't have to get a babysitter for me." Little Dan followed his brothers and sisters everywhere, and in winter the Jansen kids skated. They skated indoors and outdoors, and with the Olympic Oval so close it was no surprise he caught the bug. "It was just fun."

Jansen also credits Eric Heiden, who had won his five gold medals in the 1980 Olympic Games when Jansen was a teenager. A year later the family sent Jansen to Davos, Switzerland, for his first international meet. He won. Then he tried out for the

285

1984 Games when trials were held at the Olympic Oval. He succeeded in two events, though his brother, Mike, missed out by a tenth of a second.

Though he didn't medal that year, he did finish fourth in the 500 meters. The 1988 Olympic Games didn't go well, though Jansen was at the top of his game. His sister died a few hours before his signature race, the 500-meter speed skate. He false-started, and in the restart he fell. He fell in the 1,000 as well, just short of the finish line.

The following Games didn't go well, either. To cut costs in 1992, France held skating competitions outdoors. Rain and warm temperatures softened the ice and Jansen came away with a fourth place in the 500, and twenty-sixth in the 1,000. The 1994 Games would be his last chance, and he ended up slipping in the 500 meter. In disgust with his performance, he considered withdrawing from the 1,000 but competed anyway and held on to set a new world record and earn a gold medal after six failed attempts.

Were there any other baseball gold medalists from Wisconsin?

From Coon Valley, Wisconsin, Scott Servais (1967–) served as a backup catcher for Doug Robbins (1966–) in the 1988 Olympic Games in Seoul, South Korea. The sport was "demonstration only," not an official event, but the American team won. Even though medals were awarded, they never counted toward a country's total.

Have Wisconsin twins ever competed in the same Olympic Games?

In the 2000 Games in Sydney, Australia, twins Paul and Morgan Hamm (1982–) of Waukesha, Wisconsin, became the first set of twins to compete in the Olympics in the same year. Neither made a good showing in gymnastics—Paul came in fourteenth, Morgan fifty-seventh. As with many Olympians, the second time around was different.

In 2004 Paul became the first American to win the all-around title at the World Championships. At the Olympic Games, the American team (including Paul and Morgan Hamm) scored silver—only the second time America medaled in gymnastics since 1932. Though Paul didn't feel quite right, he led the individual field after his floor routine. He was still first after the pommel horse. After the rings—still first. He landed wrong after the vault and nearly crashed into the judges table. His poor score dropped him to twelfth with two events to go.

Hamm's performance on the parallel bars pushed him back to fourth place, and he later said it was his best routine ever. He hoped to do well enough on the high bar to score silver, but after a score of 9.837, Paul Hamm became the first American to win gold in the all-around. His margin of victory was only 0.012.

Why was there such a controversy with Paul Hamm's gold medal?

After Hamm dropped to twelfth and returned to win gold, the South Koreans argued the ruling. Their competitor said he'd been given a difficulty rating of 9.9 when it should have been 10.0. If the appeal was upheld, Hamm would lose his gold medal. After a careful review, the judges did note an error in the start value that could support that claim.

The review also revealed the South Korean had a slip-up in his routine. He'd performed four hangs and only three were allowed. The penalty of 0.2 would more than offset any difference in the start value for difficulty. A later appeal to an international gymnastics body (FIG) wasn't accepted, since all appeals needed to be filed immediately, not after the medals had been delivered.

The argument went on for months. Eventually the FIG appealed directly to Paul Hamm. They sent a letter to him through the US Olympic Committee, asking him to voluntarily give up his gold medal in "an action that would be recognized as the ultimate demonstration of Fairplay [sic]." The letter further stated the IOC "would appreciate the magnitude of this gesture." But at that point only Paul Hamm could make that decision.

The USOC was incensed. So was the IOC, which resented an athlete being put in that situation and did not support the claims of the FIG letter. The response of the USOC asserted that the FIG rules and public statements indicated Hamm was the winner of the gold medal. The request for him to give up the medal "undermines the very spirit of the Olympic Games." The USOC even refused to show the letter to Hamm.

A month later an arbitration body took up the case. A month after that they upheld the original decision of Paul Hamm winning the gold medal. "An error identified with the benefit of hindsight, whether admitted or not, cannot be the ground for reversing a result of a competition." Hamm was the gold medalist.

Was that the only controversy Paul Hamm was involved in?

After the South Korean objections, Hamm didn't perform up to his usual excellence. He had four more opportunities to medal and went on to score fifth in floor, sixth in pommel horse, and seventh on the parallel bars. The high bar was his final chance to win another medal, and he followed a Russian champion who performed brilliantly. The judges, however, only gave him a score of 9.725. The audience objected so loudly the judges were forced to reevaluate, and after a fifteen-minute delay upped his score to 9.762. The spectators still weren't happy. And Hamm stood waiting for his turn.

The South Korean objections weighed on him. Warmed up and ready to perform, he was forced to linger awkwardly while the crowds booed. Hamm said, "Eventually I had to ask [the Russian champion] to get up on the podium and gesture to the crowd to calm down."

Olympic gymnast Paul Hamm was born in Washburn. He and his twin brother, Morgan (not pictured), both competed in the 2004 Athens games.

When Hamm mounted the high bar, the audience finally quieted. He performed well enough to claim the silver medal after a tiebreaker—his third medal in the 2004 Athens Olympic Games, and his final.

Do Olympic athletes earn anything?

The IOC does not compensate athletes appearing at their Games, nor is their training paid for by that organization. Olympian hopefuls, however, are typically world-class athletes with endorsements and sponsors. The richest American participant in the 2014 Games was Sean White (1986–), who received twenty million dollars from endorsements and other income.

Medalists do earn cash from the USOC, in addition to their medals. Gold medal winners are paid $25,000, those earning silver medals pick up $15,000, and those awarded a bronze medal receive $10,000. President Barack Obama (1961–) signed a bill in 2016 to let medalists keep those earnings tax free.

Have any Wisconsin Olympians become notorious?

Suzy Favor Hamilton (1968–), a runner in three summer Olympic Games (1992, 1996, and 2000), faked an injury in her last race. Her brother had committed suicide shortly before her 2000 appearance, and her goal had been to honor his memory with a victory. Favor Hamilton's slight build (104 pounds, or forty-seven kilos) couldn't maintain the grueling pace of preliminary events followed so closely by the main competition. With the finish line a half-minute away, she broke stride and fellow runners passed her. She fell—on purpose—as panic struck. She would not win for her brother.

Favor Hamilton retired from running, married, had a daughter, and eventually became a real estate agent in the Madison area. After a visit to Las Vegas, Nevada, she became a high-priced escort and prostitute. A reporter found her in Las Vegas, and she told her story. The Big Ten removed her name from the rolls of Female Athlete of the Year, and she retreated into privacy.

Eventually Favor Hamilton was diagnosed as bipolar. Her husband knew all about her double life and had warned her about the reporter. The two are working to restore their marriage. Her story is detailed in her book *Fast Girl*.

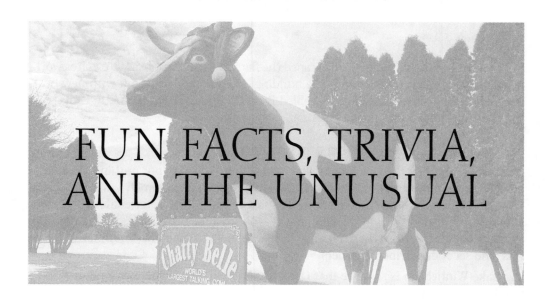

FUN FACTS, TRIVIA, AND THE UNUSUAL

What is Wisconsin's oldest city?

Wisconsin's oldest settlement is Green Bay, which was founded by French and Indian settlers in the 1600s—although, scientifically speaking, Ojibwe people had been living in the Green Bay area for thousands and thousands of years. Green Bay's first white family arrived in 1765 and immigrant workers flocked to the city afterward.

Wisconsin's second-oldest city is Prairie du Chien, which began as a fur-trading post in the 1700s.

What is the oldest structure in Milwaukee?

Though it is not the oldest originally constructed building in Milwaukee, the St. Joan of Arc chapel is the oldest structure in Milwaukee, having been built first in the early fifteenth century in the Rhone Valley.

In the 1920s, Gertrude Hill Gavin, heiress and devotee of Joan of Arc, learned of the chapel, which was thought to have been used by the young saint. Gavin purchased it, had it taken apart, and had it shipped to her home in Long Island where it was put back together near a French Renaissance chateau that she also purchased, had disassembled, moved, and had reassembled on her property. Gavin also purchased other treasures that were said to have been touched by St. Joan, and she hired a Boston artist to create stained glass windows for her new endeavor.

The chapel, which had been called the St. Martin de Seyssuel for its entire existence until then, was renamed in honor of St. Joan. In 1933, Pope Pius XI gave permission for Mass to be said in the chapel.

In 1962, she sold it and the chateau to Mark Rojtman, president of J. I. Case, a construction equipment manufacturer, and his wife. The Rojtmans, who had narrowly escaped a fire in the chateau, contacted officials at Marquette University to see if they might want the chapel, which had escaped the flames. Several months later, after workmen had once again disassembled the building, slightly modernized it with new heating and cooling systems, and reassembled it on the grounds of Marquette University, the chapel was open for business in 1966.

How many lakes are within Wisconsin's borders?

Minnesota might be the "Land of 10,000 Lakes," but they ain't got nuthin' on us: Wisconsin boasts more than 15,000 lakes! Lake Winnebago in Calumet, Winnebago, and Fond du Lac Counties is the largest, at 215 square miles (557 square kilometers)—or about 30 by 10 miles (78 by 16 kilometers)—of boating, swimming, and fishing fun. Primary tributaries from the Wolf and Fox Rivers help to make Lake Winnebago what it is, and secondary tributaries help.

Lake Winnebago is so large that Oshkosh, Neenah, Menasha, and Fond du Lac all touch upon the lake's shores.

Wisconsin's deepest lake—at 237 feet (72 meters)—is Green Lake, which is located in Green Lake County.

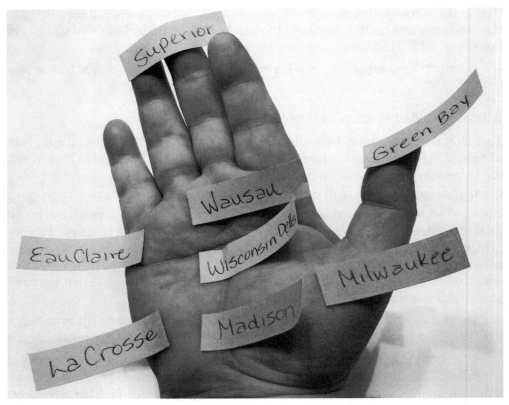

So when someone asks where in Wisconsin you live, the way to show them is to give them a hand.

What are some of the quirky museums found in Wisconsin?

The Fennimore Doll & Toy Museum, established in 1991, doesn't just have dolls. There are all kinds of toys, cars, games, dollhouses, miniatures, doll accessories, puzzles, and thousands of dolls on display from the 1800s to the turn of this century and it's sure to have the toys you loved. Their website promises new and rotating displays. Bonus: admission is inexpensive and group tours are available. For more toys, check out the Spinning Top Museum in Burlington; also, Bloomer calls itself the Jump Rope Capital of the World.

If you've never had the pleasure of standing inside a fish, head for the Fresh Water Fishing Hall of Fame in Hayward. It's a museum dedicated to fishing and its history, and the entire museum is located in a giant 143-foot-long fiberglass muskie fish that sits on the edge of a pond that holds 88,000 gallons (333,000 liters) of water.

Established in 1959, the Circus World Museum in Baraboo isn't necessarily weird, but it is your chance to go to the circus any day of the week, all summer long! There, you can see a show under the Big Top, check out the animals, and learn a lot of history about the American circus. While you're there, check out the Ringling Mansion.

It should also be noted that, in addition to Baraboo, circuses once located their winter quarters in Delavan. Sheboygan was also the home to at least two circuses. History didn't leave much of anything tangible for them, in either case.

What would a good Wisconsin polka be like without an accordion? You don't have to wonder, once you've visited A World of Accordians Museum in Superior. The 1,300+ accordions there will give you reason to dance.

The Hamburger Hall of Fame is located in Seymour. That's where, in 2001, officials grilled a burger that weighed in at over 8,200 pounds (3,720 kilograms). The museum

The Potosi Brewery is on the National Registry of Historic Places and also houses the National Brewery Museum.

also pays homage to Charles Nagreen (1870–1951), who was supposedly the inventor of the hamburger as we know it.

If you love hot dogs, visit the National Mustard Museum in Middleton. Harry Houdini lived in a "castle" in Appleton when he was a boy, and you can visit The History Museum at the castle there. The National Brewery Museum is located in the Potosi Brewery in Potosi. Check out the Clark County Jail Museum in Neillsville, a home-and-jail Victorian building constructed in 1897. You'll feel positively heavenly when you visit the Angel Museum in Beloit. There's so much to see!

How did a Chicago whiskey distiller land a big one in a Wisconsin county?

When Bob and Fannie Kutz of Hayward had the idea for a tribute to the best freshwater fishermen (and women) in the country, they envisioned something that would make, well, a big splash. That was in 1960, but it took nine years before any meaningful progress was made. In 1969, five other Hayward locals decided that the time was right to look for money for the project.

The federal government didn't seem to be interested. Grants weren't available for their endeavor and so they decided to look instead at corporations that might have something to do with fishing, even if remotely. The goal was to raise a million bucks.

Here and there, a few individuals came up with a little bit of cash toward the goal but it wasn't until the Jim Beam corporation, distillers of whiskey, stepped in with an unusual offer. According to the Fresh Water Fishing Hall of Fame & Museum website, Beam offered to produce collectable fish decanters, and a portion of the sales would go to the new Hall of Fame for a period of ten years. This would not only guarantee several hundred thousand dollars of money to support the Freshwater Fishing Hall of Fame, but it would also generate tons of publicity.

In 1971, the first collectable decanter was issued, which netted a small amount of monetary support that year. Within five years, there was enough funding to allow for a small museum to be opened and visitors were "encouraged" to make a donation for entrance. And the rest is fishing history.

As it indicates on the website, Jim Beam can truly be called the Father of the Fresh Water Fishing Hall of Fame.

What unique geological spot is found in the northern half of Wisconsin?

The "45 × 90 points" are four places on Earth that are halfway between geographical poles, the Prime Meridian, the equator, and the 180th Meridian. Two of them are found in the middle of oceans. One of them is located in a remote region of China. The fourth one is found in Poniatowski, Wisconsin, a tiny little unincorporated town west of Wausau in Marathon County. Yes, you can visit it, and stand on the exact center of the Northwest Hemisphere.

Does Wisconsin have any ties with the White House?

Like many presidents in the early twentieth century, Calvin Coolidge wanted to escape the hot Washington, D.C., weather. That's why Coolidge and his wife spent the summer of 1928 at The Cedar Island Lodge in Brule.

Imagine the work that needed to be done before the president lived in your town! New phone lines were run and the town was spiffed up for the president and first lady and everyone began to refer to Brule as the "summer White House." A small detachment of the 3rd Infantry Regiment were dispatched from Fort Snelling in Minneapolis to guard the president, who arrived around mid-June, spent his summer relaxing and fishing, and departed Wisconsin after Labor Day.

The 3rd Infantry Regiment, by the way, was reactivated in 1948 and still serves as Escort to the President.

While certainly Coolidge spent the most time in Wisconsin, other U.S. presidents have visited for the recreation: All together, five presidents fished the Brule: Dwight Eisenhower, Coolidge, Grover Cleveland, Herbert Hoover, and Ulysses Grant.

How did one Wisconsin business put the lock on a master escape artist?

Master Lock began in Milwaukee when engineer Harry Soref devised a new kind of small lock that was much, much stronger than any other padlock anyone had ever devised before. In 1924, Soref was making locks in a small storeroom in Milwaukee with a few industrial tools and a staff of five employees. Within a year, Soref's knowledge and reputation had grown; he was supposedly so knowledgeable about locks that Harry Houdini heard about Soref and reached out to the Master Lock master.

It turns out that the great Harry Houdini had been unable to escape from a pair of handcuffs and it frustrated him so he consulted with Harry Soref. Soref reportedly gave the escape artists a few ideas and pointers, many of which history indicates Houdini incorporated into his acts.

Master Lock was also instrumental in another historical event: during Prohibition, the state of New York purchased nearly 150,000 locks for use in closing any establishments that dared to sell alcohol.

What almost-fatal historical event happened in Wisconsin?

It was 1912, and President Theodore Roosevelt very much wanted to be president again for four more years. The election wasn't far off—just a few weeks—and incumbent president William Howard Taft and Democratic nominee Woodrow Wilson were tough opponents. Roosevelt was busy on his multistate campaign tour when he made a stop in Milwaukee so that he could speak publicly to voters at the Milwaukee Auditorium.

Normally a robust, go-get-'em kind of guy, Roosevelt wasn't feeling well on that day. He had, perhaps, the beginning of a cold—or maybe his throat was irritated because of the ten to twenty speeches he had been giving daily. At any rate, some in his team watched as he climbed to the dais, unaware that Roosevelt had been followed since he left New Orleans a few days before and that he was seriously injured.

John Flammang Schrank (1876–1943) was a thirty-six-year-old immigrant who came from Bavaria with his parents when he was a toddler. His time in America wasn't kind: over the years, Schrank lost his mother and his father, an aunt and an uncle, and the woman he loved, and by the fall of 1912, he was overwhelmingly distraught. Indeed, he had inherited a bit of property, but it wasn't enough to keep him stable, and he sold what he owned in order to become a drifter. It's known that he was opposed to Roosevelt in principle, and some surmise that a weird dream Schrank claimed to have had, in which the ghost of former president William McKinley blamed his death on Roosevelt, put Schrank over the edge.

John Flammang Schrank, a saloonkeeper from Bavaria, was found guilty by reason of insanity of trying to kill former president Theodore Roosevelt while he was campaigning in Milwaukee.

On October 14, 1912, he followed Roosevelt as the ex-president's motorcade traveled from Milwaukee's Pfister Hotel. As Roosevelt waved to the crowds from his automobile, Schrank aimed, and fired a .38 revolver, striking Roosevelt in the chest on his right side, rather than the head (which was where Schrank had supposedly aimed). Bodyguards tackled Schrank and bystanders began to beat him as Roosevelt continued to the auditorium; Roosevelt always said he didn't know he was shot until he felt the blood on the inside of his heavy coat.

But then, rather than ask for medical assistance, and rather than die, Roosevelt continued to the dais and announced to all that he'd been shot. He showed the audience the blood on his side, and then he showed them a fifty-page manuscript for the speech, which had likely, in part, saved his life by slowing the bullet.

After giving his speech, as he'd intended, Roosevelt then agreed to treatment for his bullet wound. Doctors found that the bullet had lodged between two of his ribs; had it not gotten stuck, it was clearly on a path to Roosevelt's heart. It was also agreed that it was safer to leave the bullet intact, exactly where it had lodged in Roosevelt's body.

As for Schrank, he was arrested and committed to the Central State Hospital for the Criminally Insane in Waupon, where he died of pneumonia in 1943.

What quirky things might be hiding in Wisconsin's Apostle Islands?

Created when the glaciers came through this part of the continent, the Apostle Islands are up near Green Bay and Bayfield. Along the 12 miles of mainland, twenty-one islands make up the Apostle Islands, and rumor has it that at some point, they were awfully irresistible to somebody (or somebodies) who wanted to hide ill-gotten booty.

Oak Island is said to be where a band of pirates buried their treasure in the 1700s. Sadly, there's little verification, except that a group of pirates were known to have clashed with French fur traders on Hermit Island (a little south of Oak Island) in the 1700s. They lost the fight and were executed. Whether or not they were the same bad guys who buried treasure is up for discussion.

In 1868, businessman Frederick Prentice (1822–1913) opened quarries on three of the Apostle Islands and became wealthy for it. In about 1890, he built a beautiful home on the island but it's unsure whether he lived there or not; at any rate, when Prentice died, very little money was recovered on the house's premises. Some say that his wealth is buried somewhere on Hermit Island.

Prentice was followed on Hermit Island by barrel maker William Wilson (c. 1792–1861), who was, appropriately, a hermit; because of a minor gentlemen's agreement and a subsequent donnybrook, Wilson left nearby La Pointe to live on the island. He, too, was said to be enormously wealthy but when he died, no money was found.

In both cases, it's assumed that the island dwellers buried their money.

During the British occupation of the Wisconsin area, soldiers are rumored to have buried treasures on several islands, including Hermit Island and Sand Island.

It's been said that a copper mine was established in the early 1700s, with permission of the local Native American tribes, but a disagreement caused the white businessmen who owned the mine to close it. Rumor says that there was a cache of money involved but nothing has ever been discovered. The mine itself is likewise lost to history.

Maybe the real treasure is the islands themselves, home to wildlife and beauty. Only one of the Apostle Islands is populated—Madeline Island. The rest are under the protection and direction of the National Parks Service.

A fun fact about the Apostle Islands: York Island used to be two islands, until a sand bridge (called a tombolo) connected the two.

Does Wisconsin have any naval honors?

Two U.S. naval warships are named after the Dairy State: BB-9 and BB-64.

Commissioned in the early years of the 1900s, the U.S.S. *Wisconsin* (BB-9) was the first ship to be named after this state. She was an Illinois-class warship with a weight of about 11.5 tons, a length of almost 374 feet (114 meters), and a speed of about 16 knots. She was built in San Francisco, California, in early 1897 and launched in late 1898. She was commissioned in February of 1901, decommissioned in November 1906, recommissioned in 1908, and decommissioned for the final time in 1920. Sadly, you can no longer visit the U.S.S. *Wisconsin* (BB-9); her parts were sold for scrap in 1921.

The U.S.S. *Wisconsin* (BB-64) was 52,000 tons when full. She was 880 feet long, 108 feet wide (268 meters long and 33 meters wide), and 36 feet (11 meters) at her draft (which is the distance between the waterline and the bottom of the keel). The U.S.S. *Wisconsin* (BB-64)'s construction was authorized by Congress in 1939 and in 1941, her keel was laid in Philadelphia Navy Yard. Nearly three years later, the wife of Governor Walter S. Goodland launched the ship at the Naval Yard.

Throughout World War II, the *Wisconsin* was heavily involved, and it survived a typhoon that could have capsized the ship.

By 1947, she was mostly used for Naval Reserve Training exercises; it was first decommissioned to Norfolk, Virginia, in 1948. In 1951, the *Wisconsin* was recommissioned for battle in the Korean War but was placed out of commission in 1958 and sent to Norfolk for overhaul.

The U.S.S. *Wisconsin* rests in a harbor in Norfolk, Virginia. Photographs don't do this ship justice; if you're ever in Norfolk, it's an absolute must-see (photo by Mark Moen).

In 1988, the *Wisconsin* was commissioned for the third time and sent to Puerto Rico and the Gulf of Mexico; later, she was utilized again for the Iraq War. In 1995, the *Wisconsin* was decommissioned once again and sent to Norfolk, Virginia, where she sits now. If you've got the time, you can tour most of the ship today.

How did Wisconsin make radio history?

If you've ever visited the UW-Madison building that Wisconsin Public Radio calls home, you may have seen a small plaque that proudly proclaims WHA as the nation's oldest radio station. Some may disagree, but here's proof:

Following the sinking of the *Titanic* in 1912, the use of wireless communication was a hot topic among Americans. In 1914, Professor Edward Bennett of the university's electrical engineering department secured a government license and the call letters 9XM and then donated both to the university's physics department and Professor Earle M. Terry, who urged his students to make what they couldn't find for their experiments. It was rather fortuitous that the glass-blowing lab was next to the physics lab, since glass tubes were instrumental in creating a radio station.

On Monday, December 4, 1916, the new "radio station" made its first broadcast from the basement of Science Hall; it was a weather report and because radios were rare then (there were only a few hundred of them in Wisconsin at the time), it's unknown how many people actually heard it.

Still, Terry persevered in his experiments until the dawn of World War I, when President Woodrow Wilson worried that wireless broadcast technology might fall into enemy hands. Terry and his students tore apart their equipment, as per government orders, but they were allowed to reassemble their technology soon afterward, when the Navy wished to use it for communications experiments.

In January of 1922, Earle Terry's radio station was relicensed with the call letters WHA, which are the call letters the station has today.

What environmental landmark is found in Wisconsin?

Horicon Marsh, established as part of the Horicon National Wildlife Refuge, was established on July 16, 1941. Its history goes back much further than that.

In the earliest part of Wisconsin's history and through the 1800s, the Horicon Marsh was rife with ducks—all kinds of ducks, because marshes are where ducks like to nest. In the 1920s, state and federal governments officially protected the marsh by establishing it as a waterfowl nesting area; two decades later, it was established as a waterfowl migratory resting area. Not long afterward, local duck hunters lobbied for restoration of the marsh, and the National Wildlife Refuge created a nesting area for the redheaded ducks. Horicon Marsh is the largest nesting area for the redheaded duck in the country; some three thousand ducks arrive each year at Horicon to lay their eggs and rear their young.

Although ducks always made their homes in Horicon, the focus on waterfowl at this marsh is at least partially on behalf of hunters. State and federal laws carefully manage the fowl through a strict hunting season; also, licensing and other fees from hunting contribute to the purchase and maintenance of wildlife properties.

In the years following World War II, concerted effort was made to manage the marsh for Canada geese. Populations of the Canada geese have been growing ever since.

The Horicon Marsh is also the nation's largest freshwater cattail marsh.

Where was Wisconsin's first state park?

About an hour north of Minneapolis, Minnesota, is Wisconsin's first state park, Interstate State Park, which was established near St. Croix Falls 1900 but was created some 10,000 years ago by glaciers.

Between its creation and its establishment as a state park, tourists coming upriver knew about the area's lush greenery, its cliffs and valleys, and the loggers that used the river to transport product. Before them, French fur traders and Native Americans knew about the wildlife along the St. Croix River and the great swimming there. As visitors do today, they likely marveled at the naturally carved holes in the rock, made by melting glaciers.

If you visit the park, be sure to view those potholes (but be careful; some of them are deep!) and take advantage of hiking trails, swimming areas, and beautiful scenery. Bring your camera!

What quirky, bewitching thing happened in Wisconsin?

TV's Agnes Moorehead (1900–1974) was born in a small town near Boston, Massachusetts, to a Presbyterian minister-father and a mother who was a singer. Moorehead was encouraged to participate in church programs as a child, which is perhaps where the acting bug bit her; by age ten, she was performing with the St. Louis Municipal Opera as a dancer and singer. Though she was obviously very good at performing, her father insisted that young Moorehead continue with her education and so she attended college at Muskingum College in Ohio. From there, she transferred to the University of Wisconsin-Madison, where she received a master's degree in English and public speaking. Later, she added a doctorate in literature from Bradley University.

Actress Agnes Moorehead (shown here in her well-known role as a witch's mother in the TV comedy series *Bewitched*) was a teacher in Wisconsin during the 1920s.

When her parents moved to the Reedsburg-Soldier's Grove area in the 1920s, Moorehead went to work at a local public school as a teacher. Her students learned English and drama from her before she headed forward to fame, fortune, and *Bewitched*.

What fun things are there to know about Wisconsin cheese?

- Most cheese tastes better at room temperature. That goes doubly for curds.
- Don't cut cheese early; wait until you're ready to use it. Doing so will keep it from drying out, which is icky. Also, it's really not a good idea to freeze cheese; it changes the food's basic taste.
- You don't necessarily have to refrigerate most cheeses, as long as you keep them at room temperature. That means taking Wisconsin cheese to Grandma's on your next vacation will need extra precaution. Cheese travels well, under the right circumstances.
- The USDA regulates the size of the holes in all Swiss cheese.
- Eating Wisconsin cheese after a meal is said to promote dental health. Bonus: it tastes delicious and it's good for you.
- With more than 350 varieties on its menu, Wisconsin is the nation's largest producer of cheese.

What mooooo-ving thing happens in Wisconsin each year?

For many decades, Wisconsin has been known for its cows—and for good reason: some 1.3 million cows call the state "home."

Cows are generally milked two or three times per day, depending on the individual dairy operation, and that goes on for the better part of a year. To do that, each cow will eat nearly 36,500 pounds (16,556 kilograms) of food and drink thousands and thousands of gallons of water.

What that adds up to here, well, we're talking superheroes: each cow gives an average of just over 2,700 gallons (10,221 liters) of milk annually, which is nearly 22,000 tall glasses of moo-juice per year.

- The Chalet Cheese Co-op in Monroe is the only place in the United States where you can get the old-school, smelly variety of limburger cheese, made like it used to be made.

- It takes around 10 pounds (4.5 kilograms) of milk to make a pound of cheese, give or take.

- If you're an average person, you'll eat more than a ton of cheese in your lifetime.

- Blame it on the grass: it's been said that our mild grass is why Wisconsin cheese tastes best!

- Colby cheese was invented in (guess where?) Colby, Wisconsin, in 1885.

How does Wisconsin fly high?

Cornell University students Ron Sauey and George Archibald loved cranes.

No, they really loved cranes and, knowing that the birds were overall struggling to survive in the wild, the ornithologists dreamed of a place where they could breed, raise, and ensure that the world's cranes would never become extinct.

That was in 1971. Two years later, the Sauey family rented their horse farm for $1 a year to the pair, and the International Crane Foundation took flight in Baraboo.

Since then, the International Crane Foundation has completed important research on the birds, as well as methods to capture and reintroduce them safely into the wild. Collaboration efforts have made a big difference, and the foundation has helped ensure that millions of acres of wetland and grasslands are protected for generations to come—generations of both human and bird.

While the almost 300-acre (120-hectare) Baraboo site is still the International Crane Foundation's main campus with some 100 cranes representing all 15 species, the foundation also has a facility in China and they collaborate with organizations in several other countries and the state of Texas. Visitors are welcome to the Baraboo site for a self-guided tour, a hike, or just to relax and watch cranes.

Some "firsts" for the International Crane Foundation:

- For several years in the late 1970s and early 1980s, the foundation celebrated the first of many species of crane to hatch in captivity. These notable "firsts" were important because they were proof that cranes could be hatched outside of the wild and, therefore, possibilities existed for better survival of chicks.

- From 1984–1986, foundation members honed "isolation rearing" methods so that chicks would not imprint on humans, ensuring that the birds could be reintroduced in the wild.

- In 1985, the foundation became the only facility in the world to have at least one pair of each of the 15 known species of crane.

- In 1993, the International Crane Foundation became the first organization to successfully breed each of the 15 known species of crane.

Which patriotic holiday got its start in Wisconsin?

The year was 1885 and for well over one hundred years, the nation had marked July 4 as Independence Day and a "birthday" of sorts for America.

But Bernard Cigrand (1866–1932) thought that wasn't enough. He was a teacher at Public School, District 6 in Fredonia (near Waukesha) and when the 108th anniversary of the adoption of the Stars and Stripes as America's official flag came around on June 14, 1885, he encouraged his young charges to celebrate a "Flag Birthday," which was ultimately shortened to "Flag Day."

Communication was slow at that time in history, and so Cigrand spent many years giving speeches and writing articles about his idea—and, of course, telling his students of the importance of Flag Day. Word spread enough that, in 1889, a kindergarten teacher in New York brought the idea to his class and the celebration was slowly adopted by cities and school boards across the country.

Because of the decades of celebration in pockets of the country here and there, on May 30, 1916, President Woodrow Wilson proclaimed a holiday known as Flag Day. It was not until August of 1949, when President Harry Truman signed an Act of Congress, that Flag Day officially became June 14 of every year.

Which Wisconsin county has the most dairy farms?

In 2017, Wisconsin proudly boasted just over 8,000 dairy farms and on those farms we had some cows. Almost 1.3 million of them, to be exact, and that doesn't count the bulls, steers (castrated boy cattle), and calves being raised for food or future milk. Those cows collectively give more than 3 billion gallons (11.4 billion liters) of milk each year. The average Wisconsin farm has 134 cows in the barn.

Wisconsin is known for its dairies, and Clark County has the most dairy farms of any county in the state—over eight hundred!

Ninety-six percent of all dairy farms in Wisconsin are family owned. As of this writing, Clark County has the most with some 850 dairy farms (and an additional 1,450 that are listed as producing some sort of agricultural product). Clark County also leads the state with the highest milk production and the most cows of any county in Wisconsin.

Which Wisconsin politician put most of us to shame in the gym?

Senator William Proxmire (1915–2005) was a big proponent of physical fitness.

The *New York Times* once reported that Proxmire got out of bed and started his day by running in place for several minutes. Breakfast was sparse, usually a can of sardines or tuna and a small bit of fresh fruit. According to Proxmire's own account, he did 100 push-ups and 200 sit-ups each morning before running five miles to his job in the Senate in Washington, D.C.; running, he claimed, wasn't something he did until he turned 50 years old. In the evening, he walked that distance back home.

In 1973, while he was in office, Proxmire even wrote a book promoting his lifestyle and health regime, entitled, *You Can Do It! Senator Proxmire's Exercise, Diet, and Relaxation Plan*

How many dairy farms are there in Wisconsin?

In 1935, Wisconsin reached its peak for dairy farms. That year, more than 180,000 farms dotted the state. Today, there are nearly 9,000 farms in Wisconsin. Sadly, census data shows that that number is shrinking.

301

Ninety-six percent of all Wisconsin farms are family farms, which means that they are run by a single family (with possible employees) and not by a corporation.

What do you call that sausage-like food at Miller Stadium?

It's a brat and, for the uninitiated, that's not an indication of an ill-behaved child, if you pronounce it right. In Wisconsin, a brat is a yummy edible in a bun, slathered with sauerkraut, and it rhymes with "dot."

When German immigrants came to Wisconsin in the 1800s, they brought lots of things with them: polkas, farm ways, and their favorite foods from home—including the bratwurst, one word that comes from two: "brat," meaning finely-ground meats, usually scraps; and "wurst," which means, basically, "sausage." So a bratwurst, in its original form, is a sausage made from scraps of meat. That meat can be anything but most bratwurst here in America is made with pork.

Now, sausage is an old food—it goes back thousands of years, dating to at least the early 1400s, most likely before—and cold-weather Europeans knew how to make it best. When temperatures fell in the fall, sausage-making was a great way to use up what hadn't made it to the smoke-house whole. Those scraps were ground up and put in a casing to be fried or grilled over a fire—often before sundown the same day, as unprocessed meats tend to spoil quickly. Indeed, bratwurst is often a breakfast food in Germany.

It was natural, then, that immigrants would want to bring comfort food to Wisconsin with them and the brat was it. If you've never had one, have napkins: the first bite is a juicy one as the brat casing breaks and releases spices on your tongue. Ask for your

---

What is lefse?

Side-by-side with fabulous German dishes, lefse is a traditional Norwegian dish that's also a Wisconsin favorite.

As with the Germans, when Norwegian immigrants came to Wisconsin more than two hundred years ago, they brought comfort food with them, including one traditional dish that's especially popular in the southwest part of the state: lefse.

Lefse looks like a tortilla, but tastes more like a potato—which is about right, since lefse (pronounced LEFF-sa) is made from finely cut potatoes, flour, butter, and milk and cooked flat on a large griddle; the mere making of it can be a social event, as generations of women usually gather to make lots of it.

Lefse is often made as a treat for the fall and winter holidays and is usually served at room temperature with butter and sometimes sugar. You may also find lutefisk served with your lefse; lutefisk (LOO-ta-fisk) is dried whitefish soaked in lye.

brat with or without sauerkraut (another German favorite). And don't forget the German potato salad on the side; no Brat Fest is without it!

How much milk does it take to make butter?

It takes over 21 pounds (9.5 kilograms) of unprocessed, raw milk to make one pound of butter.

Did you know that you can make butter at home?

To do it, you'll need either high-butterfat-content raw milk (if you know a nearby farmer), or purchase cold heavy whipping cream from your local grocer.

Pour 2/3 of a cup of the cream into a jar with a sturdy lid. Shake, shake, shake the jar without resting until there are lumps inside. That's butter, but keep shaking until the lump solidifies a bit more and the liquid buttermilk is clearly separated from the lump. Strain the mixture with a very fine strainer until all the buttermilk is out of the lump of butter—you can drink the buttermilk, if you want—then wrap the butter in plastic wrap or put it in a container with an airtight lid and refrigerate it until you need it.

Old-school readers who prefer homemade butter to the store-bought stuff may be able to find a butter-churn at antique outlets or farm-supply stores.

What did the state of Wisconsin do to protect its workers?

As the number of industries grew in the state, Wisconsin officials recognized the need to protect valuable, fully trained workers. Good employers always try to make their workplace a safe place but accidents do happen. That's part of the reason why Wisconsin was the first state in the union to create laws to care for victims of work-related accidents or illness, which provided medical expenses, wage loss protections, and / or death benefits to workers' families. The Wisconsin Workmen's Compensation Act of 1911 was passed on September 1, 1911.

What's the temperature like up dere den, hey?

Wisconsin weather is usually pretty tolerable, but don't be surprised if there's a 110 degree difference *or more* between the hottest day of the year and the coldest day of any given year. It happens, although average January daytime temperatures are about 19° Fahrenheit (–7° Celsius) and average July daytime temps are in the upper 70s Fahrenheit (mid-20s Celsius).

So far, the coldest temperature recorded in Wisconsin happened on January 24, 1922 in Danbury. It was –54° F (–48° C), which isn't very good sledding weather. The hottest day happened in Wisconsin Dells on July 13, 1936, when it was 114° F (46° C) and probably a good day to get wet.

Which ethnic group is the largest to call Wisconsin home?

According to the 2000 U.S. Census, 44 percent of all Wisconsinites reported at least some German ancestry. It's been that way since rebellions in Europe upset the German way of governing and when the dust settled, many Germans were ready to flee the continent for a better life. In the mid-1800s, German immigrants arrived in Wisconsin just in time to see treaties signed with the Native Americans here, which meant that fertile farmland was available to the newcomers. Even well into the twentieth century, German immigrants continued to arrive in Wisconsin—which is why Germans are the number one ethnic group in Wisconsin.

What quirky thing happened on Wisconsin roads?

When President Dwight D. Eisenhower (1890–1969) signed the Federal-Aid Highway Act of 1956 on June 29 of that year, his plan was to connect the east side of America to the west side of America with a 41,000-mile system of roads that would, he said, address safety issues and allow expedient evacuation in case of nuclear disaster (this was, remember, in the middle of the Cold War, when people built bomb-shelters and being bombed was a big fear). The Federal-Aid Highway Act of 1944 had started this ball rolling by authorizing the highway itself, but that act didn't explain how the highways were going to be funded; Eisenhower finally made it happen. Reportedly, he considered the signing of his bill and the creation of the Interstate Highway system as one of the greatest things he did while in office.

Building that highway system started almost immediately. It made travel easier and commerce more readily available. But Wisconsin didn't complete its portion of the Interstate Highway system until 1969—some thirteen years after Eisenhower signed his bill to create the system.

In 1972, the death toll on Wisconsin roads was 1,168 people which is, so far, the highest number of loss tracked.

Which fan-favorite food came from Wisconsin?

Strictly speaking, if you look for the history of the hamburger, you'll see that ground or minced meat has been around for quite some time—at least back to the time of Genghis Khan, and probably before. "Hamburg" beefsteak was known, for sure, in the 1700s in some countries; Germany, in particular.

And so, one must be more specific and say that the *American* hamburger may have been invented by Charlie "Hamburger Charlie" Nagreen (1870–1951) at the Seymour Fair in 1885.

Born in Hortonville, Charlie was an enterprising young man: at age fifteen, he spent his summer by walking twenty miles from his home to Seymour to sell his meat-and-onion meatballs. But, of course, with so much to see at the fair, people wanted to keep moving, rather than sit and eat a meatball sandwich, and their meatballs kept falling out of the bun. Charlie came up with a solution: he flattened the meatballs into patties and voila! Instantly portable food! He called his creation the "hamburger" because young Charlie was an entrepreneur, but he was also a born marketer and he understood that his customer base was likely mostly German. Hamburg is a place in Germany where ground-up beefsteak is a popular dish.

For most of the rest of his life, Charlie continued to appear at the Seymour Fair, but there's evidence that his creations could also be found at other fairs in the area. Today, you can pay homage to Hamburger Charlie by visiting the Hamburger Hall of Fame in Seymour, "Home of the Hamburger."

What famous game was invented in Wisconsin?

In 1967, when Gary Gygax (1938–2008) founded the International Foundation of Wargaming (IFW), he may have had big plans. One has to wonder just *how* big he imagined the future—or even where that future was, but one year later, Gygax was host to the first Lake Geneva Wargames Convention (Gen Con) at his hometown.

Game designer Gary Gygax (pictured in 2007) invented the role-playing fantasy board game *Dungeons & Dragons* with Dave Arneson at the Lake Geneva Wargames Convention.

By 1970, Gygax's interested was leaning toward medieval periods of warfare and so he formed The Castle & Crusade Society and tacked it on to the IFW as a subgroup. Almost immediately, other IFW members join his new group. Members—including Gygax—could see that there was interest in games set during that part of history.

In 1973, while attending the UW-Madison, Gygax and his friend, Dave Arneson, created the game *Dungeons & Dragons*. Gygax then teamed up with another friend, Don Kaye, to form Tactical Studies Rules. Along with a third friend, Brian Blume, they began forming official rules for their new warfare game.

In January of 1974, one thousand copies of a three-booklet game were printed and sold; by November of that year, all those copies were sold with 3,000 sold the following year. Not long afterward, Tactical Studies Rules dissolved and became TSR.

Since its birth, many versions of Dungeons & Dragons have been sold, both in physical games and for computer. After they purchased TSR in 1997, Wizards of the Coast sold D&D.

Which television shows were set in Wisconsin?

Go make the popcorn—you can see Wisconsin by just turning on your television. Here are some of the TV shows set in real cities in Wisconsin:

- *Happy Days* (1974–1984) was a show that used nostalgia for the 1950s as its main theme. It was set in Milwaukee.

- *Laverne and Shirley* (1976–1983) was also set in Milwaukee. It was about two women who worked at a local brewery and their foibles as single women in the 1950s.
- *American Dreamer* (1990–1991) was set in Kenosha and was a show about small-town life.
- *Picket Fences* (1992–1996) was set in Rome, Wisconsin. It was a drama/mystery show with undertones of weirdness and the unknown. Note: there are two towns in Wisconsin named "Rome." It was never determined which—if either—town was the true setting for the show.
- *Agents of S.H.I.E.L.D.* (2013–) is set primarily in Milwaukee. It's a drama based on a Marvel Comic series.
- *Raising Miranda* (1988) was a sitcom set in Racine.
- *A Whole New Ballgame* (1995) was a sitcom about baseball set in Milwaukee.
- *Aliens in America* (2007–2008) was set in Chippewa Falls. It's a comedy about a family who takes in a Pakistani foreign exchange student.
- *Step by Step* (1991–1998) was a family sitcom about a blended family in Port Washington.
- *The George Wendt Show* (1995) was a sitcom set in Madison.
- *Liv and Maddie* (2013–2017) was set in Stevens Point. It was a show about teenage twin sisters; its target audience was young girls.

Here are some shows set in fictional cities in Wisconsin:

- *ChalkZone* (2002–2008) was a cartoon set in the fictional town of Plainsville, Wisconsin.
- *That '70s Show* (1998–2006) was a comedy with nostalgia as a theme. It was set in a fictional suburb of Kenosha, Wisconsin.
- *Life with Louie* (1994–1998) was a cartoon set in the fictional town of Cedar Knoll, Wisconsin.
- *A Minute with Stan Hooper* (2003) was a sitcom set in the fictional town of Waterford Falls, Wisconsin.
- *My Talk Show* (1990–1991) was a parody-comedy set in the fictional town of Derbyville, Wisconsin.
- *The Young and the Restless* (1973–) is a daytime drama set in Genoa City. There *is* a real Genoa City in Wisconsin but it's not the Genoa City of *this* television show—although there have been occasional references to Waukesha County through the years.

How do I speak Wisconsin?

That's a trick question, really. Wisconsinites speak English, but we also have our colloquialisms.

- Say "Booyah!" to a group of people from Wisconsin, and they'll grab their bowls and a spoon. Booyah is a large pot of chicken-burger-vegetable soup.
- "Guys" in Wisconsin aren't necessarily of the male persuasion. "You guys" is generally used for people as a whole, with no gender specified.
- When you're driving and you have to stop at an intersection, that's sometimes called a "stop and go light" in Wisconsin. Just so you know. Because that's what we do.
- As in most places, Wisconsinites are polite. So instead of profanity, you might hear "For Cripe's sake" when someone is exasperated. Or you may hear "F'r Cri-yi" or "Fer Cri."

"Booyah" is a popular chicken, burger, and veggie soup that is well-loved in Wisconsin.

- "Don'chaknow" is just a quick way of saying "Don't You Know?" Its meaning is the same—are you not aware?—but it's also used as punctuation. As in "Get back in here! It's cold outside, don'chaknow."
- "Uff-Da" (pronounced OOOF-dah) comes from those of us who enjoy a Norwegian background. It's used in place of the too-common "Wow" or "Holy cow!" both of which are just too mild. It's used thusly: "Uff-Da, dat cow gives a lot of milk, don'chaknow."
- "'Scansin" is an alternate way to say the name of our state. Also: "Sconnie."
- "Enso" is another word used as punctuation. It asks for—but doesn't demand—agreement. "The whole family will be happy if we grill brats this weekend, enso?"
- "The Pig" refers to Piggly Wiggly, which is a regional grocery store chain.
- "Go by" is to visit. "After the Pack wins, why'n't we go by Grandma's to celebrate?"
- "Yooper" refers to someone from Michigan's Upper Peninsula, or the UP. Say "U.P." slowly and you'll understand.
- "Start with me last" is a request to move the speaker last in a roster. Often said to a waitress at Friday night's Fish Fry.
- "Borrow me…" is a Wisconsin request that something be lent to the speaker.
- "Couple-two-tree" is a number, without being too specific. "I had a couple-two-tree donuts at work today."
- "Tree." The number after "two."
- "Up Nort" is generally how Wisconsinites refer to the area nearer to Lake Superior, but also Hayward, Green Bay, Wausau, and parts geographically closer to the upper border of the state.

307

- "Da Frozen Tundra" is Green Bay. Lambeau Field. Packers Country. Duh.
- "Hey, dere!" is a greeting or the prelude to more conversation.
- Depends on where you ask: Is it a bubbler or a drinking fountain; sub sandwich or hoagie; soda or pop; distance given in miles to drive, or time to drive that distance? The answer will differ in various parts of the state.

What quirky places do Wisconsinites have their evening meal?

The difference between a supper club and a regular old restaurant? It's subtle and individual. No real, definitive answer to that question was found.

Why is Wisconsin a perfect place for big liars?

It's true: The city of Burlington is known for the Burlington Liars Club, which has held a competition for the biggest whopper since 1934.

While some say (lie?) that Otis C. Hulett started the competition, Mannel Hahn may have been the Father of Liars: a 1940 newspaper article indicates that he created the good-natured fun so that his staff of newspaper reporters, working on a holiday, would have something to look forward to each year. From there, the Liars Club expanded and included decades of never profane, always fun-spirited tall tales and whoppers meant to entertain. And yet—to add to the whole who-started-it issue—Hulett is also said to have had more than just a big hand in the competition; he was, after all, a good friend of Hahn's. Either way, Hulett proclaimed Hahn as the first president of the Burlington Liars Club.

Nearly a century later, the Burlington Liars Club still thrives. As of this writing, the most recent winners of the competition all came from Wisconsin and their entries are, well, pretty tall tales. If you want to become a well-known liar, visit the Burlington Liars Club museum devoted to liars and tall-tale-tellers, or send in an entry of your own for the next competition.

You can do it. No lie.

What color are Wisconsin license plates?

The first license plates issued in Wisconsin were black and silver aluminum, issued in 1905. Then, as now, it was required by law that citizens register their vehicles. Nowhere on those plates did it say "Wisconsin"; there was, however, a prominent "W" on each plate. One wonders if officials were concerned about a few cars from Wyoming or Washington that might have visited the Dairy State then.

Silver figures on a black background were in effect in Wisconsin until at least 1911; until 1914, the numbers were riveted onto the plates. Starting in 1914, numbers and letters were embossed directly onto the plates.

Through the Depression years, various color combinations were used for Wisconsin license plates; "Wis" or "Ws" was embossed on the plates starting in 1921.

From 1968 to 1986, Wisconsin license plates were various shades of cheddar-yellow with red or black letters / numbers.

In 1986, a small representation of a dairy farm was screen-printed on the top right of the plate, as well as a sailboat and other iconic Wisconsin figures. Letters and numbers were blue or red. This is the "base" plate used today for most of Wisconsin's license plates. You can, however, for an extra fee, get one of any number of personalized plates, including plates celebrating children, endangered wildlife, the Milwaukee Brewers, and military service plates.

How many roads can be traveled and explored in Wisconsin?

The short answer is that there are over 112,000 miles of state and local public roads in Wisconsin. Of that, 11,753 are state highways, which contain 4,600 bridges and which carry nearly 35 billion vehicle miles per year. This number does not include interstate roads.

In 1918, when it was determined that state highways needed organization, Wisconsin became the first government entity in the world to have signs for state-numbered highways. In 1955, the idea of having toll roads into Wisconsin at strategic places of high traffic was investigated; it was determined then that the idea wouldn't work. At the time of this writing, Wisconsin does not have toll roads.

As for county roads, Wisconsin favors a letter system, which came into effect after World War II. There are no set rules for how a county might name its roads; some names reflect the counties a road connects, while some roads are given letters corresponding to a bisecting or parallel road. Furthermore, roads may have just one letter, two, or up to three letters as designation. Because leeway is given to each county, it's common to have similarly named county roads in several different counties.

Which school district is Wisconsin's smallest? Which is the largest?

As of the writing of this book, Wisconsin's smallest school district is in the northeast community of Washington Island. The district's enrollment—well fewer than 100 students in pre-kindergarten through 12th grade—operates on a budget that's almost entirely funded by local taxpayers.

The largest school district is the Milwaukee School District, with over 75,000 students. The Madison Metropolitan School District runs a distant second with just over 27,000 students.

In the 2017–2018 school year, there were more than 860,000 students enrolled in more than 2,200 Wisconsin public schools.

Another fun fact about Wisconsin's schools: Long before slavery was abolished in the United States, Pleasant Ridge Community in Grant County had an integrated school.

What fabulous things were invented in Wisconsin?

Wisconsin inventors are a prolific bunch! Here are some of the more notable inventions that come from the Dairy State....

- Though the basic idea was apparently floated some 150 years before its invention, the typewriter was created by Wisconsinite Christopher Latham Sholes (1819–1890), with help from his friends, Carlos Glidden and Samuel Soules, in 1873. A politician by profession, Sholes was also a telegraph operator and inventor and he came up with the idea and the so-called QWERTY keyboard, which was so devised because its layout didn't cause a key-jam when typing.

- The electric blender was created by Stephen Poplawski (1885–1956) in 1922. It was altered in 1937 by engineer Frederick Osius (1865–1935), who initially named it the Miracle Mixer. When he received financial backing from his friend, Fred, Osius named the contraption after him, calling it the Waring Blender.

- Until 1910, silos were basically pits dug into the ground and lined with straw. Most of them were rectangular, which resulted in a lot of loss of feed. That year, though, University of Wisconsin agricultural scientist Franklin Hiram King (1848–1911) came up with a round silo that was a big improvement over the old method of storing grain and feed. Engineering-wise, silos will withstand the pressure of what's inside of them—as long as they are at least 24 feet (7.3 meters) high.

The electric blender was invented by Polish immigrant Stephen Poplawski, and then it was improved upon by Frederick Osius of Racine. Osius was the founder of Hamilton Beach Brands.

- Professor Edwin Witte (1887–1960) created the basis for Social Security in 1935, by request from President Franklin Roosevelt. This not only promised out-of-work individuals a bit of money to survive, but it ensured that seniors wouldn't be without resources in their golden years. It also considerably boosted the economy at the end of the Great Depression.

- The first bone marrow transplant did not happen in Wisconsin, but UW-Madison's own Dr. Fritz Bach (1934–2011) invented the method used to determine patient-donor compatibility. It was first tested in 1968.

- There's some controversy for this one: Wisconsin lays claim to the invention of the ice cream sundae. Legend says that the sundae was created in 1881 in Two Rivers when soda fountain jerk (that's what they called them then) Ed Berners (1863–1939) had a customer who asked for ice cream topped with chocolate syrup. A nearby shop owner in Manitowoc heard of this delicious dish and decided to only serve it on Sundays. Now, take this story with a grain of salt (or a scoop of ice cream), because two other cities in two different states also claim the invention as their own.

- Margaret Schurz (1833–1876) brought an idea from her native Germany to Wisconsin when she came and founded the country's first kindergarten in Watertown in 1856.

- Wisconsin's northern economy can thank a former resident of Sayner in Vilas County for the snowmobile. It was originally created out of skis mounted on parts of a Model T car, a small engine, and a few bike parts. Carl Eliason created it so that he could keep up with his hunting party.

- Since 1873, nearly a hundred different makes of vehicles have been manufactured in the state. That includes the nation's first steam-powered self-propelled car made by Racine inventor J. W. Carhart. In 1907, by the way, speed limits on Wisconsin's city streets was proposed by the legislature to be eight miles per hour; twelve MPH on rural roads.

What are some Wisconsin "Firsts"?

- Though the technology came from New Yorker Thomas Edison's ideas, the nation's first hydroelectric plant began operating in Appleton in 1882.

- 1882 was also the year that the Ringling Brothers held their first circus performance in Mazomanie.

- The nation's first automobile race was held in 1878. Even by today's standards, it was a surprisingly long race: from Green Bay to Madison, and it was won by Alexander Gallagher of Oshkosh. According to the Wisconsin Historical Society, Gallagher's vehicle traveled like the wind at an average speed of six whopping miles per hour.

- Wisconsin was the first state to use the national highway numbering system. Ultimately every state in the country adopted it, too.

- The first man to milk a cow on an airplane was Wisconsinite Elsworth W. Bunce. It happened on February 18, 1930, on a flight over Missouri.

- The nation's first Gideon Bible was left in a hotel in Boscobel in 1898. Traveling salesman John Nicholson was said to have wanted a way to support the faith of traveling Christians; he and fellow salesmen Samuel E. Hill and W. J. Knights formed the Christian Commercial Travelers' Association of America in Janesville and placed their first Bible shortly thereafter.

- In 1895, Wisconsin's Legislature created the Wisconsin Free Library Commission with Lutie Sterns and Frank Hutchins appointed to the board of directors. Stearns was tasked with creating a traveling library, the first of which was in Dunn County.

- A dubious honor, indeed: Wisconsin was one of the first states to adopt an income tax.
- Wisconsin was the first state to ratify the Women's Suffrage Amendment.
- In 1961, Senator Gaylord Nelson officially signed a law that required all vehicles sold in Wisconsin to have front-seat safety belts, beginning with the 1962 models.

Are there any large animals that live in Wisconsin?

Yes, a lot more than you think:

Mastodon bones were once pulled out of two sites in Richland County, about 30 miles apart. Most mastodon bones have been discovered on the European and Asian continents, so these two creatures—both discovered by local children—were quite the surprise. You can visit a composite display made from parts of the two fossilized creatures at the Geology Museum at the UW-Madison.

At the time of this writing, the World's Tallest Living Horse lives in Poynette. Big Jake stands 20 hands 2.75 inches, which is nearly 83 inches (211 centimeters) at the withers. That's unshod, by the way; horseshoes could add a bit more height.

Summerfest is the largest music festival in the nation and home to the biggest PARTY animals. Held over the course of several days with some 2,500 performers and more than a million attendees, it's a Guinness Record Holder.

The World's Largest Self-Sustaining Population of Lake Sturgeon is found in Lake Winnebago, near Fond du Lac. Once considered endangered, the fish have made a rebound—enough for the population to endure a sixteen-day sturgeon-spearing season each winter. Lake Winnebago is one of just two places in the country where sturgeon can legally be speared. Lake sturgeons can grow up to six feet (1.8 meters) long and two hundred pounds (91 kilograms); males live into what we would consider middle-age (50 to 55 years), but it's believed that female lake sturgeon may live up to 150 years. It's estimated that a fully grown female lake sturgeon can lay up to 800,000 eggs per spawning season.

Wow, Wisconsin really IS a land of giants! What other kinds of BIG things will you find in the Dairy State?

The "largest" things you can see in Wisconsin: The World's Largest Six-Pack (La Crosse); the World's Largest Grandfather Clock (Kewaunee); the World's Largest Muskie (Hayward); a memorial to the World's Largest Nightcrawler (Herman the Nightcrawler, also of Hayward); the World's Largest Hamburger (Seymour); the World's Largest Corkscrew (Hurley); the World's Largest Barber Pole (Elkhart Lake); the World's Largest Penny (Woodruff); the World's Largest Letter M (Platteville); the World's Largest Mustard Collection (Middleton); the World's Largest Badger (Birnamwood); the World's Largest Talking Cow (Chatty Belle in Neillsville); the World's Largest Roasted Chicken (Elkwood); the World's Largest Soup Kettle (Laona); the World's Largest Stuffed Black Bear (Glidden); and the World's Largest White Pine Log (also in Glidden). Note: this is not a definitive list.

"Chatty Belle," the world's largest talking cow, is a can't-miss sight if you stop in Neillsville and go to the Wisconsin Pavillion. The cow was originally on display at the 1964 World's Fair.

Which religions are most practiced in Wisconsin?

More than half of all Wisconsin residents affiliate themselves with a specific religion. Of those who do, half are Protestant; breaking it down further, the largest majority of Wisconsin Protestants worship at Lutheran churches.

Catholics are the second-largest group of those Wisconsinites affiliated with a religion. It's interesting to note that while nearly every major world religion is represented, however meager, in Wisconsin's places of worship, 15 percent of us claim no religious affiliation.

What interesting comparison can be made about two Wisconsin employers?

The Marshfield Clinic was founded in 1916 when six physicians gathered together to form a group practice. They named their business after their central Wisconsin community. In 1924, the clinic became a part of the UW's medical preceptor program, which means that it accepted students from the university, for further learning; in 1926, the first clinic building was constructed in downtown Marshfield. Ultimately, the clinic was connected to St. Joseph's Hospital in Marshfield.

313

Though the clinic stayed open during World War II, financial problems caused definite problems; it persevered and by 1956, twenty-six doctors practiced there permanently. That number expanded threefold in the 1960s.

Today, the Marshfield Clinic system is located in more than fifty locations in the central part of Wisconsin and has expanded to include a large campus in Marshfield.

The Marshfield Clinic employs more people than does the City of Milwaukee.

What nickname was given to Green Bay, and why?

Your tushy should be very happy to know that Green Bay is known for its football but also as the Toilet Paper Capital of the World.

Long before plumbing came inside homes, people used whatever substances they could find for hygiene: leaves, moss, grass, any kind of paper they could find, and sometimes even bark from nearby trees. When paper mills began producing paper specifically for the potty, their methods weren't exactly refined in the beginning and so, because paper is made from trees, toilet paper often was rough. It sometimes had slivers of wood stuck in it. It was splintery, and you can imagine the discomfort—plus, once outhouses came inside, that rough stuff wasn't flushable.

In 1901, Northern Paper Mills of Green Bay began selling "Northern Tissue," packed in 1,000 4-by-10-inch sheets. By the 1920s, Northern Paper Mills was the largest seller of TP in the country—but still, the splinters.

Northern's engineers were on the case, though, and by 1935, they'd perfected the product and their ad-men had taken the benefit and made it a catch-phrase. Northern Tissue packages all boasted of "Splinter-Free!" paper and tushies everywhere celebrated.

Oh, and by the way—yes, Green Bay is also known as Titletown because of the Packers and their NFL Championships and Super Bowl wins.

What fictional lady hails from Wisconsin?

As the story goes, Ruth Handler noticed one day that her daughter had all but stopped playing with her baby dolls; instead, the girl loved her paper dolls, which were modeled after older teens and had extensive paper wardrobes. Handler tucked that information away in her mind and, later, created the Barbie doll, which some say was modeled on a German joke-toy for men. She said that she wanted to create a fashion doll for little girls that would inspire them to be whatever they wanted to be when they grew up. With more than a billion Barbie dolls sold worldwide and three more sold every second, it's safe to say that she achieved her goal.

In the years since her creation, Barbie has had several hundred different careers, made dozens of friends, had all kinds of pets, cars, and houses, and worn hundreds of thousands of fashions by designers and by handy mothers with crochet hooks.

Barbie Millicent Roberts, according to her official biography, is from the fictional town of Willows, Wisconsin, and attends Willows High School.

314

The original Barbie doll had a fictional biography that described her as coming from the fictional town of Willows, Wisconsin. Today, Barbies are sold all over the world by the millions.

Not fictional: the American Girl Dolls headquarters is in Middleton, Wisconsin.

Is there anything interesting about Wisconsin's ethnic make-up?

Yes! Several things:

Of all the states in the United States, Wisconsin has the highest percentage of people of Polish descent. The majority of Wisconsin residents claim German ancestors.

Wisconsin is less diverse than most other states: more than 82 percent of Wisconsin residents identify themselves as white. And yet—racial minority populations increased by 500 percent in the latter part of the last century, as opposed to a mere 50 percent for white populations.

Wisconsin has a higher concentration of Mexican and Puerto Rican immigrants than does the rest of the nation.

In Milwaukee and Madison, African Americans are the largest minority; in Green Bay and Kenosha, Hispanics are the largest minority; in rural areas, especially in the western, central, and northern areas, Native Americans are the largest minority. The latter group is not growing nearly as quickly as are other minority groups.

Which iconic farmer's magazine has called Wisconsin home for more than a century?

In late January of 1885, William Dempster Hoard sat down to write a "journal devoted to dairy farming." His journal was intended to be an insert for the newspaper he founded, the *Jefferson County Daily Union*, and it proved to be very popular.

315

Hoard was born in New York in 1836. His interest in dairying came from a childhood friend and from his grandfather, a successful New York dairyman who taught young Hoard everything he knew about cows.

At age twenty-one, Hoard moved to Wisconsin but he didn't become a dairy farmer at that time—dairy farming would take another eleven years to take hold of him again. He kept his fingers in the field, though, and he considered starting a farm organization for the betterment of dairymen. Finally, in February of 1872, the Wisconsin Dairymen's Association was organized, and Hoard was appointed secretary.

Hoard's Dairyman magazine has been in print nonstop since 1885 and part of its success is that it's written from experience: the staff runs a farm located near Ft. Atkinson that includes the nation's largest continually run registered Guernsey herd.

Founder William Dempster Hoard went on to be elected governor in 1888, and that further allowed him to help Wisconsin's dairy industry to thrive and grow. He died at his home in Ft. Atkinson on November 22, 1918.

What wild thing may (or may not) be caught in northern Wisconsin?

For more than a century, if you're up in Rhinelander and you're very observant, you might be able to spot the Hodag. Catching him might be another matter....

The first Hodag ever "captured" was caught by Eugene Shepard in the North Woods near Rhinelander in 1893. Few other men have been so lucky (or so prankish, since

This photo from 1893 supposedly shows a Hodag being captured near the town of Rhinelander.

Shepard was known to be quite the imp). Few have even seen the Hodag's den, except in photographs.

The Hodag is a horned beast with dino-like spikes on its back, fearsome teeth and claws, and fine green fur. He's a stout one, growing up to seven feet (2.1 meters) long and weighing up to almost 300 pounds (136 kilograms). Definitely, that's not a beast you want to be messing with in a Wisconsin forest—or anywhere, for that matter. Fortunately for you, Hodags don't favor people for dinner; they like water snakes and turtles, oxen, and white bulldogs—but they'll only eat the latter if it's Sunday and they're hungry.

Witnesses say the Hodag is not only hard to catch, but it's also somewhat of a trickster. You can blame pretty much every missing thing on a Hodag, and a lot of things that go wrong as well. It's been that way for decades, ever since lumbermen started telling tales about the Hodag around the lumber camps....

What local tourist attraction came from above?

The Rock in the House attraction happened totally by accident: on April 24, 1995, a 55-ton, two-story, disc-shaped boulder rolled down a hill near Fountain City and came to rest in the master bedroom of the home belonging to Maxine and Dwight Anderson. The house had recently been remodeled, the Andersons were awake when it happened, and neither was hurt but the intruder, needless to say, shook them up a bit.

Not wanting to stay, the Andersons sold the house (and the rock) to real estate investor John Burt, who still owns it. The house is just another house like all others, until you walk in on a very large boulder instead of a bed in the bedroom. Burt didn't try to move the rock; it made a great attraction and besides, moving it might prove impossible, given the size and location of the rock.

Should *you* want to try moving it, though, you can visit the Rock in the House for the princely sum of $2 per person, payable on the honor system. You can actually touch the rock and try to move it (good luck with that), and you can also read about a similar accident that happened in 1901 on the same site, in which a Mrs. Dubler was killed as she slept.

Where would you find Wisconsin's largest population?

One-third of Wisconsin residents live in the five-county metro that surrounds Milwaukee.

How can you be a Packers fan forever?

No doubt about it, Packers fans are do-or-die loyal and they're that way 'til the end. Proof is in many average Wisconsin newspaper obituaries, but now you can show the world that you're a Packers fan for all eternity with a Green Bay Packers coffin.

Tastefully crafted with a white interior and green-and-gold outside, you'll spend eternity cheering on the Pack as you're reclining forever in style. Perfect for anyone who wants to be buried in his or her lucky jersey, it's also a great way to say "Go Pack Go" when it's your time to go.

How does Wisconsin make boaters, swimmers, and waders smile?

Put all of Wisconsin's waterways, rivers, and streams together and you'd have nearly 27,000 miles (43,500 kilometers) of wet riverbank.

Strictly speaking, if you look at its entirety, the Mississippi River is the longest, although it does not run the entire length of Wisconsin (to the north) and it extends hundreds of miles past the state's southernmost border.

The longest river that is within the state is the Wisconsin River, which is 430 miles (692 kilometers). The Rock River trails it, at just 299 miles (481 kilometers) long.

Lake Winnebago is Wisconsin's largest lake, at nearly 138,000 acres (55,850 hectares). Lake Winnebago is thirty miles long and ten miles at its greatest width. It's 15 feet (4.6 meters) deep, at its deepest.

It should come as no surprise that every Wisconsin county has an abundance of streams and creeks—and many are excellent places to be, if you're a trout fisherman!

Which "Lucky" man had brief Wisconsin ties?

Charles Lindbergh (1902–1974) was born in Detroit, Michigan, the son of a lawyer and congressman. After young Charles was born, his parents moved to a farm in Minnesota, where Charles spent his childhood. There, he developed a keen curiosity and an aptitude for mechanics and engineering. It would be no stretch to think of him as he must've looked at the sky and imagined being among the clouds.

In about 1920, Lindbergh attended the University of Wisconsin to study engineering, which had been his love for years. He was there for two years, but the new and growing field of aviation caught his interest and engineering fell by the wayside. That's when the

Famous aviator Charles Lindbergh attended the University of Wisconsin and received an honorary degree from the institution in 1928.

man they'd eventually call "Lucky" Lindbergh left the UW and dropped out to learn how to fly. Nevertheless, just a year after making history by becoming the first human to make a solo flight across the Atlantic in an airplane, Lindbergh received an honorary degree from the University of Wisconsin in 1928.

How did Wisconsin almost make biblical news?

For sure, no one could accuse David Oyer Van Slyke (1818–1890) of being a non-believer. While the details of his childhood have been lost to history, Van Slyke, in his adulthood, became a fierce abolitionist, to the point that he even volunteered for battle in the Civil War to fight against the South.

After the War, Van Slyke came to Wisconsin and began traveling the state, preaching to any group that would have him. Most sources say that he was never officially ordained, but he was as knowledgeable as any preacher: he claimed to have read the Bible, front-to-back, more than twenty times and was an excellent orator.

It was on one trip through the Galesville area that Van Slyke began to notice features and specific surroundings. He studied the terrain, looked at the crops grown in and near Galesville, compared it to the words of Genesis, and in 1886, published a very small pamphlet proclaiming that Galesville was the original Garden of Eden.

Van Slyke saw proof in the four rivers that come together near Galesville; not the Pishon, Tigris, Euphrates, and Gihon, but the Trempealeau, Black, La Crosse, and Mississippi Rivers. He saw the bluffs that surround Galesville and insisted that the area looked garden-like—and, of course, snakes can be found in the area, as they can in many places in Wisconsin. Had he lived in the twentieth century, Van Slyke would have no doubt pointed to Galesville's famous apple growers and nodded his sage head.

Van Slyke died in 1890, positive that he had discovered the place where Adam and Eve met their fate. If you travel to Galesville, you can visit a statue that honors Van Slyke. As for the definitive Real Garden of Eden moniker, several other U.S. locales have tried to boast the same claim.

In what unique way did Wisconsin's schoolchildren contribute to the efforts during World War II?

During World War II, many products were diverted for war use, and it was difficult to get other products—and that included kapok, a product that came from Asia and was used to make flotation devices. It became obvious that a different product was needed to make life jackets and save lives, which is where Dr. Boris Berkman of Chicago stepped in.

For years, Berkman had been championing the use of milkweed for various products but because milkweed was mostly considered a weed, few paid attention to his ideas. That all changed when the U.S. Navy did tests and discovered that, yes, milkweed fluff could keep an average-weight sailor afloat for several hours. But where would the Navy get that much milkweed fluff?

Enter Wisconsin's schoolchildren! On their way to school, on their way home, or just while helping in the fields, when they found milkweed pods, they picked them and turned them into adults who made sure the pods ended up where they were most needed. Children all over the United States were called upon to look for milkweed and, in the end, Wisconsin's schoolchildren collected more than 280,000 bags of milkweed fluff and, by doing so, saved countless lives.

What does Wisconsin law say about capital punishment?

Plenty. Most of it negative. Just one person has ever been put to death under Wisconsin law: John McCaffary killed his wife, Bridget, and was executed in May of 1851. Shocked by his death, opponents of capital punishment lobbied for legislation to prevent it from happening again; on July 12, 1853, Governor Leonard Farwell signed the legislation, making Wisconsin one of the first states to abolish capital punishment and the only state that has performed exactly one execution in its history.

What dubious claims-to-fame does Wisconsin hold in endangerment of species?

In the spring of 1871, something happened that was so astounding that it was recorded for posterity: hundreds of millions of passenger pigeons made Central Wisconsin their nesting area. Reports were that there were so many passenger pigeons in the tree that people could barely see the leaves. It was the largest recorded mass of passenger pigeons ever recorded and hunters were overjoyed. Millions of passenger pigeons were shot and sold for food on the commercial market. Such hunting was common; passenger pigeons were once one of the more common birds in North America and everyone believed that there was an unlimited supply of them in nature. Alas, in 1914, the last passenger pigeon, a captive female named Martha, died at the Cincinnati Zoo in Ohio.

Before that, though, the last wild passenger pigeon was shot and killed in Wyalusing State Park in Babcock, Wisconsin, in the fall of 1899.

Which animals originally came from Wisconsin?

In about the mid-1800s, hunters who wanted help bringing down and harvesting game began to rely on the help of a dog that seemed to originate in the Fox River and Wolf River Valley areas. They knew that the dogs loved water and were excellent swimmers, but past that, they probably never gave the dogs much thought.

At around the turn of the twentieth century, Dr. Fred J. Pfeifer of New London noticed that all those little brown spaniel dogs seemed to be of the same breed, and he thought that the dogs deserved some sort of official recognition. He lobbied several dog registries and in 1920, the United Kennel Club finally recognized the American Water Spaniel. Twenty years later, the American Kennel Club did, too.

Standing 15 to 18 inches (38 to 46 centimeters) at the shoulder and weighing 25 to 45 pounds (11 to 20 kilograms), the American Water Spaniel is an excellent companion but is also a great hunting dog. Like most spaniels, AWSs are very active and love to please their owners.

The American Water Spaniel club calls the American Water Spaniel a "rare breed"

The American Water Spaniel, recognized as a unique breed by the United Kennel Club, traces its roots back to Wisconsin's Fox River and Wolf River Valley areas.

with fewer than 3,000 dogs in known existence. Designated as the Wisconsin State Dog in 1986, the American Water Spaniel is the only dog native to Wisconsin.

What U.S. president almost lost his life in northern Wisconsin?

When President Franklin Roosevelt (1882–1945) was small, he visited Superior with his father to watch the launching of a whaleback ship. As a typical youngster, the ten-year-old future U.S. president was fully absorbed in what he was witnessing and he wasn't fully paying attention. Young FDR was knocked into the waters by a wave and almost drowned. A member of the Superior Fire Department fished him out of the lake and saved him.

Which Wisconsin town enjoys a unique method of getting its mail?

In the Lake Geneva area, the mail for some homes is still hand-delivered by boat and mail jumpers; in fact, in the summer months—from about mid-June to mid-September— some seventy-five lakeside homes receive their letters and magazines this way.

Slow-moving mail boat companies hire for the summer teenage mail jumpers who are fleet of foot. As the mail boats cruise past summer houses, the mail jumpers leap off the front side of a boat and onto a dock, drop off the mail as quick as they can, run to catch the boat, and jump back aboard on the end of it. And yes, some of them miss the jump-back and get wet.

If you're fleet of foot and so inclined, you can try out to be a mail jumper; if you'd rather not risk accidentally falling into the lake, you can catch a tour boat and watch the jumpers in person.

What are some of the truly quirky places can you visit in Wisconsin?

If you love visiting really odd and weird places, come to Wisconsin. You're in luck here!

The Troll Capital of the World is in Mt. Horeb. It all started in the late 1970s, when a Scandinavian gift store placed a few trolls outside its doorway and it trollballed from there. If you love little creatures with funny features, it's the place to be.

If something's got your goat, it surely would be Al Johnson's Swedish Restaurant in Door County. Yes, indeed, those are goats on the sod roof of the restaurant. And they don't mind pictures.

It's worth the slight drive to see Pinkie the Elephant. Bring your camera and turn off on I-90/94 onto Highway V, then look for the gas station. Pinkie is hard to miss.

Where but Wisconsin can you visit a bit of Russian history? Indeed, on September 6, 1962, a piece of the Sputnik IV crashed down on Main Street in Manitowoc, much to pretty much everyone's surprise. You can not only see the crash site, but you can also see what crashed at the Rahr-West Art Museum in Manitowoc.

Who wouldn't want to stand next to the World's Largest M? Of course you do, so head to Platte Mound, where students of the former Wisconsin Mining School created a 241-foot-by-214-foot (73-by-65-meter) "M" that can be seen thirty miles away.

And while we're on the subject of superlatives, you can visit the World's Largest Bicyclist in Sparta. Ben Bikin' is a 32-foot-(10-meter-) tall sculpture on an old Victorian bike. Take a picture and listen to what Ben has to say about his favorite city.

And if weird names are your thing, visit Wisconsin and you can say you've been to Avalanche (Vernon County); Fence (Florence County); Ixonia (Douglas County); Random Lake (Sheboygan County); and Mishicot (Manitowoc County).

Which movies were filmed in Wisconsin?

Wisconsin is a great place to bring your movie crew! In fact, for the last few years, the Wisconsin Tourism Board has encouraged film studios to consider Wisconsin when making a movie.

Some movies shot in (or partially shot) in the state of Wisconsin:

Ben Bikin' welcomes everyone to the Sparta-Elroy bike trail, a thirty-two-mile trail that takes riders along for a nice ride. Opened in 1967, the trail features three railroad tunnels that are each more than 140 years old. The trail is open year round and it links to other bike trails. Camping along the Sparta-Elroy bike trail is also available.

- *Transformers: Dark of the Moon* (2011) was partially filmed in Milwaukee
- *Bridesmaids* (2011) was partially filmed in Milwaukee and Bay View
- *Back to School* (1986) was shot at the UW-Madison
- *Public Enemies* (2009) was filmed in several locations across Wisconsin
- *Major League* (1989) was filmed at County Stadium in Milwaukee
- *The Last Kiss* (2006) was filmed at the UW-Madison campus
- *Meet the Applegates* (1990) was filmed in Oshkosh, Appleton, and Neenah
- *I Love Trouble* (1994) was filmed in Baraboo and Madison
- *Chain Reaction* (1996) was filmed in Madison, Williams Bay, and Lake Geneva
- *The Blues Brothers* (1980) was partially filmed in Milwaukee
- *The Giant Spider Invasion* (1975) was filmed in Merrill
- *Rudy* (1993) was partially filmed in Milwaukee
- *Mrs. Soffel* (1984) was filmed in Freedom
- *The Deep End of the Ocean* (1999) was partially filmed in Madison

- *The Big One* (1997) was filmed by Michael Moore in Madison and Milwaukee
- *The Amityville Horror* (2005) was partially shot in Silver Lake
- *American Movie* (1999) was shot in Milwaukee

What's quirky about Wisconsin's upper "thumb"?

In the summer months, the population of Door County will expand times ten (about 2,500 people during the off-season versus some 250,000 people in the summer). Something similar happens in Warrens in the fall: the little town of 400 swells to about 100,000 during Cranberry Festival time in September / October.

How wet does it get at the Wisconsin Dells?

At just over 19 square miles (49 square kilometers) and under 6,000 permanent residents, the Wisconsin Dells area is a beautiful place to visit, period. The surrounding bluffs, pines, lakes and rivers made "The Dells" a popular place for swimming, boating, hiking, or just for vacation relaxing. There were a few touristy things you could do and you could catch a show, but it was pretty tame by comparison.

All that changed in 1994 when Polynesian Resort Hotel owner Stan Anderson put a roof over the kiddie water sprays. According to the Wisconsin Dells own website, that "launched the waterpark craze...."

Today's Wisconsin Dells is something to behold while wearing a swimsuit. If you added all the waterpark attractions together, they hold more than sixteen *million* gallons (61 million liters) of water! At 125,000 square feet (11,600 square meters), the Kalahari Resorts & Convention is Wisconsin's largest indoor waterpark; Noah's Ark, at seventy acres (twenty-eight hectares) and with three miles of slides, is the largest outdoor waterpark in the United States. With as much space as twelve football fields, Wilderness Resorts is the largest combined (indoor and outdoor) waterpark resort in America.

That's a lot of wet!

How has Wisconsin made racing history?

In 1903, the Milwaukee Mile opened, and the first auto race was held on a dirt track. Every year since then (except during World War II), a race has been held on the oval track, which was finally paved in 1954. There is also a 1.8-mile (2.9-kilometer) paved road circuit, which was also home to the Green Bay Packers from 1934 until 1953.

What college degree can you only get in Wisconsin?

Wisconsin is the only state in the nation that offers a Master Cheesemaker's degree. You can get yours at the UW-Madison but first, it's going to take a lot of planning: you must be an active, licensed cheesemaker in the state of Wisconsin for at least a decade before starting the program.

Today's Milwaukee Mile is a part of the State Fair Park in West Allis and is considered to be the world's oldest operating motor speedway. As of this writing, the future of the Milwaukee Mile itself is not secure; officials are studying the situation, and may close the track forever.

What Mississippi River summertime phenomenon might make you shiver?

It's not easy being a mayfly.

As an egg, you're valued as food for a Mississippi River fish. As a nymph, you spend a whole year in the mud, just hanging out and hoping you're not a tasty (but accidental) snack. On the evening when you become an adult—which usually happens around July 4, but can happen any time during the summer—you officially hatch and fly to a nearby place, mate, lay eggs, and die.

Yes, the lifespan of an adult mayfly is *one day*. Mayflies haven't even developed mouth parts because mating is their sole focus and there isn't time to eat.

That doesn't allow a single mayfly to make much of an impact, but when the waterway is healthy, the water temperature hovers right around 68 degrees, and there are a lot of mayflies to hatch (and we mean *a lot*), then something interesting happens....

Trillions and trillions of mayflies swarm from the water onto land in their search for mates. Evolutionarily, they always navigated by natural light (the moon, specifically) but since the invention of electricity, they tend to swarm around any kind of light, looking for love in all the right places.

Male mayflies fly in an up-and-down motion, while females fly in a relatively straight line. It's a good definition of frenzy: mating happens on the wing when a male grabs a female, and it's quick—just about thirty seconds, upon which the female returns to the water to lay her eggs and die. The male will spend a little time looking for another conquest but ultimately, he, too, dies before long.

On less-heavy hatch years, mayfly swarms are just a mild nuisance but on heavier years, they can show up on weather radar and they can cause accidents because their carcasses on asphalt are messy and slippery. One year, in La Crosse, snowplows were deployed to rid the Cass Street Bridge over the Mississippi River of dead bugs. The good news is that if a mayfly lands on you, it's disgusting but totally harmless.

They don't, after all, have any mouth parts to bite you.

What part of the 1964 New York World's Fair still exists in Wisconsin?

When officials from the state of Wisconsin decided to participate in the World's Fair in Flushing Meadow, New York, in 1964–1965, they didn't know that their exhibit would be such a hit. According to a press release dated August 5, 1964, millions of people visited the pavilion, ate at the restaurant, had a cold one in the authentic Beer Garden, and peeked at the indoor and outdoor attractions designed to highlight the state's industries and pastimes.

The Wisconsin Pavilion was moved from its site in New York's 1964 World's Fair, to Neillsville. Today, it houses a gift shop and radio station WCCN. The Wisconsin Pavilion is on Highway 10; while there, you can also come visit Chatty Belle, the World's Largest Talking Cow.

Originally, the Wisconsin Pavilion boasted nearly 60,000 square feet (5,574 square meters) of space over a complex of five buildings; the display was anchored by a 48-feet-in-diameter, 46-feet-high (14.6-by-14-meter) rotunda in the shape of a teepee with no 90-degree angles inside it. A spire graced the tip-top of that teepee, making the whole building some 80 feet (24.3 meters) high. It was created by designer John Steinmann of Monticello, Wisconsin.

Food and drink were available at the Wisconsin Pavilion, but that's not all: also in the Wisconsin exhibit was the World's Largest Cheese, made in Denmark, Wisconsin. The cheese was six-and-a-half feet wide, five-and-a-half feet tall (2 by 1.67 meters), weighed more than seven tons, and was displayed in a glass-sided, refrigerated semi-truck.

After the fair was over, the pavilion teepee was purchased for $5,000 by Ivan Wilcox, who toured the building when it was at the New York World's Fair. He had it dismantled and taken to Boscobel, where he reportedly planned to use it as a dance hall. In 1967, his plans unfinished, Wilcox sold the World's Fair teepee to two partners who brought it to Neillsville to be reassembled along Highway 10.

Today, the Wisconsin Pavilion of the 1964 New York World's Fair is home to a radio station and a gift shop. Chatty Belle, the World's Largest Talking Cow, stands nearby and will tell you more for a few coins; Chatty Belle's "calf," Bullet, and a replica of the World's Largest Cheese were removed from the grounds around the turn of the 21st century.

The building was added to the National Register of Historic Places in 2012.

What are the most important things you need to know about Wisconsin?

Wisconsinites are fierce about: cheese curds (fresh and squeaky or fried); brats, and Friday Fish Fries. We love the Packers, shorts whenever the temp gets above 40 degrees, NASCAR, brats, and Brewers. We get along fine with snow.

And we love our cows. Enso?

SPOOKY WISCONSIN

Is there really anything all that paranormal about the state?

Wisconsin is not without paranormal activity, and reports of weirdness go back many centuries: Ancient Wisconsin Native American cultures have passed down stories of alien visitations for centuries. Some of the legends disappeared or went unproven for so long that they now seem quaint or silly, while others have lingered well into the twenty-first century or are still actively being investigated due to recent sightings or case studies. Lock the doors, turn on all the lights, and read on....

MONSTERS

What kind of monsters might I encounter when I'm in Wisconsin?

Wisconsin might be known for cows and cheese, but within the borders of the state lurk water monsters, wolfmen, giant hairy beings, fierce and ferocious beasts, and some of the most frightening creatures you should never hope to see.

What is the story behind the Beast of Bray Road?

Werewolves are not uncommon in Wisconsin: sightings were reported as early as the mid-1930s, although it's a safe bet that such creatures were spotted but not reported much earlier in state history.

Our story of the Beast of Bray Road begins, aptly, on Halloween of 1999, when Elkhorn resident Doristine Gipson was driving down Bray Road when she thought she'd accidentally hit something, perhaps an animal. Getting out of her car to check, she saw a form rushing toward her at a considerable speed. Alarmed, of course, she got back into her car but not before seeing a large, muscular form and hearing stomping from "heavy feet." As Gipson tried to drive away, the creature jumped on the back of her car but it slid off and she escaped. The next day, she told a neighbor what had happened. That opened the floodgates, and Elkhorn residents began adding their stories, some of which had happened a decade or more before.

At a height much taller than even the tallest human, the Beast of Bray Road (also known as the Wisconsin werewolf) must be a sight to behold. The creature, seen by few but made famous by journalist, author, and expert researcher Linda Godfrey (1951–) is described as "dog-like" but bipedal, hairy from head-to-toe but smooth-faced, and he possesses a wolf-like face, fangs, yellow eyes, and pointy ears. He is said to favor fresh meat and is often seen eating or having just eaten. Most often presumed to be a male, he also has notably-muscled thighs, huge calves, and either paw-like feet or long fingers. The one thing witnesses young and old agree on is that the Beast can easily keep pace with an automobile on a Wisconsin country road, running upright much faster than any other creature they've seen run. Eyewitnesses are also adamant that he has a human-like quality to his demeanor and that he seemed hateful and dangerous.

While the Beast of Bray Road was originally spotted in the country near Elkhorn and Delevan, the creature seems to have expanded his territory. Seen by people of many walks of life, including some former skeptics, he's been spotted in several different parts of the state. Or perhaps there are more Beasts than we actually know about....

What are Pepie the Pepin Lake Monster and his siblings?

Here's an example of a Wisconsin monster that's been reported since before Europeans came to the area: Native Americans told of a lake monster of considerable size, living in

Lake Pepin in Pepin County in westernmost Wisconsin is the puported home of "Pepie," a monster similar to the one supposedly inhabiting Loch Ness in Scotland.

Lake Pepin, between the Wisconsin-Minnesota border. Modern-day humans gave it the cute moniker of "Pepie," although eyewitnesses say the creature is anything but cute: it's said to live just beneath the surface of the lake, it's gray and large, and it appears serpent- or even dinosaur-like (but also like a log, an errant water wave, or general lake flotsam).

If this sounds a lot like another Loch Ness Monster story, you're pretty close. The difference is that Pepie has been investigated thoroughly by Eau Claire author and lecturer Chad Lewis who found nothing, even though he used sonar, underwater cameras, and his own body as bait. Because rumors persist, Lewis, together with businessman Larry Neilson of Lake City, Minnesota, has put up a $50,000 reward for the irrefutable proof that Pepie is a real lake serpent.

Grainy pictures have surfaced (no pun intended) as have shaken eyewitness accounts, but the desired proof has not been offered yet. The reward was offered nearly five years ago; so far, it has gone unclaimed.

A similar monster was reported by fishermen in 1887 in Lake Koshkonong in Jefferson County. This beast rose ten feet (three meters) out of the water and was estimated to be at least 40 feet (12.2 meters) long. Instead of fleeing, however, the fishermen claimed that they rowed toward the creature but they weren't fast enough, and it slipped beneath the water, never to be seen again.

Jenny, who lives in Lake Geneva, has been reported since at least 1902. She is said to closely resemble an extremely long, very thick snake that prefers deep water. It's possible that Jenny, if she did indeed live, has died, since fewer sightings have been reported in this century.

Other lake serpents have been reported through the years in Lake Mendota, Devil's Lake (of course!), Pewaukee Lake, Rock Lake, and Lake Winnebago.

Are there any creatures like Bigfoot in Wisconsin?

Seen in various places at various times for at least a century, it's hard to describe Bigfoot in detailed terms because each tale seems to be just a little bit different. Most Bigfoots (Bigfeet?), however, are commonly said to be tall, bulky, and hairy, and they reportedly smell bad. The color of their hair (which is all over their bodies, head to toe) appears to be mostly brown or shades of brown, but black hair has also been reported. All Bigfoots walk upright.

It shouldn't come as any surprise that many of the Bigfoot sightings have come from northern Wisconsin counties. The northern part of Wisconsin, after all, boasts more and denser forests than in the southern and eastern parts. Marinette County is a particular Bigfoot hotspot; the most recent sighting happened just a few years ago, when a former police officer (a credible witness, in other words) saw a Bigfoot as it strolled across the highway.

Oneida, Price, and Vilas Counties have a combined 3,000 square miles (7,770 square kilometers) of woodland and nearly twenty Bigfoot sightings have been recorded there in recent years. Local campgrounds appear to be stomping grounds for the creature(s), in case you want to try your luck. Pick a site near wetlands and spots where a Bigfoot might lurk, and don't forget your camera.

South Central Wisconsin has recorded many sightings of Bigfoot in recent years. Bigfoot has been spotted in the Mirror Lake / Devil's Lake area, Sauk Prairie, and Blue Mound ... maybe Bigfoot likes The Dells, too?

In Clark County, a newspaper deliveryman witnessed a "mighty, mighty big" creature walking on two legs and carrying a goat, presumably for dinner.

As for a Yeti, there's a possibility that a Wisconsin Yeti could just be a Bigfoot in the snow—which they're said to not mind one bit.

What is the Goatman of Hogsback Road?

Since the latter part of the 1870s, people traveling Hogsback Road near Hubertus have reported spotting a creature with the lower body of a goat and the upper body of a human. In 2003, what had been brushed off as folklore became a real possible creature when two men saw a goat-like creature cross the road on two legs. The Goatman, they said, was enormous, at well over 6 feet (1.8 meters) tall.

Others who claim to have spotted the creature say that he has horns and fangs, and that the hair on his haunches is long and red. Legend has it that the Goatman stalks and brutally kills people who have car trouble in the area around Holy Hill and Hogsback Road (which is already creepy enough, with switchbacks and cemeteries dotting its path), and lovers who dare to tryst while parked in the area.

It should be noted that Hubertus is near the Kettle Moraine, which would offer plenty of places for a creature like the Goatman to hide, in case you're thinking of looking for him. It should also be noted that several other places in Wisconsin have their Goatman legends (indeed, several other states boast their own Goatman)—although none seem quite as creepy as this one.

Are there vampires in Wisconsin?

Since at least March of 1981, sightings of a vampire have terrorized the tiny town of Mineral Point, in central Wisconsin. The first report of the Mineral Point Vampire said that a tall, thin, cape-wearing, black-clad person was lurking near the Graceland Cemetery and when police confronted the person, he ran off and escaped over a six-foot fence at the edge of the cemetery. When officials returned the next morning, with hopes of following footsteps left in the snow ... *there were no footprints left in the snow.*

In 2004, almost exactly twenty-three years after the first sighting, the creature (always a male) was again spotted sitting in a tall tree and was said to have attacked at least one person by dropping down on the victim as the victim tried to enter a nearby apartment complex. When police came to investigate, the ethereal man disappeared after leaping a ten-foot fence. Again, the creature was not apprehended.

Four years later, in 2008, the creature was a little more brazen. A man and a woman out for a fishing trip saw the pale-faced creature, who chased them when it realized that it had been spotted. The couple were able to make it safely to their vehicle, but the creature chased them as they drove away. They said that the creature was inhumanly speedy. When police investigated, they found the couple's fishing gear was right where they'd left it, but a flashlight that they'd thrown at the creature was gone.

So where is the Mineral Point Vampire now? No one has spotted him in at least a decade, but vampires are supposed to be eternal, you know....

What are Thunderbirds?

For centuries, Wisconsin's Menominee and Winnebago Indians told various stories of gigantic birds that lived in a faraway mountain. Their legends say that Thunderbirds were large and strong enough to carry away something as large as a human (gulp!); they were ferocious, wild-eyed, and fearless. That said, they were actually heroic: legend has it that Thunderbirds were brave enough to do battle with evil water spirits and they were enemies of horned snakes. Legend says that it's thanks to the birds that the planet wasn't taken over by the snakes. One of the most epic water battles is said to have happened near Devil's Lake, back when time was young.

An artist's interpretation of a Thunderbird, a mythological, huge bird that is part of the folklore of many American Indigenous people, including those in Wisconsin.

Other legends say that Thunderbirds were able to control the weather.

The chilling thing is that gigantic birds actually did once live in Wisconsin. Fossilized remains have been discovered in Wisconsin, proving that massive birds with 14- to–20-foot wingspans once darkened the skies over what's now the Dairy State.

But do Thunderbirds still exist?

Eyewitnesses say yes. Gigantic birds with huge wingspans have been spotted in the Lake Geneva area by a group of motorcyclists who raced to escape it; perhaps Thunderbirds don't like motorcycles, because motorcycles appear in other sightings. Linda Godfrey reports another case of a witness who saw a "silvery-feathered" bird with a 22-foot wingspan in northwest Wisconsin. A tall bird was witnessed standing on a bridge near Black River Falls in recent times. The Native American woman who saw the creature believed it to be a Thunderbird.

Skeptics have tried to say that so-called "Thunderbirds" were condors, herons, emus, or even escaped ostriches. Eyewitnesses say that the birds they encountered were much, much larger than condors and herons, and ostriches and emus can't fly.

What event takes place in Wonewoc each summer?

Each year, from roughly the middle of June or so until around Labor Day, the Western Wisconsin Spiritualist Camp is open in Camp Wonewoc near Wonewoc, southwest of Mauston and about 30 miles west of Wisconsin Dells.

Attend for a day or stay for a week, the gathering boasts rooms and cabins to rent and camping available. The event offers classes and workshops on things like psychic development, communicating with your pet, natural healing, mediumship, using chakras, and honing your spiritualist skills. Ordained ministers are on-site, and various church services are available.

The real appeal for laypeople, however, is that dozens of mediums and psychics stay all summer at Spiritualist Camp, which means you can get a psychic reading, a reading with artwork, get help with your chakra, speak with a spirit, receive Reiki massages, or ask someone to check back in time with past life regression sessions. Stick around for Spirit Circles in a group setting, or for church services.

The grounds are available for weddings or group gatherings. As for individuals—perhaps those who are traveling on the nearby bike trail—there is no admission to stop by, walk the grounds, or to visit the healing tree. There is always a charge for any service done on your behalf, however.

Since 1874, spiritualists have been gathering at the Wonewoc Spiritualist Camp. The first group mostly consisted of spiritualists from New York; psychics and seers today come from all over the country.

Where in Wisconsin might you see unidentified flying objects?

Fans of Little Green Men, listen up: Wisconsin boasts not one … not two … but three UFO Capitals of the World: Belleville, Dundee, and Elmwood.

Belleville, Wisconsin, is a small city that straddles Green and Dane Counties, southwest of Madison. In January 1987, a spate of unidentified flying object sightings rocked the community; the first sighting came and went in the early evening on an otherwise normal Thursday; one witness, a police officer, ignored what he saw, thinking it might be an airplane or something perfectly innocent.

He and fellow police officer then spotted the UFO in the form of a stationary group of blinking lights in the night sky over Belleville, making it the second sighting. They watched the phenomena for a while as it hung in the sky, unmoving.

More than six hours later, the original spotter and a neighbor went to a high spot overlooking Belleville and watched the lights for several minutes before calling the Dane County dispatch, to see if anyone else had witnessed and reported lights over the village.

The answer was negative and eventually, some time later, the lights slowly moved away and were never seen in Belleville again.

UFOs are still seen in Belleville, however, in the form of floats and signs: Belleville celebrates UFO Day every year on the last Saturday of October.

Dundee, Wisconsin, is a small unincorporated village within the town of Osceola in Fond du Lac County, located very near Campbellsport, Wisconsin, also in Fond du Lac County. Between the two villages, which are a few miles apart, are many believers who swear that UFOs have (and do) stop to visit—and that the UFOs do it often.

If you ask around, you'll learn that a lot of people in the area have seen at least one UFO; one local watering spot even claims to have a small, dark-eyed alien pickled in a jar. Even despite that (possibly horrifying, for an alien) claim, local residents swear that they welcome UFOs to the area and, to that end, they celebrate UFO Daze each summer on the third Saturday of July at Benson's Holiday Hide-A-Way near Long Lake, which fans from all over the country say is apparently a UFO "hotspot."

Elmwood, Wisconsin, is a small town near Chippewa Falls, a few dozen miles from Minneapolis. Their status as the UFO Capital of Wisconsin started in 1976 when a thirty-year veteran of the local police force spotted an extremely bright "glow" near his home by a hill. The second time he saw it, he assumed it to be something on fire, and so he drove to the top of the hill, only to find a large, hovering object with windows on all sides. Through the windows, he claimed to have seen shadowy figures that were moving about inside the object. He radioed dispatch to make a report, when the object flew directly upwards and a beam of light fell onto him, stopping all mechanicals on his squad car and stunning him for an undetermined amount of time.

Had it just been one person—albeit, someone in a position of authority—the claim might have been brushed away but others in Elmwood also saw the skyward object and dogs were said to have acted "weird."

After the sightings, a landing area for UFOs was suggested but the idea was quashed by scoffers and nonbelievers, despite enthusiasm from a local Chippewa Falls business-man. Instead, Elmwood hosts UFO Days each year on the last full weekend in July.

Readers may also want to note that UFOs have officially been seen in other spots in Wisconsin, including a 1961 face-to-face contact with black-and-blue-suited men in Eagle River; a reported alien abduction in 1997 in Bloomer; a frightening encounter with weird little beings in Frederic in 1974; and an alien abduction near La Crosse in 1988 and one in Antigo in 1974. All these makes one wonder if some sort of crossroad lies in the skies above Wisconsin.

What was the cause of the BOOMs in Clintonville?

For four days in the early spring of 2012, residents of Clintonville were awakened (and very perturbed) by a series of loud, thunderous booms that shook their homes and frightened them. Sounding like the loud slamming of a mega-gigantic car door, the booms often went on for hours. Residents understandably tried to find the cause, blam-

The town of Clintonville experienced thunderous booms in 2012 that were eventually explained as being earthquakes shaking the bedrock beneath the city.

ing the booms on military exercises, sand fracking, and gas explosions. Some said it was water, sinking beneath the ground. Others had different and often otherworldly explanations, but the reason for the booms wasn't thunder, a car door, fireworks, a loud speaker, or anything nefarious or weird.

The booms and shaking, as it turned out, was caused by something much more natural: the U.S. Geological Society eventually determined that they were caused by very minor earthquakes beneath the bedrock of Clintonville, located northeast of Madison.

GHOSTS

Does Wisconsin have a long history of ghostly occurrences?

Because Wisconsin's history goes back into ancient times, it should come as no surprise that ghost stories abound in the Badger State. Oral Native American legends tell of magical beings, winged things, and tricksters who came from out of this world. Such tales were often shared around the fire on long winter's nights, or they explained things that were then unexplainable.

Modern tales run similarly and just as unexplainably. While these are nowhere near a complete telling of Wisconsin ghost stories, here are some things to read about, if you're feeling brave.

What are some famous haunted places in the state?

Built as a fishing lodge in 1900 and remodeled by its owner, Secretary of Commerce Robert Lamont in 1916, Summerwind Mansion in the far northern reaches of Wisconsin in Land O'Lakes is said to have been haunted on the first day it was built. The Lamont family's staff complained about weird noises and strange events going on in the house, but the family appeared to have ignored those things—until the night that Mr. Lamont shot at an ethereal intruder that wasn't there and the Lamont family fled the house on that night, never to return. Subsequent families who've owned the house or stayed in it also reported odd happenings. Even after the house burned to the ground in 1988, paranormal activity was spotted on the site for decades.

Brumder Mansion in Milwaukee is 8,000 square feet (743 square meters) of fright: built in 1910, the mansion is now a B&B but one of the visitors is said to be the sister of the original owner. Reportedly, she loves the manse but hates it when people redecorate.

Also in Milwaukee, the Pfister Hotel is said to be haunted by the man it's named after. Long after guests have checked in, it's said, the ghost of Charles Pfister walks noisily around their rooms without leaving footprints.

The Bodega Brew Pub in La Crosse is said to be haunted by an early owner who died on-site. He likes to tap patrons on the shoulder and when they turn around, no one is there. He's also responsible for noises, moved items, and other unexplained phenomena, and he's been spotted walking around his bar many times. Several other places in downtown La Crosse are likewise said to be haunted, too.

The ghost of William Wilson is said to still haunt Hermit Island on Lake Superior, about two miles north of Madeline Island. As the story goes, Wilson originally lived on Madeline Island but got into a donnybrook with the local law there. When he lost his battle, he set up camp on Hermit Island—and that's where he lived until some time in the winter of 1861–1862, when Wilson was discovered, dead, the victim of an apparent murder. He might have RIP'd, except that a very rich man, Frederick Prentice, disturbed Wilson's beloved island by building a large mansion and it's said that Wilson's ghost was having none of that. Even Prentice's bride took one look at the mansion and fled back to the mainland the same day she saw the place and the house was ultimately abandoned. In the end, you could say, Wilson won: Hermit Island is a part of the Apostle Islands National Lakeshore today, and is protected from development forevermore.

Boy Scout Lane in Stevens Point is said to be a *do*-miss. It's supposedly a dead-end (of course) road named to honor several Boy Scouts who were discovered, dead, some years ago. No definitive reports say how they died, but stories agree that there was some sort of fire and on certain nights, you can still spot the light of a lantern carried by either the spirit of one of the dead boys, or by the one who started the fire.

The Clark County Insane Asylum in Owen is said to be one of Wisconsin's most haunted (former) hospitals. Stories tell of shrieking ghosts, odd noises, and other phenomena attributed to the dead who once were treated—most often, it's said, horribly— by staff and others.

Near there, at the St. Joseph's Hospital building in Marshfield, reports are that people have seen a man in dark robes walking around and entering and exiting rooms on the West Wing. Who he is (or was) is unknown, as is why he's even haunting the hospital.

Depending on who you ask, there's a bridge near Stevens Point that was (or was not) the site of a car crash in which a new bride died on her wedding night. Some swear that if you're on the bridge on the wrong night, you might spot the bride wearing white, but covered in red (blood). Some say that she's hitchhiking but she disappears, once inside a vehicle, while some say she just jumps in the car, whether you stop or not. Others say it's just a story made up to scare people. But would you be brave enough to take your chances and find out?

What are the creepiest cemeteries?

Whatever you do, if you go to Riverside Cemetery in Appleton, stay away from the grave of Kate Blood. Said to have been a witch, a murderess, a child snatcher, and more, even her name is chilling—made more so by the fact that her grave is somewhat isolated from other graves.

The most popular tales about Kate have said that she killed her husband and children or that she was killed by her husband. The truth is likely to be neither: she died long before he did, although it wasn't his fault, and it's unclear whether or not she was ever someone's mother. Was it her name that makes folks shudder when they see her tall, aging, granite gravestone? Who knows, but people who are brave enough to go to the cemetery at night report a dark figure that scares and then vanishes; and some say they've seen blood on Blood's tombstone.

Plainfield Cemetery, the resting place of Ed Gein (see below), is said to be haunted. It's creepy in the first place, having been where Gein found two of his victims; reportedly, one of them can occasionally be seen, walking around above ground.

Dartford Cemetery in Green Lake is said to be creepy *and* a sacred area for Native Americans. Stories are told of a Chief Highknocker who drowned near the site in 1911; other reports are of Civil War soldiers marching between the gravestones. There's also a mausoleum on the south end of the cemetery and it's said that if you sit on the mausoleum at night, the ghost of the child buried inside will push you off.

The Forest Hills Cemetery in Wisconsin Rapids has a baby section. Reports are that if you're there on the right night, you'll hear babies crying but there are no infants in sight.

Walnut Grove Cemetery in Glenbeulah is said to be haunted by, among other spirits, the ghost of a man who hung himself at that very site. Things are said to disappear in Walnut Grove Cemetery and other things just simply ... *vanish*!

Visitors to the Burlington Cemetery in Burlington have reported feeling very unsettled when they're walking among the graves there. Some have run from the grounds, saying they felt as though they were being chased.

St. Kilian's Catholic Cemetery in Lake Geneva might seem to be doubly haunted: reports of a ghostly priest have been reported, mists and cold spots have been felt, and some say they've heard an ethereal church bell pealing—even though the church that was there burned to the ground many years ago. Rumors are that the church basement was used for dark purposes and that the very grounds exhibit paranormal activity that is particularly dangerous. Visit at your own risk!

DISAPPEARANCES

Why did some Wisconsin villages and towns disappear?

It's hard to imagine an entire town disappearing, but that's what happens when your village is by-passed for a railroad stop, a business, or it just plain can't sustain itself any longer. That's what happened to Donaldson, near Land O'Lakes, abandoned after the mill burned; Pokerville, which was the first city in Dane County and was once a hotspot on the map but is now Blue Mounds West; Sinnippee, which was located in the south-eastern corner near Dubuque, Iowa, and once hosted a U.S. president and a Confederate president; Ft. Howard, on the Fox and Wisconsin Rivers, which was abandoned due to a plague of malaria; Dover, which was superseded by Mazomanie and the railroad—as was Cooksville, Wisconsin; Belmont, which was almost the state capital; and Ulao, a former port in Ozaukee County, once the home of the man who assassinated President James Garfield.

Where is Evelyn Hartley?

The short answer is: since late 1953, nobody knows.

Here's the back story: On October 23 of that year, La Crosse residents were excited about football and not much else. Local La Crosse State (later, the University of Wisconsin-La Crosse) was playing rival River Falls in La Crosse for the latter's homecoming, and it seemed that everyone was going to the game to cheer.

Everyone, that is, except children whose parents were lucky enough to have found a babysitter. One of the babysitters available in the area was Evelyn Hartley (b. 1937), who was just fifteen years old that almost-Halloween night.

Professor Viggo Rasmussen was lucky to have hired her; the game was the thing but Evelyn, the responsible, scholarly daughter of a professor herself, agreed to stay with Rasmussen's toddler daughter instead of watching football. The weather in Wisconsin at that time of year is usually pretty chilly, so Evelyn might have actually preferred to stay inside; besides, homecoming didn't hold much allure for her and, according to her father, neither did dating because she believed herself too young for that.

To put the time into perspective, 1953 was a very innocent year. When you think of 1953, you should think of sock hops and drive-in movies that never had anything even remotely R-rated in them. People knew their neighbors in small-town Wisconsin then, and they trusted other folks. Few locked their doors and nobody thought a thing about it. In this case, however, the Rasmussens *did* lock their house up. All except one basement window that remained unlocked....

By 6:30 that October night, Evelyn had met her small charge and received instructions on the little girl's care; a few minutes later, the Rasmussens and their older, school-age daughter left for the football game. It's believed that a man—authorities always presumed the abductor was a man—was already looking for a victim by that time, and that he didn't have Evelyn in mind, specifically. Police believe that he tried to break into other houses but he settled on the Rasmussen home.

He didn't want jewelry or monetary valuables. He overlooked the silver, papers, and the gems. Instead, whoever last saw Evelyn Hartley alive came up the basement steps at around 7 P.M.—neighbors reported hearing a scream or two at around that time—*and he took her.*

She was supposed to have called her father—a check-in call, normal for any parent—at 8:30 but when the time passed, nobody worried. At the end of the game, Evelyn's father stopped by the Rasmussen house for a look and saw trouble through the window: a shoe and broken eyeglasses on the floor. He went back around and noticed a screen torn out from a basement window, entered, saw that the toddler was unharmed but Evelyn was gone. Just before ten o'clock, he called the police.

On October 24, 1953, it seemed that the entire town of La Crosse turned out to find Evelyn. Bloodhound trails ended on a southside road; blood was also discovered behind some of the houses in the neighborhood, making it obvious that the abductor had dragged Evelyn away through several back yards, and he most certainly drove her off in a car. In weeks to come, other possible clues came to light: police in a nearby area found a man's shoe with tread identical to footprints left in the Rasmussen home, a man's jacket, blood that was the same type as Evelyn's, and bloody underwear that may or may not have been hers.

Evelyn Hartley herself has never been found.

On October 23, 1953, La Crosse State won their homecoming game. But on that same night, people in La Crosse lost their innocence and one family lost their daughter.

TRUE CRIME

What ties did John Dillinger have with Wisconsin?

Our tour on a Wisconsin crime spree begins with the gangster John Dillinger (1903–1934), who was born in Indianapolis and died in Chicago.

For many folks in nearby Chicago, Wisconsin's north woods represent a great place to escape: it's quiet up there, secluded, and there are places where you can drive for miles and not see a single soul. And if that sounds appealing to you, imagine how great that would sound if you were on the lam.

Indeed, Chicago's gangsters and mobsters knew full well that Wisconsin was the place to be in the early years of the last century. Al Capone was supposedly a regular visitor and had a home near Hayward where he received bootleg whiskey from Canada; Joe Saltis is said to have loved to hunt in Wisconsin; and Roger Touhy was said to have shown up now and again to fish. It was Dillinger, however, who really put Wisconsin on a crime map, so to speak.

In 1934, Dillinger was known nationwide for being the FBI's Most Wanted Bank Robber, for having masterminded a series of heists. That, and his willingness to escape from custody and use a gun, made him one of the FBI's Public Enemies. And so, on April 22, 1934, according to FBI historian Dr. John Fox, when the Feds learned that Dillinger and some of his men had fled north of Rhinelander to Manitowish Waters, J. Edgar Hoover's men were *on it.*

The Feds rallied in Chicago and began to plan. Someone had a map of Little Bohemia, the two-story lodge to where Dillinger had supposedly run. It was a lovely site, perfect for a weekend of swimming, hiking, and leisure. Quietly, FBI agents headed north and when they got there, they took the dirt-and-gravel road to the lodge.

There were, says Fox, more agents than there were cars, however, and so several agents had to hang on the side of the vehicle on the road to Little Bohemia. The cars startled dogs in the area, which started to bark. Once at the lodge, the agents fanned out and, at about that time, three men who'd obviously been having fun, exited a lodge and began to drive away.

Gangster John Dillinger is commonly associated with his days in Chicago, but he spent a considerable time hiding out in Wisconsin.

FBI agents ordered them to stop but it's thought that the men didn't hear and so the agents opened fire, killing an innocent man.

That, of course, alerted Dillinger and his cohorts and they began to return fire with the FBI agents. At some time during this battle, Dillinger escaped out the back of the Little Bohemia and fled again, and Baby Face Nelson arrived and quickly joined the melee. When it was over, Dillinger and Nelson and their cohorts were gone to another Wisconsin hideout—Dillinger, north; Nelson, west—a civilian and an agent were dead, and at least one local was seriously injured.

This story—which embarrassed the FBI greatly—ended shortly after the bungled raid. The following July—nearly three months later to the day—the Feds finally caught up with Dillinger at the Biograph Theatre in Chicago and killed him. Baby Face Nelson died after being shot on the side of an Illinois highway a few months later.

Who was Ed Gein and why was he infamous?

Rumored to have "inspired" Alfred Hitchcock's *Psycho* and other horror flicks, no book about Wisconsin would be complete without a few dozen words on Ed Gein (1906–1984).

Born Edward Theodore Gein in 1906 in either Plainfield or La Crosse (sources differ), Ed might have enjoyed a simple childhood—first, as the son of a greengrocer and then on a farm in Plainfield around 1915—except that his father was a raging alcoholic and his mother was domineering, even abusive, and tried to disallow Ed from having any friends. Further trauma came when Gein's beloved older brother, Harry, died in a mysterious fire in 1944. Because Ed pretended that Harry was missing, but had led police straight to the body, it was obvious that Ed was odd, even then.

Because his father died in 1940, Ed was left alone on the farm when his mother died in 1945. Though he had certainly suffered from her overwhelming personality, it's said that he set aside parts of the ramshackle home that she used, and that he rarely used those spots himself. He was a thirty-year-old bachelor with little experience with women but, because government subsidies meant that he didn't even have to run the farm anymore and he'd let the land go fallow, he worked odd jobs for local residents in Plainfield. Also at about this time, he cultivated a deep, almost-depraved curiosity of the female body and began collecting medical books and adult literature. This led Ed to regional cemeteries, where he excavated female corpses and took them home to study, to use as a sort of garish costume, to make household items from, and to eat.

And that led to murder.

In 1957, Plainfield hardware store owner Bernice Worden was missing and because she and Gein had been spotted together recently, police went to Gein's farm to question him. There, they found Worden's corpse, decapitated, and the corpse of tavern owner Mary Hogan, who had also been killed by Gein. As stunned investigators looked around, they noticed other body parts from other women that Gein had stolen from graves. There were an estimated fifteen bodies, in part or in whole, although Gein couldn't recall exactly how many women's corpses he'd stolen.

In the end, Ed Gein admitted to having killed two women and he pleaded guilty by reason of insanity. Later that year, he was sent to Center State Hospital in Waupun and then to Mendota in Madison; he was finally tried in 1968 and was found guilty but insane at the time of the crime. He returned to institutional life in Mendota Hospital in Madison, where he died of respiratory illness and complications of cancer in 1984.

For many years, Ed Gein's tombstone in Plainfield was vandalized. In 2000, it was stolen almost completely and was recovered in 2001, halfway across the country in Seattle. Today, Gein's tombstone is in storage, under lock and key.

Who was Jeffrey Dahmer and what crimes did he commit?

Another must-discuss, if you're talking about true crime in Wisconsin, is Milwaukeean Jeffrey Dahmer (1960–1994).

Born in Milwaukee to parents who were have said to have doted on him, Jeffrey Dahmer once remembered tension in his house because his mother suffered from weakness and anxiety and his parents argued a lot. When he was eight years old, his family moved to Ohio, which is where young Dahmer began collecting insects, roadkill, and dead animal parts—although the fascination with such things might have already been established inside Dahmer's head long before the move.

Ten years later, it was at his parents' Ohio home that Dahmer committed his first murder: just a few weeks after graduating from high school, authorities said that Dahmer lured a hitchhiker home, killed him, destroyed the body, and buried what was left in the nearby woods.

With his parents arguing more and his alcoholism out of control, Dahmer reportedly tried to start college classes but could not keep focus. His father then forced Dahmer to join the Army, where Dahmer was a medic stationed in Germany from 1979 until 1981. After his discharge, and with his father fed up with his addiction, Dahmer was sent to live with his grandmother in West Allis, four years after his first murder. There, he was said to be a kind-hearted young man who accompanied his grandma to church, helped her with tasks around her house, and secured a good job as a phlebotomist at a local blood plasma center (later, he worked as a candy maker). Even so, by the mid-1980s, he had one indecent exposure arrest on record; he'd also begun to frequent local gay bathhouses and had been accused of drugging men and raping them.

Though he was still living with his grandmother at the time, in late 1987, Dahmer met twenty-five-year-old Steven Tuomi and took him to a hotel room at which Dahmer had previously registered. The next morning, Dahmer denied remembering exactly what happened but when he awoke, Tuomi had been battered to death. Dahmer stuffed Tuomi's body into a suitcase and took him back to Dahmer's grandmother's house. A week later, he dismembered the body and ridded himself of it, though he kept the victim's skull for some time before he got rid of that, too. This murder and its aftermath seemed to have opened a gruesome door in Jeffrey Dahmer's mind; in 1988, he left his grandmother's home and found an apartment relatively near Milwaukee's downtown, and he began killing young men and defiling their corpses. In 1990, he killed four men and by the summer of 1991, he was killing an average of one man per week.

On July 22, 1991, Milwaukee police stopped thirty-two-year-old Tracy Edwards as he walked naked and handcuffed down a city sidewalk. Edwards, an African American man, told them that a "weird dude" had drugged and had sex with him and when they took Edwards back to Dahmer's apartment, Dahmer handed the police the keys to the handcuffs. That was when one officer saw photographs of dismembered bodies, and Dahmer was arrested.

All in all, Jeffrey Dahmer was said to have killed at least 17 young men and the details of his crimes are gruesome; suffice it to say that he dismembered and consumed some of his victims and kept body parts of others for months.

His trial started in late January of 1992 and less than a month later, he was found guilty on 15 counts of murder. Sentenced to fifteen consecutive life terms, Dahmer was beaten to death by a fellow inmate at the Columbia Correctional Institution in Portage on November 24, 1998.

How did Netflix shine a light on a Wisconsin crime-not crime?

Beginning just before Christmas of 2015, *Making a Murderer* captivated Netflix viewers with the true-crime story of Steven Avery (1962–), who was convicted of a crime he didn't commit. Here's the story:

In the early 1980s, Avery was just an average guy with a new wife, starting his life in Manitowoc County. A little over a year after his wedding, he was charged with indecent exposure for having exposed himself to a couple of women he didn't know; later, his cousin reportedly spread the story and Avery confronted her and her husband.

Not long afterward, he was picked out of a lineup by a woman who was assaulted on a nearby Lake Michigan beach and Avery was arrested, even though he had proof that he was with his wife some thirty miles away from the crime scene. Despite witnesses in his defense, he was convicted of attempted first-degree murder, attempted assault, and false imprisonment and was sent to prison.

In 1995, the Wisconsin Innocence Project picked up Avery's case and discovered that new DNA technologies proved that Avery didn't commit the crime. In 2003, he was released from prison and moved to live near his family's salvage business.

In October of 2004, twenty-five-year-old Teresa Halbach went missing after having finished the three appointments she had scheduled that day. The last place Halbach visited was Avery Auto Salvage. Within days of her disappearance, her car was found at Avery Auto Salvage, half-hidden, but Halbach herself was nowhere to be found. Police quickly secured the area and Avery was asked about Halbach. He claimed that he saw her, she took photos, and drove away, but he was arrested for possession of a gun found on his premises.

A few days later, police find bone fragments and teeth behind Avery's trailer and other evidence inside his home. On November 15, 2004, Avery was arrested for Teresa Halbach's murder and held on a $500,000 bond. He pleaded guilty in January of 2006, just before Avery's nephew, sixteen-year-old Brendan Dassey was also arrested and confessed to being involved in the murder.

In 2015, Laura Ricciardi and Moira Demos brought this long and convoluted story to Netflix and it instantly captivated the imaginations of viewers. Surprisingly (or not, depending on which side you stand), a significant number of viewers were sympathetic to Avery's situation and they demanded that he be pardoned. The full story has a lot of twists, many inconsistencies, legal wrangling, an insinuated frame-up and, it's suggested, a tale that relied on viewers' kind-heartedness.

One can be forgiven for wondering if the story is truly over. Stay tuned....

Who is Slender Man and what was he doing in Wisconsin?

Next, what would compel two beautiful teenagers to try to entrap and kill their equally lovely friend? Slender Man, a fictional entity, that's who.

Created as an entry in a contest in 2009, the incredibly thin, extremely tall, faceless, suited Slender Man was conceived by Eric Knudsen and used as a meme on creepypasta, which are online stories crafted and told by posters and fans. The story that goes with the long-limbed creature is that Slender Man (sometimes "Slenderman") lives deep in a wooded area, where he lures children who are unaware or unafraid. There, he's said to kill them before he goes after their families; currying favor and becoming one of his disciples, or "proxies," is supposedly the only way for a teen to save him- or herself, grandparents, parents, and siblings.

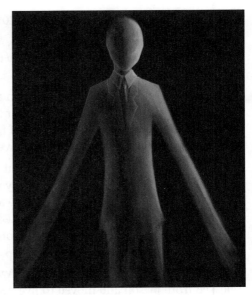

An artist's concept of what Slender Man looks like.

Twelve-year-old Anissa Weier had become familiar with Slender Man on a video game about a year before; Weier had then introduced twelve-year-old Morgan Geyser to the figure and the girls became fast fans. Neither girl, it's been said, was "popular"; they and their friend, Payton "Bella" Leutner, hung out together and were best friends, but it's been said that they weren't into boy bands or cheerleading like most pre-teen girls tend to be. They did have active imaginations, however.

One weekend, those imaginations got completely out of hand.

On the morning of May 31, 2014, following Geyser's twelfth birthday sleepover the night before, the three girls asked permission to walk to David's Park in Waukesha, supposedly to "play." Instead, apparently, Geyser had also decided that months of planning on behalf of Slender Man would finally happen; indeed, on the way to the park, according to Weier, Geyser showed Weier a knife she'd hidden beneath her shirt. Minutes later, eschewing the knife, Geyser and Weier attacked Leutner near the park's restrooms in what has been described as more roughhousing than a malicious attack. Leutner naturally resisted and her friends said they tried to calm her and themselves; it was then that Geyser and Weier suggested they play hide-and-seek in the wooded area of the park.

You may wonder why, if she was attacked once already, Leutner would want to stick around. Again, it's been suggested that perhaps she thought the attack was some sort of play—she wasn't hurt by it, after all—and she decided to continue hanging out with her friends. Heading into the woods, there was some hiding and some seeking before Weier told Geyser to proceed, and Geyser stabbed Leutner nineteen times before telling Leutner to lie down among the leaves, and the girls fled.

For much of the rest of the afternoon, Geyser and Weier wandered around Waukesha, until police caught up with them. In the meantime, a weak and wounded Leutner had managed to crawl up onto a bicycle path, where she was found by a biker who helped get her to the hospital by calling 911.

During their police interviews, both Geyser and Weier insisted that they had tried to kill Leutner to please Slender Man. They both considered the murder as necessary, a kind of test to ensure that Slender Man would accept them, take them into his mansion in the forest, and turn them into prototypes of himself, thereby protecting them and their loved ones. According to sources, the girls also spoke during interviews of other fictional fantasy and science fiction characters as though they were real.

After a stay in a juvenile detention facility and, for Geyser, a short stint at the Winnebago Mental Health Institute, the girls went on trial in adult court. Both were deemed mentally fit for trial.

In October 2017, Geyser, who'd received a diagnosis of schizophrenia while at Winnebago Mental Health Institute, pled guilty to a charge of attempted first-degree intentional homicide, hoping to avoid jail time; by Wisconsin law, she was found not guilty by reason of mental disease or defect. On February 1, 2018, she was sentenced to forty years in a psychiatric facility.

Two months prior to Geyser's sentencing, Weier pled guilty to being a party to attempted second-degree intentional homicide and was sentenced to twenty-five years in a mental hospital.

Who—or what—else was a Wisconsin killer?

And finally, just to show that humans aren't the only nefariously minded creatures around, we bring you the story of Romeo the Killer Elephant.

In the mid-to-late 1800s, dozens of circuses called Wisconsin home, the first one being the Mable Brothers U.S. Olympic Circus, the first national circus to land in the territory (Wisconsin wasn't quite a state then). They came to Delevan, then called "the Circus Capital of the World," and they brought along their nearly 11-foot-tall, 10,500-pound (3.3-meter, 4,763-kilogram) star performer, Romeo the Elephant.

It should come as no surprise that Romeo was not alone: of course, there was a Juliet who was slightly smaller and much sweeter in personality. She arrived at the Mable Brothers U.S. Olympic Circus in 1851 and the two pachyderms got along famously; their act consisted, quite literally, of a music-and-dance number and crowds loved them.

Alas, like the Shakespearean tragedy, Juliet died one winter in Delevan. Legend has it that Romeo was tasked with dragging her body to the middle of the ice on Lake Delevan, with the idea that her body would disappear when the ice melted (her body is said to still be at the bottom of the lake). Another legend says that he witnessed the death of another elephant when he was forced to let go of her, and she fell over a bridge. It's hard to say what really happened, but it's true that something did.

Romeo went wild.

In the space of some seventeen years, Romeo was responsible for the deaths of five handlers, impaling one with his tusk and crushing the others. At one point, the elephant escaped from his winter barn and spent three days terrorizing the area around

343

Delevan and Lake Geneva. Another time, he tore his way out of a performance center, nearly destroying the building, and wandered the streets of Chicago for an hour.

Shortly after his last murder, Romeo was rarely exhibited, mostly due to failing health; he was, after all, said to be nearing fifty years old then. In early 1872, his owners said he was still in good health, but that was not quite true; Romeo the Elephant died in Chicago on June 7, 1872, of an infection brought on by foot surgery two days prior.

His remains were meant to have been preserved for display but, because of the heat and a reported delay in action, the window of opportunity closed early. Romeo's carcass was instead ignominiously hauled off to the local municipal dump and abandoned.

Today, you can see a life-size statue of Romeo at the corner of E. Walworth Avenue and 2nd Street North in Delevan. It's a rare—and seemingly upbeat-happy—statue of a rogue murderer.

Is there any truth to the Smiley Face Killer?

For more than twenty years, a controversial mystery lingered along the Wisconsin border near the Mississippi River, specifically in La Crosse, but also in other areas of Wisconsin. While the crimes—if they were, indeed, crimes—may have started earlier, the focus on *this* mystery begins in 1997 and extends for twenty years afterward, and it concerns the Mississippi River drownings of eleven young men.

The loss of eleven lives is a tragedy, made even more so by the way things generally are said to have unfolded: usually speaking, the victim was out with friends for a night of revelry and drinking. Often, one thing led to another and the group was separated; later, someone would realize that the victim had gone missing. In hours to come, the body of the young man would be found dead in the Mississippi River and, in some cases, a graffiti-scrawled smiley-face was also spotted nearby, rumored to have been placed where he entered the water.

So was a killer—or killers—to blame?

A good Internet search indicates that *if* there were multiple killers, they were prolific and highly organized: the so-called Smiley Face Killer, as the possible *single* perpetrator was dubbed, committed their crimes near several rivers and in several states during those twenty years, killing dozens of young men. Overall, the strongest indication to link those crimes together was that graffiti.

In La Crosse, though, the drownings seemed to happen in a more concentrated area and the similarities were chilling: the general age of the victims was the same (college-age), the racial identity was the same (most were white), and the fact that most had been seen out having fun before disappearing made rumors swirl. The whole idea that the deaths were the work of a mass murderer or even a group of organized killers was frightening but, well, it just didn't completely add up—especially when you consider that the most notable similarity was that each body had a high blood-alcohol content.

The FBI got involved and blamed the drownings on alcohol. One criminal profiler supposedly scoffed at the whole idea of a killer being at fault. Parents of the young men also expressed skepticism that a killer was about. But famed coroner Dr. Cyril Wecht pointed a finger again at the list of coincidences. Experts weighed in, magazine articles and entire books were written, and rumors swirled. Paranormal experts were consulted. There was even a documentary made about this mystery.

In the end—and it looks like there might be an end to this—the drownings were blamed on one thing: over-imbibing.

Here in Wisconsin, a patrol was organized to walk Riverside Park in La Crosse, on the edge of Mississippi. Officials and patrol organizers say that since the patrol started, they've stopped many young people from walking out to the Mississippi River for a quick dip after a night of fun with friends, and they've ensured that those people got home safely. Drownings similar to what happened in those twenty years have all but stopped, proving that drink may have indeed been the reason for the terrible deaths. This success, they say, indicates that there never was a Smiley Face Killer.

NOTABLE SONS AND DAUGHTERS

Who are Wisconsin's most famous architects?

Frank Lloyd Wright (1867 or 1869–1959) was born in Richland Center, the son of a preacher who took his family along on his circuit. Wright was nearly 10 years old before he could call one place a permanent home. Later, after his parents divorced during his early years at the University of Wisconsin, young Wright took a job as an assistant to the dean of engineering; it was a job that portended good things. In 1887, he left the University of Wisconsin to study in Chicago, where he worked under the great architect Louis Sullivan, honed his skills, and developed his own personal style.

Houses were perhaps Wright's most famous endeavors—his lovely Taliesin homes as examples—and he designed churches as well as the S. C. Johnson Co. office building in Racine. A true Renaissance man, Wright was also known as a teacher and an author.

Architect and construtor Alex Jordan Jr. (1914–1989) is the brain behind of the House on the Rock, a tourist attraction located in Spring Green, Wisconsin, said to be "bizarre," "weird," and a "hoarder's paradise."

Legend has it that Jordan landed a meeting with Frank Lloyd Wright, with the hopes of a chance to work with the famous architect; instead, Wright dismissed Jordan with a supposed insult. Angered, Jordan decided on his way home from the disastrous meeting to out-do Wright's Taliesin and he secured a large, formidable rock on which to build his home. Opened in 1959 with a small collection of oddities, the House on the Rock now includes twenty-one rooms, a full-size merry-go-round, sea creatures, unique musical instruments, a massive library, and other entertaining items that Jordan decided to add as the years went by.

As for Jordan himself, legends and stories abound, books have been written, articles have been printed, and he remains somewhat of an enigma.

Who are Wisconsin's most famous artists?

Elmer P. Peterson (1928–) is a sculptor, born in Racine. Sculpture was not much of an interest in Peterson's early days; he didn't take to it much until he was in college at the University of Wisconsin. After graduation, Peterson moved to Texas but his heart remained in Wisconsin. In the late 1970s, he returned to Wisconsin and rediscovered his love of sculpture.

Peterson's perhaps-most famous sculpture is the World's Largest Buffalo, which sits in South Dakota, although many of his works can be found in and around La Crosse. That includes the statue of Native Americans playing in La Crosse, which welcomes visitors to the city, and the large eagle that dominates the entry to Riverside Park. Peterson currently lives in Galesville.

Georgia O'Keeffe (1887–1986) was born to childhood sweethearts, the second of seven children and named after her mother's father. She grew up in Sun Prairie, where she developed a deep love of nature. Even as early as the very beginning of her teenage years, O'Keeffe is said to have already known that she wanted to become a painter; her mother encouraged it by arranging for the girl to have lessons from a local artist. O'Keeffe attended high school in Madison and continued there, even when the rest of her family moved to Virginia. She joined them there and attended boarding school for a while, but around 1904 she she returned to the Midwest to attend school in Chicago; in 1907, after a bout with typhoid fever, O'Keeffe traveled to New York City, supporting herself with her talents. She continued to travel to be with family and to strike out on her own until her later years, when she finally settled in New Mexico. There is where her ashes were scattered upon her death.

In 1970, O'Keeffe received the National Institute of Arts and Letters' Gold Medal; in 1977, she received the Medal of Freedom.

John Colt (1925–1998) was born in Madison to a father who founded Colt School of Painting in Madison and who helped nurture John's career as an artist. As a young man, Colt entered World War II as a Navy electrician and worked on a submarine; in 1946, he returned home to Madison to become an art teacher. Colt instructed students at various schools throughout Wisconsin and he was a professor at the UW-Milwaukee and a visiting art professor in Indiana and Michigan, as well as a teacher overseas. He died in Amherst, Massachusetts, in 1998.

Known for her paintings of desert landscapes, flowers, and skyscrapers, artist Georgia O'Keeffe was born in Sun Prairie, Wisconsin.

348

Colt is considered to be one of Wisconsin's most important twentieth-century artists by many university professors and museum officials. His paintings have hung in galleries worldwide.

Who are Wisconsin's most famous authors?

Linda Godfrey (1951–) started out as a Janesville area newspaper reporter when she learned of several reports of a "beast" that was sighted in and around Elkhorn, near Janesville. The sightings—and the Beast—intrigued her, and she dug deeper into the phenomena and that of other cryptozoology in Wisconsin. Today, Godfrey is one of the country's foremost experts on werewolves and other monsters. She is the author of *The Beast of Bray Road, Monsters Among Us,* and other books. She lives in Elkhorn.

Jerry Apps (1934–) was born in Waushara County and grew up on a farm where his love of Wisconsin and the state's natural beauty sprung. Apps worked as a county agent and was a teacher before becoming a writer; he is the author of dozens of books, including *Barns of Wisconsin, The Quiet Season, Never Curse the Rain,* and *The Travels of Increase Joseph.* Apps lives in Wild Rose.

Michael Perry (1964–) was born and raised on a family farm in New Auburn. After graduating from high school, he attended nursing school, paying for it by working as a hand on a Wyoming ranch. Later, when he returned to Wisconsin, he became an EMT and volunteer firefighter, the stories of which framed his first book. Today, Perry is a humorist, author, and member of "The Long Beds" band, and lives in northwestern Wisconsin with his wife and daughters. He is the author of several books, including *Population 485* and *Truck.*

Jacqueline Mitchard (1956–) was born in Chicago and moved to Milwaukee as an adult to work at the *Milwaukee Journal Sentinel.* Later, at the recommendation of novelist-friend Jane Hamilton, she began writing fiction. Mitchard's first novel, *The Deep End of the Ocean,* was Oprah Winfrey's first Book Club Pick in 1996. Mitchard currently lives in Massachusetts.

Ben Logan (1920—2014) was born in Seneca and grew up on a farm, where his love of the land and its people seemed to have been nurtured. During World War II, Logan served in the Navy in the Mediterranean and continued to write for radio; later, he wrote for TV and film production. He was also an advocate for natural conservation for most of his life. In 1986, Logan and his wife returned for good to the Seneca area and retired; Logan's wife died in 1990 and Logan died in Viroqua in 2014. Ben Logan's best-known work was *The Land Remembers,* which was published in 1975.

Thornton Wilder (1897–1975) was born in Madison but spent some of his childhood and young adulthood overseas. Returning to the United States, he served in World War I and then began writing his first novel. Wilder won a Pulitzer Prize in 1927 for *The Bridge of San Luis Rey*; a second Pulitzer in 1938 for his book, *Our Town;* and a third Pulitzer in 1942 for *The Skin of Our Teeth.*

Victoria Houston (1945–) is a mystery writer who was born and raised in Rhinelander and, she says, has always had "an aptitude for writing." She attended college in Vermont and worked as a magazine and newspaper writer (both, fodder for her nonfiction books) and she worked in publicity for a major book publisher, rubbing elbows with cartoonists and advice columnists. She returned to Rhinelander in 1996 and began writing her mysteries. As a child, Houston says she always loved to fish Wisconsin's waters; perhaps that's why her *Loon Lake Mystery Series* features Wisconsin's north woods and fishing in particular. Today, Houston still lives in Rhinelander.

August Derleth (1909–1971) was born in Sauk City in south central Wisconsin, one of just two children in the family. He attended parochial school in Sauk City and claimed that his writing career had already been "decided upon" by the time he became a teenager. At sixteen, he sold his first story. Derleth attended the University of Wisconsin, worked briefly in Minneapolis as a book editor, and continued to write as he returned to Wisconsin and became active in his community. Perhaps best-known for his horror / science fiction and detective-story novels, Derleth himself, toward the end of his life, estimated that more than three thousand individual works of his had been published throughout the years.

Laura Ingalls Wilder (1867–1957) was born in Pepin, about two years before her family moved to Kansas, an experience on which she would base her first book. Wilder did, indeed, have an older sister named Mary and a younger sister named Carrie; she also had two other siblings, one of whom died as an infant. In 1878, the Ingalls family returned to Wisconsin and then moved to the Dakota Territory a year later. For the most part, Ingalls had little of what we might call formal education; because the family moved often, her schooling was catch-as-catch-can; even so, Ingalls knew enough to earn her teaching certificate and she began working at a rural school in South Dakota. While there, she met her husband, Alonzo. In 1910, Wilder's daughter encouraged Wilder to write about the experiences she learned as the child of a self-sufficient pioneer; the book was rejected and Wilder persisted. In 1932, her first book, *Little House in the Big Woods*, was published when she was sixty-five years old. Wilder finished her last book in her "Little House" series in 1943, when she was seventy-six years old.

Edna Ferber (1885–1968) was born in Kalamazoo, Michigan, and had a difficult childhood almost from the start—in part because Ferber was Jewish and often suffered anti-Semitism. When she was five years old, her family moved to Ottumwa,

Born in Pepin County, Laura Ingalls Wilder became famous for her "Little House" series about a settler family in the American frontier.

Iowa, a town she later remembered as particularly brutal toward Jews. Undaunted, Ferber claimed to have stood up to them on a daily basis. As a young woman, Ferber fell in love with the theatre but in 1897, after the family moved to Appleton, she gave up her dreams of becoming an actor and landed a job as a reporter at an Appleton newspaper. In 1905, she fell ill; while recovering, she began to write fiction and ultimately became a playwright, novelist, short-story writer, and a Pulitzer Prize winner in 1935 for her novel *So Big*.

Zona Gale (1874–1938) was born in Portage and knew at a very young age that she wanted to be a writer. She attended the University of Wisconsin and worked for six years after graduation as a newspaper reporter and writer. In 1901, she moved to New York City to work for a newspaper there; in 1903, she sold her first short story and in 1905, her first romance novel was published. At around that time, she returned to Portage to write novels and became one of the most popular authors of the Jazz Age. Zona Gale won a Pulitzer Prize for drama in 1921 for her own adaptation of *Miss Lulu Bett*.

Aldo Leopold (1887–1948) was born in Burlington, Iowa, where he spent much of his childhood observing and drawing birds and other wildlife. He attended Yale Forest School in 1909 and, following his dreams, left for work in Arizona and New Mexico, where he moved his way up the job ladder. In 1924, Leopold was transferred to Wisconsin where, in 1933, she published a textbook on wildlife management and accepted a chair position in wildlife management at the UW-Madison. Two years later, Leopold and his family began planting pine seedlings along the Wisconsin River near Baraboo, and they worked to restore Wisconsin prairie. Leopold followed the endeavors closely and journaled about the project and his observations on nature in general. One week after he learned that the book he wrote, *A Sand County Almanac*, was to be published by a major publisher, Leopold died of a heart attack.

Marguerite Henry (1902–1997) was born in Milwaukee, the youngest of five children. Her father was a publisher of books, and that may have shaped her wish to become an author; it didn't hurt that when she was seven years old, he gave her a set of her very own tools to be an author; at age eleven, Henry was a published author of a magazine article, for which she was paid a reported $12. After graduating from college, Henry worked as a teacher but, because writing was always her first love, she continued to also work for national magazines. This led to a decision to write children's books. Legions of little girls have thrilled to her *Misty* horse series. Among her many other awards, Henry won a Newbery Honors Award for her book *Justin Morgan Had a Horse* in 1946 and another in 1948 for *Misty of Chincoteague*; she finally got her Newbery Medal in 1949 for *King of the Wind*.

Peter Straub (1943–) was born in Milwaukee and grew up only wanting to learn to read, which he taught himself to do through comic books and memory. This gave him a jump-start in school. Later, Straub graduated from the University of Wisconsin and became a teacher in Milwaukee and, hoping to write, he left the country to live in Ireland and London, where *Ghost Story* was written. In addition to that terrifying tale, Straub's horror novels have been translated into several languages; he is the winner of eight

Bram Stoker Awards. His books include *Ghost Story, Shadowland,* and *The Talisman* (with Stephen King).

Frank King (1883–1969) was born in Cashton and moved to Tomah with his parents when he was just four years old. He loved to draw while growing up; as a young man, he entered contests with his artwork and he doodled wherever he could. One of his doodles was seen by a traveling salesman, who arranged for young King to speak to an editor at the *Minneapolis Times.* He left there to attend school in Chicago, where he found work. In 1919, King began penning his most famous cartoon strip, *Gasoline Alley.*

Sterling North (1906–1974) was born near Edgerton, where North loved to explore the outdoors. He lost his mother at age seven and suffered from a bout of polio that nearly killed him, but he healed enough to leave home to move to Chicago as a young man, where he landed a newspaper job. In his position there, he publicly denounced comic strips as dangerous to "youth." By 1929, he was a published writer of books; his most famous work, *Rascal,* the story of his friendship with a raccoon, was published in 1963.

Lorena Hickok (1893–1968) was born in East Troy and later became a journalist. Hickok is perhaps best remembered as a very close friend of First Lady Eleanor Roosevelt.

Alice Sebold (1963–) was born in Madison into the tumultuous home in which she was often left for her older sister to care for. In 1980, she moved to New York to attend college, where she was attacked and raped on her way home to her dorm room; her experience was the basis for her memoir, *Lucky.* It was her second, most famous book, *The Lovely Bones,* published in 2002, that earned her the most accolades: for it, Sebold won a Bram Stoker Award for First Novel, an American Booksellers Association Book of the Year Award for Adult Fiction, and the book was made into a movie.

Hamlin Garland (1860–1940) was a novelist and writer from West Salem, best known for his slice-of-prairie-life novels. That comes as a surprise when one notes that Garland wasn't a fan of such a life; when he was a young man, he left for Boston in 1884, looking for a career that was more stable than the constant change of being a sustenance farmer on the unsettled prairie. Self-educated, he entered the literary society in Boston and began writing about the hard lives and frustrations of being a pioneer. Garland was also a politician who worked to further the work of reform candidates. His book, *Daughter of the Middle Border,* won a Pulitzer Prize in 1921.

Did any Wisconsinites work on behalf of the environment?

John Muir (1838–1914) was born in Scotland but moved with his parents and siblings when he was small, first to Fountain Lake and then to Portage. Muir's father was said to be a harsh taskmaster and worked his children from sunup to sundown; when young John had any free time, he used it to educate himself on the land around him and by studying the wildlife on his father's homestead. Despite having little formal education, he ultimately enrolled at the University of Wisconsin. In 1867, after having been blinded in one eye by a work accident, Muir began a journey of a thousand miles from Indianapolis to the Gulf of Mexico, to Cuba, Panama, and then to California, which became his home (or, home as much as Muir had one, since he continued to travel). For his wanders, Muir became known for his descriptions of plants in Wisconsin and across the country and was one of the founders of the Sierra Club, which, he said, would "do something for wildness and make the mountains glad." He died in a hospital in Los Angeles.

Roy Chapman Andrews (1884–1960) was born in Beloit in a house that was near enough to be "city" but far enough away to have been bordered by meadow, which is where young Roy loved to explore as a boy. As a young man, Andrews attended Beloit College and studied archaeology and was known for his research on whales; in 1906, he began working at the American Museum of Natural History as an assistant and janitor. By 1934, he'd worked his way up to being director of the museum. Ever the adventurer, Andrews took many a scientific group on expeditions to several countries around the world, including to the Gobi Desert, where his group discovered the first known nest of dinosaur eggs. Andrews died in California in 1960 and his cremated remains were interred in the family plot in Beloit.

Although born in Scotland, legendary environmentalist John Muir was raised and educated in Wisconsin.

Increase Lapham (1811–1875) was born in New York to Quaker parents, the fifth of thirteen children. He got his first job cutting stone at age thirteen. A year later, he began making money with his map-drawing abilities—a talent that grew in proficiency and notoriety. Almost totally self-taught, Lapham came to Wisconsin in 1836, having landed a job as a surveyor and, two years later, he settled in Milwaukee. A scientist at heart, he was a "first" in many ways: Lapham wrote the first book ever published in Wisconsin, drew the first accurate Wisconsin maps, founded several of its schools, and was one of the first white men to study effigy mounds and other notable and interesting parts of Wisconsin land and history. In addition, Lapham was instrumental in helping pass environmental laws; he also helped found the Milwaukee Public Library, the State Historical Society, and the National Weather Service.

Gaylord Nelson (1916—2005) was born in Clear Lake. With eleven siblings to play with, Nelson loved enjoying what the outdoors had to offer, and he loved exploring the area. Though his main interest as an adult was politics, Nelson remained concerned about the environment all his life; in the late 1960s, he held "teach-ins" to educate Wisconsinites on the environment; by 1970, that "teach-in" had become Earth Day and has since been honored every April around the country. For more on Gaylord Nelson, check out the "Politics and Law" chapter.

Who took the Dairy State to Hollywood?

Don Ameche (1908–1993) was born Dominic Felix Amichi in Kenosha, attended college in Dubuque, Iowa, and had worked first as a lawyer until he discovered theatre. In addition to his many radio, film, television, and theatre appearances (most often as a leading man), Ameche won an Academy Award for Best Supporting Actor for his 1985 role in the movie *Cocoon* and was inducted into the Radio Hall of Fame in 1992.

Ellen Corby (1911–1999) was born Ellen Hanson in Racine and made her screen debut at age twenty-four in 1935's *Speed Limited*. For the most part, her early career consisted of bit parts, though she did receive an Academy Award nomination in 1948 for *I Remember Mama*. That didn't garner the wild fame she

Three-time Oscar winner Willem Dafoe was born in Appleton.

wanted, and she continued to land smaller parts until she took on what is arguably her best-known role as Grandma Walton in *The Waltons* TV show.

Willem Dafoe (1955–) was born in Appleton. His first role came in 1979 for the ill-fated *Heaven's Gate,* for which Dafoe was fired long before the film was completed. He has been nominated for Academy Awards for Best Supporting Actor three times: in 1986 for his role in *Platoon*; in 2000 for *Shadow of the Vampire;* and in 2017 for *The Florida Project*.

Tyne Daly (1946–) was born Ellen Tyne Daly in Madison. She's perhaps best known for her role as Mary Beth Lacey in the TV series *Cagney & Lacey*. Daly has won six Emmy Awards for her work and has received two Tony Award nominations and one Tony Award for *Gypsy* in 1990. Today, Daly is also known for her activism.

Tom Wopat (1951–) was born Thomas Steven Wopat in Lodi and grew up on a dairy farm. He fell in love with the limelight at age twelve by acting in school plays; after studying at the UW-Madison, Wopat dropped out to play in a band that performed for stage productions. Having decided to pursue acting as a profession, he appeared off-Broadway and then on Broadway in 1978. One year later, he was well-known for his role as Luke Duke on *The Dukes of Hazzard.* In 1983, Wopat began a second phase of the performing life by releasing a country & western music album; in 2000, fans found one filled with love songs.

Chris Farley (1964–1997) was born Christopher Crosby Farley in Madison. He moved to Chicago after graduating from Marquette University; he was a cast member with the Improv Olympic Theatre and with Second City Theatre; at the latter, he was dis-

How many Miss Wisconsins have won the Miss America pageant?

Two Miss Wisconsins went on to win the Miss America pageant. Terry Meeuwsen of De Pere won the competition in 1973, and Laura Kaeppeler of Kenosha was crowned Miss America in 2012.

covered performing by Lorne Michaels and he then became a regular cast member of *Saturday Night Live*. Farley died in Chicago from an overdose and complications of his obesity. During his time on *SNL*, Farley also made movies, including *Tommy Boy, Billy Madison,* and *Black Sheep*. After his death, *Almost Heroes* was released.

Alfred Lunt (1892–1977) was born in Milwaukee and attended Carroll College in Waukesha until he was called to the theatre. In his long career in film and stage, Lunt was the winner of three Tony Awards—in 1954 for *Ondine;* in 1955 for *Quadrille;* and a Special Award in 1970 that also included his wife, actress Lynn Fontanne (1887–1983); neither Lunt nor Fontanne were ever seen in an Oscar-nominated Best Film, although both were nominated as Best Actor and Best Actress for their roles in 1932's *The Guardsman*. During their years in Hollywood, Lunt and Fontanne kept a small farm Genesee Depot, near Waukesha; today, they are buried side-by-side in Forest Home Cemetery in Milwaukee. Amusingly, it's been said that Fontanne refused to give her actual birthdate; her husband died believing that she was years younger when the exact opposite was true!

Fredric March (1897–1975) was born Ernest Frederick McIntyre Bickel in Racine and started his adult life as a banker. The acting bug bit and he enjoyed a stage and screen career, after leaving finance behind, shortening his name, and altering his mother's maiden name (Marcher) for use as a stage name. March was seen on-screen primarily in the 1930s and 1940s although he continued to make films into the 1970s. He won the Oscar for Best Actor in 1932 for *Dr. Jekyll and Mr. Hyde* and again in 1947 for *The Best Years of Our Lives*. He also won two Tony Awards and had the honor of having a theatre named after him at the UW-Oshkosh.

Pat O'Brien (1899–1983) was born William Joseph Patrick O'Brien in Milwaukee and grew up with an eye toward entering the seminary and becoming a priest. He was perhaps best known as a character actor, having appeared in *Angels with Dirty Faces* and *Some Like It Hot*. Fans might find it amusing that O'Brien's last professional acting gig was for the TV show, *Happy Days*, which was set in his hometown.

Charlotte Rae (1926–2018) was born in Milwaukee, one of three daughters of Jewish parents. Though Rae grew up on a farm, she knew early in her life that she wanted to perform; at first, she wanted to be a serious actress but her sense of humor won out and she embraced comedy as her main talent, although she did a bit of theatre and some minor parts on TV. Rae, born Charlotte Rae Lubotsky, is perhaps best known for her role as Edna Garrett in the TV series *The Facts of Life*.

Gena Rowlands (1930–) was born Virginia Cathryn Rowlands in Madison, into a political family; her father was a member of the State Assembly and later worked for the U.S. Department of Agriculture. A TV, stage, and movie actress, she is a four-time Emmy Award winner and the winner of two Golden Globes. As the wife of the late director John Cassavetes, Rowlands is one of a very small handful of women to have been nominated for an Academy Award for Best Actress for a film directed by her husband.

Famous for such films as *Boys Town, Captains Courageous,* and *Guess Who's Coming to Dinner,* Spencer Tracy was a Milwaukee native.

Spencer Tracy (1900–1967) was born Spencer Bonaventure Tracy in Milwaukee and wanted to be a doctor when he grew up. He was at Marquette University when World War I broke out and Tracy enlisted; following his service, he returned to Wisconsin, to Ripon College where one of his teachers supposedly noticed his gift with debate and suggested that Tracy become an actor. Tracy was nominated nine times for an Academy Award and won twice: for his roles in *Captains Courageous* in 1937 and *Boys' Town* in 1938. He died of a heart attack just weeks after finishing his last movie, *Guess Who's Coming to Dinner.*

Orson Welles (1915–1985) was born George Orson Welles in Kenosha, the son of an inventor and a piano player, both of whom died when Welles was a young boy. Sent to live with a family friend in Chicago, Welles spent some time fueling the wanderlust his father had instilled in him, and he tried to break into the theatre in Great Britain. The year 1934 was a big one for Welles: he got married, joined a road company, directed a film short for the first time, and made his dramatic radio debut. Welles is familiar with a wide audience because of his enduring legacies: he was co-producer of *The War of the Worlds;* director, producer, and star of *Citizen Kane;* and TV pitchman for a brand of wine.

Heather Graham (1970–) was born Heather Joan Graham in Milwaukee, the daughter of a book author and an FBI agent. Voted as "Most Talented" by the students in her high school, Graham was a model for a time and also worked at a retail store before starting her acting career. She has appeared on TV in *Scrubs, Portlandia, Twin Peaks,* and other shows; her movie appearances include *Boogie Nights.*

Mark Ruffalo (1967–) was born Mark Alan Ruffalo in Kenosha but grew up in Virginia and California. In the latter locale, he cofounded the Orpheus Theatre Company and became somewhat of a Renaissance man there. At that time, he tended bar to make ends meet until he finally landed his first role in a play. Ruffalo is also a filmmaker, and activist, but is perhaps best known for his role as the Incredible Hulk.

Tony Shaloub (1953–) was born Anthony Marcus Shaloub in Green Bay and was raised there. At the tender age of six, he landed his first role in a school production and that was that: Shaloub graduated from the University of Southern Maine and Yale School of Drama. Though Shaloub has had several smaller parts in several movies, he is perhaps best known for his role as Adrian Monk in TV's *Monk*.

Gene Wilder (1933–2016) was born Jerome Silberman in Milwaukee to parents of Russian Jewish descent. Almost from the outset of his career, Wilder turned heads: his Broadway debut won him a Clement Derwent Award. He continued acting on-stage until he made the transition to movies with the 1967 movie *Bonnie and Clyde.* He received an Oscar nomination for Best Supporting Actor for his role in *The Producers;* in addition to that film, Wilder is perhaps best known for his movies, such as *Willy Wonka and the Chocolate Factory, Young Frankenstein,* and *Silver Streak.*

Kathy Kinney (1954–) was born in Stevens Point. She is best known for her role as Mimi Bobeck in TV's *The Drew Carey Show.*

Fred MacMurray (1908–1991) was born Frederick Martin MacMurray in Kankakee, Illinois, but moved to the Madison area with his family when he was a small boy. He graduated from Beaver Dam High School, where he was an athlete and sports star, though he really wanted to be a musician. He attended Carroll University in Waukesha but did not graduate; by 1930, he'd already landed a few rather prestigious music gigs with famous singers. Also in 1930, he appeared on Broadway and, within four years, signed a contract with Paramount Pictures. MacMurray had an impressive film résumé, including work for Walt Disney Studios, but modern generations probably know him best for his role as Steve Douglas in TV's *My Three Sons*. He was the first individual honored as a Disney Legend in 1987. Fred MacMurray, it's said, also never forgot his small-town roots.

Chris Noth (1954–) was born Christopher David Noth in Madison; his mother was a TV reporter. After attending college in Vermont and at the Yale School of Drama, he jumped feet-first into drama with his first role in TV's *Law and Order* in 1990 before tackling the role of Mr. Big on HBO's *Sex and the City*. His credits include roles on *Sex and the City* and *Law & Order*. He also owns a bar, The Cutting Room, in New York City.

Greta Van Susteren (1954–) was born Greta Conway Van Susteren in Appleton and attended the University of Wisconsin, and then studied at Georgetown Law Center, where she received a degree in law; return-

Appleton native Greta Van Susteren is a successful television journalist who has reported for CNN, NBC, and Fox News.

357

ing to Wisconsin, she worked as an attorney. In 1991, Van Susteren became a legal analyst for CNN (where she covered the 1994 O. J. Simpson trial), as well as the co-host of a legal talk show; in 2002, she migrated to Fox News; in 2017, she moved to MSNBC. At the time of this writing, Van Susteren works for Voice of America.

Jane Kaczmarek (1955–) was born Jane Frances Kaczmarek in Milwaukee, the oldest child of four. She attended the University of Wisconsin, where she was a theatre major but also hoped to become a teacher; later, after encouragement from her friend, Tony Shaloub (see above), she attended Yale University. Though Kaczmarek has appeared in several roles, she is best known for her role as Malcolm's mother on TV's *Malcolm in the Middle;* Kaczmarek is a three-time Golden Globe winner and has been nominated for an Emmy seven times.

Al Molinaro (1919–2015) was born Umberto Francesca (also said to be Francesco) Molinaro in Kenosha, so-named in honor of an Italian prince. Molinaro might have been satisfied to live his life quietly in Kenosha working for the city, but when he was twenty years old, a friend strongly urged him to move to California and become a movie star. His first movie job was as an animator, and he might have been satisfied at that, were it not for a union strike. To make ends meet, Molinaro then became a bill collector, but he persisted in looking for acting roles. Five years after he came to Hollywood, his dream finally happened with a stage role in a Chekhov play. Though Molinaro had a long and, apparently, varied career, he is perhaps best known for his role as Al Delvecchio on TV's *Happy Days*, and for Officer Murray Greshler on *The Odd Couple* with Tony Randall and Jack Klugman.

Daniel J. Travanti (1940–) was born Danielo Giovanni Travanti in Kenosha but spent part of his childhood in Iowa. He was a football star in high school but found his love of acting at the University of Wisconsin. Travanti was reportedly offered football scholarships but turned them down to attend the Yale School of Drama; once done there, he landed his first important role almost immediately, in a touring company with Colleen Dewhurst (1924–1991). His career is wide and varied, but Travanti is undoubtedly best known for his role as Frank Furillo on TV's *Hill Street Blues*.

Tom Snyder (1936–2007) was born in Kenosha. Though he began his career as an actor, he was better known for his work as a newsman and talk show host. Snyder was most often seen on NBC in the 1970s and 1980s and on CBS in his later career.

Allen Ludden (1917–1981) was born Allen Packard Ellsworth in Mineral Point. Though his career was a long one, he is mostly known today as an emcee and game show host, particularly that of the TV game show *Password*.

David (1947–) and Jerry Zucker (1950–) were born and raised in Milwaukee. They are writers and film producers best known for their comedies *Airplane!, Top Secret!* and the television show *Police Squad*, created with their friend Jim Abrams (1944–), who was born in Shorewood. The three grew up together. Fans may like to know that the Zucker brothers often cast their mother in a small role in their movies.

Deidre Hall (1947–) was born Deidre Ann Hall in Milwaukee, a twin whose sister, Andrea Hall, often plays her twin on TV. Deidre Hall is best known for her role as Dr. Marlena Evans on the daytime drama *Days of Our Lives*. She's enjoyed many accolades: Hall was once voted Best Television Role Model; she received an American Women in Radio and Television Award in 1994, five Best Actress awards from *Soap Opera Digest*, and several nods from *TV Guide* for her sense of style.

Carole Landis (1919–1948) was born Frances Lillian Mary Ridste in Fairchild, the youngest child of a woman whose husband abandoned the family soon after little Frances was born. At age fifteen, Landis graduated from high school and promptly got married; the marriage lasted just weeks before the couple divorced, but they soon re-married before moving to California. Almost immediately, Landis landed work as a dancer / singer and not soon afterward, she got a studio contract with Warner Brothers. She received her big break in 1940 with the film *One Million B.C.* At age twenty-nine, and with almost fifty films under her belt in a short fourteen year career, Carole Landis committed suicide by overdose.

Bill Weir (1967–) was born William Francis Weir in Milwaukee. Weir was formerly a reporter for ABC News and a *Nightline* anchor; he is now with CNN.

Tom Laughlin (1931–2013) was born Thomas Robert Laughlin in Milwaukee and went to high school there where he once reportedly admitted to being a "greaser." A trained expert in judo, Laughlin is best known for his title role in the *Billy Jack* movies, although some may remember him for his politics and his ill-fated run for president in 1992, which he announced in his hometown. He also ran in 2004 and 2008.

Eric Szmanda (1975–) was born Eric Kyle Szmanda in Milwaukee and participated in community productions there as a child. After graduating from high school in Muk-wonago, Szmanda moved to Los Angeles to pursue acting, but he landed an internship with BMG Music, which led to a move to Chicago to work in the music industry. Months later, he moved back to California to work onstage. It didn't take long for Szmanda to land work on the small screen. Though he lists independent films and a handful of TV appearances on his biography, Szmanda is best known for his role of Greg Sanders in the CBS drama *CSI: Crime Scene Investigation*. In case you're wondering, Szmanda is the great-nephew of Menard's pitchman Ray Szmanda (1926–2018).

Amy Pietz (1969–) was born Amy Kathleen Pietz in Milwaukee and, though she initially trained for ballet, she spent much of her childhood acting in local performances. She attended the Milwaukee High School of the Arts and graduated from DePaul University's Theatre School before heading to Hollywood. Pietz is best known for her role as Annie Spadaro in NBC's *Caroline in the City*.

Jackie Mason (1931–) was born Jacob Moshe Maza in Sheboygan, the brother of three rabbis—something Mason himself became after years of being a cantor. Three years later, he left the synagogue in favor of acting. The winner of several awards and an actor in many films, Mason was on the *Ed Sullivan Show* the famous night the Beatles appeared in 1964. Today, he performs as a stand-up comedian.

Which musicians came from Wisconsin?

Woody Herman (1913–1987) was born Woodrow Charles Herman in Milwaukee and knew by the time he was eight years old that he wanted to lead his own band. To achieve it, he took lessons in music and dance and played in a children's group. By the time he was a teenager, Herman was playing with a touring band; he finally achieved his dreams with his own band in 1936; for a time, Alan Greenspan played saxophone for Woody's band, the Thundering Herd. The Big Band and Jazz Hall of Fame inducted Woody Herman in 1981.

Bobby Hatfield (1940–2003) was born Robert Lee Hatfield in Beaver Dam. He was a singer, best known for being half of the Righteous Brothers, with hits such as "You've Lost That Lovin' Feelin'" and "Unchained Melody."

Liberace (1919–1987) was born Wladziu Valentino Liberace in West Allis to a family whose musical talents ran strong.

It might be a surprise that a performer so flamboyant as pianist Liberace could come from the mellow land of cheese, lakes, and forests, but Liberace was, indeed, born in West Allis to Polish and Italian immigrants.

Young Wladziu started studying music at age four; three years later, he won a scholarship to the Wisconsin College of Music. By age ten, he was playing music professionally; as a teenager, he performed a solo with the Chicago Symphony and attended the Wisconsin College of Music; he also worked under the stage name of Walter Busterkeys. In 1939, as he was performing for an audience, someone requested a popular tune and Liberace, ever the showman, played the tune, tongue-in-cheek, in classical style. The audience went wild and by 1940, he had incorporated that and more into his act, complete with enhanced piano and that iconic candelabra. Much as he loved live performances, Liberace appeared in a handful of films throughout his long career but was also incredibly popular as a TV host and guest while also selling out in such venues as Madison Square Garden. In the heyday of his career in the 1960s and 1970s, he was one of America's highest-paid entertainers. Among his accolades, Liberace was named Best Dressed Entertainer, Entertainer of the Year, received two Emmy Awards, and laid claim to six gold albums.

Les Paul (1916–2009) was born in Waukesha and was always fascinated with electronics; he built his first radio tuner when he was just nine years old. By the time he was a teenager, he was performing at concerts; at that time, he figured out how to amplify a guitar, how to harness broadcast radio, and how to record sound. He continued to play professionally with and without his wife, Mary Ford (1924–1977), even after a devastating accident almost cost him the use of his right arm. He's also renowned for his iconic guitars. Among his many honors and awards, Les Paul was inducted into the Rock & Roll Hall of Fame in 1988.

Steve Miller (1943–) was born in Milwaukee into a musical family; Les Paul and Mary Ford were close friends of Miller's parents. He formed the Steve Miller Band in 1966; their first major hit was "The Joker" in 1973.

Al Jarreau (1940–2017) was born Alwyn Lopez Jarreau in Milwaukee to a minister father and a piano-playing mother. Though he loved singing—particularly in church—young Al went to school to become a counselor. Still, his love of singing led to gigs at clubs, where he was discovered by the president of Warner Brothers Records. Al Jarreau's first album was released in 1975; over his career, he won five Grammy Awards.

Justin Vernon (1981–) was born Justin DeYarmond Edison Vernon in Eau Claire. He is the founder of indie band Bon Iver.

Eric Benét (1966–) was born Eric Benét Jordan in Milwaukee. He is a Grammy-nominated R&B singer and winner of three Wisconsin Area Music Industry awards.

Robin Zander (1953–) was born in Beloit. He is the lead singer and guitarist for the rock band Cheap Trick. Fans might also know that Zander has appeared as an actor in three major motion pictures.

Who else came from (or had strong ties to) Wisconsin?

Velvalea "Vel" Phillips (1924–2018) was born in Milwaukee. Upon graduation from high school, she landed a scholarship and attended the University of Wisconsin—Madison Law School and became the first African American woman to graduate from the prestigious school. She and her husband moved to Milwaukee where, in 1956, she gained a seat on the City Council; by the early 1960s, she was active in the Civil Rights Movement and, in 1962, wrote and presented a Fair Housing Law to help eliminate racial bias in housing in the city. The city adopted the law in 1968.

In 1971, Phillips was the first African American woman in Wisconsin to become a judge when she was appointed to the Milwaukee County Judiciary; alas, she lost the seat to a white candidate in a later election. In 1978, she became the first woman and the first African American to be elected as secretary of state, which also made her the highest ranking female official in the state of Wisconsin in the twentieth century.

Jeane Dixon (1904–1997) was born Jeane L. Pinckert in Medford. An American psychic, she is perhaps best known for having predicted John F. Kennedy's assassination. In that prediction, made years before the actual event, Dixon said that the winner of the 1960 election would die in office; years later, she claimed that she specifically said he'd be assassinated, but her interviewer then refused to use that word. After her vision came true, Dixon became extremely in demand as a psychic. She was the subject of two best-selling books and became an author herself, as well as the columnist of an astrology column. By the early 1980s, Dixon had had enough incorrect predictions that her star was waning and critics were brutal; even so, it's said that in her day-to-day life, Dixon's prophesies were still eerily uncanny.

Harry Houdini (1874–1926) was one of the greatest escape artists and musicians ever. Born Ehrich Weisz in Hungary, when little Ehrich was small, his parents moved to Appleton (the city where he often claimed he was born) and set about raising their growing family. Ehrich took note of his family's poverty when he was a teenager, and he devised a quick street show that took advantage of his fascination with magic. Be-

fore long, he began traveling with another traveling magician, naming and billing themselves after French magician Jean-Eugene Robert-Houdin. On his own a few years later, Houdini (the name he'd assumed) hired a young assistant named Bess and married her. At age twenty-four, he finally reached fame with his Challenge Act, which consisted of a complicated series of hurdles from which he had to extricate himself. At this time, though he'd also performed now and again as a "spiritualist" (an act that even he knew was a sham), Houdini began to work to debunk "real" spiritualists. His efforts to that end didn't stop when he died at age fifty-two after an unfortunate accident related to a performance gone awry: Houdini reportedly left instructions with Bess for communication in his afterlife. Alas, he was correct: nothing ever came from it.

Deke Slayton (1924–1993) was born Donald Kent Slayton and raised in Sparta. After graduating from Sparta High School, he entered the Army Air Force. In 1943, Slayton "received his wings" and served during World War II as a B-25 pilot with the 340th Bombardment Group; at war's end, he attended the University of Minnesota, where he received a bachelor's degree in aeronautical engineering and he then worked for Boeing for a time before being recalled to the Minnesota National Guard in 1951. In 1955, he attended USAF Test Pilot School to be a test pilot; four

Born in Hungary, the great escape artist Harry Houdini was brought to Appleton as a child.

years later, Slayton was tapped as one of the original Mercury 7 astronauts but was grounded due to a heart condition. Even so, he continued to work for NASA on various projects and in various positions until his retirement in 1982. When he died, he was working as the president of Space Services, Inc., a company he founded.

Mark Lee (1952–) was born in Viroqua. After graduating from Viroqua High School in 1970, Lee attended the U.S. Air Force Academy, where he received a bachelor of science degree in civil engineering. Originally trained as a pilot, Lee became an astronaut candidate in 1984, and has flown four space flights, including thirty-three days in orbit for a total of more than thirteen million miles in over five hundred trips around the world. Lee is the recipient of several honors, including Distinguished Flying Cross and four NASA Space Flight medals.

James Lovell (1928–) was born in Ohio and moved to Milwaukee with his mother when he was just five years old. Always fascinated with flying, rockets, and space, he graduated from Juneau High School, where he was an Eagle Scout with the Boy Scouts. For two years, he attended the University of Wisconsin but left there to attend the U.S. Naval Academy at Annapolis; there, he earned a bachelor of science degree in 1952. Commissioned to the Navy, Lovell became a pilot and an expert in nighttime landing of jets at sea. In 1958, Lovell entered Naval Test Pilot School and some five years later, in the fall of 1962, he was selected by NASA to be an astronaut. Lovell was aboard the Gemini 7 in 1965, the commander of Gemini 12 in 1966, navigator and command module pilot of Apollo 8 in 1968, and commander of Apollo 13 in 1970. In 1973, he retired from the Navy and NASA, both simultaneously. James Lovell had a cameo role in the movie *Apollo 13*.

Golda Meir (1898–1978) came to Milwaukee from Russia in 1905 as an eight-year-old; there, she went to school, then teacher's college, before she married Morris Myerson in 1917 (she later shortened her name to Meir). In 1921, she left Wisconsin for Palestine, worked for the government, and became an activist for the Zionist movement. Meir was elected to the Israeli Parliament after Israel became a country; she was later appointed to minister of labor and social insurance. From 1956 to 1966, Meir served as Israel's foreign minister and became prime minister in 1969. She resigned that position in 1974 and subsequently retired.

Golda Meir, who was prime minister of Israel four times, was brought to Milwaukee as an eight-year-old and lived there for sixteen years.

Ellen Sirleaf (1938–) was born in Liberia but came to the United States and attended college at the UW-Madison, receiving a degree in accounting. She also attended the University of Colorado at Boulder and Harvard University before returning to her home country where she worked as the assistant minister of finance under President William Tolbert. When Tolbert was killed in 1980 and Liberia was thrown into turmoil, Sirleaf went into exile and lived for a time again in the United States. Returning to Liberia in 1985, she attempted to run for a seat in that country's Senate but instead landed in jail; three years later, she returned once again to the United States. In 1997, she once again returned to the country of her birth and quickly got involved in politics again. In 2005, Sirleaf took over Liberia's Unity Party and was elected president. As the twenty-fourth president of Liberia, she served from 2006 to 2018, and was the first elected female head of state in Africa.

Marissa Mayer (1975–) was born in Wausau and has said in interviews that she enjoyed a typical Wisconsin small-town upbringing, complete with ice skating and ballet lessons. Always a quick study with numbers and math, she graduated from Wausau West High School and headed for Stanford University, where she fell in love with computers and received both a bachelor of science and a master's degree for computer science. Her knowledge was such that she received fourteen job offers upon graduating and she took the one offered by what would ultimately become Google. There, she spent a decade absorbing and working and in mid-2012, she accepted a job as the CEO of Yahoo! as the fifth executive hired in as many years. She resigned her position with Yahoo! in 2017, after almost exactly five years with the company.

Rosemary Kennedy (1918–2005) was born in Massachusetts, the first daughter of Joe and Rose Kennedy. As the story goes, her mother was in labor, and the obstetrician had not yet arrived, so the birth attendant held baby Rosemary in her mother's birth canal, thus inadvertently depriving the infant of oxygen. It was apparent almost immediately that Rosemary was "different" from her two older brothers and the other children to come: she suffered from seizures, was mercurial in her behavior, and was not quite mentally or physically able to keep up with her siblings, although many who knew her only slightly claimed that she could be witty and charming and could easily hold a lively conversation. Even so, because mental illness was shameful in the 1920s, Rose Kennedy pulled her daughter from school and hired a tutor; later, she turned Rosemary over to nuns at a Catholic school, where the girl was said to have flourished. Though it's debatable how well Rosemary might have done had she been left on that path, there's no way of knowing what would have happened. In a misguided effort to help his daughter, Joseph Kennedy sought out a controversial doctor and, supposedly without the knowledge of the rest of the family or the consent of his daughter, ordered that Rosemary undergo a lobotomy. Rosemary was twenty-three years old and the operation backfired. Instead of a cure, she was left unable to walk or talk. She underwent physical therapy and was able to return to her family for a time, but it ultimately became obvious that they couldn't care for her as she needed to be cared for. In the late 1940s, Rosemary Kennedy was quietly moved to Saint Coletta's, a care facility near Waukesha, which is where she died.

Carrie Chapman Catt (1859–1947) was born in Ripon but moved to Iowa when she was still young. There, she grew up and entered college, the only woman in her class at Iowa State Agriculture College, where she studied to be a teacher. As a teen, young Carrie realized that her father could vote but her mother couldn't, and it angered her; by the later 1800s, she had started to work for women's suffrage and joined the National American Women Suffrage Association. She became president of the organization in 1900. In 1904, she took her efforts global, by founding the International Women Suffrage Alliance; in 1904, she took some time off to care for her dying husband, but she returned in 1915; some five years later, the Nineteenth Amendment was ratified, giving women the right to vote. Mission accomplished, Catt continued with the political life and, among other endeavors, founded the League of Women Voters, an organization aimed at educating women on current and political events. She was honorary president of the organization until her death.

King C. Gillette (1855–1932) was born in Fond du Lac and moved to Chicago as a young boy; there, because of the Fire of 1871 and the subsequent loss of his family's belongings, young King was forced to find odd jobs to help out and worked as a time as a traveling salesman. Still, he liked to tinker and people noticed, including an employer who advised Gillette to invent something that kept people coming back for more. In 1985, Gillette recognized his first product: a razor with a removable blade that could be thrown away, thus ensuring that customers would need more blades. It would have been a classic Eureka! moment, except that Gillette had no manufacturing knowledge. Still, he persevered and in 1903, the Gillette Safety Razor Company sold a whopping fifty-one razors and just over 150 blades. A year later, Gillette's invention had taken off spectacularly with sales of more than twelve million blades. While his blades are what he's probably best-known for, Gillette also owned patents for valves, faucets, and taps, and he was also an author and near-founder of a planned utopian society in Arizona.

Ron Kovic (1946–) was born in Ladysmith but was raised in Long Island, New York. In high school, he became a star athlete and considered pursuing a career in Major League baseball but instead joined the Marines upon graduation in 1964 and was sent to Vietnam. On January 20, 1968, Kovic was wounded in the spine and was paralyzed from the waist down; though he received a Purple Heart, Kovic felt a lot of guilt for the things he'd seen overseas. After recovering from his wounds in a veteran's hospital, Kovic enrolled in college in New York but, with his experiences as a veteran and recent indignities suffered at a veteran's medical facility, he became outspoken on behalf of veterans and against the Vietnam War. Deeply political, he interrupted Richard Nixon's speech at the Republican National Convention in 1972 and continued to speak out well beyond the war. In 2003, he became an activist against the Iraq War. Kovic's book, *Born on the Fourth of July*, was a best-seller in 1976 and became a movie starring Tom Cruise in 1989.

Kato Kaelin (1959–) was born Brian Gerard Kaelin in Milwaukee and grew up in an average middle-class home, the fifth of six children in the family. "Kato," a name that came from a TV show, attended the University of Wisconsin Eau Claire, where he hosted a campus talk show; it was so popular that he left school after two years and moved to Hollywood in 1979 in order to pursue fame. Despite that he's appeared in several roles on TV and in movies, his career didn't take off as he expected, and he made ends meet by waiting tables. In 1992, he met Nicole Brown Simpson (1959–1994) and they became fast friends; he moved into her condo in exchange for odd jobs and babysitting. It was there, at her guest house, where he was living when Simpson was murdered in 1994—subsequently, Kaelin's fame has come from being a witness during the O. J. Simpson murder trial in 1994–1995.

Mitchell Red Cloud (1925–1950) was born in Hatfield, went to school in Neillsville and Black River Falls, and joined the Marines in 1941. On November 5, 1950, Red Cloud was guarding a command post on a ridge in Korea when Chinese forces came upon his location. He warned his fellow soldiers and began firing at the Chinese, which gave his company opportunity to organize and return fire; in the meantime, Red Cloud was severely injured but he did not leave his post. Eyewitnesses say that he pulled himself up and, leaning on a tree, continued to fight until he was mortally wounded. Red Cloud was Wisconsin's first Native American Medal of Honor recipient for bravery during the Korean War.

William Harley (1880–1943) and Arthur Davidson (1881–1950) were childhood friends in Milwaukee, and they loved bicycles! As adults, they remained close friends and decided to make a motorized bicycle. The two invited Davidson's brothers to join them in their endeavor; they later pulled the Davidson's father into the business as well. By 1906, Harley and the Davidsons were making motorized bicycles full-time and the rest is "potato-potato-potato" history.

John Ringling (1866–1936) was born in McGregor, Iowa. John's family moved to Wisconsin shortly after John's birth. He and his brothers loved the circus so much, they decided to form their own troupe. Ringling himself initially played a clown; later, he became manager then owner and president of the American Circus Corporation. Though he moved to Sarasota, Florida, in his later years, the site of his former circus can still be seen in Baraboo.

Governors
of Wisconsin

Territorial Governors

Name	Appointed by	Years in Office
Henry Dodge	Andrew Jackson	1836–1841
James Duane Doty	John Tyler	1841–1844
Nathaniel P. Talmadge	John Tyler	1844–1845
Henry Dodge	James K. Polk	1845–1848
John Catlin*		1848–1849

*When the State of Wisconsin was admitted to the United States on May 29, 1848, only part of the territory became the State of Wisconsin. Catlin was Henry Dodge's Secretary of the Territory, and became Territorial Governor when Dodge was elected to the U. S. Senate.

State Governors

Name	Party	Years in Office
Nelson Dewey	D	1848–1852
Leonard James Farwell	Whig	1852–1854
William Augustus Barstow	D	1854–1856
Arthur MacArthur	D	1856–1856
Coles Bashford	R	1856–1858
Alexander William Randall	R	1858–1862
Louis Powell Harvey*	R	1862–1862
Edward Saloman	R	1862–1864
James T. Lewis	R	1864–1866
Lucius Fairchild	R	1866–1872
Cadwallader Colden Washburn	R	1872–1874
William Robert Taylor	D	1874–1876
Harrison Ludington	R	1876–1878
William E. Smith	R	1878–1882
Jeremiah McLain Rusk	R	1882–1889
William D. Hoard	R	1889–1891
George Wilbur Peck	D	1891–1895
William H. Upham	R	1895–1897
Edward Scofield	R	1897–1901

Name	Party	Years in Office
Robert M. La Follette, Sr.	R	1901–1906
James O. Davidson	R	1906–1911
Francis Edward McGovern	R	1911–1915
Emanuel Lorenz Philipp	R	1915–1921
John James Blaine	R	1921–1927
Fred R. Zimmerman	R	1927–1929
Walter Jodok Kohler, Sr.	R	1929–1931
Philip Fox La Follette	R	1931–1933
Albert George Schmedeman	D	1933–1935
Philip Fox La Follette	WI Progressive	1935–1939
Julius Peter Heil	R	1939–1943
Orland Steen Loomis+	WI Progressive	
Walter Samuel Goodland	R	1943–1947
Oscaar Rennebohm	R	1947–1951
Walter Jodok Kohler, Jr.	R	1951–1957
Vernon W. Thompson	R	1957–1959
Gaylord Anton Nelson	D	1959–1963
John W. Reynolds	D	1963–1965
Warren P. Knowles	R	1965–1971
Patrick J. Lucey	D	1971–1977
Martin J. Schreiber	D	1977–1979
Lee Sherman Dreyfus	R	1979–1983
Anthony Scully Earl	D	1983–1987
Tommy George Thompson	R	1987–2001
Scott McCallum	R	2001–2003
Jim Doyle	D	2003–2011
Scott Walker	R	2011–2019
Tony Evers	D	2019–

*Governor Harvey held office from January 6 to April 19, 1862. He was taking medical supplies to Wisconsin troops wounded in the Battle of Shiloh when he fell into the Tennessee River and drowned. His body wasn't recovered for two weeks, and had floated sixty-five miles (105 km) downstream.

+Died December 7, 1942, prior to inauguration.

Further Reading

BOOKS

Balkan, Gabrielle. *50 Cities of the U.S.A.* London, England: Wide Eyed Editions, 2017.

Benson, Margie, and Nancy Jacobson. *Awesome Almanac—Wisconsin.* Fontana, WI: B&B Publishing, Inc., 1993.

Davis, Kenneth C. *More Deadly Than War.* New York: Henry Holt, 2018.

Epting, Chris. *The Birthplace Book: A Guide to Birth Sites of Famous People, Places & Things.* Mechanicsburg, PA: Stackpole Books, 2009.

Godfrey, Linda, *The Beast of Bray Road: Tailing Wisconsin's Werewolf.* Trails Books: Madison, WI, 2003.

Heim, Michael, compiler. *Exploring America's Highways: Wisconsin Trip Trivia.* Wabasha, MN: T.O.N.E. Publishing, 2004.

Hintz, Martin. *Forgotten Tales of Wisconsin.* Charleston, SC: The History Press, 2010.

———. *Wisconsin Portraits.* Black Earth, WI: Trails Media Group, 2000.

McCann, Dennis. *The Wisconsin Story.* Brookfield, WI: Milwaukee Journal Sentinel, 1998.

Minnich, Jerry, general editor. *The Wisconsin Almanac.* Madison, WI: Trails Books, 2006.

Numbers, Ronald L., and Judith Walzer, editors. *Wisconsin Medicine: Historical Perspectives.* Madison, WI: University of Wisconsin Press, 1981.

Rash, Patrick J., compiler. *Bella Danger: Steamboat Disasters on the Mississippi River Between Trempealeau and Victory, Wisconsin.* Grand Excursion 2004 Committee: Genoa, WI, 2004.

Rath, Jay. *The W-Files: True Reports of Wisconsin's Unexplained Phenomena.* Madison, WI: Trails Media Group, Inc., 1997.

Rogers, Norm, and Chris Dinesen Rogers. *101 Things to Do on the Wisconsin Great River Road.* Peoria, IL: McVicker Press, 2002.

Stotts, Stuart. *Books in a Box: Lutie Stearns and the Traveling Libraries of Wisconsin.* La-Farge, WI: Big Valley Press, 2005.

WEBSITES

Amish in Wisconsin, http://www.amishinwisconsin.com

The Bobber / Discover Wisconsin, http://bobber.discoverwisconsin.com

KeyLogRolling.com, https://keylogrolling.com

Master Locks, https://www.masterlock.com/about-us/history

Milwaukee Public Museum, https://www.mpm.edu

Peshtigo Fire Museum, http://peshtigofiremuseum.com

TravelWisconsin.com https://www.travelwisconsin.com

Wisconsin 101, http://www.wi101.org

Wisconsin Department of Health Services, https://www.dhs.wisconsin.gov

Wisconsin Department of Military Affairs, https://dma.wi.gov

Wisconsin Department of Natural Resources http://dnr.wi.gov

Wisconsin Historical Society, https://www.wisconsinhistory.org

Wisconsin Public Radio, https://www.wpr.org

WisconsinHistoricalMarkers.com http://www.wisconsinhistoricalmarkers.com

WisContext.org, https://www.wiscontext.org

WisDells.com https://www.wisdells.com

Index

Note: (ill.) indicates photos and illustrations.

376

INDEX

379

384

N